THE DEATH PEN

THE DEATH PENALTY

A Worldwide Perspective

Third Edition—Revised and Updated

ROGER HOOD

Fellow of All Souls College
Professor of Criminology
and
Director, Centre for Criminological Research
University of Oxford

OXFORD
UNIVERSITY PRESS

OXFORD

UNIVERSITY PRESS

Great Clarendon Street, Oxford OX2 6DP

Oxford University Press is a department of the University of Oxford.
It furthers the University's objective of excellence in research, scholarship,
and education by publishing worldwide in

Oxford New York

Auckland Bangkok Buenos Aires Chennai
Dar es Salaam Delhi Hong Kong Istanbul Karachi Kolkata
Kuala Lumpur Madrid Melbourne Mexico City Mumbai Nairobi
São Paulo Shanghai Taipei Tokyo Toronto

Oxford is a registered trade mark of Oxford University Press
in the UK and in certain other countries

Published in the United States
by Oxford University Press Inc., New York

British Library Cataloguing in Publication Data

Data available

Library of Congress Cataloging in Publication Data

Data available

ISBN 0–19–925129–0
ISBN 0–19–925128–2 (pbk)

3 5 7 9 10 8 6 4

Typeset in Garamond
by Cambrian Typesetters, Frimley, Surrey
Printed in Great Britain
on acid-free paper by
Biddles Ltd,
Guildford and King's Lynn

Foreword

Every human being has the inherent right to life: this is set forth in both Article 3 of the Universal Declaration of Human Rights and Article 6 of the International Covenant on Civil and Political Rights. It is with regard to the protection of this right that the main objective of the United Nations is to progressively restrict the number of offences for which capital punishment might be imposed, with a view to its eventual abolition, as emphasized in various resolutions of the General Assembly (e.g. General Assembly resolution 2857 (XXVI) and 32/61) and the Economic and Social Council (e.g. Economic and Social Council resolution 1574 (L), 1745 (LIV), 1930 (LVIII)). It is also from this perspective that, on 15 December 1989, the United Nations General Assembly adopted the Second Optional Protocol to the International Covenant on Civil and Political Rights aiming at the abolition of the death penalty (resolution 44/128). The Protocol affirms that the abolition of the death penalty contributes to the enhancement of human dignity and the progressive development of human rights.

In this third, enlarged and thoroughly revised edition of *The Death Penalty—A Worldwide Perspective,* Professor Roger Hood, builds upon his earlier study for the United Nations on the question of the death penalty and new contributions of the criminal sciences in the matter, prepared in pursuance of resolutions 1986/10 and 1989/64. It documents the changes in attitude of many countries and societies towards the question of the death penalty since the second edition was published in 1996.

The present version makes good use of the report of the Secretary-General of the United Nations entitled *Capital punishment and implementation of the safeguards guaranteeing the protection of the rights of those facing the death penalty* (E/CN.15/2001/10). This is a revised, updated version of the sixth quinquennial report on this subject, which covered the period 1994–1998 ((E/2000/3), for which Professor Hood acted as the consultant to the United Nations Centre for International Crime Prevention of the Office of Drug Control and Crime Prevention.

It should be recognized that, while the Secretary-General's report was based on replies received from 63 Member States of the United Nations, only 13 of the replies came from countries which actively retained the death penalty. This meant that Professor Hood has had to make strenuous efforts to collect the relevant information from a wide variety of other sources. Furthermore, although it is difficult to draw conclusions by comparing the results of the Secretary-General's survey with previous ones—a number of countries that had replied in the past did not respond on this occasion—nevertheless, the picture that emerges is that the rate at which countries have embraced abolition has remained unchanged and at a much higher level than in previous periods. At the end of 2001 there were 89 abolitionist states (either for all crimes or for all ordinary crimes in peacetime) whereas at the end of 1995 there had been 73. With regard to the Safeguards, this study reveals that mandatory death

sentences still exist in various countries, providing no leeway for mitigating circumstances. Other countries still face the challenge to guarantee respect for those Safeguards relating to fair trial, especially within the jurisdiction of military or special
tribunals at times of perceived national crises or emergencies. Accordingly, the information received reconfirms the urgent need for a more effective application and
dissemination of the Safeguards.

It is hoped that this newly updated and expanded study by Roger Hood will serve
as a basis for well-informed discussions on the issue of the death penalty, both at the
national and international levels. In this context, the United Nations will continue
to be a reliable partner in assisting Member States in their efforts to promote peace,
development and security, while guaranteeing the protection of the rights of all
human beings, including those who have committed serious crime.

Eduardo Vetere
Director, Centre for International Crime Prevention
Office for Drug Control and Crime Prevention
United Nations Office at Vienna, Austria
September 2002

Acknowledgements

In the six years that have elapsed since the second edition of this book was published there have been many changes in the status of capital punishment worldwide. I was fortunate to have the honour of being invited again by the United Nations to act as its consultant on the death penalty and to draft for the Secretary-General his Sixth Report on *Capital Punishment and Implementation of the Safeguards Guaranteeing the Rights of those Facing the Death Penalty*, the final version of which (E/CN.15/2001/10) brought the information, as far as possible, up to date until the end of the year 2000. The book also draws, of course, on the large number of reports (official and from non-governmental organizations), books, and articles that have appeared since the last edition.

In preparing this third edition of the book I have tried to be as up to date as possible. It has been like trying to pin down a moving target. The situation as regards the status of capital punishment worldwide is as I understood it to be at the end of 2001, but I have also been able to include some significant reports (such as the Report of Governor Ryan's Capital Punishment Commission in Illinois), court judgments and articles that appeared before the manuscript went to the printer at the end of June 2002.

As usual there are more people to thank than I can name, but special thanks must go to Pat Wilkinson and her colleagues at Amnesty International for much assistance; to Peter Hodgkinson, Director of the Centre for Capital Punishment Studies at Westminster University, for a constant stream of information; to Saul Lehfreund for keeping me up to date on Caribbean issues; to David Baldus, William Bowers, Deborah Denno, C. Raj Kamur, James Liebman, Vaughan Lowe, Michael Radelet, David Rose, and William Schabas for answering my queries; to Christopher de Souza for taking time out to help me; and, as always, to Eric Prokosch.

As I gratefully acknowledged when preparing the first two editions of this book, one can only take on a task like this if one has first-class research assistance. Jessica Skinns, immediately after graduating in Law from New College, Oxford, helped me by developing a database so as to bring together the materials for the Secretary-General's Sixth Quinquennial Report in 2000. She was extremely efficient and helpful and I am most grateful to her.

When that report came to be updated and revised with material from a further batch of replies for the report submitted in 2001, Martina Feilzer, Research Officer at the Oxford Centre for Criminological Research, came to my aid. She continued to assist me in very many ways with this book, especially in keeping abreast of the materials that piled up around us. She has done her best to make sure that I have not made too many errors in the revisions I have made to this new edition. I thank her most warmly for her dedication and for the special contribution she has made to this work.

R.H.

Oxford
30 June 2002

For Eric Prokosch
who set me on this path

Contents

List of Tables

Introduction

1. SOURCES OF INFORMATION

This book, now in its third edition, began life as a report to the United Nations Committee on Crime Prevention and Control in 1988. That report was commissioned following a resolution of the Economic and Social Council of the United Nations (ECOSOC), which had called for 'a study of the question of the death penalty and new contributions of the criminal sciences in the matter'.[1] The main aim was to bring up to date the survey of world trends that had been provided, some years earlier, by two influential reports. Both of these reports, *Capital Punishment* (the Ancel Report, 1962) and *Capital Punishment: Developments 1961–1965* (the Morris Report, 1967), were based on replies to a questionnaire sent to member states of the United Nations (as well as to certain non-member states) by the UN Secretary-General, seeking information on the de jure and de facto status of capital punishment and the number of judicial executions carried out annually. These surveys were subsequently carried out every five years as a regular feature of UN activity in the area of capital punishment.

Since 1985 attempts have also been made to discover the extent to which countries that have yet to abolish capital punishment abide by nine 'Safeguards Guaranteeing Protection of the Rights of those Facing the Death Penalty' which were promulgated by resolution of ECOSOC in 1984 and endorsed by the General Assembly later that year, on the understanding that 'they would not be invoked to delay or prevent the abolition of the death penalty'.[2] These safeguards can be summarized as follows: to ensure that capital punishment is only implemented for the most serious, intentional crimes with lethal or other extremely grave consequences; to protect convicted persons from retrospective applications of the death penalty and to provide for the possibilities of lighter punishments; to exempt those under 18 years of age at the time of the commission of the crime, pregnant women, new mothers, and those who are or have become insane; to ensure that it is only applied when there is no possibility of wrongful conviction, and only after a fair trial with legal assistance; to provide for appeals and the possibility of a pardon or commutation of sentence and to ensure that no executions are carried out until all such procedures have been completed; and where capital punishment does occur, to carry it out so as to inflict the minimum possible suffering.

After receiving a report (the first edition of this book), which reviewed the extent to which these safeguards were being implemented, ECOSOC recommended that

---

[1] In pursuance of Economic and Social Council (ECOSOC) Resolution 1986/10, s. X, and Resolution 1989/64.

[2] Economic and Social Council Resolution 1984/50, Annex. General Assembly Resolution 29/118, 1984.

they should be strengthened by adding four more injunctions.[3] These related to providing adequate time and facilities to prepare a defence against a capital charge; providing for a mandatory appeal or mandatory review with provision for clemency or pardon in all cases; establishing a maximum age beyond which no death sentences or executions may be imposed; and ensuring that no person suffering from mental retardation or extremely limited mental competence should be sentenced to death, let alone executed. The Seventh United Nations Congress on the Prevention of Crime and the Treatment of Offenders, held in 1989, requested the Secretary-General to publicize these safeguards widely, as well as the procedures necessary to implement them and this was reiterated by ECOSOC in 1996. They are set out in Appendix 3, along with the text of Articles 6, 14, and 15 of the International Covenant on Civil and Political Rights, which incorporate nearly all these safeguards.

In 1996 the second edition of this book was published. It was based, in part, on replies to the Fifth Quinquennial Survey, covering the years 1989 to 1993, which I had been commissioned to analyse for the United Nations. This third edition likewise draws on responses to the UN survey, this time the Sixth Quinquennial Survey, which covered the years 1994 to 1998, which again I was privileged to analyse and to draft the Secretary-General's Report.[4] But, as in the previous editions, I have drawn on materials far wider in scope, as will be apparent throughout this book and its Bibliography.

In earlier editions I pointed to the paucity of information on the situation regarding the death penalty in many parts of the world. This was because many retentionist countries failed to respond to the Secretary-General's request, and even those that did could not be relied upon to provide accurate information on all aspects of the law and procedure governing the use of capital punishment, or statistics on the number of people sentenced to death and executed. In some cases there was an obvious avoidance of the questions, especially as regards the scale of executions.

As far as the Sixth Survey was concerned, the situation had not improved. Only 63 countries eventually responded. Again, it was the abolitionist countries that were most likely to reply—41 of the 87—and they accounted for two-thirds of the 63 replies. In contrast, only 13 (18 per cent) of the 71 countries that retained the death penalty at the end of the year 2000, and had carried out executions within the past ten years, returned the questionnaire.[5] These did not include countries which, according to official announcements, press reports, and other sources, have most frequently executed offenders in recent years: China, Egypt, Iran, Nigeria, Saudi Arabia, Taiwan (Province of China), Vietnam, among them.[6] Iraq did reply, but failed to provide any statistics on death sentences imposed or persons executed.

---

[3] Economic and Social Council Resolution 1989/64, para 1.

[4] United Nations, *Capital Punishment and Implementation of the Safeguards Guaranteeing Protection of the Rights of those Facing the Death Penalty*, E/CN.15/2001/10 (May 2001).

[5] Forty-nine countries responded to the first capital punishment survey (1969–73); 74 to the second survey (1974–8); 64 to the third survey (1979–83); 55 to the fourth survey (1984–8); 73 to the survey on safeguards in 1987; and 69 to the fifth survey (1989–93).

[6] Japan and Thailand, which replied to all six surveys, and Bahrain, the Philippines, Singapore, and Tunisia, which replied to four of them, are the exceptions among the countries which retain the death penalty. Among the countries and territories that could have replied to all six surveys, covering the thirty-

It is difficult to obtain data from other sources, because several of the retentionist countries publish no regular official statistical returns of death sentences or executions, or even if they do they may be unobtainable outside the country in question. And although Amnesty International keeps a tally of reported death sentences and executions gathered by its representatives in countries around the world, and publishes the figures in its Annual Report, there is no way by which it can ensure that the data it has obtained is always accurate and up to date. In particular, there is frequently no follow-up information on reports of death sentences imposed to confirm whether or not they resulted in executions. This is especially a problem in relation to China, where statistics on any aspect of capital punishment are still regarded as a state secret. It will be apparent to anyone who studies Amnesty International's *Death Penalty Log* (which collates reports of death sentences imposed and executions reported in newspapers across China) that, informative as it is, the *Log* can provide only a snapshot of some aspects of capital punishment in this vast and important country. It will be impossible to present an accurate picture of capital punishment until all states in the world take seriously their obligations to collect systematically statistical data on this subject and to report their practice, as requested, to the United Nations.

No claim can be made, therefore, to provide in this book a completely accurate picture of the situation regarding capital punishment around the world. Even if information had been forthcoming from every country, there would have been many gaps between the law and procedure as set out in statutes and the way in which the death penalty is applied in practice, which no officially compiled questionnaires would be likely to have revealed. Thus, questions in the UN survey that ask whether the various safeguards guaranteeing the rights of those facing the death penalty are in force are almost invariably answered in the affirmative. When countries are asked whether they guarantee a fair trial to those accused of capital crimes, how many can be expected to say 'no'? Furthermore, as any socio-legal scholar knows, theory and

---

year period 1969 to 1998, there were 42 that did not reply to any of them, not including six very small abolitionist states whose failure to reply to such a detailed questionnaire on all occasions may be more understandable: Andorra, the Vatican City State, and four small island states in the Pacific. Only six of these 42 replied to the Secretariat's requests for information for the report on the implementation of the United Nations Safeguards published in 1988 and/or the Annual Surveys presented to the Commission on Human Rights in 1998 and 1999. Only seven of these non-responding countries had become abolitionist by the end of 2000: Albania, Angola, Cambodia, Côte d'Ivoire, Guinea Bissau, Honduras, and South Africa. Twelve had progressed at various stages to abolitionist de facto status: Bhutan, Central African Republic, the Republic of Congo, Dominica, Gabon, Gambia, Grenada, Mali (which replied to the 1987 survey on safeguards), Mauritania, Nauru, Papua New Guinea, and Swaziland. The majority, 23, had remained retentionist throughout the period: China (which responded to the Safeguards Survey in 1987 and to a questionnaire sent by the UN Commission on Human Rights in 1999), the Democratic Republic of Congo, Equatorial Guinea, Ghana, Iran (which sent a letter to the Commission on Human Rights in 1999 to the effect that the matter should be handled by the UN Crime Prevention and Criminal Justice Branch, but nevertheless did not reply to the sixth survey), Kenya (which replied to the 1987 survey on safeguards), Lesotho (also replied to the 1987 survey on safeguards), Liberia, Libya, Malawi (also replied to the 1987 survey on safeguards), Mongolia, Nigeria, Oman, St Christopher and Nevis, St Lucia, St Vincent and Grenadines, Saudi Arabia, Sierra Leone, Somalia, Uganda, Vietnam, Yemen, and Zimbabwe.

practice may be wide apart. Thus, the 'law in the books' and the 'law as implemented in practice' are not necessarily the same thing.

For this reason, it is necessary to turn mainly to other sources of information obtained by the United Nations, other international bodies and non-governmental organizations. Of particular value have been the reports of the UN Special Rapporteur on extra-judicial, summary, or arbitrary executions; the reports of and submissions to the UN Human Rights Committee; the reports of the Secretary-General to the UN Commission on Human Rights; the many valuable reports published by Amnesty International, other human rights organizations, and anti-capital punishment pressure groups, such as the Death Penalty Information Center in the United States; and the regular news service provided by the Centre for Capital Punishment Studies at the University of Westminster in London. In addition, of course, there is the large academic literature, including many excellent empirical studies, most of which emanate from the United States.

These sources do indeed reveal that frequently there is a disjunction between official replies on the formal state of the law and procedures, and what is discovered about the enforcement of law and the procedures adopted in practice. For example, the Federal government of the United States, in its response to the UN Sixth Quinquennial Survey, stated that: 'Our highest state and federal courts have upheld capital punishment subject to the heightened procedural safeguards required under our state and federal constitutions and statutes, which generally meet or exceed those provided under international standards and the laws of most other nations'.[7] Yet the report of the Special Rapporteur on extra-judicial, summary, and arbitrary executions on a visit to the United States in 1998[8] was highly critical of the 'serious gap [that] exists between federal and state governments, concerning implementation of international obligations undertaken by the United States Government'.[9] It is therefore hoped that, by juxtaposing official and unofficial sources, it may be possible to get closer to the realities of how the death penalty has been employed over the last twenty-five years in many parts of the world, and in particular during the six years since the second edition was published.

But such a method naturally raises problems of veracity and objectivity where allegations of failure to abide by the safeguards go unanswered or are flatly denied. Who should one believe? The stance taken in this book is to try to make plain whenever the information has been unsubstantiated and to give, wherever possible, the source for any allegation of practices officially denied.

It has also to be recognized that information based on empirical studies of the use

---

[7] *Capital Punishment*, see n. 4 above, para. 84, p. 22.

[8] E/CN.4/1998/68, Add. 3.

[9] Amnesty International has concluded: 'Far from offering the leadership necessary to begin to remedy the situation, the US Government has, for example, reconfirmed its policy of allowing individual states to violate international law in the case of children accused of capital crimes. In 1999, the US Solicitor General filed an amicus curiae brief in the Supreme Court urging the court not to examine the USA's obligations in relation to the international ban on the use of the death penalty against child offenders.' See Amnesty International (AI), *United States of America: Failing the Future—Death Penalty Developments, March 1998–March 2000*, AI Index: AMR 51/03/00, p. 6.

of the death penalty and its effects comes from only a few countries: those that have a strong tradition of such research and a body of scholars committed to challenging the legal and penological assumptions upon which support for a death penalty is often based. As West European countries have abandoned the death penalty, so have their scholars generally lost interest in it. Other than the occasional study in South Africa, Nigeria, Poland, Yugoslavia, and Canada, empirical inquiries have been concentrated on the situation in the United States, and even there, mainly, although not solely, on a few southern states. They are no less valuable for that. But they do, of course, provide a rather distorted and partial view of the death penalty looked at in its worldwide context. This is particularly so when it is recognized that the United States differs from other countries that retain the death penalty in many ways, such as: the definition of capital murder; prosecution and trial procedures; the number executed in relation to the number of homicides and per head of the population; the complex state and federal appeal processes; let alone the racial, cultural, and political factors which shape criminal policies in those states of the United States that execute offenders.

2. PLAN OF THE BOOK

Chapter 1 provides an overview of the extent to which the movement to bring about abolition of the death penalty worldwide had progressed by the end of the year 2001. Chapter 2 should be of interest to those who require a more detailed account on a region-by-region and country-by-country basis. Chapter 3 deals with the range of crimes for which capital punishment may be imposed in various countries and the extent to which in some parts of the world the range of offences for which it is available has been expanding rather than retracting. But the number of offences for which capital punishment is on the statute books is not necessarily an indication of how frequently executions will be carried out. So Section 2 of Chapter 3 provides information, as far as it is available, on the number and rate of executions carried out in the past several years; and Section 3 of that chapter discusses the extent to which countries abide by the safeguard that calls upon them to inflict it with the minimum possible suffering, including the mode of execution, the role of physicians, and the so-called 'death row phenomenon'. Chapter 4 deals with the implementation of those safeguards that are meant to protect from execution those who commit capital crimes when juveniles (under the age of 18), who are aged, pregnant women and new mothers, and the insane or mentally retarded. Chapter 5 reviews the evidence on the extent to which procedures are in place to guarantee a fair and impartial trial, adequate counsel for the defence of the accused, and the right to appeal and to seek pardon or clemency, so that no innocent persons (as well as others undeserving of such severe punishment) are sentenced to death and executed. Chapter 6 begins with a consideration of capital punishment legislation—whether it is mandatory or discretionary—and proceeds to examine the evidence from legal scholarship and social science research on the question of whether systems of capital punishment can be applied in a non-arbitrary and non-discriminatory way, or whether arbitrariness and discrimination are inevitable features of putting capital punishment into effect. Chapter 7 discusses the concept of general deterrence and analyses the research evidence on the subject—for claims that the death penalty is necessary in order to reduce the incidence of capital crimes are often brought forward by those who wish to retain, or even reintroduce, capital punishment. But deterrence is not the only factor in the debate. The book ends, therefore, with a discussion in Chapter 8 of the role of public opinion in relation to the politics of capital punishment and raises the question of what should determine this issue: opinion or principle? Appendices chart the changing status of capital punishment and the extent of ratification of international treaties to prohibit its imposition.

A word must be said about two related issues not covered by this book, both of which cannot be ignored by anyone concerned with the protection of human rights. The first is the very regrettable fact that abolition of judicial capital punishment has not always guaranteed that state forces, whether military or police, have respected the rule of law and the right to life in enforcing the law. All too often governments—even abolitionist governments—have resorted to extra-judicial killing, and in recent times this has become a policy that is in danger of becoming legitimized as a means of dealing with those defined as 'terrorists'. The second issue concerns the alternative to capital punishment. It has to be recognized that death should not be replaced by 'living death'. Conditions for long-term imprisonment must respect international standards for the humane and progressive treatment of prisoners, even those who have committed the worst of crimes. Furthermore, to offer as an alternative to capital punishment the mandatory use of lifelong imprisonment without the possibility of parole would be, in my opinion, to offer one human rights abuse in return for another. While there will be some prisoners who will have to remain in confinement, they should be kept to the minimum number necessary for the protection of the public. The experience of West European countries is testimony to the fact that a system that promotes the progressive rehabilitation of life-sentenced prisoners followed by careful selection for release based on a risk assessment does work very satisfactorily for the majority of prisoners who, in other countries, would face death or a lifetime without hope in prison.

3. THE APPROACH TAKEN TOWARDS CAPITAL PUNISHMENT

As already mentioned, this book began life as an official report, and was not intended to present an argument, as such, for the abolition of capital punishment. It was orientated instead towards assessing the extent to which the policy objectives of the United Nations are being achieved, and what impediments there appear to be in bringing them to fruition, namely 'progressively restricting the number of offences for which the death penalty may be imposed with a view to the desirability of abolishing the punishment'.[10]

---

[10] General Assembly Resolution 32/61, 8 Dec. 1977. See United Nations, 'United Nations Action in the Field of Capital Punishment', *United Nations Crime Prevention and Criminal Justice Newsletter* 12 and 13 (1986), pp. 2–4.

Yet, one would be unlikely to embark on such a task without believing that this is a desirable goal. And, certainly, my own involvement in researching this subject over the past quarter of a century has convinced me even more strongly of the case for abolition of judicial executions throughout the world.

In the Introduction to the first edition in 1989 I remarked that 'no one can embark upon a study of the death penalty without making the commonplace observation that from a philosophical and policy standpoint there appears to be nothing new to be said'. This is still true: the arguments remain essentially the same. Yet the balance has changed, and the nature of the debate has moved on. There can be no doubt that the greater emphasis on the 'human rights' perspective on the subject has added greatly to the moral force propelling the abolitionist movement. It has further 'internationalized' what was formerly considered an issue solely for national policy. And those who still favour capital punishment 'in principle' have been faced with yet more convincing evidence of the abuses, discrimination, mistakes, and inhumanity that appear inevitably to accompany it in practice.

Many protagonists of abolition believe that the death penalty is a fundamental violation of the human right to life: in essence that it is an extreme form of cruel, inhuman, and degrading punishment. For such persons any discussion of its effectiveness as a deterrent is irrelevant. But it has to be recognized that not everyone regards this 'human rights' view as valid, especially outside Europe and the European hegemony. Indeed, many people appear to believe that (at least some) criminals who violate the right to life of others by murdering them deserve to lose their own right to life. And in some countries this argument is used to justify capital punishment for other grave personal or socially injurious harms. Sometimes capital punishment is said to be sanctioned by religious authority, as in Islamic countries, and sometimes by deeply embedded cultural norms or 'mindsets', as in many Asian countries.

Yet, even where the human rights argument against capital punishment is not accepted, the case for capital punishment also often rests on assumptions about its unique deterrent effects as compared with alternative lesser punishments. If it were shown that it is unnecessary to retain the death penalty to control grave crimes, perhaps many of those who favour it would not continue to do so merely on retributive grounds to exact revenge: they might well regard it as 'useless cruelty'. The same values that proclaim the rights of victims can also be invoked to protect the rights of the accused, especially when innocent persons are subject to the death penalty or it can be shown that the system as a whole inflicts capital punishment on persons who are 'undeserving' of it, such as the mentally retarded. Nor would all those who favour capital punishment 'in principle' continue to favour it if it were to be shown that it was accompanied by unnecessary cruelty, or that the system for administering it produced arbitrary judgments or class or racial bias on an unacceptable scale. In other words, there remains a large gap between believing that some persons 'deserve to die' for the crimes they commit, and believing that a state system for the administration of capital punishment can be devised which meets the high ideals of equal, effective, procedurally correct, and humane justice that civilized societies seek to implement.

It is necessary therefore to approach the question of capital punishment from both normative (moral) and utilitarian points of view, and always in relation to how it is applied in practice. In essence, therefore, the case for retaining the death penalty—and thus resisting the movement to make its abolition an international norm—cannot rest solely on moral, cultural, or religious arguments. It would also have to be shown that it is useful and that it can be applied fairly, and without mistakes or a degree of arbitrariness and cruelty unacceptable to contemporary social and legal values. There is, as this book makes clear, sufficient evidence to indict capital punishment on all these grounds.

UPDATE

While this book was in production the Parliament of Turkey abolished the death penalty (2 August 2002) for all offences committed in peacetime (see Chapter 2 page 27). The government of Thailand announced that from 2003 all executions would be carried out by lethal injection (see Chapter 3 page 100).

1

The Abolitionist Movement: Progress and Prospects

1. THE PACE OF ABOLITION

The modern movement to abolish the death penalty has its roots in the liberal utilitarian and humanistic ideas spawned by the enlightenment in Europe at the end of the eighteenth century. Cesare Beccaria's famous treatise *On Crimes and Punishments*, published in 1764, advocated the replacement of the old regime of maximum terror, randomly inflicted, by a graded system of penalties proportionate to the crime committed and inflicted with greater certainty. Capital punishment, Beccaria declared, was both inhumane and ineffective: an unacceptable weapon for a modern enlightened state to employ, and less effective than the certainty of imprisonment. Furthermore, he argued that capital punishment was counterproductive if the purpose of law was to impart a moral conception of the duties of citizens to each other. For, if the state were to resort to killing in order to enforce its will, it would legitimize the very behaviour which the law sought to repress, namely the use of deadly force to settle disputes.

In the 1780s Beccaria's ideas were taken up by the enlightened rulers of Tuscany and Austria, who put capital punishment into abeyance for several years. In Imperial Russia, under the empresses Elizabeth and Catherine II, the death penalty was also suspended. Pressure to restrict the death penalty to only the gravest crimes began to mount in Britain, America, and several European states. Pennsylvania (in 1794) was the first American state to abolish capital punishment for all crimes except 'first degree' murder and by 1861 in England it had for all practical purposes been restricted to murder.

In 1846 the American state of Michigan became the first jurisdiction in modern times to abolish capital punishment for murder.[1] Rhode Island followed suit in 1852 (except for murder of a prison guard by a convict serving a life sentence) and one year later Wisconsin became the third abolitionist state. By the end of the first quarter of the twentieth century several European countries—Portugal, San Marino, the Netherlands, Norway, Sweden, as well as Italy, Romania, Austria, and Switzerland (all of whom later reinstated it for a time)—had got rid of the death penalty for

---

[1] Effective from 1 March 1847, although there had been no executions since it had become a state of the Union in 1837. The death penalty was retained for treason (but never used) until 1963. See William J. Bowers with Glenn Pierce and John F. McDevitt, *Legal Homicide: Death as Punishment in America, 1864–1982* (1984), pp. 6–15 at 9.

crimes committed in peacetime, and so had several South American states after gaining their independence: Brazil, Colombia, Costa Rica, Ecuador, Uruguay, and then Argentina in 1921. Venezuela in 1863 was the first country to abolish capital punishment for all crimes, whether committed in peacetime or wartime.

However, the path to abolition in these countries was not always straight. Capital punishment was reinstated and expanded by various authoritarian regimes during the twentieth century in both Europe and South America. It was reintroduced in Italy by Mussolini's Fascist regime in 1927 and in Germany was expanded beyond all recognition by the Nazis, where it was 'to be transformed from an instrument of penal policy into a tool of racial and political engineering . . . not merely a matter of retribution but also of eugenics policy'. Under the Third Reich 'some 16,500 death sentences had been passed'.[2] The demise of both these regimes at the end of the Second World War was swiftly followed by abolition of the death penalty (see Chapter 2 page 23).

(a) A Leap Forward

By 1965, when Professor Norval Morris reported to the United Nations on the status of capital punishment in the world, there were, however, still only 25 abolitionist countries. Eleven had completely abolished it[3] and a further 14 countries[4] had abolished it for ordinary crimes in peacetime,[5] plus the Australian state of New South Wales. Over the last thirty-six years (up to December 2001) the number of abolitionist countries has grown from 25 to 89, although that figure reflects to some extent, of course, the break-up of some states and the emergence from them of several newly independent nations, most notably in Africa and the former Soviet Union. Since 1965, 67 countries, including eight former states of the Soviet Union (Azerbaijan, Estonia, Georgia, Latvia, Lithuania, Moldova, Turkmenistan, and Ukraine) have changed their status from retentionist to abolitionist: 54 of them absolutely for all crimes[6] and 13 of them for ordinary

---

[2] See Richard J. Evans, *Rituals of Retribution: Capital Punishment in Germany 1600–1987* (1996), pp. 613–737 at 630 and 795.

[3] Colombia (1910), Costa Rica (1877), Ecuador (1906), Federal Republic of Germany (1949), Honduras (1956), Iceland (1928), Monaco (1962), Panama (1922), San Marino (1865), Uruguay (1907), and Venezuela (1863). In addition, one Australian state (Queensland), nine American states (Alaska, Hawaii, Iowa, Maine, Michigan, Minnesota, Oregon, West Virginia, and Wisconsin), and 24 of the 29 Mexican states had abolished the death penalty for all crimes.

[4] Austria (1950), Denmark (1933), Finland (1949), Israel (1954), Italy (1947), the Netherlands (1870), New Zealand (1961), Norway (1905), Portugal (1867), Sweden (1921), Switzerland (1942), and the United Kingdom of Great Britain and Northern Ireland (1965). Also Argentina (1921) and Brazil (1882), both of which reintroduced the death penalty under military decrees after 1965.

[5] That is, they retained the death penalty in exceptional circumstances only, notably in time of war for military crimes and for certain crimes against the state.

[6] Andorra (1990), Angola (1992), Australia (1985), Azerbaijan (1998), Belgium (1996), Bolivia (1997), Bulgaria (1998), Cambodia (1989), Canada (1998), Cape Verde (1981), Côte d'Ivoire (2000), Croatia (1990), Czech Republic (1992), Djibouti (1995), Dominican Republic (1966), East Timor (1999), Estonia (1998), France (1981), Georgia (1997), German Democratic Republic (1987), Guinea-Bissau (1993), Haiti (1987), Hungary (1990), Ireland (1990), Kiribati (1979), Liechtenstein (1987),

crimes'.[7] Nineteen of these countries had been, at the time they abolished the death penalty, abolitionist de facto,[8] meaning that they had not executed anybody for at least ten years. Passing through this phase was, at one time, assumed to be a necessary precondition for achieving full abolition (see Chapter 2 pages 24–25), but this pattern appears no longer to be so common. Indeed, a significant majority—48 of these 67 countries—had moved directly from retentionist to abolitionist status.

As more states embraced the abolitionist position it looked as if the pool of countries most likely to be responsive to change would become smaller. One might have expected the pace of change to slow down. For instance, in 1986 the distinguished German professor of criminology Dr Günther Kaiser, after reviewing the provision of international efforts to achieve abolition, had come to the melancholy conclusion that 'there appears to be little hope that international bodies, whether private or official, will be able to achieve unanimity [among] the majority of countries concerning the restriction or abolition of capital punishment'.[9] But a 'plateau' had not been reached: quite the opposite. In the twenty-three years between the survey undertaken for the United Nations by Norval Morris, and that carried out in 1988 for the first edition of this report, 17 retentionist countries abolished the death penalty completely[10] and another 12 retentionist countries abolished it for ordinary crimes in peacetime:[11] 29 in all. Furthermore, seven of the 14 countries that had abolished capital punishment for murder and other ordinary crimes by 1965 had proceeded by 1988 to abolish it for all crimes in wartime and in the military code.[12]

In the twelve years since then and up to December 2001 another 39 retentionist countries became abolitionist, 34 of them completely[13] and five for ordinary

Lithuania (1998), Luxembourg (1979), Malta (2000), Marshall Islands (1986), Macedonia (1991), Mauritius (1995), Micronesia (1986), Moldova (1995), Mozambique (1990), Namibia (1990), Nepal (1997), Nicaragua (1979), Palau (1994), Paraguay (1992), Poland (1997), Romania (1989), São Tomé and Principe (1990), Seychelles (1993), Slovak Republic (1990), Slovenia (1989), Solomon Islands (1978), South Africa (1995), Spain (1995), Turkmenistan (1999), Tuvalu (1976), Ukraine (1999), Vanuatu (1980), Vatican City State (1969).

[7] Albania (2000), Argentina (1984), Bosnia-Hercegovina (1997), Brazil (1979), Chile (2001), Cyprus (1983), El Salvador (1983), Fiji (1979), Greece (1994), Latvia (1999), Mexico, Peru (1979), and Yugoslavia (2001).

[8] Andorra, Belgium, Bolivia, Bosnia-Hercegovina, Cape Verde, Chile, Côte d'Ivoire, Djibouti, Greece, Ireland, Liechtenstein, Luxembourg, Malta, Nepal, Nicaragua, Panama, Paraguay, Vatican City State, and Yugoslavia.

[9] Günther Kaiser, 'Capital Punishment in a Criminological Perspective', *United Nations Crime Prevention and Criminal Justice Newsletter* 12 and 13 (1986), pp. 10–18 at 16.

[10] Australia, Cape Verde, Dominican Republic, France, German Democratic Republic, Haiti, Kiribati, Liechtenstein, Luxembourg, Marshall Islands, Micronesia, Nicaragua, Philippines (reintroduced the death penalty in 1994 for a wide range of offences, see p. 44 below), Solomon Islands, Tuvalu, Vanuatu, and the Vatican City State.

[11] Argentina, Brazil, Canada, Cyprus, El Salvador, Fiji, Malta, Mexico, Papua New Guinea (reintroduced the death penalty in 1991 for wilful murder), Peru, Seychelles, and Spain.

[12] Austria, Denmark, Finland, the Netherlands, Norway, Portugal, and Sweden.

[13] Andorra, Angola, Azerbaijan, Belgium, Bolivia, Bulgaria, Cambodia, Côte d'Ivoire, Croatia, Czech Republic, Djibouti, East Timor, Estonia, Georgia, Guinea Bissau, Hungary, Ireland, Lithuania, Macedonia, Mauritius, Moldova, Mozambique, Namibia, Nepal, Palau, Paraguay, Poland, Romania, São Tomé and Principe, Slovak Republic, Slovenia, South Africa, Turkmenistan, and Ukraine.

offences.[14] Of these 39 countries, 19 were formerly in Soviet-dominated Eastern Europe or were states within the Soviet Union itself. In addition, eight countries already abolitionist for ordinary offences in 1988 completely abolished it between 1988 and December 2001.[15]

Thus, the annual average rate at which countries have abolished the death penalty trebled: from roughly one a year in the period 1965–88 to three a year over the years 1989–2001. Furthermore, more countries when becoming abolitionist did away with capital punishment completely at one go, rather than first abolishing it for ordinary offences only. Moreover, the abolitionist movement has become more widespread across the regions of the world. The list of abolitionist countries in the Morris Report of 1965 included only two that were outside Western Europe and Central and South America. By December 2001 the states that had embraced abolition had spread not only into Eastern Europe, but also into Africa. Eleven African countries are now completely abolitionist, and another 11 are abolitionist de facto. While only two Asian states have so far completely abolished the death penalty, six are now abolitionist de facto (according to the ten-year criterion). Among the islands of the Pacific, 11 have abolished the death penalty (10 of them for all offences), and a further four are abolitionist de facto. At the advent of the new millennium the gathering pace of the abolitionist movement had shown no sign of faltering.

(b) Some Setbacks

There have, however, been a number of setbacks in recent years. Papua New Guinea, which had abolished the death penalty for ordinary crimes on obtaining independence in 1975, reinstated it for wilful murder in 1991, and the Philippines, which announced abolition on the overthrow of President Marcos in 1987, similarly brought back and extended the scope of capital punishment in 1993. The period of abolition in Gambia was even shorter: 1993 to 1995. In the United States New York State reinstated the death penalty in 1995 after thirty years, and Kansas, which had not enacted a new law providing for the death penalty in accordance with the *Gregg* decision in 1967 (see page 63 below), reinstated the death penalty in 1994, 29 years after the last execution had been carried out. Nevertheless, only the Philippines has resumed executions (in 1999), but while there were, at the end of December 2001, more than 1,000 prisoners awaiting executions on death row, only seven offenders have so far been executed (see page 45 below).

As mentioned above, many countries in recent years have jumped the abolitionist de facto phase in progressing to abolition. The opposite is also true. Several countries that appeared to be abolitionist de facto resumed executions after a moratorium of at least ten years. It has been proved to be no longer safe to make the assumption that after such a period of time without executions a kind of taboo would be built

---

[14] Albania, Bosnia-Hercegovina, Chile, Greece, and Latvia.

[15] Canada, Italy, Malta, New Zealand, Seychelles, Spain, Switzerland, and the United Kingdom of Great Britain and Northern Ireland.

up which would militate against their resumption. Thus, since the beginning of 1994, 10 countries that had previously been considered abolitionist de facto resumed executions[16] and in some states of the United States executions have taken place after very long periods of abeyance. For example, a 1985 execution in South Carolina was the first in that state for twenty-one years; and since 1990 Arizona, California, Colorado, Kentucky, Oregon, Washington, and Wyoming have resumed executions after a gap of more than a quarter of a century. As the new millennium got under way, both Tennessee and New Mexico resumed executions after forty and forty-one years respectively. Of perhaps even greater significance were the two federal executions, the first for thirty-eight years, of Timothy McVeigh and Juan Raoul Garza, sanctioned by the President of the United States, who decided not to exercise his power to grant clemency, in June 2001. In some of the Commonwealth Caribbean countries the appearance of de facto abolitionism reflects the successful strategies of lawyers for defendants on death row in saving them from execution, rather than government intentions (see Chapter 5 pages 142–143 below).

The concept of abolitionist de facto, based purely on the criterion of the number of years without executions, therefore no longer has the credibility at one time ascribed to it. It is for these reasons that Amnesty International has warned, 'There is good reason in practice for caution in classifying as "abolitionist in practice" any country which keeps the death penalty in law,'[17] and why it accepts some countries as genuinely intent on abolition and others as not. Indeed it lists only 22 countries as *truly* abolitionist *in practice*, not all 34 that fulfil the 'ten-year' criterion.

Given the large number of countries that have abolished the death penalty de jure, it is less necessary or politically advantageous than hitherto to treat any ten-year abolitionist de facto states as if they were a subcategory of the abolitionist group. Rather, until they have given clear indications of their intention to remove capital punishment from their legislation and to subscribe to international conventions that ban its reintroduction, it would, in my view, be more accurate and safer to classify countries that have not executed anyone for at least ten years, but still retain capital punishment on their statute books, as a subcategory of retentionist, rather than abolitionist, states. In other words 'abolitionist de facto', as far as some countries are concerned, really means 'lapsed retentionist', for there can be no guarantee that a respite in the use of capital punishment will lead to abolition de jure. They are so classified in Table 1.1.

(c) The Present Status of Abolition

To summarize: by the end of December 2001 there were 75 totally abolitionist countries, 14 abolitionist for ordinary crimes and 105 retentionist states, of which 71 have carried out executions within the past ten years, and 34 which were 'abolitionist de

---

[16] Bahamas, Bahrain, Burundi, Comoros, Guinea, Guatemala, Philippines, St Christopher and Nevis, Trinidad and Tobago, and Qatar.

[17] AI, *The Death Penalty* (1979).

TABLE 1.1

Comparison of abolitionist and retentionist countries in December 1988,
December 1995 and December 2001

Year	Complete abolitionist		Abolitionist for ordinary offences		Total retentionist		Retentionist with executions in the previous ten years		Abolitionist de facto		Total number of countries
	No.	%	No.	%	No.	%	No.	%	No.	%	
1988	35	19	17	9	128	71	101	56	27	15	180
1995	60	31	13	7	119	62	90	47	29	15	192
2001	75	39	14	7	105	54	71	37	34	18	194

facto' (for a full list of these countries see Appendix 1). Bearing in mind that the countries are not necessarily the same in 1988 as they were in 2001, the pace of change is illustrated in Table 1.1. Thus, by the end of December 2001, 46 per cent of all separate political entities had completely abolished the death penalty or abolished it for all ordinary crimes in peacetime de jure. Seventy-one (37 per cent) had actually carried out executions during the last ten years, and 65 since 1994.

The resistance to abolishing capital punishment is now concentrated mainly in the Middle East, North Africa, and the continent of Asia. The only Western jurisdictions to retain capital punishment are the Federal government and thirty-eight states of the United States and English-speaking Commonwealth Caribbean countries.

Chapter 2 will review, region by region and country by country, as far as information is available, both the progress that the abolitionist movement has made and the reasons why it has been resisted. But one can no longer deal with this issue solely on a country-by-country basis. What marks the modern period from the past, when abolition was very much regarded as an 'internal matter' of national penal policy, is the development from the late 1970s onwards of a European-led political movement to make abolition of the death penalty the touchstone of acceptable international standards of respect for human rights.[18]

2. THE HUMAN RIGHTS DIMENSION: CONVENTIONS AND POLITICS

(a) The Establishment of International Treaties

The International Covenant on Civil and Political Rights (ICCPR), adopted by the United Nations in 1966, affirmed in Article 6 (1) that 'every human being has the right to life' and that 'no one shall be arbitrarily deprived of his life', but this did not bar capital punishment. It was, however, ringed around with conditions, the most

---

[18] See Council of Europe, *The Death Penalty: Abolition in Europe* (1999).

important of which was embodied in Article 6 (2), namely that it should be restricted to 'the most serious crimes'.

It was in 1971 (Resolution 2857) and again in 1977 (Resolution 32/61) that the United Nations took the first step towards declaring abolition of the death penalty as a universal goal when it called for 'the progressive restriction of the number of offences for which the death penalty might be imposed, with a view to its abolition'.

That call was responded to first by European abolitionist politicians, most notably Dr Joseph Broda, the Austrian Minister of Justice. Towards the end of the 1970s the Committee of Ministers of the Council of Europe was invited by the Parliamentary Assembly to consider the issue of capital punishment as 'inhuman'.[19] In December 1982 Protocol No. 6 to the European Convention for the Protection of Human Rights and Fundamental Freedoms (ECHR) was adopted, and opened for signature on 28 April 1983. Article 1 provides for the abolition of the death penalty in peacetime. Article 2, however, did allow a state to make provision in its law for the death penalty in time of war or of imminent threat of war. Six years later, in December 1989, the UN General Assembly adopted the Second Optional Protocol to the ICCPR, Article 1 of which states: 'No one within the jurisdiction of a State party to the present Optional Protocol shall be executed'; clause 2 of this article establishes the important principle that 'The death penalty shall not be re-established in States that have abolished it.' Although Article 2, like the Sixth Protocol to the ECHR, allows a reservation to be made which provides for the application of the death penalty in time of war pursuant to a conviction for a most serious crime of a military nature committed during wartime, the reservation can only be made at the time of ratification or accession.

A year later, in June 1990, the General Assembly of the Organization of American States adopted the Protocol to the American Convention on Human Rights to Abolish the Death Penalty. Article 1 calls upon states to abstain from the use of the death penalty, but does not impose an obligation on them to erase it from the statute book. Thus de facto abolitionist countries may also ratify the Protocol.[20] However, those countries that have already abolished the death penalty may not reinstate it.

It will be noted that none of these instruments fully endorsed the complete abolition of the death penalty. However, a significant move was made in this direction when, in 1994, the Parliamentary Assembly of the Council of Europe recommended that a further Protocol to the European Convention on Human Rights should be established. This would provide for the complete abolition of the death penalty with no possibility of reservations being entered for its retention in any special circumstances.[21] To this effect, the Committee of Ministers adopted Protocol No. 13 in

---

[19] Hans Christian Krüger, 'Protocol No. 6 to the European Convention on Human Rights', in Council of Europe, *The Death Penalty: Abolition in Europe* (1999), pp. 69–78.

[20] On the provisions of these Protocols and questions of interpretation, see William Schabas, *The Abolition of the Death Penalty in International Law* (1997), pp. 147–191, 222–260, 273–294.

[21] Parliamentary Assembly of the Council of Europe, 1994 Session, *Recommendation 1246 (1994) on the Abolition of the Death Penalty*. Also, *European Union Annual Report on Human Rights, 2000, Annex 5,*

February 2002 in order to send 'a strong political signal that the death penalty is unacceptable in all circumstances'.

By December 2001 Protocol No. 6 to the ECHR, had been ratified by 39 countries and signed by a further three countries (see Appendix 2) and the new Protocol No. 13, which was opened for signature on 3 May 2002, had already attracted thirty-three signatures and three ratifications by 14 June 2002. Further, the Second Optional Protocol to the ICCPR had been ratified by 46 countries and signed by a further seven; and the Protocol to the American Convention on Human Rights had been ratified by eight countries and signed by one. Countries that have ratified the American Convention on Human Rights and have also abolished the death penalty completely or for ordinary crimes are, under Article 4(3) of the Convention, banned from reintroducing it. There are 18 such countries.[22] Thus, by the end of December 2001 altogether 69 countries were barred by their ratification of one or other of these treaties or conventions from reintroducing the death penalty (for a list, see Appendix 2). Several factors have been influential in this expansion of the number of countries that have committed themselves in this way to the abolitionist cause, but none so vital as the political influence and pressure exerted by European political institutions.

(b) The 'European Movement'

The Parliamentary Assembly of the Council of Europe has been particularly trenchant in its opposition to capital punishment. In resolution 1044 of 1994, and recommendation 1246 (1994)—reaffirmed by resolution 1097 (1996) and again by resolution 1187 (1999) on *Europe: A Death Penalty Free Continent*—the Parliamentary Assembly called upon 'all the Parliaments in the world which have not yet abolished the death penalty, to do so promptly, following the example of the majority of Council of Europe member states'.[23]

Furthermore, the Parliamentary Assembly has averred that 'the death penalty has no legitimate place in the penal systems of modern civilised societies, and that its application may well be compared with torture and be seen as inhuman and degrading punishment within the meaning of Article 3 of the ECHR'. In accordance with this, in 1994 the Assembly made it a precondition that any country that wished to become a member of the Council of Europe should agree to implement an immediate moratorium on executions and then sign and ratify, within a set number of years, the Sixth Protocol to the ECHR.[24] This policy had an enormous impact on the

---

EU Memorandum on the Death Penalty; 'Drafting of a Protocol to the European Convention on Human Rights Concerning the Abolition of the Death Penalty in All Circumstances', Steering Committee for Human Rights (CDDH), Final Activity Report: CDDH (2001)35, Addendum.

[22] I am grateful to Professor William A. Schabas for pointing this out to me. See Christina M. Cerna, 'The Death Penalty and the Jurisprudence of the Inter-American System for the Protection of Human Rights', Paper presented to the Conference on the Death Penalty, University of Galway, Sept. 2001.

[23] See on this subject Renate Wohlwend, 'The Efforts of the Parliamentary Assembly of the Council of Europe', in Council of Europe, *The Death Penalty: Abolition in Europe* (1999), pp. 55–67 and Appendix II, 'Europe a Death Penalty Free Continent', at 171–184.

[24] See *ibid.*, p. 57. See also Parliamentary Assembly Resolution 1097, 1996, para. 6.

countries of the former Soviet bloc in Eastern Europe, all of which wished to join the Council of Europe, as well as on several states of the former Soviet Union, including Ukraine and the Russian Federation. Although the latter has yet to abolish the death penalty formally, it has enforced a moratorium on executions since 1996 (see Chapter 2 pages 30–31). Altogether, by April 2002, 16 East European countries had abolished capital punishment and ratified the Sixth Optional Protocol to the ECHR, and three had signed it.[25] All of them had been retentionist when the first edition of this book was published in 1989.

Similarly, the European Union has made the abolition of capital punishment a precondition for membership, and in 1998 it embarked on a diplomatic policy to persuade other nations, through the adoption of Guidelines to European Union Policy towards Third Countries on the Death Penalty. This document stated that the objectives of the European Union are to 'work towards the abolition of the death penalty as a strongly held policy view agreed by all EU member states'. The guidelines stressed that 'abolition of the death penalty contributes to human dignity and the progressive development of human rights'.[26] Meeting in Nice in December 2000, the European Council, in conjunction with the European Parliament and Commission, welcomed the draft Charter of Fundamental Rights. Article 2 (2) of the Charter states that ' No one shall be condemned to the death penalty or executed', and Article 19 that 'No one shall be removed, expelled or extradited to a State where there is a serious risk that [the person] would be subjected to the death penalty, torture or other inhuman or degrading treatment or punishment.' In July 2001 the European Parliament adopted a resolution on the death penalty in the world. This reiterated 'that the abolition of the death penalty, which is iniquitous, degrading and contrary to the universal principles of justice, is essential to the affirmation of human dignity and for the progressive development of human rights, the first of which is the right to life'. Furthermore it called upon the European Commission 'to consider the abolition of the death penalty and a universal moratorium on executions as an essential element in relations between the European Union and third countries, and to take this issue into account in concluding agreements with third countries'.[27]

To this effect the European Union had already made diplomatic démarches to the United States usually in relation to individuals facing execution, to the Governors and Boards of Pardons of several US states, including Tennessee, Oklahoma, Missouri, Georgia, Texas, and Virginia,[28] as well as to other 'third countries' such as Lebanon, the Palestinian Authority, Malaysia, Sri Lanka, Japan, Guinea, and

---

[25] Ratified: Albania, Bulgaria, Croatia, Czech Republic, Estonia, Georgia, Hungary, Latvia, Lithuania, Macedonia, Moldova, Poland, Romania, Slovakia, Slovenia, Ukraine. Signed: Armenia, Azerbaijan, Russian Federation.

[26] Council of the European Union, *Guidelines to EU Policy towards Third Countries on the Death Penalty*, Brussels, 3 June 1998.

[27] *Death Penalty in the World*, adopted by the European Parliament on 5 July 2001.

[28] *EU Policy and Action on the Death Penalty* at www.eurunion.org/legislat/Deathpenalty/deathpen-home.htm.

Botswana. This diplomatic offensive marks a new phase in the campaign against capital punishment and is already making its mark. For example, the former US Ambassador to France Felix Rohatyn has publicly declared that hostility to the death penalty in Europe had opened his eyes to the issue because it was a direct challenge to the 'moral leadership' of the United States in world affairs, and turned him from a supporter of capital punishment to a sceptic who now supported a moratorium on executions so that the whole issue could be reviewed.[29] A signal of how strong European feelings have been on this issue was the resolution passed by the Parliamentary Assembly in June 2001 to remove the observer status of both Japan and the United States unless they make 'significant progress' on abolishing executions by 1 January 2003.[30]

(c) Disputed Norms

Despite the remarkable advances made in gaining commitment from so many countries to the abolition of capital punishment through international treaties and political pressure, there is obviously still a considerable way to go before it is fully accepted worldwide as an 'international human rights norm'. This appears to be mainly due to the political resistance mounted by states that regard their criminal justice system as a matter of national sovereignty reflecting their cultural and religious values, and who reject the argument that judicial execution is an infringement of basic human rights.[31] Most of the countries who opposed the adoption of the Second Optional Protocol to the ICCPR were those with a predominantly Muslim population, but also included Japan and the United States.[32] These countries have continued to oppose UN resolutions aimed at promoting abolition, and several of them have objected to the attempt to make the issue one of international morality, characterizing it as insulting and culturally imperialistic. Thus, a series of attempts at UN Congresses,[33] in the General Assembly, and at the Committee on Human Rights to secure support for resolutions calling for a worldwide moratorium on

---

[29] Felix G. Rohatyn, 'America's Deadly Image', *Washington Post*, 20 Feb. 2001, p. 23.

[30] Resolution 1253 (2001) adopted on 25 June 2001.

[31] See, for example, Joan Fitzpatrick and Alice Miller, 'International Standards on the Death Penalty: Shifting Discourse', *Brooklyn Journal of International Law* 19 (1993), pp. 273–366 esp. at 274.

[32] For an excellent account, see William A. Schabas, *The Abolition of the Death Penalty in International Law* (1997), p. 175 n. 231. The countries which voted against its adoption were: Afghanistan, Bahrain, Bangladesh, Cameroon, China, Djibouti, Egypt, Indonesia, Iran, Iraq, Japan, Jordan, Kuwait, Maldives, Morocco, Nigeria, Oman, Pakistan, Qatar, Saudi Arabia, Sierra Leone, Somalia, Syrian Arab Republic, Tanzania, United States, and Yemen. Malaysia and Sudan apparently advised the Secretariat that they had also intended to vote against. *Ibid.*, p. 175 n. 231.

[33] *Report of the Eighth United Nations Congress on the Prevention of Crime and the Treatment of Offenders*, Havana, Cuba, 27 Aug.–7 Sept. 1990, A/CONF. 144/28, 5 Oct. 1990, p. 277. Resolution: 'To consider the possibility of establishing, within the framework of their national legislation, a moratorium on its application, at least on a three year basis or creating other conditions under which capital punishment is not imposed or executed, so as to permit a study of the effects of abolition on a provisional basis'. This was rejected (despite the fact that the majority of states—48—voted in favour, with only 29 against and 16 abstentions) because it had failed to receive the two-thirds majority vote required under United Nations rules of procedure.

executions, with the aim of eventually achieving abolition, have been thwarted by counter-resolutions from states supporting capital punishment.[34] Thus, in December 1994, in response to such a resolution at the General Assembly,[35] Singapore asserted that 'capital punishment is not a human rights issue', and introduced an amendment 'affirming the sovereign right of States to determine the legal measures and penalties which are appropriate in their societies to combat serious crime effectively'. Indeed, Singapore argued that the resolution went 'some way towards dictating a particular set of values from countries which have abolished capital punishment on those which have not'.[36]

Five years later, in October 1999, a draft resolution (A/C.3/54/L.8) was introduced at the fifty-fourth session of the UN General Assembly by Finland on behalf of the European Union with 73 co-sponsors. This resolution urged all states that still maintained the death penalty to comply fully with their international obligations, to observe the safeguards, to restrict progressively the number of capital offences, to establish a moratorium with a view to abolishing the death penalty completely, and to make available to the public information with regard to the imposition of the death penalty. A series of amendments to this resolution were tabled, once again led by Egypt and Singapore, referring to the right of states to choose their own political, economic, and social systems without interference from the United Nations or other states. These amendments also attracted over 70 co-sponsors. In view of such an irresolvable difference of opinion, the co-sponsors of both the resolution and the amendments decided not to press for action on the draft resolution or the amendments when they were considered at the fiftieth meeting of the Third Committee of the General Assembly in December 1999.[37]

---

[34] In 1999 the UN Sub-Commission on the Promotion and Protection of Human Rights (previously the Sub-Commission on Prevention of Discrimination and Protection of Minorities) called upon retentionist states to apply a moratorium on executions throughout the year 2000 in order to mark the millennium and to commute the sentences of those under sentence of death on 31 Dec. 1999. The resolution was controversial not only because it was the first time that the Sub-Commission has adopted a resolution on this subject but also because the unusual step was taken of making reference to specific countries in a pre-ambular paragraph. Resolution, E/CN.4/SUB.2/RES/1999/4, 24 Aug. 1999.

[35] General Assembly, A/C.3/49/L.32, 29 Dec. 1994. This resolution invited states that had not yet abolished the death penalty 'to consider the progressive restriction of the number of offences for which the death penalty may be imposed' but encouraged them 'to consider the opportunity of instituting a moratorium on pending executions with a view to ensuring that the principle that no state should dispose of the life of any human being be affirmed in every part of the world by the year 2000'.

[36] Statement by Singapore proposing no action to L.32. Seventy-one states voted in favour of this amendment, 65 against, and 21 abstained. Many of those states which had originally sponsored the resolution for a moratorium were unwilling to accept the Singaporean amendment because it failed to uphold the universal principles of human rights and made no mention of international law. As a result, 74 countries abstained and the resolution was lost. See also similar statements by representatives of Libya, Algeria, Thailand, and the United States at the 57th Session of the UN Commission on Human Rights on 25 Apr. 2001, Press Release 25/04/01, *Commission of Human Rights Adopts Ten Resolution, Measures on the Death Penalty, Impunity, and Other Issues Concerning the Promotion and Protection of Human Rights*. It should be noted that the view that human rights, including the right to life, are culturally relative has not gone unchallenged in Singapore. See Simon S. C. Tay, 'Human Rights, Culture, and the Singapore Example', *McGill Law Journal* 41 (1996), pp. 743–780.

[37] See Ilias Bantekas and Peter Hodgkinson, 'Capital Punishment at the United Nations: Recent Developments', *Criminal Law Forum* 11(1) (2000), pp. 23–34.

There have been similar experiences at the UN Commission on Human Rights. In 1997 a resolution was adopted (27 countries in favour, 11 against, and 14 abstentions) calling on all countries that retained capital punishment to consider suspending executions with a view to completely abolishing the death penalty and to sign or ratify the Second Optional Protocol to the ICCPR, aiming at the abolition of the death penalty. Resolutions to the same effect have since been brought forward annually. The number voting in favour has remained much the same, but the number of dissenters has increased—to 18 in 2001 and 20 in 2002—and the expression of their dissent more emphatically expressed. At its fifty-seventh session in April 2001, 60 states, led by Saudi Arabia, dissented from a resolution by the UN Human Rights Commission which emphasized the obligations of retentionist states to ensure that 'the notion of "most serious crimes" should not encompass non-violent financial crimes or any non-violent religious practice or expressions of conscience; and not to impose the death penalty on a person suffering any form of mental disorder or to execute any such person'.

However, the joint statement issued by these states appeared to rest on the assumption that Article 6 (2) of the ICCPR, relating to 'the most serious offences', conveyed a justification for retaining the death penalty. Yet Article 6 (6) declares that 'Nothing in this article [Article 6] shall be invoked to delay or to prevent the abolition of capital punishment by any State Party to the present Covenant.' Furthermore, there are human rights lawyers who would argue that, notwithstanding Article 6 (2), 'a dynamic interpretation of article 7 of the Covenant ("No one shall be subjected to torture or to cruel, inhuman or degrading treatment or punishment"), ought to be interpreted to denounce any imposition of capital punishment.'[38]

Yet, despite these attempts to block or at least delay the advancement of the international movement towards final abolition of the death penalty, there can be no doubt that they are now the voices of a minority. This is further reflected in the agreement reached at the United Nations that the International Criminal Tribunals for trying cases of genocide and crimes against humanity in the former Yugoslavia and Rwanda were not given the power to impose the death penalty.[39] Similarly, the Statute of the International Criminal Court, adopted by the Rome Conference in July 1998, did not provide the death penalty for any of the exceptionally grave offences, encompassing genocide and other crimes against humanity, covered by the statute.[40]

(d) The Strategy of Non-cooperation

Of considerable, some would say cardinal, significance was the judgment of the

---

[38] See Manfred Nowak, 'Is the Death Penalty an Inhuman Punishment?', in Theodore S. Orlin, Allan Rossas, and Martin Scheinin (eds), *The Jurisprudence of Human Rights Law: A Comparative Interpretive Approach* (2000), pp. 27–45 at 44.

[39] On this generally, see Eric Prokosch, 'The Death Penalty versus Human Rights', in Council of Europe, *The Death Penalty: Abolition in Europe* (1999), pp. 17–27 at 21.

[40] *Rome Statute of the International Criminal Court*, UN Doc. A/CONF. 183/9 (17 July 1998), Art. 77. Now that 66 countries have ratified the treaty, the statute will enter into force on 1 July 2002. The Court will begin to function from 2003. On 6 May 2002 the United States announced that it was withdrawing from the treaty.

European Court of Human Rights in 1989 in the case of *Soering* v. *United Kingdom and Germany*, which prohibited extradition of an offender charged with a capital offence to the state of Virginia on the grounds that in facing the death penalty he would suffer from 'the death row phenomenon', which would amount to 'inhuman or degrading treatment or punishment', contrary to Article 3 of the European Convention on Human Rights, especially in light of the fact that the United Kingdom itself had abolished capital punishment for murder.[41] Since then, this has developed into a firm policy. The Charter of Fundamental Rights, adopted by the European Union in Nice in December 2000, prohibits the extradition of offenders to any country where the death penalty might be imposed unless a firm guarantee is given that the death penalty will not be imposed, and this, of course, includes those suspected of carrying out acts of terrorism against the United States post September 11 2001.[42]

A striking illustration of how views on the question of extradition to countries with the death penalty can change is the recent decision of the Canadian Supreme Court in the case of *United States* v. *Burns* (2001).[43] Ten years earlier the majority of the Court had ruled that it was not unconstitutional for the Canadian government to extradite a person accused of capital murder to the state of Pennsylvania, which had not entered an assurance that the death penalty would not be imposed. In reaching its judgment in *Kindler* v. *Canada (Minister of Justice)* in 1991 the majority of the Court had stated:

Extraditing an individual accused of the worst form of murder to face capital prosecution does not shock the conscience of the Canadian people, nor is it in violation of international standards ... In determining what is fundamentally just, the global context must be considered. Although there is a growing trend towards the abolition of capital punishment, the vast majority of the nations in the world retain the death penalty. There is no international norm.[44]

Furthermore, when the case came before the UN Human Rights Committee in 1993, it decided by a majority of 13 to 5 that there had been no breach of Article 6 (protecting the right to life) or Article 7 of the ICCPR (cruel and unusual punishment) by the Canadian government.[45] And yet, in February 2001 the Canadian Supreme

---

[41] *Soering* v. *United Kingdom*, Federal Republic of Germany intervening, 161 *Eur. Ct. H.R.* (ser. A) 34 (1989).

[42] Charter of Fundamental Rights of the European Union, O.J.E.C. 18.12.2000, 2000/C 364/1, Art. 19 (2). See also AI, *United States of America. No Return to Execution: The US Death Penalty as a Barrier to Extradition* (2001), AI Index: AMR 51/171/2001.

[43] William A. Schabas, 'From *Kindler* to *Burns*: International Law is Nourishing the Constitutional Living Tree', Paper presented at a Conference on Capital Punishment and International Human Rights Law, Galway, 20 Sept. 2001.

[44] *Criminal Reports* 8 C.R. (4th) (1991), at p. 4. The minority (two justices) held that the death penalty did constitute cruel and unusual punishment, and that extradition to a state with the death penalty would therefore be a breach of the Canadian Charter. See William A. Schabas, 'Note on *Kindler* v. *Canada* (Minister of Justice)', *American Journal of International Law* 87 (1993), pp. 128–133; also, Allan Manson, '*Kindler* and the Courage to Deal with American Convictions', *Criminal Reports* 8 C.R. (4th) (1991), pp. 68–81.

[45] See William A. Schabas, '*Soering*'s Legacy: The Human Rights Committee and the Judicial Committee of the Privy Council Take a Walk down Death Row', *International and Comparative Law Quarterly* 43 (1994), pp. 913–923 at 916–917.

Court in *Burns* decided that his unconditional extradition to the state of Washington for the crime of murder, without assurance that the death penalty will not be imposed, would violate Section 7 of the Canadian Charter of Rights and Freedom (right to life, liberty, and security of the person, and the right not to be deprived thereof except in accordance with 'the principles of fundamental justice'). There is no doubt that the Court was influenced by the controversy that surrounds the use of the death penalty in the United States, particularly as regards the danger of wrongful conviction. But it further made the following telling observation:

While the evidence does not establish an international law norm against the death penalty, or against extradition to face the death penalty, it does show significant movement towards acceptance internationally of a principle of fundamental justice Canada has adopted internally, namely the abolition of capital punishment . . . It also shows that the rule requiring that assurances be obtained prior to extradition in death penalty cases not only accords with Canada's principled advocacy on the international level, but also is consistent with the practice of other countries with which Canada generally invites comparison, apart from retentionist jurisdictions in the United States.[46]

In South Africa, too, the Constitutional Court made it plain that the authorities had acted wrongly in deporting to the United States illegal immigrants suspected of bombing the US Embassy in Dar es Salaam in 1998, without first obtaining an assurance from the US government that the suspect would not be executed if convicted of a capital offence.[47] This is yet another example of abolitionist countries seeking to create an international embargo on capital punishment.

Nevertheless, it would be wrong to underestimate the level of support for capital punishment in many of the countries that retain it, notably most of the Islamic states, China, and the United States of America. There is good evidence to support the view that abolition of capital punishment is linked to the development of political rights which emphasize 'human rights',[48] and it is probable therefore that many countries that face this challenge shelter behind the fact that the government of the United States, a government which regards itself as a champion of human rights, continues to support and practise capital punishment. What happens to the abolitionist cause in America may therefore be of crucial significance to the further advancement of the abolitionist movement worldwide.

---

[46] 2001 SCC7. File No.: 26129. Once the State of Washington, which had sought the extradition, had given these assurances, the prisoner and his associate were surrendered to face trial in the United States.

[47] See *Mohamed* v. *President of the Republic of South Africa and Others* 2001 (7) BCLR 685 (CC). The extradition or deportation of a Tanzanian national to the Unites States by South Africa to stand trial on federal capital charges was judged to be an infringement of the right to life, to dignity, and not to be subjected to cruel, inhuman, or degrading punishment embodied in the South African constitution. In due course this defendant was convicted of a capital offence, but the jury in New York did not impose the death penalty.

[48] An interesting and substantial attempt to test this empirically has been carried out by David F. Greenberg and Valerie West, 'Siting the Death Penalty Internationally', Paper presented to the Annual Meeting of the Law and Society Association, Budapest, July 2001.

2

Abolition and Retention: A Regional Analysis

The objective of this chapter is to chart the extent to which the abolition of capital punishment has been achieved in different parts of the world. In doing so, it draws attention to some of the main factors that have contributed to the success of the abolitionist movement as well as those that continue to hinder it.

1. WESTERN EUROPE

The roots of abolition are deeply buried in West European political culture. Portugal[1] was the first European country to abolish capital punishment for murder in 1867, and indeed no one had been executed there since 1849. It was followed soon after by the Netherlands, Romania, Italy, the Republic of San Marino, and the Federal Council of Switzerland (although two cantons quickly reverted to it). Norway, after the turn of the century, was the first of the Scandinavian countries to become abolitionist and was followed after the First World War by Sweden, Iceland, and Denmark. Finland had executed no one for murder since 1826.

With the end of the Second World War and the Fascist tyranny, capital punishment for all ordinary offences in the penal code was abandoned by Italy in 1944 (it had been restored by Mussolini in 1926 and expanded in the Penal Code of 1930), and then, after a short period of reintroduction in response to an outbreak of banditry, it was abolished in 1947 for all but military offences during wartime. The Federal Republic of Germany went further. Article 102 of its new Constitution of 1949 abolished the death penalty for all crimes in all circumstances, despite the fact that there were strong pressures to retain it.[2] Finland carried out executions for wartime offences during the Second World War, but abolished capital punishment for all ordinary crimes in 1949. So did Monaco in 1962, although no executions had been carried out there since 1847.

Thus, when Marc Ancel made his survey for the Council of Europe in 1962, executions for murder were being carried out in Western Europe—and quite

---

[1] There had been no executions for ordinary crimes since 1847 although executions for military crimes took place between 1916 and 1918 in Portugal.

[2] See Richard J. Evans, *Rituals of Retribution: Capital Punishment in Germany 1600–1987* (1996), pp. 613–737 at 630 and 795.

rarely—only in the United Kingdom, France, Cyprus (the last being carried out in that year), Greece, Spain, and Turkey. It was on the statute books for murder in the Irish Republic, but the last hanging had taken place in 1954. Luxembourg and Belgium also retained it for murder, but the last time they had carried out executions was in 1949 and 1950 respectively, and only for collaboration with the enemy and other wartime offences.

Several other countries that had long before abolished the death penalty for murder had nevertheless retained it for possible use in relation to offences against the state, such as treason in wartime and for military offences in time of war. With very few exceptions the necessity of retaining capital punishment for use in wartime was not seriously questioned until the 1970s and indeed it had been used quite extensively after the Second World War to punish quislings (collaborators) and other war criminals by Norway, Denmark, and the Netherlands. In 1962 Marc Ancel, following Cesare Beccaria, had remarked that 'even the most convinced abolitionists realise that there may be special circumstances, or particularly troublous times, which justify the introduction of the death penalty for a limited period'.[3] But such was the potency of the human rights movement in Europe that from 1972 onwards European countries began to divest themselves of this power. By the end of the twentieth century all but Cyprus, Greece, and Turkey had abandoned capital punishment completely.[4]

Marc Ancel further observed in 1962 that 'the process of abolishing capital punishment has gone through much the same stages everywhere': first the reduction of the number of crimes legally punishable by death, then the introduction of alternatives and systematic commutation, leading to de facto abolition and eventually abolition in law 'as simply the recognition of established fact. In the Netherlands, Norway, Sweden and Denmark, events followed this course to the end without any noteworthy incidents.' Neverthless, he went on to note that there was 'no uniform rule in this connection'.[5] Indeed, capital punishment was abolished completely at one go by France in 1981 only four years after the last execution.[6] In the United Kingdom capital punishment was abolished for murder in 1965 without any period of de facto abolition, yet it took thirty-three more years to wipe capital punishment completely from the statute book. It was finally abolished for the unused vestiges (piracy and treason) as well as for military offences in 1998. Italy—currently in the vanguard of the abolitionist movement—took forty-seven years finally to abolish capital punishment for wartime offences in 1994. Belgium finally abolished the death penalty in 1996 although only one execution for murder had taken place since

[3] Marc Ancel, *The Death Penalty in European Countries: Report*, Council of Europe (1962), p. 3.

[4] Greece and Cyprus has retained the death penalty for military offences, the latter on the grounds that a 'highly anomalous situation . . . has been caused by the Turkish invasion of a large part of our country since 1974'. See Roger Hood, *The Death Penalty: A World-Wide Perspective* (1996), p. 14.

[5] Ancel, n. 3 above, pp. 47–48.

[6] UK: Human Rights Act 1998, s. 21 (5); France: Textes nationaux, Abolition de la peine de mort, 1981.

1863—in 1918—and none for any offences since 1950.[7] In Cyprus there were no executions for twenty-one years before capital punishment was abolished for premeditated murder in 1983. The President of the Supreme Court attributed this to 'social evolution and changed social attitudes on capital punishment'.[8] An even more extreme example is the principality of Liechtenstein, which formally abolished capital punishment in 1987 although no one had been executed since 1x785. Thus, there has been no one pattern.

Anti-capital punishment campaigns, such as that led by the Howard League for Penal Reform and in the British Parliament by Sydney Silverman, were undoubtedly of great importance in achieving abolition.[9] So was strong political leadership from the head of state, as was demonstrated in France. François Mitterrand had, in 1981, when campaigning in the presidential election, declared his opposition to capital punishment even though opinion polls showed that 63 per cent of the public favoured retention. On his election he appointed the distinguished lawyer Robert Badinter as his Minister of Justice, a long-time opponent of the death penalty, who resolutely pushed the law to abolish capital punishment through the French National Assembly, with some support from the right as well as solid support from the left.[10]

In the United Kingdom abolition proceeded in stages, an attempt first being made (despite warnings against it from the prestigious Royal Commission on Capital Punishment 1949–53)[11] to define a narrow group of mandatory 'capital murders'— those committed in the course or furtherance of theft or robbery, by using firearms or explosives, of police or prison officers, or multiple murders—for which it was believed essential to retain the death penalty as a deterrent. The resulting Homicide Act of 1957 produced many anomalies and resulted in so few executions that much public sympathy welled up for some of those executed, whose crimes were less heinous than others which did not fall under the definition in the act, such as the infamous cases of Ruth Ellis, executed for a *crime passionnel* because she used a pistol, and Derek Bentley (later exonerated), convicted and executed as an accessory to a shooting of a policeman by an accomplice too young to be hanged himself.[12]

---

[7] See Philippe Toussaint, 'The Death Penalty and the "Fairy Ring" ', in Council of Europe, *The Death Penalty: Abolition in Europe* (1999), pp. 29–34.

[8] Quoted from the reply from Cyprus to *United Nations Safeguards Survey*, 1987.

[9] See, for example, James B. Christoph, *Capital Punishment and British Politics* (1963); E. R. Calvert, *Capital Punishment in the Twentieth Century* (1962); Elizabeth O. Tuttle, *The Crusade against Capital Punishment in Great Britain* (1961). Also, for contemporary reflections, see Leon Radzinowicz, *Adventures in Criminology* (1999), pp. 245–279, and Andrew Rutherford, 'Abolitionism: A Tale of Two Struggles', in Peter Hodgkinson and Andrew Rutherford (eds), *Punishment: Global Issues and Prospects* (1996), pp. 261–277 at 262–264.

[10] By a majority of 368 to 113 and in the Senate by 160 votes to 126. See Robert Badinter, *L'Abolition* (2000), pp. 255–315.

[11] For an insightful account based on the testimony of an influential commissioner, see Radzinowicz, n. 9 above, pp. 252–274.

[12] See *R* v. *Derek William Bentley (Deceased)* [2001] 1 Cr.App.R. 21. Lord Bingham, the Lord Chief Justice of England, concluded: 'The Court had come to the decision that the summing-up as a whole [by the former Lord Chief Justice Lord Goddard] had been such as to deny the applicant a fair trial which is the birthright of every British citizen.'

This, combined with concerns about the possible wrongful conviction of Timothy Evans (later exonerated), produced a healthy majority for abolishing the death penalty for murder in 1965 for a trial period of five years, which was confirmed in December 1969.[13]

Even so, it was not long before repeated attempts were made—13 in all—to reintroduce capital punishment at least for some categories of murder, such as causing death through terrorist acts in 1982 and 1983 or the murder of a child in 1987. They were defeated for the same reasons that the Homicide Act was scrapped; namely that to pick one or two classes of murder out as deserving of death, when there might be equally heinous offences committed in categories of murder not subject to capital punishment, would inevitably produce anomalies and a sense of injustice. But what put an end to these debates was a spate of wrongful and unsafe convictions for just such offences. The most notable were the cases of the 'Birmingham Six', the 'Guildford Four', and the Price sisters, all wrongfully convicted of terrorist offences, and Stefan Kisko, wrongfully convicted of a child sex murder. All would certainly have attracted the death penalty had it been available. This persuaded many who had previously supported the reintroduction of capital punishment to change their minds: most prominent among them was the then Conservative Home Secretary, Michael Howard. So, on the last occasion that the question of the reintroduction of capital punishment was debated in the British Parliament in 1994, the motion was defeated by a very large majority.[14]

Most West European nations have come to recognize that, even in circumstances of war, capital punishment inflicted by the state is contrary to their commitment to maintain human rights.[15] Thus, in its reply to the Fifth United Nations Survey in 1995 Switzerland stated that it had abolished the death penalty for military offences because it constituted 'a flagrant violation of the right to life and dignity . . . the arguments in favour of the abolition of the death penalty in peacetime are just as valid concerning its abolition in wartime because there cannot be two ways to guarantee human rights'. Similarly, Spain took the view 'that the death penalty has no place in the general penal system of advanced, civilised societies . . . What more degrading or afflictive punishment can be imagined than to deprive a person of his life, or can anyone conceive of anything more contrary to the philosophy of punishment enshrined in our Constitution, where punishment is seen as a means of rehabilitation,

---

[13] By 343 votes to 185. See Radzinowicz, n. 9 above, pp. 272–3.

[14] See Gavin Drewry, 'The Politics of Capital Punishment', in G. Drewry, and C. Blake (eds), *Law and the Spirit of Inquiry* (1999), pp. 137–59 at 151 and 154. Also, Lord Windlesham, *Responses to Crime*, vol. 3 (1996), pp. 60–61. However, as far as public opinion is concerned, the decline in support for capital punishment has not been very great. The British Social Attitudes Survey showed that between 1985 and 1990 the proportion of the public who were in favour of capital punishment for murder in the course of a terrorist act fell from 77% to 70%, for murder of a policeman from 71% to 67%, and for other murders from 66% to 61%. There was no further decline in the support for capital punishment between 1990 and 1994. See Lindsay Brook and Ed Cape, 'Libertarianism in Retreat', in Roger Jowell *et al.* (eds), *British Social Attitudes: The 12th Report* (1995), pp. 191–209 at 193–194. But in the latest survey on British Social Attitudes in 1999, 56.9% of respondents agreed with the statement 'For some crimes, the death penalty is the most appropriate sentence'.

[15] See AI, *The Death Penalty in Wartime: Arguments for Abolition* (1994), AI Index: ACT 50/01/94.

than deprivation of life.' And Greece expressed similar sentiments when it abolished capital punishment for ordinary offences in 1993: 'human life is of supreme value . . . [and] efficiency of the death penalty has been proven non-existent'. Yet it still retains remnants of capital punishment in its military code.[16]

As mentioned above, only one West European country, Turkey, now retains the death penalty for grave offences in peacetime. It seemed as if Turkey was moving towards abolition during the lengthy moratorium on executions between 1973 and 1980. But the military junta in power from 1980 to 1983 judicially executed 48 persons, 25 for politically related offences and 23 for common crimes. Since the return to civilian government only two executions have been carried out, both for politically motivated homicides, the last in October 1984.

Although Turkey is a long-standing member of the Council of Europe, and that has been a major factor in maintaining its abolitionist de facto status, it has yet to sign and ratify the Sixth Protocol to the ECHR or to give sufficient assurances to the European Union (for which it is a candidate member) that it intends to abandon capital punishment entirely. Turkey stated, in its response to the United Nations in 1995, that its policy was 'aimed not at abolishing the death penalty but at reducing and limiting the offences carrying the death penalty'. It had reduced the number of capital offences from 29 to 19, including abolition of the death penalty for offences relating to narcotics. Nevertheless, death sentences have continued to be imposed— between 1994 and 1998, 19 for ordinary offences and 11 for offences against the state, and in 2000 at least 80 death sentences were imposed for a variety of offences—although none can be carried out without ratification by the Turkish Parliament. In 1999 the Kurdish rebel leader Abdullah Ocalan was sentenced to death for treason and separatism, sparking international protests. His appeal to the European Court of Human Rights on the grounds that his treatment has infringed twelve articles of the European Convention has been accepted but has yet to be determined. It is widely recognized that Turkey's hopes of membership of the EU would be gravely prejudiced were Ocalan (or another 'terrorist') to be executed. On the other hand, the Turkish Parliament has taken action in relation to 'ordinary' crimes. In October 2001 a constitutional amendment was passed barring the imposition of the death penalty in all circumstances except those committed 'in times of war, imminent threat of war and for terrorism'.[17] In effect, this has made Turkey 'almost' an abolitionist country for 'ordinary crimes'.

2. EASTERN EUROPE AND THE FORMER SOVIET UNION

While communist governments held sway in Eastern Europe, the official attitude towards capital punishment had been that, while in principle it was incompatible

---

[16] Art. 33 of 2172/1993 (16 Dec. 1993); see Ilias G. Anagnostopoulos and Konstaninos D. Magliveras, *Criminal Law in Greece* (2000), paras. 207–208 at p. 104.
[17] AI, *Death Penalty News*, Sept. 2001, AI Index: ACT 53/004/2001, p. 3.

with socialist ideals, it was nevertheless regarded as 'a temporary and exceptional measure of punishment which is temporarily applied pending its complete abolition, and only for specific and extremely dangerous offences which threaten the foundations of the structure of the state and society and which are committed under especially aggravated circumstances'.[18]

The first country to cast this doctrine aside was the former German Democratic Republic, which in 1987, as part of its attempt to shore up the regime by demonstrating its concern for human rights, declared that capital punishment was no longer essential to defend socialism from violent crimes or even the legacy of Nazi war crimes.[19] Soon afterwards the advent of democracy in nearly all the states formerly under Soviet influence created the springboard for abolishing, or substantially reducing the scope of, the death penalty. And this movement was given further impetus by the desire of most of these newly free states to become members of the Council of Europe. Romania led the way by abolishing capital punishment immediately after the fall and summary execution of President Ceauşescu and his wife in December 1989.[20] In Hungary the Constitutional Court, after hearing the proposal from the League against Capital Punishment, declared the death penalty unconstitutional in October 1990 on the main ground that it violated the fundamental right to life and human dignity.[21] After 'the elimination of the totalitarian regime' (as the new government described it), the Parliament of the Federal Czech and Slovak Republic voted in May 1990 to abolish capital punishment. Two months later this was embodied in the laws of the now separate Czech Republic and Slovakia, both of which became members of the Council of Europe in that year, and ratified Protocol No. 6 in 1992.

The situation in Yugoslavia has been complicated, as in so many other ways, by the break-up of the former Federal Republic in 1991. The newly independent state of Bosnia-Hercegovina retained the death penalty, but in 1997 it was abolished when the Human Rights Chamber of the Human Rights Commission (established under the General Framework Agreement for Peace in Bosnia-Hercegovina) ruled that the death penalty could not be imposed for crimes committed in peacetime.[22] Slovenia, where there had been a strong abolitionist movement, had already abolished the death

---

[18] Reply from the USSR to the Questionnaire on the Implementation of Safeguards Guaranteeing Protection of Rights of those Facing the Death Penalty, United Nations, Crime Prevention and Criminal Justice Branch, 1987 (hereafter cited as United Nations Safeguards Survey, 1987).

[19] *Resolution of the Council of the State of the German Democratic Republic on Abolishing the Death Penalty in the GDR of 17 July 1987.* The last execution had taken place in 1981. See. Evans, n. 2 above, pp. 859–864.

[20] Under Decree Law of 7 Jan. 1990. Ironically, President Ceauşescu had, in February 1988, proposed legislation to restrict capital punishment to exceptional cases involving state security and Romanian sovereignty. Romania became a member of the Council of Europe in 1993 and ratified Protocol No. 6 in 1994.

[21] Constitutional Court Decision No. 23/1990 (X.31) AB on the constitutionality of capital punishment. See Tibor Horvath, 'L'Abolition de la peine de mort en Hongrie', *Revue Internationale de Criminologie et de Police Technique* 2 (1992), pp. 167–179. In 1990 Hungary became a member of the Council of Europe and ratified Protocol No. 6 in 1992.

[22] The new Criminal Code of the Bosnia-Hercegovinian entity of Republika Srpska, adopted in June 2000, has no provision for the death penalty.

penalty under its state law in 1989 and, on becoming independent in 1991, enshrined this in its new Constitution, Article 17 of which states, 'Human life is inviolable. There shall be no capital punishment in the Republic of Slovenia.' Similarly, Macedonia and Croatia marked their independence from Yugoslavia by making capital punishment unconstitutional. In its reply to the United Nations Fifth Survey in 1995 Macedonia cited as its reasons 'modern views in penology which negate the need for the death penalty, democratic developments in our society and the constitutional guarantees to the right to life'.[23]

The remaining parts of the Federal Republic of Yugoslavia (comprising Serbia and Montenegro) abolished the death penalty under the Federal Criminal Code in 1993, but it was not until the end of 2001 that both states took action to abolish it for aggravated murder under state law. Serbia amended its criminal code in November 2001 and in June 2002 Montenegro followed suit.

The last execution in Bulgaria took place in 1989. The following year the President commuted all death sentences to thirty years' imprisonment and established a moratorium on executions in anticipation of Bulgaria's accession to membership of the Council of Europe in 1992. It took another six years, during which the moratorium was maintained, before capital punishment was abolished completely in December 1998, following a presidential initiative that was taken up by the Legal Committee for the National Assembly.

Also in the Balkan area Albania moved rapidly towards formal abolition of the death penalty as the country prepared for membership of the Council of Europe. The last execution took place in 1995 and a year later the President of the Parliament declared a moratorium on executions.[24] In December 1999 the Albanian Constitutional Court ruled that the death penalty was unconstitutional, and in September 2000 it was removed from the Criminal Code for ordinary crimes and Protocol No. 6 to the ECHR was then ratified.

Support for abolition of the death penalty had begun to gather force in Poland in the late 1970s.[25] Articles appeared in the influential journal *Polityka*, and the Ministerial Commission for the Reform of the Penal Law, the Centre for Civil Legislative Incentives (an organ of Solidarity), and the Congress of the Polish Bar Association all called for abolition. In 1987 the Polish Ministry of Justice appointed a new Commission on the Reform of the Criminal Law, and a moratorium on executions began in 1988. The first stage of abolition came in 1990, the year prior to Poland becoming a member of the Council of Europe, when capital punishment was eliminated for the offence of organizing and directing a major economic crime. Early in 1998 capital punishment was removed entirely when the new Polish Penal

---

[23] Slovenia became a member of the Council of Europe in 1993, Macedonia in 1995, and Croatia in 1996. They ratified Protocol No. 6 to the ECHR in 1994, 1997, and 1997 respectively.

[24] *Status of the International Covenants on Human Rights, Question of the Death Penalty*, Report of the Secretary-General submitted pursuant to Commission Resolution 1997/12, Commission on Human Rights, 54th Session, E/CN.4/1998/82.

[25] See Alicja Grzeskowiak, 'Capital Punishment in Polish Penal Law', *United Nations Crime Prevention and Criminal Justice Newsletter* 12 and 13 (1986), pp. 43–46 at 44.

Code of 1996 came into effect. In its response to the Sixth UN Survey on Capital Punishment in 1999, Poland stated that the motivation for abolition was a combination of 'political will, official inquiry, and the influence of United Nations policy'.

The history of capital punishment in the former Soviet Union was turbulent. It was abolished three times, in 1917–18, in 1920–1, and for peacetime offences between 1947 and 1950,[26] but each time was soon reinstated. On each occasion the rationale for its reintroduction was based on Lenin's assertion that the death penalty was necessary to defend the revolution from its class enemies—those involved in counter-revolutionary actions, terrorist acts, or deemed to be members of organizations set on rebellion. Such a formula, of course, lent itself to elastic definition, and during the Stalinist period and the heyday of the Security Police thieves as well as dissidents were classed as 'enemies of the people' and therefore political offenders liable to the death penalty. The number of executions at the height of the purges of 1937–8 has been said to have reached 1 million: indeed, 'taking the [twentieth] century as a whole, few countries have used capital punishment so extensively, either judicially or extra-judicially'.[27]

In the 1960s the death penalty in the Soviet Union was applied not only to premeditated murder but also to certain economic crimes, aggravated rape, and hijacking.[28] However, in 1980 it was abolished for rape of an adult as part of the movement to restrict its use 'pending its complete abolition'. This was further fuelled during the period of perestroika,[29] and by 1991 the USSR in its new 'Fundamentals of Criminal Legislation' restricted the scope of the death penalty from 18 offences to five, dropping most notably economic crimes and exempting women. With the break-up of the Soviet Union in December 1991 and the abolition of the communist system, the Russian Federation adopted a new Constitution, Article 20 of which stated:

1. 'Everyone has the right to life' and
2. 'Until such time as it is repealed, the death penalty may be imposed under Federal Law as an extreme measure of punishment for particularly serious crimes against life, the accused possessing the right to have his case considered by a court with the participation of sworn assessors [meaning jurors].'

From the late 1980s the number of death sentences fell dramatically, although executions, rare in the early 1990s, were again becoming more frequent by the mid-1990s.[30] Then, in 1996, President Yeltsin issued a decree declaring a moratorium on

---

[26] A useful short history of capital punishment in Russia and the former Soviet Union can be found in Alexander S. Mikhlin, *The Death Penalty in Russia* (1999), pp. 8–22.

[27] Introduction by W. E. Butler to Mikhlin, *ibid.*, p. 4.

[28] See Ger P. van den Berg, 'The Soviet Union and the Death Penalty', *Soviet Studies* 35 (1983), pp. 154–174.

[29] *Moscow News* 50 (1987). Another pronouncement calling for abolition had come from Professor Alexander Maksimovich Yakovlev, Head of the Theory and Sociology of Criminal Law Section of the USSR Academy of Sciences' Institute of State and Law. See *Current Soviet Press* (1988), p. 10.

[30] See Ger P. van den Berg, 'Russia and Other CIS States', in P. Hodgkinson and A. Rutherford (eds), *Capital Punishment: Global Issues and Prospects* (1996), pp. 77–103 at 84–88. In 1985, 448 persons were sentenced to death and 40 executed. Death sentences averaged around 150 between 1991 and 1996 and

all executions in the Russian Federation.[31] The catalyst for change was Russia's desire to ally itself with Europe and to become, eventually, part of the European Union. Upon accession to the Council of Europe in 1996, Russia undertook, as a condition of membership, to abolish the death penalty and ratify Protocol No. 6 to the ECHR within three years. Yet by the end of 2001 the Russian Criminal Code and Constitution had still not been amended so as to abolish the death penalty in law.

Nevertheless, capital punishment was in effect made redundant by a ruling of the Constitutional Court in February 1999, which laid down (in conformity with Article 20 (2) of the Constitution) that it could only be imposed when all citizens in all the Federation's 89 republics, regions, and territories had been granted the right to jury trial. At present this is only available in nine of the republics. In June 1999, according to information provided by the Organization for Security and Cooperation in Europe (OSCE), the President signed a decree commuting the sentences of all convicts on death row to either life sentences or terms of 25 years' imprisonment.

Thus, in practice (although not strictly according to the ten-year rule), the Russian Federation has become an abolitionist de facto state. It appears that what stands in the way of abolition de jure is the political sensitivity of pushing legislation through the Duma at a time when political and public opinion is sensitive to the need to react vigorously to a very serious and mounting crime problem. Indeed, early in 2002 a large majority of the members of the State Duma, supported by a petition signed by 100 prominent citizens, appealed to President Putin to reinstate capital punishment because of the country's high murder rate.[32] But President Putin resisted this pressure and committed himself to uphold the moratorium on the death penalty. However, there has been no sign that the Russian Federation is about to honour its commitment to ratify Protocol No. 6 to the ECHR.[33] The situation as regards the necessary legislation finally to abolish capital punishment appears to be 'frozen' until better times arrive.[34]

By December 2001 eight of the other 14 independent states that had emerged out of Russia's former empire had abolished capital punishment. Again, the main impetus appears to have been the desire to join the Council of Europe and eventually the European Union. Moldova led the way in 1995 on accession to membership of the Council of Europe[35] but several other countries found it difficult to achieve abolition so soon after accession. Thus Estonia, which had ceased executions in 1991,

the number of executions was: 1 in 1992, 4 in 1993, 19 in 1994, 86 in 1995, and 53 in 1996; see Mikhlin, n. 26 above, pp. 7 and 118.

[31] However, executions continued in the breakaway republic of Chechnya under Islamic law in 1997, 1998, and 1999. See AI, *Report 2000*, p. 202.

[32] Van den Berg, n. 30 above, p. 90, above, described the frequency of murder in Russia as 'appalling', about 20 homicides per 100,000 inhabitants in 1993–5. Since then it has remained at this very high level: considerably more than twice as high as the United States.

[33] See AI News Release, AI Index: EUR 46/017/2001.

[34] I am grateful to Academician Professor Vitaly Kvashis for keeping me informed about the situation in Russia. According to a report in the *Moscow Times*, 26 Nov. 2001, amendments to abolish capital punishment were due to be submitted to the Duma in December 2001, but nothing came of this.

[35] Although the self-proclaimed Dnestr Moldavian Republic remains retentionist. No executions have been reported.

took five years from its accession in 1993 to abolish capital punishment finally in 1998. Lithuania, which had acceded in 1993, and Latvia, in 1994, both carried out executions after this date before finally abolishing the death penalty in 1998 and 1999 respectively.

Ukraine agreed to an immediate moratorium on executions and to ratify Protocol No. 6 to the ECHR within three years from the date of its accession to the Council of Europe in November 1995.[36] But executions continued on a considerable scale— a total of 180 from the beginning of 1996 until the moratorium was eventually put into effect on 11 March 1997. The then Minister of Justice, Serhiy Holovatiy, a committed abolitionist, accused the President of Ukraine of failing in political leadership by not signing the decree to implement the moratorium, but it is also true to say that there was very strong public and press opposition to abolition. Indeed opinion polls showed that only six per cent were in favour of immediate abolition and that 62 per cent wished to see the death penalty more intensively applied.[37] It is therefore not surprising that attempts by the Ukrainian Cabinet to abolish the death penalty through a provision of the new Criminal Code failed to gain the support of the Ukrainian Parliament. However, in December 1999 the Supreme Court of Ukraine ruled that all provisions of the Criminal Code relating to the death penalty were incompatible with Articles 27 and 28 of the Ukrainian Constitution.[38] Finally, in February 2000 the Ukrainian Supreme Council (Parliament) removed provisions on the death penalty from the Ukrainian Criminal Code, Code of Prosecutions Procedure, and the Penitentiary Code.

The desire to gain membership of the Council of Europe was not the only reason why former states of the Soviet Union decided to abandon capital punishment. The importance of political leadership in this region was demonstrated in Georgia, where capital punishment was abolished on the initiative of its president, Eduard Shevardnadze, in 1997, well before becoming a member of the Council of Europe in 1999.[39] Similarly, the complete abolition of the death penalty by the Parliament of Azerbaijan in February 1998, following a moratorium on executions since June 1993, was the result of a bill introduced by the President of the Republic in support of human rights, despite the strong Islamic influences in that country.[40]

---

[36] See AI News Release, AI Index: EUR 50/16/95.

[37] Serhiy Holovatiy, 'Abolishing the Death Penalty in Ukraine: Difficulties Real or Imagined?,' in Council of Europe, *The Death Penalty: Abolition in Europe* (1999), pp. 139–151 at 145 and 147.

[38] See Organization for Security and Cooperation in Europe (OSCE), *The Death Penalty in the OSCE Area: A Survey, January 1998–June 1999*, Review Conference, Sept. 1999, Background Paper 1999/1 (1999), pp. 23–24; Council of Europe Compliance with Member States Commitments AS/Inf. (1999) 2, pp. 124–125; and Holovatiy, n. 37 above, pp. 139–151.

[39] Death sentences do, however, continue to be imposed in the disputed region of Abkhazia (an internationally unrecognized entity). However, no executions have been carried out there since Georgia abolished capital punishment. There have been no reports of death sentences being imposed in the other Georgian disputed area of South Osetia, which uses the criminal code of Russia. See AI, *Report 2001*, p. 107. And OSCE, n. 38 above, pp. 15–16.

[40] AI, *Concerns in Europe, January–June 2001*. AI Index: EUR 01/003/2001. In May 2001 Azerbaijan also followed the policy of the European Union in forbidding extradition to countries where the death penalty would be carried out.

The change in policy and practice in Turkmenistan (where 89 per cent of the people are Muslim) was also remarkable. Although no official figures were published, it was thought that well over 100 people were executed in each of the years 1994, 1995, and 1996—one of the highest ratios in the world, in relation to population. The new Criminal Code adopted in 1997 provided the death penalty for as many as 17 offences, yet on 1 January 1999 the President announced a moratorium on executions and by December of that year had abolished the death penalty completely by Presidential Decree.[41]

Other countries formerly in the Soviet bloc have responded more gradually. Armenia reduced the number of capital offences and has executed no one since 1991. In its reply to the United Nations Sixth Survey in 1999 the government reported that it intended to abolish the death penalty, but the new Criminal Code has yet to be approved by the Armenian Parliament.[42] Although death sentences have continued to be imposed,[43] Armenia classifies itself as abolitionist de facto and signed Protocol No. 6 to the ECHR in January 2001 as an indication of its intentions not to revert to executions.

Kyrgyzstan also abolished capital punishment for economic crimes as well as for several other offences. The process began when a bill was introduced in 1997 supported by the President. A year later he established a moratorium on executions, and a new Criminal Code was expected to be introduced in 2001, which would totally remove the death penalty from the crimes (terrorism, murder, aggravated rape, and state treason) for which it is still prescribed. So far, however (July 2002), the President has only gone so far as to issue a policy decree stating that 'one of the objectives for Kyrgyzstan in the field of human rights is the gradual reduction of the application of the death penalty and its eventual abolition'.[44]

The scope of the death penalty has also been considerably reduced in law in several other countries which have predominant or large Muslim populations. Tajikistan, where 85 per cent of the people are Muslim, reduced its list of capital crimes in 1998 from 44 to 15;[45] and in Kazakhstan (where about half the people are of the Muslim faith) the scope of capital punishment in 1998 was reduced from 15 to three peacetime offences.[46] It is reported that the President of Kazakhstan plans to replace capital punishment with life imprisonment by 2003, or earlier if international aid could be obtained to build the necessary new prisons.

---

[41] See OSCE, n. 38 above, pp. 22–23.

[42] United Nations, *Report of the Human Rights Committee*, General Assembly, Official Records Fiftieth Session, vol. 1, suppl. no. 40, 1996 (A/50/40) p. 37; and OSCE, n. 38 above, p. 12.

[43] AI, n. 40 above.

[44] Reported in *Agence France Presse*, 5 January 2002.

[45] AI, *Report 2001*, p. 237. See also OSCE, n. 38 above, pp. 20–21. The list includes: rape, terrorism, hijacking, drug trafficking, and illegal cultivation of crops containing narcotic substances. However, according to a report on a conference held in Tajikistan in December 2001, around 100 people had been executed that year: a very high rate in relation to a population of less than 6 million.

[46] Premeditated murder, aggravated murder, and genocide, plus treason in time of war and eight military crimes. See OSCE, n. 38 above, p. 16.

Although the number of capital offences in Uzbekistan (where 88 per cent of the population are Muslims) had been substantially reduced—from 13 to eight and then in October 2001 to four—as evidence of its policy 'to abolish the death penalty by stages', there have been continuing reports to Amnesty International of large numbers of death sentences and executions. The government of Uzbekistan has been severely criticized by the UN Human Rights Committee for refusing to make this information available, without which it is impossible to say how far the authorities in practice are sincere in their claims to be moving towards abolition.[47]

Belarus also reduced the number of capital offences in 1995, most notably by declaring that 'under the new socio-economic conditions it [capital punishment] was inappropriate' for economic crimes such as the taking of bribes under aggravating circumstances and the theft of state property in particularly large amounts. However, the death penalty is still available for a wide range of offences including, in addition to premeditated murder, for political offences (treason, plotting to seize power, terrorism, sabotage, bombings that threaten public safety) as well as undermining the work of a prison and aggravated rape. There has been no moratorium on executions: far from it. They continue to be carried out on a very considerable scale (see page 91 below).

Thus, the new countries of the former Soviet Union have responded in different ways to capital punishment. Just over half have taken the principled view, no doubt influenced by the 'human rights culture' of the Council of Europe and European Community, that the death penalty cannot be reconciled with the values of a democratic state that respects human life and human rights. Others, in the context of major economic, social, and cultural changes, have clung to the old justifications that 'conditions are not yet ripe' and 'the public is not yet sufficiently prepared and educated to accept it'. Underlying this viewpoint is the belief that the abolition of the supreme sanction may be taken as an indicator of a lack of resolve by the state to deal effectively with crime.

Sixteen states in Eastern Europe had by the end of 2001 ratified Protocol No. 6 to the ECHR and three had signed it.[48] Nine of these countries have also ratified the Second Optional Protocol to the ICCPR, and a further two of them have signed it.[49]

---

[47] See AI, Uzbekistan. *The Rhetoric of Human Rights Protection: Briefing for the United Nations Human Rights Committee*, AI Index: EUR 62/006/2001, June 2001, pp. 9–14, 16–21; concluding observations of the Human Rights Committee on Uzbekistan, CCPR/CO/71/UZB. 67, 6 Apr. 2001; also *Uzbekistan. Mothers Against the Death Penalty* (2002), AI Index: EUR 62/009/2002.

[48] Albania, Bulgaria, Croatia, the Czech Republic, Estonia, Georgia, Hungary, Latvia, Lithuania, Poland, the Republic of Moldova, Romania, Slovakia, Slovenia, Macedonia, and Ukraine ratified Protocol No. 6, and Armenia (2001), Azerbaijan (2001), and the Russian Federation (1997) signed it.

[49] Azerbaijan, Bulgaria, Croatia, Georgia, Hungary, Romania, Slovakia, Slovenia, and Macedonia ratified the Second Optional Protocol to the ICCPR, and Lithuania and Poland signed it. Bosnia-Hercegovina, Turkmenistan, and Yugoslavia have ratified the Second Optional Protocol only.

3. THE MIDDLE EAST AND NORTH AFRICA

Most of the states of the Middle East and North Africa continue to express their strong support for the death penalty and few have shown any signs of abolishing it. In fact, the trend is towards expansion of the scope of capital punishment and, in several countries, a vigorous enforcement of it.[50] The exception is the state of Israel, which abolished capital punishment in 1954 for all crimes except those connected with the Holocaust, for which there has only been one notorious execution, that of Adolf Eichmann in 1962.

Every one of the 11 countries in this region which replied to the United Nations Survey on Safeguards in 1987 said that there were 'no official initiatives or plans to abolish the death penalty for any . . . offences'.[51] Very few of them have considered it appropriate to respond to subsequent United Nations surveys on capital punishment.[52]

Tunisia is the only country in this region which seems to be committed to its abolitionist de facto status. Its reply to the United Nations in 1995 stated that 'Even after the death sentence has been passed, the President of the Republic . . . does not in practice authorize execution of the death penalty.' Indeed, no executions have taken place since 1991. Four other countries in this region have also gone through long periods when the death penalty has not been enforced, giving the impression that they had become abolitionist de facto, yet executions were resumed. In 1977 Bahrain carried out executions after a lapse of twenty years, and followed this by another nineteen years of de facto abolition before carrying out another execution in 1996 for the premeditated murder of a police officer. Qatar executed two men and a woman for murder in 2000, eleven years after its last execution. Libya was de facto an abolitionist country for twenty-three years until executions were resumed in 1977. Despite Colonel Qaddafi's public announcement in 1988 that he favoured total abolition, several executions have been reported since then.[53] The Libyan position has hardened. In voting against the resolution in favour of abolition, a moratorium, or restricting the scope of the death penalty, at the fifty-seventh session of the UN Commission on Human Rights in April 2001 (see Chapter 1 page 20 above), the Libyan representative argued that the resolution 'disregarded the dignity of the

---

[50] It should be noted, however, that in 1975 the Yemen Arab Republic abolished capital punishment for adultery and rape, and in 1976 the Yemen People's Republic reduced the number of political crimes liable to the death penalty. These countries were united as the Republic of Yemen in 1990.

[51] These were: Algeria, Bahrain, Egypt, Iraq, Jordan, Kuwait, Morocco, Qatar, Sudan, Syria, and United Arab Emirates.

[52] Only Morocco, Tunisia, and Qatar responded to the Fifth Survey in 1995, and only Bahrain, Iraq (although no figures on the number of death sentences or executions were provided), Lebanon, and Morocco to the Sixth Survey in 1999.

[53] See AI *Report 1993*, p. 194, reporting six executions in 1992 for criminal offences including murder and rape, and AI, *Report 1998*, p. 237, reporting eight executions in 1997, six for 'passing defence secrets to foreign states'.

victims who were killed or assassinated . . . The death penalty concerned the justice system and was not a question of human rights.'[54]

Lebanon had also been classified as abolitionist de facto until a man was hanged in 1994, eleven years after the previous execution. Between 1994 and 1998, 14 executions took place. However, early in 2000 it was reported that the Prime Minister had refused to sign the decree of execution of two people, stating that it was inconsistent with his convictions,[55] and in July 2001 the Lebanese Parliament unanimously abolished the mandatory death penalty for premeditated murder and gave judges discretion to impose it only in extreme cases. In December 2001 Amnesty International reported that Prime Minister Emile Lahoud had made a commitment to impose a moratorium on executions during his term of office.[56]

It is well over a decade since the government of Algeria informed the United Nations that it did not regard it as 'inconceivable that in time a de facto abolition of capital punishment will be witnessed'.[57] However, since then the security situation has deteriorated and a state of emergency has existed since February 1992. As a result, some of the repealed provisions of the emergency legislation relating to the death penalty have been incorporated into normal penal law, resulting in an increase in the number of offences punishable by death.[58] Although some executions of persons convicted by special courts of anti-terrorist law took place in August 1993, by December of that year a moratorium was announced and this has prevailed—despite the fact that extra-judicial killings and massacres by rebel groups and security forces have continued on a horrifying scale, and several hundred persons remain under sentence of death.

All of these examples show that although capital punishment is retained in these Islamic countries, none of them appear to be committed to it as a regular means of enforcing their criminal laws.

On the other hand, many other countries in this region appear to be fully committed to supporting capital punishment. Egypt has maintained the use of the death penalty, not only for premeditated murder and rape associated with kidnapping, but also for serious drug offences. In response to the violent protests of militant fundamentalists, the government extended the death penalty through an amendment to the Penal Code in 1992 to cover 'terrorist offences' and this led to a substantial rise in the number of death sentences—from 21 in 1992 to 78 in 1995. According to Amnesty figures, at least 108 people were sentenced to death in 1999, nine of them *in absentia* by military courts, and three women and 13 men were executed. In 2000 at least 79 people were sentenced to death and six women and 16

---

[54] UN Resolution E/CN.4/RES/2001/68 and Press Release 25/04/01, *Commission on Human Rights Adopts Ten Resolutions, Measures on the Death Penalty, Impunity, and Other Issues Concerning the Promotion and Protection of Human Rights*, Commission on Human Rights 57th Session, 25 Apr. 2001.

[55] AI, *Lebanon: Amnesty International Calls for Immediate Death Penalty Moratorium*, AI Index: MDE 18/003/2000.

[56] AI, News Release, *Pakistan: Young Offenders Taken off Death Row*, AI Index: ASA 33/029/2001.

[57] M. J. Bossuyt, *The Administration of Justice and the Human Rights of Detainees* (1987), p. 25.

[58] *Report of the Human Rights Committee*, General Assembly, Official Records 53rd Session, vol. 1, suppl. no. 40, 1998 (A/53/40), p. 81.

men were executed. In both years the majority of death sentences were handed out following conviction for murder.[59]

Since 1989 the scope of capital statutes has been extended in 14 Middle Eastern countries, notably for the production of and trafficking in drugs, but also in some of them for sexual and economic crimes (see Chapter 3 pages 82–84 below). The countries concerned are Bahrain, Brunei Darussalam, Iran, Iraq, Syria, Jordan, Kuwait, Libya, Oman, Qatar, Saudi Arabia, Sudan, the United Arab Emirates, and Yemen.

While only two countries in this region—Saudi Arabia and Yemen—(and formerly the Taliban government of Afghanistan) apply Islamic law in its entirety, it has nevertheless had a pervasive influence on penal thought throughout the Muslim world. Punishments in Islamic law are intended to be 'preventative before the event, and intimidating and salutary after the event', but free from any hint of vengeance or torture. Thus, the justification for capital punishment is based on both just retribution and utilitarianism. The death penalty is the mandatory penalty for certain Hudud crimes (punishments laid down by the Koran or the Sonna, over which the judge has no discretionary power and no pardon or amicable settlement is possible): for rebellion, or obdurate apostasy of Islam, for certain cases of highway robbery involving homicide, and for adultery by a married person, provided very stringent standards of proof are adhered to.[60] Death is also the punishment for premeditated murder, but the discretion whether to enforce it lies with the victim's family. They may seek retaliation (Qisas), but they may also pardon the murderer or accept 'blood money'—compensation or forfeited rights of inheritance (Diya). The Koran appeals for such forgiveness, promising absolution of sins for those who extend a pardon. According to a Saudi Arabian source, the government 'does its utmost, before the execution of Qisas to convince the relatives of the victim to commute the Qisas into . . . Diya, in some cases these efforts have succeeded while in other cases they have failed'.[61] Yet it has been pointed out that this procedure much better protects Saudi nationals than it does foreign workers sentenced to death, many of whom do not have these familial resources to save them from execution.[62] The death penalty can also be imposed as a 'Ta 'zir' punishment (one adopted by the State to fulfil 'the needs of society') under the Shari'a for espionage and for sodomy, although with the same very stringent evidential restrictions required in order to obtain a conviction for adultery.

[59] See AI, *Report 2000*, p. 96, and AI, *Report 2001*, p. 92. Also AI, *Egypt. Increasing Use of the Death Penalty* (2002), AI Index: MDE 12/017/2002.

[60] See N. Hosni, 'La Peine de mort en droit égyptien et en droit islamique', *Revue Internationale de Droit Pénal* 58 (1987), pp. 407–420 at 415–20. Also the useful discussion in M. Lippman, S. McConville, and M. Yerushalmi, *Islamic Criminal Law and Procedure* (1988), pp. 37–53 and 82–89.

[61] See Sheik Mohammed Ibn Ibrahim Al-Hewesh, 'Shari'a Penalties and Ways of their Implementation in the Kingdom of Saudi Arabia', in *The Effects of Islamic Legislation on Crime Prevention in Saudi Arabia* (1980), Kingdom of Saudi Arabia in collaboration with UNSDRI, Rome, pp. 349–400 at 377. Also, William A. Schabas, 'Symposium. Religion's Role in the Administration of the Death Penalty: Islam and the Death Penalty', *William and Mary Bill of Rights Journal* 9 (2000), pp. 223–236.

[62] See AI, *Saudi Arabia: Defying World Trends: Saudi Arabia's Extensive Use of Capital Punishment*, AI Index: MDE 23/105/2001, p. 8.

What is striking is that there is no publicly voiced opposition to capital punishment in these countries: no vestiges of an abolitionist movement. Apparently, to oppose the death penalty openly in Saudi Arabia would put the advocate in danger of being classified as apostate or 'corrupt on earth': crimes that are themselves subject to the threat of capital punishment.[63] In Egypt the retention of the death penalty is said to be 'essential for the maintenance of law and order',[64] and Iraq, where Amnesty International claims 'hundreds of political prisoners are executed every year', has contended that abolition would be incompatible with its 'religion, historical heritage and cultural values'.[65] At the UN General Assembly, late in 1994, Sudan expressed these views in uncompromising terms: 'Capital punishment is a divine right of some religions. It is embodied in Islam and these views must be respected.'

4. AFRICA SOUTH OF THE SAHARA

When the Morris Report (covering the years up to 1965) was published, no country in the African region south of the Sahara had abolished the death penalty. Twenty-two years later, in 1987, the then Chief Justice of Zimbabwe told an international conference on the death penalty: 'Looking at Africa the depressing fact is . . . all African countries retain the death penalty'.[66] Only two small countries in the region (as defined by the United Nations)—Seychelles (for ordinary crimes only, 1979) and Cape Verde (1981)—had done away with capital punishment and only five were abolitionist de facto.[67]

The intervening years, up to the end of 2001, have witnessed a remarkable transformation towards the abolitionist position among African countries. Nine have eliminated capital punishment completely: Mozambique and Namibia in 1990, when it was prohibited by their new Constitutions; Angola in 1992; Guinea Bissau in 1993; and South Africa (by a decision of the Constitutional Court in 1995 and the Criminal Law Amendment Act of 1997). In addition, São Tomé and Principe, which had previously retained the death penalty for mercenary and military crimes, became completely abolitionist in 1990. The Prime Minister of Mauritius announced in 1987 that 'no death sentence is to be carried out for the time being',

---

[63] AI, *Saudi Arabia*, p. 11.

[64] A. Wazir, 'Quelques aspects de la peine de mort en droit pénal islamique', *Revue Internationale de Droit Pénal* 58 (1987), pp. 421–429.

[65] In their reasons for voting against the draft resolution on the abolition of the death penalty (A/C3/37/L.60/Rev.1) of the United Nations Commission on Human Rights in 1982. See Bossuyt, n. 57 above, pp. 30–31.

[66] E. Dumbutshena, 'The Death Penalty in Zimbabwe', *Revue Internationale de Droit Pénal* 58 (1987), pp. 521–532 at 524.

[67] There had been no executions in Madagascar for twenty years, the President always exercising his right to grant clemency; and none for over ten years in Côte d'Ivoire, Niger, and Senegal. São Tomé and Principe had become independent in 1975 and retained the death penalty for mercenarism and military crimes. No death sentences had been imposed.

and by November 1995 the National Assembly had voted, for the second time, to abolish the death penalty: the President then being obliged to sign this into law, having refused to do so on the first occasion because he was dissatisfied with the length of alternative imprisonment proposed.[68] Djibouti, which abolished the death penalty in 1995 (only one person having received a—later commuted—death sentence since the country became independent in 1977), informed the United Nations that this had been achieved through a combination of public opinion, political will, and empirical evidence. The turn of the century was marked by yet another African nation embracing abolition for all crimes, when the Côte d'Ivoire, after the government of President Bédié had been overthrown, adopted a new Constitution by referendum in July 2000, which banned capital punishment. Several of these countries—Cape Verde, Mozambique, Namibia, and the Seychelles—have ratified the Second Optional Protocol to the ICCPR and Guinea Bissau and São Tomé and Principe have declared their intention to do so by signing it.

Moreover, by the end of December 2001 the ranks of the de facto abolitionist nations in Africa had swollen to 11: Benin, Burkina Faso, the Central African Republic, the Republic of Congo, Eritrea, Gabon, The Gambia, Mali, Mauritania, Togo, and Swaziland. In July 1997 the President of Malawi commuted all death sentences, having signed no execution orders since taking up office in 1994.[69] However, three abolitionist de facto countries in sub-Saharan Africa resumed executions—Burundi, Comoro, and Guinea, the latter after seventeen years.[70]

The change in South Africa, a country that had been renowned for its extensive use of the death penalty, was particularly remarkable. The Society for the Abolition of Capital Punishment in South Africa had been established in 1971, but while apartheid persisted the government had rejected all calls for inquiries into the system. However, with the release of Nelson Mandela in February 1990 and the beginning of negotiations for constitutional change, the death penalty became one of the touchstones of commitment to a new social order. President F. W. de Klerk announced an immediate moratorium on executions, the last one having taken place on 2 February 1989, and in July 1990 the Criminal Law Amendment Act abolished capital punishment for housebreaking with intent to commit a crime or with aggravating circumstances, and made the death penalty for murder discretionary rather than mandatory. A tribunal was set up to review death sentences imposed before July 1990 and, as a result, the Minister of Justice announced in 1992 that all executions would continue to be suspended, pending the introduction of a Bill of Rights for the

---

[68] See AI, *Death Penalty News*, Sept. 1995, AI Index: ACT 53/03/95. Previously, under an amendment to the Dangerous Drugs Act 1986 (in Apr. 1992), the death penalty was made mandatory for drug trafficking.

[69] See the Report of the Secretary-General submitted pursuant to Commission Resolution 1997/12, Commission on Human Rights, 54th Session, *The Question of the Death Penalty*, E/CN.4/1998/82.

[70] It was reported that the Minister of Justice of Guinea stated in relation to the executions which took place in February 2001: 'It is not the government that decided to execute them [four men who had been sentenced to death for murder in 1995], but the judicial system and it will from now on be this way. Whoever is found guilty of murder will be executed.' AI, *Death Penalty News*, Mar. 2001, AI Index: ACT 53/002/2001, p. 2.

new South Africa. Despite the fact that the South African Transitional Constitution of 1993 was silent on the matter of whether or not the death penalty was permissible, the Attorney-General, in line with President Mandela's long-held belief that the death penalty was barbaric, brought a case before the Constitutional Court, arguing that the death penalty should be declared unconstitutional. The Court, in the landmark judgment of *The State* v. *T. Makwanyane and M. Mchunu* in 1995, decided that capital punishment was incompatible with the prohibition against 'cruel, inhuman or degrading' punishment and with a 'human rights culture' which made the rights to life and dignity the cornerstone of the Constitution.[71] A further influential argument was that it would be inconsistent with the spirit of reconciliation, post-apartheid. Thus, despite widespread concern about a tide of violent crime, and strong political pressures to reinstate the death penalty,[72] the South African Parliament endorsed the opinion of Judge Chaskalson, the President of the Constitutional Court, that the way to reduce violence was to create a 'human rights culture' which respects human life. In 1997 the Criminal Law Amendment Act removed all references to capital punishment from the statute book.

Of particular significance is the change in policy evident in Nigeria. For many years, and especially under military rule, Nigeria had one of the highest rates of execution in the world, the death sentence was mandatory for armed robbery, and public mass executions took place by firing squad. But since the country's return to civilian rule in 1999 no executions have taken place and President Obasanjo, who is personally opposed to capital punishment, granted an amnesty, early in 2000, to all those under sentence of death.[73] Yet the use of Islamic law in the northern provinces of Nigeria, where several death sentences have been imposed and an execution was carried out in 2001, suggests that the achievement of abolition, even de facto abolition, throughout Nigeria will be difficult to achieve.

This is also the case in several other African countries. In Zimbabwe, following the Report of the Advisory Committee on Law Reform in 1982, a draft law was eventually published in 1991 which aimed to limit death-eligible crimes to murder, treason, and some military offences. Eight years later, in November 1999, the Constitutional Commission recommended that the Constitution should retain the death penalty solely as an optional punishment for murder (it is currently mandatory for murder and treason). However, the necessary legislation has yet to be passed, and hopes that executions had become a thing of the past were shattered when they

---

[71] Case No. CCT/3/94 *State* v. *T. Makwanyane and M. Mchunu*; judgment was delivered on 6 June 1995. Reported in the *International Herald Tribune*, 7 June 1995. It was a moot point as to whether this judgment would apply to the offence of treason committed in time of war. This possibility was referred to by the Court but no argument was heard on it. See Raoul Wallenberg Institute of Human Rights and Humanitarian Law, *The Abolition of the Death Penalty in South Africa*, Report No. 23 (1997), Lund.

[72] See AI, 'Backlash Follows South African Ruling', *Death Penalty News*, Sept. 1995, AI Index: ACT 53/03/95. According to Professor B. Naude's report *Criminal Justice and the Death Penalty in South Africa: A Criminological Study* (1992), a public opinion survey published in the *Pretoria News*, 15 Aug. 1990, found that '74% of blacks believed that the abolition of the death penalty would lead to an increase in crime, whereas 70% of white and 63% of coloureds and Asians held this view'.

[73] See AI, *The Death Penalty Worldwide: Developments in 2000*, AI Index: ACT 50/001/2001, p. 9.

resumed in 1995 after a seven-year gap. The human rights situation in Zimbabwe has since deteriorated, and reports of extra-judicial executions have increased. Furthermore, three men were hanged for murder in October 2001, the first since April 1998.[74]

Zambia reduced the scope of capital punishment in 1990 by making it discretionary for murder rather than mandatory. Consideration was given to abolition in the mid-1990s by the Constitutional Review Commission, but it reported in favour of retaining capital punishment.[75] At a conference held in September 2000 the Minister of Justice stated that he would like to see the death penalty abolished as soon as 'the public would accept it'. Yet, although no executions have taken place since 1997, concern has been raised by the number of death sentences that continue to be handed down by the courts—at least 97 between 1998 and 2000, 59 of them for treason.[76]

Zaire, which subsequently became the Democratic Republic of Congo, seemed to be taking the path towards abolition until the outbreak of civil war. Between 1998 and 2000 serious concerns were expressed about the high number of executions being carried out (see page 91 below)[77] despite repeated assurances given to Amnesty International and the UN High Commissioner for Human Rights that the government would impose a moratorium on executions.[78]

It is particularly notable that several senior judges in African states have expressed sentiments in favour of abolition. The highly respected former chief justice Dumbutshena of Zimbabwe was a noted advocate of abolition. In the High Court of Tanzania, Justice James L. Mwalusanya ruled in a murder case in 1991 that the death penalty violated the Constitution because it was 'a cruel, inhuman and degrading punishment and or treatment and also that it offends the right to dignity of man in the process of execution of the sentence'.[79] It is interesting to note that the Tanzanian Court of Appeal agreed that capital punishment was 'cruel, inhuman and degrading' but nevertheless held that 'there was no conclusive proof regarding its effectiveness and it was for society to decide what was reasonably necessary': it was thus saved by Article 30 (2) of the Constitution of Tanzania, which provides for derogation from fundamental rights in the public interest.[80] The crux of its argument was that capital punishment could not be abolished while there was still such strong support for it. Indeed, it is these concerns that appear to be responsible for the reversal of abolitionist tendencies in several African countries, especially when

---

[74] AI, *Death Penalty News*, Dec. 2001, AI Index: ACT 53/001/2002, p. 4.

[75] See John Hatchard and Simon Coldham, 'Commonwealth Africa', in P. Hodgkinson and A. Rutherford (eds), *Capital Punishment: Global Issues and Prospects* (1996), pp. 155–191 at 160.

[76] AI, *Zambia: Time to Abolish the Death Penalty*, AI Index: AFR 63/004/2001 (July 2001), pp. 1–4.

[77] AI, *Report 2000*, p. 79, and AI, *Democratic Republic of Congo: 61 People Face Imminent Execution*, AI Index: AFR 62/006/2000.

[78] AI, *Report 2001*, p. 78.

[79] *Republic* v. *Mbushuu alias Dominic Mnyaroje and Kalai Sangula*, Criminal Sessions Case No. 44 of 1991, [1994] *Tanzanian Law Reports* 146–173 at 173.

[80] *Mbushuu* v. *Republic* [1995] LRC (Law Reports of the Commonwealth), 269 at pp. 216–217 and 232.

connected with civil unrest or even military *coups d'état*. The Gambia abolished the
death penalty completely in 1993, yet the Armed Forces Provisional Ruling Council
issued a decree in August 1995 which reintroduced capital punishment. In Sierra
Leone alleged plotters of a coup were summarily executed in 1992 to the accompani-
ment of international protests.[81] In 1997 Comoros carried out its first executions
since it gained independence in 1975: two men convicted of murder were executed,
one in public by firing squad. And Burundi executed six people in 1997 for participation in the massacres of Tutsi civilians in 1993, the first executions since 1981.
Executions were resumed after a periods of abeyance not only in Zimbabwe (see
above), but also in Botswana (where they were carried out in 1987, 1995, and 2001),
Cameroon (in 1988 and then in 1997), and Ethiopia (in 1991 and then not until
1998).

Since gaining independence in 1956, Sudan has witnessed a cycle of democratic
governance alternating with military and authoritarian rule. In 1983 Shari'a law was
introduced into the Sudanese Penal Code by President Numeiri and remained in
force under the rule of both the National Islamic Front and the military junta which
succeeded it in 1989: and it was extended to Northern Sudan in 1991. The death
penalty can be imposed for a wide range of crimes, including sexual and political
offences. Some indication of the extent of its use was given by the Sudanese Minister
of Justice in 1998 when he stated that 112 of the 894 sentenced to death since 1989
for murder and armed robbery had been executed.[82] The return to normal political
activity in 2000 has so far not had any effect on the issue of capital punishment.
Indeed in June 2002 Amnesty International reported that at least nineteen people
had been executed in the Dafus region of western Sudan after being convicted by
'Emergency' courts of offences such as armed robbery, banditry, and murder.

It has been claimed that support for the death penalty in many African countries
is rooted in 'customs and culture' that assume that 'for particularly reprehensible
crimes such as murder, death is the only fitting punishment'.[83] However, such opinions are just as prevalent in many abolitionist states, no doubt including South Africa
and Mozambique. Perhaps it is more significant that countries which suffer from
high rates of crime, weak policing, and fears of political instability often regard the
threat of capital punishment as an essential instrument of security, the abandonment
of which would be interpreted as a sign of weakness in the apparatus of state
control.[84] Yet, the fact that South Africa has abandoned the death penalty, despite
having one of the highest crime rates in the world, on the grounds that it infringes
fundamental principles of human rights, gives grounds for optimism.

---

[81] See AI, *Report 1993*, pp. 254–7. Also, Reuters, 5 Jan. 1993.

[82] AI, *Report 1998*, AI, *Report 1998*, p. 314.

[83] See D. D. N. Nsereko, 'The Death Penalty in Botswana' (1987), mimeo. Also, D. D. N. Nsereko
and M. J. A. Glickman, 'Capital Punishment in Botswana', *United Nations Crime Prevention and
Criminal Justice Newsletter* 12 and 13 (Nov. 1986), pp. 51–53.

[84] A. A. Adeyemi, 'Death Penalty: Criminological Perspectives. The Nigerian Situation', *Revue
Internationale de Droit Pénal* 58 (1987), pp. 485–502.

5. Asia and the Pacific

When Marc Ancel presented the first report on capital punishment to the United Nations in 1962 (covering the period up to 1961), the Australian state of Queensland was the only territory in the Pacific area in which the death penalty had been abolished completely. New South Wales and New Zealand were abolitionist for ordinary crimes but not for treason and military offences. Since then, all the Australian states have abolished the death penalty absolutely, the last one to do so being Western Australia in 1984, and so did New Zealand in 1989.

Hong Kong (while under British administration) abolished capital punishment completely in 1993, and the Chinese authorities, under the 'one nation two systems' form of government, have not sought to restore it.[85] However, several jurisdictional problems have arisen involving enforcement of the death penalty against residents of Hong Kong who have been tried in China, as well as those who have fled to Hong Kong from the Chinese mainland. These remain to be resolved.

A number of Pacific Island states, when they became independent of Britain, Australia, or New Zealand, continued the policy of these countries and did not introduce capital punishment—Kiribati (1979), Marshall Islands (1986), Micronesia (1986), Solomon Islands (1978), and Tuvalu (1976), followed by Palau and Vanuatu in 1994. Fiji had become abolitionist for ordinary crimes in 1979, but only after a good deal of hesitation. Yet, following the sentencing to death of George Speight for treason in March 2002 and the setting aside of that penalty for life imprisonment, the Fijian Parliament unanimously voted to abolish capital punishment. In December 2001 East Timor, on declaring independence from Indonesia, also abolished capital punishment.

Elsewhere in Asia there has been little support for the abolitionist movement, even in those countries that were former colonial territories of Western powers. Only two states have so far permanently abolished capital punishment: Cambodia and Nepal. At the end of its civil war and terrible holocaust Cambodia decided to abolish the death penalty completely so as to mark with a powerful symbol the end of the Pol Pot regime: and this was confirmed in 1993, when the Constitutional Assembly adopted Article 32 of the Constitution, which explicitly stated that 'there shall be no capital punishment'.

Nepal had been abolitionist for ordinary offences since 1945, but the death penalty was reintroduced for certain murders and terrorist offences in 1985. Nevertheless, by 1990 capital punishment was again abolished, both for offences against the state and for murder. Article 12 of the Constitution of the Kingdom of Nepal, which came into effect in 1990, stated that 'no law should be made which provides for capital punishment'. However, despite this constitutional prohibition, the death penalty for 'exceptional crimes' was retained in Nepal, mainly, it seems, as an assumed protection for the royal family. It was not until 1997 that the Supreme

---

[85] See Mark Gaylord and John F. Galliher, 'Death Penalty Politics and Symbolic Law in Hong Kong', *Howard Journal of Criminal Justice* 33 (1994), pp. 19–37.

Court of Nepal ruled that these exceptions were inoperative, and two years later the death penalty was formally abolished when royal assent was given to amend the laws that still provided for it.

The Philippines was the first Asian country to abolish capital punishment, but has since reintroduced it. Following the overthrow of President Marcos in 1987, the new Constitution of the Philippines, promulgated by the government of President Aquino, abolished the death penalty for all offences on the grounds that it infringed human rights, but with an important proviso. It was still possible under the new Constitution of 1987 for Congress to provide for capital punishment should there be an 'alarming upsurge of heinous crimes' that 'undermine the people's faith in the government and its ability to maintain peace and order in the country'.

By 1994 proponents of the death penalty had convinced the National Assembly that lawlessness in the country was such that it met these conditions, passing Republic Act 7659 (otherwise known as the Law Reimposing the Death Penalty for Heinous Crimes). Anti-death penalty campaigners—in particular the Free Legal Assistance Group (FLAG) and the Coalition Against the Death Penalty and Catholic Bishops' Conference—have argued, however, that there were certainly no 'compelling reasons' at the time to justify the reintroduction of the death penalty.[86] In any case, the spirit of the proviso was severely breached, for capital punishment was reintroduced for a very wide variety of offences, covering 10 categories of crime in 46 defined circumstances: including treason, murder (including parricide and infanticide not committed by the mother or maternal grandparents), robbery (accompanied by rape, intentional mutilation, arson, or homicide), qualified bribery, plunder, kidnapping for ransom, drug trafficking, rape (if committed in front of others, if the victim becomes insane, is under 18, or the offender is a parent, step-parent, guardian, common-law-spouse, etc.), qualified piracy, hijacking, arson, and serious illegal desertion. In 21 of these circumstances the death sentence was made mandatory.

Many death sentences were then imposed and executions resumed, after a period of twenty-three years, in February 1999 when a man was put to death for the rape of his stepchild, the Philippines Congress having refused to review the death penalty statute after the Supreme Court had adjourned consideration of the case to give Parliament the opportunity to do so. Six more executions followed (three for rape and two for robbery with homicide) before President Estrada announced in March 2000 that there would be a moratorium on executions for the remainder of the year and that he would commute 107 death sentences that had been confirmed by the Supreme Court. Thirteen had been signed before his fall from power in March 2001. It appeared that his successor, President Arroyo, a former opponent of capital punishment, had also decided to suspend executions during her period of office. But in October 2001, in response to an increase in cases of kidnapping involving foreign-

---

[86] Free Legal Assistance Group (FLAG), *Position Paper on the Death Penalty Bills.* Given in evidence before the Joint Meeting of the Committee on Revision of Laws and the Committee on Human Rights, Congress of the Philippines, House of Representatives, 10 Dec. 2001. See *FLAG Newsletter*, Dec. 2001.

ers, including Chinese businessmen and holidaymakers, she announced that she would permit the execution of persons convicted of murder and kidnapping.[87] She has remained ambivalent, having expressed support for 16 Senators who introduced a bill early in 2002 to repeal the death penalty and put in its place the penalty of thirty years' imprisonment, to be served in its entirety. In May 2002 the House of Representatives Commission on Revision of Laws and Civil, Political, and Human Rights also passed bills to repeal the death penalty and forwarded them to the House of Representatives for debate.[88] Meanwhile (December 2001) there were 1,023 prisoners under sentence of death (981 still awaiting the outcome of the Supreme Court's review of their cases), more than half of them convicted of rape—the majority of incest-rape or statutory rape (unlawful sex with a person too young to be able to give legal consent).

Papua New Guinea, where the last execution occurred in 1950, also experienced a period of abolition de jure between 1974 and 1991. In that year the Prime Minister, Rabbie Namaliu, justified its reintroduction for wilful murder as a response to 'the endless succession of vicious and mindless murders that are becoming a part of our daily lives'.[89] However, after the first death sentence was imposed in 1995, his successor, Sir Julius Chan, declared at a meeting of the judiciary that he was opposed to the death penalty, believing it to have no deterrent effect and to be nothing more than 'society looking for quick and easy answers'.[90] A year later the prisoner was exonerated on appeal. By the end of December 2001 no one had been executed. Thus, Papua New Guinea remains in practice abolitionist de facto, capital punishment having no more than symbolic significance.

Over the last thirty years several Asian and Pacific countries have become abolitionist de facto: no executions have taken place in the Maldives since 1952, in Brunei Darussalam since 1957, in Bhutan since 1964, or in Tonga since 1982. Nor have any executions taken place in Western Samoa and Nauru since they attained independence in 1962 and 1968 respectively. By December 2001, by virtue of the 'ten years without executions' rule, two further countries had just become *abolitionist* de facto—Laos and Myanmar (formerly Burma). No death sentences have been reported from Laos since 1993, but they continue to be imposed in Myanmar. Although no judicial executions have taken place in Myanmar since 1989, there have been many reports of extra-judicial killings of ethnic-minority civilians.[91]

An official Commission on Capital Punishment in Sri Lanka (formerly Ceylon) recommended the experimental dispensation of the death penalty for murder as long

---

[87] See AI, *Philippines: Alarm Bells Ring for Human Rights as President Announces About-Turn on the Death Penalty*, AI Index: ASA 35/005/2001; and AI, *Philippines: Executions Put on Hold*, AI Index: ASA 35/03/00, and *Death Penalty News*, Mar. 2001, AI Index: ACT/53/002/2001, p. 1.

[88] See *Flag Newsletter*, Jan.–Mar. 2002 and May 2002.

[89] See AI, *Papua New Guinea: Possible Reintroduction of the Death Penalty*, AI Index: ASA 34/03/90.

[90] AI, *Death Penalty News*, Mar. 1995, AI Index: ACT 53/01/95, p. 2.

[91] See AI, *Report 2001*, p. 176.

ago as 1959.[92] But it was not until 1976 that executions ceased. A year later the death penalty was officially suspended. However, when serious crime began to rise, demands began to mount for a tough response, and in 1995 there were calls in the Sri Lankan parliament for the death penalty to be implemented for 'extreme cases of murder which shock the public conscience'. In 1999 and again in each of the following years the government announced that it was seriously contemplating the resumption of executions for murder as well as for drug trafficking. However, in May 2002 the President commuted the sentences of all the 196 prisoners who were then on 'death row' to life imprisonment, which in practice means twenty years less further reductions granted on religious anniversaries for good behaviour. It appears therefore that the abolitionist de facto status of Sri Lanka is no longer under a serious threat of reversal.

At the end of 1995 it looked as if Thailand might soon join the de facto abolitionist countries, the last execution having taken place in 1987. Yet despite the fact that the Deputy Interior Minister was reported to have said in 1993 that capital punishment should be banned in Thailand,[93] executions were resumed in January 1996. The government held public hearings on the issue during 1999 and claimed that these showed that 'the majority of the Thai people were still convinced that it is necessary to retain the death penalty as a crime deterrent measure as well as to ensure protection of the rights of the victims and their families'.[94] Early in 2001 the recently elected government of Prime Minister Thaksin embarked on a new wave of executions, when five drug traffickers were shot on the same day.[95] Leading the protests against the executions was the chairman of Thailand's Senate Foreign Affairs Committee, who declared: 'I disagree with the executions. I suggest that the government conduct a referendum . . . to see if such highly-publicised executions, which treat human beings like animals, is the right thing to do.'[96] Thus, opinion in Thailand remains divided.

Several other countries in this area have also made cautious moves in the abolitionist direction. Amendments to the Mongolian Criminal Code in 1993, similar to those in other former Soviet territories, reduced the number of capital offences to five, although the list still included aggravated rape of a minor and three offences against the state involving violence. Taiwan abolished the death penalty for corruption and made it discretionary rather than mandatory for serious drug offences, kidnapping, gang robbery, and other violent crimes in January 2002, but capital punishment is still the mandatory penalty for about 60 offences and is optional for a further 96, 156 offences in all.[97] In practice, however, it is less extensively used

---

[92] See Donovan Moldrich, *Hangman—Spare that Noose* (1983), who notes that Buddhist organizations have not supported abolition, being either indifferent or in favour of the death penalty, p. 165. In several Asian countries prisoners under sentence of death have had their sentences commuted to mark national celebrations.

[93] Reported in *The Nation*, 16 Jan. 1993.

[94] See UN Commission on Human Rights, 57th Session, Apr. 2001, Press Release, 25 Apr. 2001.

[95] Altogether 7 of the 10 people executed in 2001 had been convicted of drugs offences.

[96] Reported in *The Nation*, 20 Apr. 2001.

[97] AI, *Report 1999*, pp. 324–325.

than these legal powers would suggest (see page 92 below). The Vice-Minister of Justice of Taiwan informed an Amnesty International seminar in 1990 that his country intended to abolish the death penalty, 'but only when social conditions and public opinion favoured such a move'.[98] That date appears to be moving closer, for in 2001 the new Minister of Justice announced that he hopes to have achieved abolition by the end of his first term of office on 20 May 2004.[99] The number of persons executed fell from 38 in 1997 to 10 in 2001.

The question of abolition has been raised in the Republic of Korea (South Korea) a number of times. In the late 1980s the Minister of Justice instructed a Special Committee on the Reform of the Criminal Code to consider the reduction of the number of capital offences and the abolition of the death penalty. In 1990 the Act Concerning Aggravated Punishment for Specified Crimes and the Act Concerning Aggravated Punishment for Specified Economic Crimes were revised to remove the death penalty from 15 clauses, and in 1995 the revised Criminal Code eliminated the death penalty from a further five clauses.[100] There appears to be a lively debate on the justification for retaining the death penalty, and a Council for the Abolition of the Death Penalty was formed in 1989. Early in 1992 the Constitutional Court heard argument on a petition submitted on the part of two prisoners who claimed that the death penalty violated Article 10 of the Constitution, which guaranteed 'human worth and dignity and the right to pursue happiness', and Article 12, which guaranteed the liberty of the person.[101] Yet, the Court rejected this petition, on technical grounds, so avoiding the issue, and apparently one of the prisoners was executed before the Court made its ruling.[102] Nevertheless, in 1998 the President of the Republic, Kim Dae Jung, told Amnesty International that he personally opposed the death penalty, and since then there have been no executions.[103] The public debate he believed was necessary before any change in the law could occur received a fillip in 2000, when a bill, backed by ninety-two parliamentarians, was for the first time brought before the National Assembly with the object of replacing capital punishment with life imprisonment.[104] It is significant that in October 2001, 155 members submitted a new bill, for it appears that the tide is sweeping ever nearer the 273-member majority that will be required to put it into law.[105]

Little is known about the situation in North Korea. The authorities maintain that the last execution took place in 1992, but according to Amnesty International, it 'continues to receive reports of both public and secret executions of suspected criminals and political prisoners'.[106]

---

[98] AI, *Taiwan: 'Hsinchu Crime Ring' Death Sentences Upheld*, AI Index: ASA 38/01/91.

[99] See Nick Roberts, 'Death Penalty Developments around the World', *Amicus Journal*, 3 (2001), p. 5.

[100] State Party Report to the Human Rights Committee, *Republic of Korea*, CCPR/C/114/Add. 1, 20/08/98.

[101] AI, *South Korea: Facts about the Death Penalty and Calls for Abolition*, AI Index: ASA 25/06/93.

[102] AI, *South Korea: Threat of Imminent Executions*, AI Index: ASA 25/42/93.

[103] See AI, *Report 1999*, p. 227.

[104] See AI, *The Death Penalty Worldwide: Developments in 2000*, AI Index: ACT 50/001/2001, p. 5.

[105] See AI, *Death Penalty News*, Dec. 2001, AI Index: ACT 53/001/2002, p. 2.

[106] AI, *North Korea: Human Rights under Scrutiny at the UN*, AI Index: ASA 24/001/2001.

When Indonesia became independent from the Netherlands in 1950, there were no provisions in the Penal Code for the death penalty. However, it was introduced during the 1950s for hoarding and market fixing and in 1963, by Presidential Decree, for subversion. Premeditated murder was also made a capital offence and in 1975 so was drug trafficking. According to Amnesty International, 'few executions took place before . . . President Suharto came to power following the failure of the coup attempt in 1965'.[107] In 1973 executions began when an army officer was put to death for subversion, and between 1985 and 1995, 33 prisoners were executed, including members of the banned Communist Party and Muslim activists convicted of killings in the course of rebellion, as well as common murderers.[108] There was then a pause until May 2001, when the first executions in five years took place (in West Timor), the two prisoners having been under sentence of death for a multiple murder since 1989. In November 2000 legislation on the establishment of a Human Rights Court in Indonesia was passed, which ironically included the death penalty as the maximum penalty for a number of serious human rights violations.[109] By the end of 2000, 34 people were on death row.

The abolition of capital punishment by the new government of East Timor immediately after this former Indonesian territory had gained its independence is yet a further example of the association with tyranny with which this supreme punishment is so often connected.

In 1975 Malaysia introduced capital punishment as the mandatory penalty for possession and importation of drugs (see Chapter 3 page 81), in addition to murder and several other offences. Between 1970 and 1996, 349 people were hanged, and 150 of them (the first in 1980) had been convicted of drug offences.[110] In November 2000 executions were resumed after a gap of four years, when two men were executed for trafficking in 123 and 132 grams of heroin respectively, offences for which they had been sentenced to death in 1988.

Revision of the Japanese Penal Code, which has been under consideration since 1963, was expected to reduce the number of crimes subject to the death penalty from 18 to nine. However, recommendations from the Legislative Council of the Ministry of Justice, which 'urged that it would be desirable to limit the application of the death penalty as far as possible . . . and that a new provision be stipulated to make the application of the death penalty especially careful', have not been translated into law because other proposals from the Council met with opposition.[111] Despite support for a growing abolitionist movement, in which the distinguished former

[107] AI, *When the State Kills* (1989), p. 148.

[108] AI, *The Death Penalty* (1979), AI Index: ACT 05/03/79. In 1990 the Chief Justice of Indonesia voiced his support for the death penalty for those convicted of political subversion. See AI, *Indonesia: Four Political Prisoners Executed,* AI Index: ASA 21/04/90.

[109] AI, *Indonesia: First Executions in Five Years—a Step Back,* AI Index ASA 21/016/2001.

[110] AI, *Malaysia: First Executions in Four Years—a Step Backwards for Human Rights,* AI Index: ASA 28/011/2000.

[111] Japan's reply to the *Fifth Survey on Capital Punishment and on the Implementation of Safeguards Guaranteeing Protection of the Rights of those Facing the Death Penalty* (1995), United Nations Crime Prevention and Criminal Justice Branch.

Supreme Court judge Dr Shigemitsu Dando has played a prominent part, the Japanese government has remained firmly committed to retaining the death penalty on the grounds that a very large majority of public opinion favours it. And indeed an officially sponsored opinion poll in 1994 found that 74 per cent of the respondents believed that 'the death penalty can be applied in some cases'.[112] Yet, for over three years between November 1989 and March 1993 there was a de facto moratorium, three consecutive Ministers of Justice having refused to sign execution orders. However, their successor reversed this policy on the grounds that 'personal feelings should not come into play', and executions resumed.[113] The position of the Japanese government, according to its response to the UN Sixth Quinquennial Survey in 2000 appears to be that 'although it is necessary to refer to the trends and experiences of other countries . . . the issue of retention or abolition of the death penalty should be left to the independent decision of each country'. Nevertheless, the practice of capital punishment in Japan continues to give rise to concern among lawyers and politicians, and it has recently been made the subject of an official inquiry by the Japanese Bar Association: 'The Association is studying the abolition of the death penalty with the idea that human rights must be protected in accordance with international standards.'[114]

Over the last forty years there has been pressure in India to restrict the use of the death penalty. A challenge to its constitutionality in the case of *Bachan Singh* v. *State of Punjab* (1980) failed to convince the Supreme Court of India, which declared: 'it cannot be said that the provision of the death penalty as an alternative punishment for murder, in Section 302, Penal Code, is unreasonable and not in the public interest'. Nevertheless, Sarkaria J giving judgment emphasized that

The extreme penalty can be inflicted *only* in gravest cases of extreme culpability . . . life imprisonment is the rule and the death sentence an exception . . . A real and abiding concern for the dignity of human life postulates resistance to taking life through law's instrumentality. That ought not to be done save in the rarest of rare cases when the alternative option is unquestionably foreclosed.

The Court had in mind offences where 'the murder has been committed after previous planning and involves extreme brutality' of grave danger to the society at large.[115] Subsequently, the Court has continued to uphold the constitutionality of the death penalty as applied on the 'rarest of rare cases' principle. The Law Commission of India has also insisted that 'having regard to the conditions in India,

---

[112] The Japanese opinion poll was published by the Prime Minister's Office, Minister's Secretary (Management and Coordination Agency) (1994), with an English summary.

[113] AI, *Japan: The Death Penalty: A Cruel, Inhuman and Arbitrary Punishment*, AI Index: ASA 22/03/95, p. 27. See S. Dando, *Shikei Haishi-ron (On Abolishing the Death Penalty)* (1995).

[114] Daini Tokyo Bar Association, Judicial Reform at www.dntba.ab.psiweb.com/english/activities.html.

[115] *Bachan Singh* v. *State of Punjab* [1980] 2 SCJ 474 at 522 and 524. See also the full judgment of the court which includes the dissent of Bhagwati J, who found the death penalty to be unconstitutional, *Bachan Singh* v. *State of Punjab* [1983] 1 SCR (Supreme Court Review) 145 at 250, 252, and 256. More generally, see David Pannick, *Judicial Review of the Death Penalty* (1982), pp. 142–144 and 151 n. 15.

to the variety of social upbringing of its inhabitants, to the disparity in the level of morality and education in the country, to the vastness of the area, to the diversity of its population and to the paramount need for maintaining law and order in the country at the present juncture, India cannot risk the experiment of the abolition of capital punishment'.[116] Indeed, there has been a strong feeling in India, expressed by the Supreme Court, that Western experiences and arguments based on Western statistical studies are not necessarily relevant to the social conditions and educational level of India.[117] Political assassinations, such as those of Indira and Rajiv Ghandi, and other upheavals have also played a part in India's reluctance to abolish the death penalty.

In recent years there has even been an extension of the death penalty in India to various 'terrorist offences', to causing death through the use of illegal arms or ammunition, and for a second conviction of drug trafficking. However, there is little doubt that executions are reserved for the gravest class of murderers. As Subhash C. Gupta has pointed out, political leaders have remained in two minds on the issue. While being inclined towards abolition in theory, they have nevertheless recognized the existence of extremely heinous cases which, in their view, 'shock the conscience of society' and deserve death.[118] Thus, the number of death sentences in relation to the size of the population of the country has remained very small in recent years—49 in the five years 1996 to 2000—and the number of executions even smaller, apparently only five during the same period, the last in 1997.[119]

Perhaps a major impediment to abolition has been, until very recently, the absence of a coherent voice in India to campaign on the issue. Indeed, it was only in July 2000 that the first national conference of activists was held in New Delhi under the auspices of a new umbrella organization, the Campaign Against the Death Penalty. It is significant that it called not for immediate abolition, but for abolition only after a ten-year moratorium on executions.[120] At least 60 people remained on death row at the end of 2000, and legislation to extend the use of the death penalty to offences of rape was still pending.[121]

Far from there being any sympathy with the abolitionist cause, there is strong support for the death penalty in a number of Asian countries, most notably,

---

[116] *Report of the 35th Law Commission of India*, pp. 354–355, quoted in Mahendra P. Singh, 'Capital Punishment: Perspective and the Indian Context', in R. S. Agarwal and S. Kumar (eds), *Crimes and Punishment in New Perspective* (1986), pp. 28–39 at 33.

[117] See A. R. Blackshield, 'Capital Punishment in India', *Journal of the Indian Law Institute* 21 (1979), pp. 137–226 at 143–144.

[118] See Subhash C. Gupta, *Capital Punishment in India* (1986), p. 107. Also, AI, *India: The Death Penalty* (1989); this reports that the former Chief Justice of the Supreme Court had changed his mind by 1989 and was now opposed to the death penalty. AI Index: ASA 20/13/89. However, in abstaining from the resolution in support of abolition at the 57th Session of the UN Commission on Human Rights in April 2001, the spokesman for India stated that the international community had thus far not reached a consensus on the issue of capital punishment and defended India's use of it for 'the rarest of rare cases'. See UN Press Release, n. 54 above.

[119] I am grateful to C. Raj Kumar for making the investigation which provided these figures.

[120] See AI, *The Death Penalty Worldwide: Developments in 2000*, AI Index: ACT 50/001/2001, p. 5.

[121] AI, *Report 2001*, p. 124.

Singapore, Pakistan,[122] Bangladesh, and Myanmar. In Singapore, which has the highest per capita rate of executions in the world (see Chapter 3 page 91), the majority of persons executed have been convicted of drug trafficking, often on the basis of the possession of quite small amounts of illegal substances. The Singaporean government, as pointed out in Chapter 1, is one of the most vociferous supporters of the death penalty, although a recent opinion poll has suggested that a majority of the population may favour abolition.[123]

In Pakistan the death penalty is available for a wide variety of offences, as it is in Bangladesh, where it was extended in 1995 to offences of kidnapping and trafficking women and children.[124] In March 2001 Bangladesh carried out its first execution for four years, when a man convicted of murder in 1991 was hanged. At the end of 2000, 160 prisoners were reported to be on death row.[125]

In Vietnam death sentences can be imposed for 29 offences, including crimes against national security, murder, rape, drug trafficking, and economic crimes,[126] but there was some amelioration in July 2000 when new legislation came into force allowing the death sentence on pregnant women and mothers of children aged up to 36 months to be changed to life imprisonment.[127] In 2000 as many as 112 death sentences were recorded, seven for economic offences such as fraud and forgery but most for drug trafficking, and executions have continued to be carried out on a considerable scale.

Although the official and academic view in the People's Republic of China is that the death penalty will be abolished when conditions are appropriate sometime in the future, its use was fully endorsed for a substantial range of crimes, even at a time when Chinese scholars claimed that the crime rate in China was among the lowest in the world.[128] There is said to be deep-seated support among the Chinese people based on traditional values of Chinese culture, which proclaim that 'the killer should be killed'[129] and that to fail to take this into account would have serious consequences

---

[122] When Benazir Bhutto was elected president in 1988, she declared a moratorium on executions and commuted 2,000 death sentences, but after the Islamic Democratic Alliance had come to power in 1990, executions were resumed in 1992. See AI, *Death Penalty News*, Feb. 1993. Also, Joan Fitzpatrick and Alice Miller, 'International Standards on the Death Penalty: Shifting Discourse', *Brooklyn Journal of International Law* 19 (1993), pp. 273–366 at 358–360.

[123] AI, *Death Penalty News*, June 2001, AI Index: ACT 53/003/2001, reported that an Internet poll of 1,135 respondents found that 68.5% opposed the death penalty. But of course the sample may have been biased towards certain sections of the population.

[124] AI, *Report 1996*, p. 88. [125] AI, *Report 2001*, p. 43.

[126] AI, *Newsletter*, Sept. 2000, AI Index: NWS 21/005/2000, p. 4.

[127] AI, *Report 2001*, p. 266.

[128] See Yu Shutong, 'Le Système de la peine capitale dans le droit pénal chinois', *Revue Internationale de Droit Pénal* 58 (1987), pp. 689–695. See also Jerome Cohen, *The Criminal Process in the People's Republic of China 1949–1963* (1968), quoting the leading Chinese Criminal Law text of 1957: 'A correct estimate of the death penalty's active role in the struggle against crime by no means implies the need to retain the death penalty forever. On the contrary our country is in the process of creating conditions for the gradual abolition of the death penalty.' For a very helpful summary of the history of the death penalty in China, see Michael Palmer, 'The People's Republic of China', in P. Hodgkinson and A. Rutherford (eds), *Capital Punishment: Global Issues and Prospects* (1996), pp. 105–141 at 105–112.

[129] See Liu Hainan, 'The Effect on the Capital Punishment by the Chinese Traditional Theory of the Criminal Law', in M. Nowak and Xin Chunying (eds), *EU–China Human Rights Dialogue: Proceedings of*

for political and social stability. Furthermore, a good deal of emphasis is placed on the necessity of providing a sufficient deterrent, not only to murder but also to counteract gangsterism and economic exploitation.[130] Professor Gao Ming Xuan, for a long time the leading Chinese expert on capital punishment, affirmed:

If we abolish the death penalty, which is a means to suppress these heinous hostile elements and saboteurs, the most important interests of the state and all citizens would lose its powerful guarantee . . . If we abolish the death penalty now, no other punishment would be sufficient to express the negation of such monstrous crimes . . . the goal of reinforcing the law-abiding attitude by way of punishment would then be unattainable.[131]

Recent political, economic, and social changes have undoubtedly brought with them a rising tide of crime, which is probably all the more significant in fuelling anxiety because of the low levels of crime experienced during the Maoist era. The need to control this upsurge of crime, which threatens not only the social but also the political order, is now regarded as the main justification for retaining capital punishment for a wide range of offences in China.

Furthermore, the speed with which the market economy is developing in China—it hopes soon to accede to the World Trade Organization—has caused a renaissance of behaviour which the revolution had appeared to have largely eradicated, such as gambling, drug trafficking, organized prostitution, dissemination of pornography, and economic corruption. The latter has invaded the Communist Party and various other organs of the state and created concern for the reputation and legitimacy of government and the communist system as a whole. Thus, capital punishment is viewed as a necessary preventive measure in order to stave off anti-socialistic corrupting influences and as a symbol of the state's determination to ensure its legitimacy with the masses. Thus, the *People's Daily*, commenting on the death sentences handed down for bribery and corruption imposed in 2000 on two high officials, the Deputy Governor of Jiangxi province and the former Vice-Chairman of the National People's Congress Standing Committee, both of whom were executed, stated that: 'A criminal who has committed such a very serious crime must be put to death in order to uphold national law and satisfy popular indignation and in order to rectify Party work ethics and fight against corruption; no less penalty will suffice'. The execution of such a high official was said 'to further strengthen the confidence of the party members and cadres and the masses in the struggle against corruption'.[132]

---

the Second EU–China Legal Experts, Seminar Held in Beijing on 19 and 20 October 1998 (2000), pp. 99–120 at 120. Also, Palmer, n. 128 above, pp. 112–126 n. 115.

[130] For a historical perspective, see Jerome T. Monthy, Comment, 'Internal Perspectives on Chinese Human Rights Reform: The Death Penalty in the PRC', *Texas International Law Journal* 33 (1998), pp. 189–212.

[131] Gao Ming Xuan, 'A Brief Dissertation on the Death Penalty in the Criminal Law of the People's Republic of China', *Revue Internationale de Droit Pénal* 58 (1987), pp. 399–405 at 400–402, and his book (in Chinese), *The Main Idea in General Provisions of the Criminal Law* (1986), sect. 5.

[132] Quoted in Marina Svensson, 'State Coercion, Deterrence and the Death Penalty in the PRC', Paper presented to the Annual Meeting of the Association for Asian Studies, Chicago, 22–5 Mar. 2001.

In addition, increased freedom of expression has been perceived by the authorities as a threat to state security and public order, especially when it is associated with 'separatism', as is the case in Tibet and with the Uighurs of Xinjiang province.

According to one of the leading scholars of the younger generation, Dr Hu Yungten:

. . . Chinese scholars . . . think that China, when conducting the construction of the market economy and social reform, needs a stable and orderly environment and [to] curb and reduce as [many] crimes, especially those which seriously endanger China's development and human rights, as [it] can.

Moreover, a study of popular opinion on the subject in 1995 revealed 'that the overwhelming majority of Chinese citizens hold affirmative attitudes towards the death penalty'.[133] As Professor Hans-Jörg Albrecht has pointed out:

The firm belief in the death penalty is also shown in the reservations that the country has introduced when signing the International Covenant on Civil and Political Rights in September 1998. These reservations are comparable to those that have been made by the United States of America when ratifying the International Covenant in 1992. The [People's Republic of China] is stating in these reservations that in the current stage of social and economic development the death penalty cannot be abolished and that the restrictions mentioned in Art.7 of the International Covenant regarding the use of cruel, unusual and degrading punishment cannot be understood as prohibiting the imposition and enforcement of the death penalty.[134]

The official policy has been characterized as one of 'killing only a few' as 'negative examples', a popular slogan being 'execute one as a warning to a hundred'. Thus the Criminal Law and the Criminal Procedure Law of 1979 (which had 28 capital crimes) had stated that the death penalty is 'only to be applied to criminal elements who commit the most heinous crimes' (Article 43). This did not prevent the extension of capital punishment through Decisions of the Standing Committee of the National People's Congress in the early 1980s to many new offences encompassing crimes of violence, abduction of women and selling into prostitution, organized criminality and gangsterism, corruption and serious economic crime, and serious offences of smuggling and trafficking in narcotics.[135]

The latest reform of China's Criminal Law in 1997 included the abolition of capital punishment for more than 10 offences previously punishable by death, most notably theft (except of cultural relics and very large sums of money from financial institutions), but it still contains 51 articles stipulating the death penalty for at least 68 capital crimes, 21 of which relate to national security and the military. Although official policy remains that executions should be confined to 'criminals who have

---

[133] Hu Yunteng, 'On the Death Penalty at the Turning of the Century', in M. Nowak and Xin Chunying (eds), *EU–China Human Rights Dialogue: Proceedings of the Second EU–China Legal Experts, Seminar Held in Beijing on 19 and 20 October 1998* (2000), pp. 88–94 at 91–92.

[134] H-J Albrecht, 'The Death Penalty in China from a European Perspective', in Nowak and Xin (eds), n. 133 above, pp. 95–118 at 99.

[135] Palmer, n. 128 above, pp. 112–116. See also Ch. 3 p. 86 below.

committed particularly serious crimes of extremely profound subjective evil, when social order could not be maintained if they were not killed',[136] those who may be subject to the supreme penalty still include offenders convicted of grave offences against economic order, violent crimes, dereliction of duties, and sales of drugs (see Chapter 3 pages 86–87).[137] Furthermore, the authorities have continued to employ the death penalty as an exemplary punishment through 'strike hard' campaigns (known as Yanda), when large numbers of persons are executed during a crackdown on criminals,[138] the last one being put into effect in the spring of 2001.

Despite the fact that the Chinese authorities have stated that the 'standard of death penalty applicable to some crimes' has been raised, indicating that capital punishment would only apply to the most serious cases, it is nevertheless the case that that they have interpreted the injunction in Article 6 (2) of the ICCPR, to restrict the death penalty to 'intentional crimes with lethal or extremely grave consequences' in a very wide manner. They have not restricted it to a few types of crime, but to what they regard as 'the most serious forms' of *many* types of crime. Furthermore, they have undoubtedly given a wider interpretation to the concept 'extremely grave consequences' than Article 6 (2) was intended to convey.

At present there is no way of assessing whether or not the proportion of serious offenders who are executed is high or low, declining or increasing. Nor is it known how many death sentences are suspended for a period of two years (as the law allows) to give the convicted person an opportunity within two years, subject to hard labour, to show that they have repented—and of these how many fail and are eventually executed. This is because the Chinese authorities have shrouded the collection and publication of any systematic data on capital punishment by deeming it to be a state secret. A system which is not transparent and openly accountable is, of course, difficult to assess and to change.[139] As Professor Michael Palmer has pointed out, 'China is unlikely to cast off easily its traditions of, and ideological commitment to, capital punishment.'[140] The process of abolition is therefore predicted to be slow. Indeed, when in 1998 Chinese lawyers began a discussion on 'The Way towards the Abolishment of the Death Penalty in China', they pointed to the fact that it took almost 200 years to abolish the death penalty in Britain and France. In their view, China has already made great strides in this century by reducing from more than 940 capital crimes at the beginning of the twentieth century to the present number.[141] It

---

[136] 'China's Legislative Guarantees for Human Rights in the Judicial Field', *Guangming Daily*, 6 Oct. 1998, quoted in AI, *People's Republic of China: The Death Penalty in 1998*, AI Index: ASA 17/57/99, p. 2.

[137] Albrecht, n. 134 above, pp. 96–97.

[138] See Daniel C. Turack, 'The New Chinese Criminal Justice System', *Cardozo Journal of International and Comparative Law* 7 (1999), pp. 49–70 at 50–52. Also, John T. Boxer, 'China's Death Penalty: Undermining Legal Reform and Threatening National Economic Interest', *Suffolk Transnational Law Review* 22 (1999), pp. 593–618 at 604.

[139] See Roger Hood, 'The Value of Statistical Returns and Empirical Research in Discussions on the Death Penalty', Paper presented to the EU–China Human Rights Seminar, Beijing, 11–12 May 2001.

[140] See Palmer, n. 128 above, p. 131.

[141] Hu, n. 133 above, pp. 89–90. Under the Kuomintang Government in 1936 the Criminal Law of the Republic of China had stipulated 20 capital crimes.

may be that the recent willingness of the Chinese authorities to discuss the death penalty in its human rights seminars and dialogues with European countries is the signal that a change is in the air. However, it would be premature to be too optimistic, for at the same time that the subject was being placed on the agenda of the EU–China Human Rights Seminar in Beijing in May 2001, a new and intensive 'strike hard' campaign was in progress, resulting in at least 1,781 executions between April and July 2001[142] and at least 2,468 by the end of the year.[143]

The general reluctance to abandon capital punishment in the Asian and Pacific area is evident when one reflects on the fact that only Australia, New Zealand, and Nepal have ratified the Second Optional Protocol to the ICCPR.

6. SOUTH AND CENTRAL AMERICA

South and Central America has been in the vanguard of the abolitionist movement. Venezuela, Costa Rica, and Brazil, which had already abolished capital punishment by the end of the nineteenth century, were followed soon afterwards by Ecuador, Uruguay, Colombia, Argentina, Panama, and most of the Mexican states. Many of them got rid of the death penalty for all crimes, whether under civil or military law, in peacetime or wartime.[144]

In 1956 these nine countries were joined by Honduras, where no executions had taken place since 1940. Article 66 of the Constitution of Honduras (modified in 1985) prohibits the death penalty. When the revolutionary government of Nicaragua came to power in 1979, it immediately abolished capital punishment for all crimes. Four years later, in 1983, El Salvador abolished it for ordinary crimes, and although it was retained under military law, Article 28 of the Constitution of the Republic states that the death penalty may only be imposed when the country is at war. All attempts to reintroduce it for common crimes have been resisted by the government.

Paraguay, which had been abolitionist de facto for decades, finally abolished the death penalty for all offences in 1992 under the new Constitution, 'following the world trend towards abolition of the death penalty'. According to the Constitution

---

[142] See AI, *China's Execution Frenzy, The Wire*. Also, Ch. 3 pp. 88–91 below.

[143] See AI, *Death Sentences and Executions in 2001*, AI Index: ACT 51/001/2002.

[144] Argentina (for political offences in 1853 and for all ordinary offences in 1921), Brazil (last execution in 1855, abolished for ordinary offences in 1882 and in the Constitution of 1891), Colombia (incorporated as Article 29 of the Constitution of 1886, and abolished by legislation for all crimes in 1910), Costa Rica (1877 for all crimes and incorporated into the Constitution by decree in 1882), Ecuador (for political crimes in 1851, for all crimes except parricide in 1878 and totally abolished in the Constitution of 1906, now Article 19 of the Constitution, as amended in 1983), Mexico (abolished for political offences in 1917 and for all ordinary crimes in the Federal Penal Code of 1931), Panama (in effect, for all crimes, since independence from Colombia in 1903, and in the Penal Code of 1922), Uruguay (1907, for all crimes, prohibited by Article 163 of the 1918 Constitution, now Article 26 of the 1967 Constitution), and Venezuela (for political offences in 1849 and all offences in 1863, prohibited by Article 58 of the Constitution of 1961). See AI, n. 107 above; and Hands Off Cain, *Towards Abolition: The Law and Politics of the Death Penalty* (1998).

of Bolivia of 1967, which was amended in 1995, Article 17 prohibits the use of the death penalty. Despite this prohibition, the Penal Code of 1973 still provided for capital punishment. To bring the law into line with the Constitution, the Bolivian Congress, by Law 1768 of 1997, formally abolished the death penalty by removing all remaining capital offences (parricide, murder, treason, and other crimes against the security of the state) from the statute book.[145] Although it has yet to be formally abolished for all offences under the military code, the Bolivian Constitution provides the overriding legal authority and the Bolivian government has confirmed, in a response to the United Nations, that capital punishment is banned entirely from civil and military law.[146]

The last execution in Chile took place in 1985 and the death penalty was abolished for a number of crimes in 1989. Unsuccessful attempts were made in both 1990 and 1997 to achieve total abolition for ordinary crimes, but finally both the Senate and Chamber of Deputies passed a bill by a considerable majority to replace capital punishment with life imprisonment for a minimum of forty years. The new law was signed by the President in May 2001, leaving the death penalty available only in the Code of Military Justice for times of war.[147]

Surinam and Belize are de facto abolitionist states; the last executions took place in Surinam in 1982 and in Belize in 1985. In the early 1990s concern was expressed that Belize might soon resume executions.[148] Although this has not materialized, nine people were on death row at the end of 2000.[149] Death by hanging had been mandatory for murder in Belize, but the 1994 Criminal Justice Act introduced the option to pass a sentence of life imprisonment in special extenuating circumstances.[150]

Although it extended the death penalty in 1992 to drug-trafficking activities resulting in the death of others, and in 1995 to kidnapping (contrary to its obligations under Article 4 (2) of the American Convention of Human Rights),[151] Guatemala had also appeared to be abolitionist de facto. Nobody had been executed since 1983 and the Chief Judge of the Supreme Court of Justice had stated that the death penalty should be abolished 'provided that, in accordance with the San José pact, prison achieves the purpose of reintegrating the convicted parties into society, through a process of re-education and rehabilitation'.[152] Despite this, Guatemala executed the first persons for thirteen years in 1996—two men convicted of the rape

---

[145] See AI, *The Death Penalty Worldwide: Developments in 1997*, AI Index: ACT 50/04/98, p. 2.

[146] See Capital Punishment and Implementation of the Safeguards Guaranteeing the Protection of the Rights of those Facing the Death Penalty: *Report of the Secretary-General to the Commission on Crime Prevention and Criminal Justice*, E/CN.15/1996/19, para. 24. Also see Hands Off Cain, n. 144 above, pp. 138–184.

[147] AI, *Death Penalty News*, June 2001, AI Index: ACT 53/003/2001, p. 2.

[148] See AI, *Belize, Update: Death by Hanging: The Death Penalty in Belize*, AI Index: AMR 16/01/94.

[149] AI, *Report 2001*, p. 47.

[150] AI, *Government Commitments and Human Rights in Belize*, AI Index: AMR 16/003/2000.

[151] See Christina M. Cerna, 'The Death Penalty and the Jurisprudence of the Inter-American System for the Protection of Human Rights', Paper presented to the Conference on the Death Penalty, University of Galway, Sept. 2001.

[152] Reply to *UN Fifth Quinquennial Survey* (1995) in 1994.

and murder of a child. A further execution was carried out in 1998 and two more in June 2000, when two men were put to death by lethal injection for the kidnapping and murder of a woman—executions that were televised.[153] However, in November 2000 the Constitutional Court of Guatemala revoked the death sentences of five men sentenced to death under the law extending capital punishment to kidnapping, and declared that in matters of human rights international law prevails over national legislation.[154]

Despite the early advance of the abolitionist movement in South America, there have been several setbacks during periods of political instability and military rule. Both Argentina and Brazil reintroduced and then again abolished the death penalty. Brazil, which had abolished capital punishment for ordinary offences as long ago as 1882, twice reimposed the death penalty: for politically motivated crimes of violence between 1937 and 1945 and, under a military government, for political crimes against national security between 1969 and 1979. This turned out to be of little significance because no death sentences were handed down during either of these periods. Since 1979 such offences have only been punishable by death in time of war. An attempt to reintroduce capital punishment for robbery, rape, and kidnapping leading to murder was overwhelmingly defeated in the Constituent Assembly in Brazil in February 1988 (392 votes to 90) and another move was defeated in 1991. In 1995 Brazil informed the United Nations that 'the death penalty is not contemplated in the Brazilian juridical system'.[155]

The Constitution of Argentina prohibited the use of the death penalty for political offences as long ago as 1853, and it was abolished for ordinary criminal offences in 1921. However, military governments have tried to reintroduce it at various times. For example, in 1971 a military junta restored capital punishment for political offences. Such was the fierceness of the opposition from Argentinian jurists that they were forced to abolish it a year later, in 1972 (except in the Military Penal Code). In 1976, following a military coup, the death penalty was reintroduced for a variety of violent crimes, including rape and robbery, but no death sentences were imposed by the courts. When the military junta fell, the civilian government again abolished capital punishment for all crimes except offences committed during wartime under the Code of Military Justice. In the 1990s there were several political initiatives aimed at reintroducing the death penalty, but they all failed to get parliamentary approval after the Roman Catholic Church and several other influential organizations had expressed strong opposition.

Peru, which had become abolitionist for ordinary crimes in 1979, made way for the possible reintroduction of the death penalty, following approval by a national referendum, under Article 140 of the Constitution of 1993, for two offences against the state: treason and terrorism carried out within the country (it was already a capital offence to commit these acts in the context of a foreign war). The Peruvian

---

[153] AI, *Report 2001*, p. 114.
[154] AI, *Death Penalty News*, Dec. 2000, AI Index: ACT 53/001/2001.
[155] Reply to *Fifth UN Quinquennial Survey* (1995). See also AI, n. 107 above, p. 111.

government stated that this extension was a special measure in response to the civil war waged by 'criminal bands', but so far no legislative provisions have been introduced into the Peruvian Criminal Code to specify in criminal law the acts for which the death penalty can be imposed or to determine the relevant criminal procedures, nor have any persons been sentenced to death under these provisions. In October 1994 a popular initiative to abolish the death penalty was submitted to the Peruvian Congress so as to modify the Peruvian Constitution, but by the end of 2001 complete abolition had yet to be achieved.

Mexico provides a good example of a country which has retained capital punishment under its Constitution but which nevertheless appears to have no intention of using it. Although the Political Constitution of the United Mexican States of 1917 provides for the death penalty for several categories of murder, in fact the Penal Codes of the Mexican states make no provision for it. The last execution took place in the state of Puebla in 1937.[156] And while the Code of Military Justice provides for capital punishment for specific offences under Article 130 of the Code, in practice the death sentence is always commuted to long-term imprisonment. Indeed, the government regards it as a 'dead letter'. Thus Mexico is abolitionist as far as ordinary criminal offences are concerned, and in relation to military offences should be, according to the government's official reply to the United Nations, 'regarded as de facto abolitionist'.[157]

The only country in South and Central America to carry out executions in recent years is Guyana (which is culturally part of the Caribbean world), where prior to 1985 there had been a fifteen-year moratorium on executions. Guyana's abolitionist de facto status was undermined when a newly elected government resumed executions for a period of six years. However, when they ceased in 1991 it did not, as abolitionists hoped, mark a return to a long moratorium, for in 1996 a prisoner named Rockliffe Ross was executed despite having an application or a review of his case pending before the UN Human Rights Committee. In 1999 the government of Guyana withdrew from the Second Optional Protocol to the ICCPR only to rejoin it the same day with a reservation preventing the Human Rights Committee from considering petitions from individuals that their human rights have been violated by capital proceedings brought against them. With this move Guyana followed Jamaica and Trinidad and Tobago—the only countries to withdraw from the ICCPR to date (see page 62 below).

The hundred-year tradition of abolition in South America now holds sway over almost the entire region. Nine South American countries have either ratified or signed the Second Optional Protocol to the ICCPR[158] and six of them plus Brazil have ratified the Protocol to the American Convention on Human Rights to Abolish

---

[156] By 1965, 24 of the Mexican states had abolished the death penalty, and none of the 33 Mexican states have included the death penalty in their penal codes today.

[157] Reply of Mexico to the United Nations Fifth and Sixth Quinquennial Surveys.

[158] Chile, Colombia, Costa Rica, Ecuador, Panama, Uruguay, and Venezuela have ratified, and Honduras and Nicaragua have signed the Protocol.

the Death Penalty.[159] Eighteen South American countries which have abolished the death penalty completely or for ordinary crimes have also ratified the American Convention on Human Rights and are thus banned from reintroducing capital punishment.

7. THE CARIBBEAN

During the past thirty years the death penalty has been abolished in the Dominican Republic (1966), Haiti (1987), Bermuda (1999),[160] and the French territories of Martinique and Guadeloupe (which are part of metropolitan France), and those islands which remained British dependencies.[161]

It may have appeared that Cuba could be heading in the abolitionist direction when it reduced the scope of capital punishment in 1988 by abolishing it for crimes against 'collective security', for robbery with violence, and for certain crimes against 'peace and international law'. But this was not so, for in 1999 the death penalty was extended to include serious involvement in drug trafficking, corruption of minors, and armed robbery. It can now be imposed for 79 violations of state security and for 33 common crimes, although no executions have taken place since 1999.[162]

A feature of this area is the number of countries that have appeared to be abolitionist de facto, yet have resumed executions after long periods of abeyance (Guyana has already been mentioned in the section above). Grenada executed five men in 1977 and 1978 after a lapse of fifteen years and nobody has been executed since; after eleven years without executions St Christopher and Nevis hanged a man in 1985 and then the next hanging did not take place until 1998. In 1995 St Lucia resumed executions after a lapse of nine years and St Vincent after a lapse of four years, but no further executions have since been reported in either country. The execution of a man for murder in the Bahamas in 1996 was the first since 1984. Then further executions were carried out in 1998, when two men convicted for murder were hanged despite having petitions pending before the Inter-American Commission on Human Rights.

Both Dominica and Antigua–Barbuda earned the status of abolitionist de facto under the 'ten-year criterion' in 1996 and 1999 respectively, but there is no indication that either island state is intending to abolish the death penalty. In 1979 a consultant appointed by the Barbados government recommended abolition of the death penalty and, as a result, a committee was established to review the question. It

---

[159] Brazil, Costa Rica, Ecuador, Nicaragua, Panama, Uruguay, and Venezuela have ratified, and Chile and Paraguay have signed the Protocol to the American Convention.

[160] In 1977 Bermuda executed two men for a politically motivated murder—the first executions for thirty-four years and the last before abolition was achieved twenty years later. In 1989 a bill had been introduced to abolish the death penalty, but it had been rejected in a referendum in 1990.

[161] In 1999 it was abolished in all of the small British dependencies: Anguilla, Bermuda, Cayman Islands, Montserrat, the Turks and Caicos, and the Virgin Islands.

[162] As of 31 Dec. 2001.

concluded that the issue should be decided by Parliament. However, the only change achieved was the raising of the minimum age to 18 in 1989. By 1994 Barbados had become abolitionist de facto, but there appears to be no legislative impetus to make the country abolitionist de jure. In many of these island states executions would probably have been carried out more frequently had it not been for successful appeals to the Judicial Committee of the Privy Council in London and internationally aroused pressure. Thus, despite the fact that many may at times appear to be abolitionist de facto, they have not in fact forsaken their attraction to capital punishment.

Trinidad and Tobago had executed nobody since 1979, but warrants for execution continued to be issued. In June 1988 the Senate established a Commission of Inquiry into Capital Punishment. The Prescott Commission, which reported in 1990, recommended the replacement of the mandatory death penalty by a distinction between capital and non-capital murder, but nevertheless staunchly supported capital punishment as a deterrent.[163] A fifteen-year moratorium on executions was finally broken when Glen Ashby was executed for murder in July 1994, even though legal proceedings aimed at obtaining a further stay of execution were under way (see Chapter 5 page 168). Since then a further 10 executions have taken place and in 2000 the Offences against the Person Act (Amendment) came into effect, making the death penalty the mandatory sentence for those who have committed more than one murder and one of three different categories of murder (see Chapter 6 page 174).[164]

The movement towards abolition in the English-speaking Caribbean appears to have been frustrated by concerns generated by the extent of violent crime. This is especially the case in Jamaica, where the murder rate has been climbing inexorably to reach more than 42 murders per 100,000 population in the year 2001. In April 1976 a four-year moratorium on executions commenced, and although the Jamaican House of Representatives decided in 1979, on a free vote, to retain capital punishment, it was agreed that all outstanding death sentences should be reviewed. As a result, a Committee of Inquiry (the Fraser Committee) was set up to examine the question, and its report in 1981 recommended that, in principle, the death penalty for murder should be abolished. Nevertheless, it bowed to public concern by suggesting that this should be done in stages and that at first the penalty should be restricted to murder committed by the principal party in offences committed with firearms or explosives. Executions resumed in 1980 and were carried out on a considerable scale in relation to Jamaica's population until 1988. Despite the fact that the death penalty had been condemned by the Prime Minister, the leader of the Opposition, and the Attorney-General, and that informed opinion in the legal profession favoured abolition, public opinion was felt to be too hostile for the government to press through legislation.[165]

Eleven years passed before the Offences against the Person Amendment Act of

---

[163] *The Death Penalty in Trinidad and Tobago*, Report of the Commission of Inquiries into the Death Penalty (Chairman Elton A. Prescott), 27 Sept. 1990.

[164] AI, *Report 2001*, p. 243.

[165] AI, *Report 2001*, p. 140.

1992 created a distinction between capital and non-capital murder (modelled on the defunct and discredited UK Homicide Act of 1957), the former being defined as: murders of persons involved in the administration of criminal justice, and murders committed in the course of certain felonies, such as robbery, burglary, arson, and sexual offences, murder for hire, multiple murders, and murder after a previous conviction for murder. For these offences the death penalty was mandatory. As this law was applied retroactively, all those under sentence of death were administratively reclassified. Over 60 per cent of them were defined as non-capital and their death sentences were commuted to life imprisonment. Concern was expressed about the fairness of this procedure.[166] Of those remaining under sentence of death no one had, by the end of 2001, been executed, but there has been no explicit commitment to a moratorium. Although Jamaica has become abolitionist de facto, according to the 'ten-year rule', the Jamaican government has indicated that it may follow Trinidad and Tobago and resume executions.

The Constitutions of all the Commonwealth Caribbean countries, with the exception of Belize, contain 'savings clauses'. According to the leading barrister Edward Fitzgerald QC, 'Either they rule out altogether any constitutional attack on the laws in existence at the time of independence, or, at the least, they prohibit any attack on the specific colonial *penalties* or *punishments* in existence at the time of independence based on the alleged cruelty or inhumanity of those punishments.' For this reason, Fitzgerald has argued, 'Such savings clauses inhibit the sort of dynamic or evolutionary approach to the development of human rights protections that other constitutions, and international human rights conventions, have adopted throughout the world.'[167]

It is of considerable significance, therefore, that in April 2001 the Eastern Caribbean Court of Appeal (covering the jurisdiction of Antigua and Barbuda, Dominica, Grenada, St Kitts and Nevis, St Lucia and St Vincent, and the Grenadines) held the mandatory death penalty for murder to be unconstitutional, and in March 2002 this was confirmed on appeal in a judgment of the Judicial Committee of the Privy Council (see Chapter 6 page 174). If a similar judgment were to be obtained in relation to the more limited mandatory death penalty for capital murder in Jamaica, Trinidad and Tobago, Barbados, Guyana, and the Bahamas, it would have a considerable impact on the number of persons sentenced to death in those countries.

The final court of appeal for death-sentenced prisoners in the Commonwealth Caribbean is the Judicial Committee of the Privy Council, which sits at the House of Lords in London. While the Privy Council has no constitutional power, because

---

[166] AI, *Jamaica: Moves to Resume Hangings* (Jan. 1993), AI Index: AMR 38/01/93. See generally, Edward Fitzgerald, 'The Commonwealth Caribbean', in P. Hodgkinson and A. Rutherford (eds), *Capital Punishment: Global Issues and Prospects* (1996), pp. 143–153.

[167] Edward Fitzgerald, 'Savings Clauses and the Colonial Death Penalty Regime', in Penal Reform International, Simons Muirhead and Burton, Foreign and Commonwealth Office, Attorney General's Ministry (Belize), *Commonwealth Caribbean Human Rights Seminar*, 12–14 Sept. 2000 (2001), pp. 113–126 at 113.

of the savings clause, to abolish the death penalty in Caribbean countries, its judgments in recent years—particularly with regard to limiting the length of time that persons can be kept on death row awaiting execution (see Chapter 3 page 112)—have upset those Caribbean states that are keen to enforce the death penalty more frequently. It remains to be seen whether the Caribbean Court of Justice, when it eventually comes into existence, will take a different stance to that taken by British judges sitting on the Judicial Committee of the Privy Council in London.

Meanwhile, another problem has arisen in respect of appeals made by prisoners under sentence of death to international bodies, namely the UN Committee on Human Rights and the Inter-American Commission on Human Rights. The time taken for decisions to be taken in such cases has been interpreted by Guyana, Trinidad and Tobago, and Jamaica as a means of frustrating their attempts to carry out capital punishment, given the decision of the Privy Council that no one should be executed after remaining more than five years under sentence of death (see Chapter 3 page 112). The decision of Jamaica, Guyana, and Trinidad and Tobago to try to avoid their international commitments to abide by rulings of the UN Human Rights Committee under the ICCPR, and by Trinidad's withdrawal from the American Convention on Human Rights (see Chapter 5 page 169), is a clear indicator of their determination to resist abolition of capital punishment.

8. NORTH AMERICA

The process of abolition in Canada, as in Britain, went through various stages. In 1961 the death penalty was limited to a separate class of 'capital' murder, and in 1966 it was limited still further to the killing only of on-duty police officers and prison guards. Ten years later capital punishment was finally abolished for all ordinary crimes. No one had been executed since 1962. An attempt was made to reintroduce it in June 1987, but this was defeated by a substantial majority of Members of Parliament. It was finally expunged from Canadian law in 1998 when all references to the death penalty for military offences and treason were removed from the National Defence Act.

After the end of the Second World War the number of executions carried out in the United States of America began to decline sharply. During the 1930s, 1,670 persons had been executed, in the 1940s, 1,288, and in the 1950s, 717. The annual average for the years 1955 to 1959 was 61, but by 1963 the number executed had fallen to 21, to 15 in the following year, and finally to two in 1967.[168] Shortly afterwards the Supreme Court, faced with the pressure of many challenges to the death penalty orchestrated by the Legal Defence Fund of the National Association for the Advancement of Colored People, ordered a moratorium until the question of the

---

[168] See W. J. Bowers, *Legal Homicide: Death as Punishment in America, 1864–1982* (1984), pp. 25–26 and 53–55. Fifty three per cent of executions in the 1960s took place in southern states, including 26 men executed for rape; *ibid.*, p. 58.

constitutionality of capital punishment could be settled.[169] When all death penalty statutes then in force were ruled unconstitutional by the Supreme Court in 1972 in *Furman* v. *Georgia*, it seemed to many that capital punishment had finally been eliminated in the United States.[170] In fact, the Court did not hold that the death penalty was cruel and unusual punishment and therefore unconstitutional per se, rather that it was unconstitutional because it was being applied in an arbitrary, capricious, and discriminatory manner contrary to the Eighth and Fourteenth Amendments of the Constitution of the United States. So all but two of the previously 38 retentionist states decided to redraft their statutes to restrict and more carefully define the class of murder subject to capital punishment so as to avoid the objection of arbitrariness. These new capital statutes were subsequently ruled to be constitutional by the Supreme Court in *Gregg* v. *Georgia* and several other cases in 1976 (see Chapter 6 pages 180–181).

It is common for people, when discussing the attitude of America and Americans towards capital punishment, to speak as if the death penalty is on the statute books of all states. This is not so. Indeed 13 jurisdictions in the United States do not have capital punishment. They are (with the date of abolition): Alaska (1957), District of Columbia (1973), Hawaii (1957), Iowa (1872, reinstated in 1878 and abolished in 1965), Maine (1887), Massachusetts (1984), Michigan (1846 for all crimes except for treason, total abolition in 1963), Minnesota (1911), North Dakota (1915, except for murder by a prisoner serving a life term for murder, total abolition in 1973), Rhode Island (1852, restored the death penalty in 1882 for any murder by a prisoner serving a life sentence, total abolition in 1984), Vermont (1965, total abolition in 1987), West Virginia (1965), and Wisconsin (1853).[171]

Nevertheless, in recent years there have been attempts to reinstate the death penalty in several abolitionist states. In 1999, for example, bills were brought forward to reintroduce the death penalty in Iowa, Maine, Massachusetts, Minnesota, and even Michigan. All of them failed. The situation in Massachusetts proved to be particularly dramatic. A bill to reinstate capital punishment for murder had been passed by both legislative chambers in 1997, but when it came forward the next year for ratification, one supporter defected, leaving the vote tied at 80–80. The attempt by the Governor to resolve this deadlock by submitting the bill again in 1999 failed by 80 votes to 73,[172] and in 2001, when again reintroduced by the much larger margin of 94 to 60.[173]

In retentionist states many bills were introduced during the 1990s to expand the range of aggravating circumstances and to streamline processes of appeals so as to

[169] See Michael Meltsner, *Cruel and Unusual: The Supreme Court and Capital Punishment* (1973), pp. 106–148; also Bowers, n. 168 above, pp. 16–18.

[170] See F. E. Zimring and G. Hawkins, *Capital Punishment and the American Agenda* (1986), p. 26.

[171] These dates have been compiled from Bowers, n. 168 above, p. 9, and the Death Penalty Information Center at www.deathpenaltyinfo.org/nodp.html.

[172] See Brian Hauck, Cara Hendrickson, and Zena Yoslov, 'Symposium. The Death Penalty Debate: Capital Punishment Legislation in Massachusetts', *Harvard Journal on Legislation* 36 (1999), pp. 479–503.

[173] AI, *Death Penalty News*, Mar. 2001, AI Index: ACT 53/002/2001, p. 3.

speed up executions.[174] The vast majority of them failed to be passed, but nevertheless their very consideration signifies the mood of legislatures at this time.

The death penalty was successfully reintroduced in two states. In 1995, following the defeat of Mario Cuomo, who, as Governor of New York, had continually resisted attempts by the legislature to reintroduce capital punishment,[175] the new Governor, George E. Pataki, reinstated capital punishment—thirty-two years after New York's last execution. Furthermore, Kansas, twenty-nine years after the last execution, brought back the death penalty in 1994 despite the Governor's opposition, who allowed it to pass into law without her signature. Thus, the total number of retentionist jurisdictions is 40: 38 states, the Federal Government, and the United States military.

Executions recommenced in 1977, after a ten-year moratorium, with the dramatic execution of Gary Gilmore by firing squad in Utah, after he had determined to abandon all appeals.[176] When material for the first edition of this book was gathered ten years later in 1988, 25 of the 36 states which had retained capital punishment had not yet executed a prisoner. By the end of 2001 only four of these states (Connecticut, New Hampshire, New Jersey, and South Dakota), plus Kansas and New York and the US military, had not carried out an execution. Owing to the lengthy appeals process, it is still too early to say categorically, with the exception of New Hampshire (see below), whether any of these states can be regarded as truly abolitionist de facto.

The Supreme Court has remained deeply divided on the legitimacy of capital punishment, and has rejected systemic challenges to the constitutionality of death penalty statutes by only a narrow majority of 5 to 4 in two landmark cases: *McCleskey* v. *Kemp* (1987) and in *Blystone* v. *Pennsylvania* (1990).[177] Public opinion has oscillated, the polls showing that American citizens have changed their minds on this issue. Whereas in 1953 six out of ten adults supported its use, by 1965 only four out of ten did so. By 1994, 76 per cent were again in favour of the use of the death penalty, and by 1998 it appeared that as many as 80 per cent of the population were in favour. Since then, following concerns about the possibilities of wrongful conviction (see below),

---

[174] For example, in 1999 Alabama extended capital punishment to several types of intentional killings, California to killing a peace officer at a hospital, and in 1998 New Jersey extended it to killing in violation of a domestic violence restraining order. Bills extending aggravating circumstances failed in California, Connecticut, Florida, Georgia, Maryland, Missouri, Texas, and Washington. Bills to extend the death penalty to aggravated rape in Georgia and in Mississippi for the use of firearms, even if no death had resulted failed to be passed (see Chapter 6 pages 188–189).

[175] New York had abolished capital punishment in 1965, except for the murder of a police officer on duty or for murder committed by a prisoner serving a life sentence.

[176] A story dramatically told by Normal Mailer in *The Executioner's Song* (1979).

[177] See Welsh S. White, *The Death Penalty in the Nineties: An Examination of the Modern System of Capital Punishment* (1994), pp. 11–14. According to John C. Jeffries Jr., *Justice Lewis F. Powell, Jr.: A Biography* (1994), Justice Powell, who wrote the majority opinion in *McCleskey* v. *Kemp*, has changed his mind, stating that, if he were still a member of the Court he would now vote against the death penalty: 'I have come to think that capital punishment should be abolished.' Quoted in AI, *United States of America: Developments on the Death Penalty during 1994*, AI Index: AMR 51/01/95, p. 4.

support dropped to around two-thirds in 2001, yet still a substantial majority (for a fuller discussion, see Chapter 8).[178]

The application of the death penalty was effectively restricted to murder in the United States when the Supreme Court ruled it unconstitutional for rape in 1977 (*Coker* v. *Georgia*). Although the courts have accepted that this decision prohibits the imposition of the extreme penalty for all crimes not resulting in death, several states have left untouched the capital felony statutes which provide it for such offences as kidnapping and rape of a child. Furthermore, a few others have extended the scope of the death penalty by passing statutes which ensure that it applies to murders committed in particular contexts, either by increasing the number of aggravating features or by specifying murders relating to drug dealing, sexual assault, of informants, or judicial officers (for more details see Chapter 6 pages 188–189).

Under federal law the death penalty had been available in the pre-*Furman* period for a substantial number of offences, but only one of them (relating to air piracy) had been amended by Congress since the *Furman* decision in order to bring it within the constitutional requirements of death penalty statutes which had been laid down in *Gregg*. Whether the other death penalty provisions, relating for example to the murder of a member of Congress, were constitutional had never been tested by the Supreme Court.[179] However, since 1988 the scope of the death penalty has been expanded under the Federal Criminal Code. In that year the Anti-Drug Abuse Act amended earlier legislation aimed at controlling the involvement of 'continuing criminal enterprises' in drug trafficking, so as to enable the Federal government to seek the death penalty for murder committed while engaged in illegal drug activity and for killing a law enforcement officer in order to avoid apprehension for a drug violation.[180] The Violent Crime Control Act of 1994 not only made capital punishment a discretionary penalty for more than 50 offences in which death had ensued as a consequence, but also introduced it for several crimes in which death was not a consequence: the attempted assassination of the President, for large-scale drugs offences as part of 'a continuing criminal enterprise', and for a leader of such an enterprise who 'in order to obstruct the investigation or prosecution of the enterprise or an offence involved in the enterprise, attempts to kill or knowingly directs, advises, authorises, or assists another to attempt to kill any public officer, juror, witness, or members of the family or household of such a person'. The Act also laid down the 'constitutional procedures for the imposition of the sentence of death' and prohibited it for those under the age of 18.[181]

---

[178] According to the Gallup Poll. See AI, *United States of America: Failing the Future—Death Penalty Developments, March 1998–March 2000*, AI Index: AMR 51/003/2000, p. 47. See generally, Phoebe C. Ellsworth and Samuel R. Gross, 'Hardening of the Attitudes: Americans' Views on the Death Penalty', in Hugo Adam Bedau (ed), *The Death Penalty in America: Current Controversies* (1997), pp. 90–115.

[179] See Charles W. Williams, 'The Federal Death Penalty for Drug-Related Killings', *Criminal Law Bulletin* 27 (1991), pp. 387–415 at 388 n. 12.

[180] *Ibid.*, pp. 393–398. This involved any violation under the Continuing Criminal Enterprise Act (21 U.S.C.) ss 841 (b) (1) (A), 960 (b) (1). The Anti-Drug Abuse Act was codified at 21 U.S.C., s. 848 (e) 1998.

[181] *Violent Crime Control Act*, P.L. 103–322, Title VI—Death Penalty, ch. 228, s. 3591 (b) (1 and 2), s. 3593.

Since then the 1996 Anti-Terrorism and Effective Death Penalty Act has expanded the scope of capital punishment still further by providing the death penalty for crimes where death is caused, even if only proximately, by the use of explosives or arson.[182]

Until June 2001 no prisoner had been executed for a federal offence since 1963. But in that month federal executions began when Timothy McVeigh's life was ended by lethal injection for the infamous Oklahoma City bombing of a federal building with the loss of 168 lives. His execution aroused enormous interest and widespread support throughout the United States and condemnation from many countries. The Council of Europe called it 'sad, pathetic and wrong'.[183] Later in the same month a second prisoner, Juan Raoul Garza, was executed for drug-related murders, although this time with much less publicity. A moratorium lasting thirty-eight years had been broken.

In June 1992 the United States ratified the ICCPR but made a reservation in respect of Article 6, which prohibits the execution of persons whose crimes were committed when they were below the age of 18 years. Indeed it stated: 'That the United States reserves the right, subject to its Constitutional constraints, to impose capital punishment on any person (other than a pregnant woman) duly convicted under existing or future laws permitting the imposition of capital punishment, including such punishment for crimes committed by persons below eighteen years of age.' The United States has stuck to this position even though the UN Human Rights Committee has stated that the US reservation is invalid because Article 4 of the ICCPR forbids derogation from Article 6, even in time of emergency. The Committee called upon the US Supreme Court to carry out its own examination of the issue—but so far the Court has refused to consider the matter again (see Chapter 4 pages 114–120).

The United States also made a reservation to Article 7, which concerns cruel and unusual treatment or punishment, which, according to the United Nations Human Rights Committee, prohibits the use of the gas chamber as a method of execution. In its reservation it stated it could only agree to be bound by Article 7 'to the extent that "cruel, inhuman or degrading treatment or punishment" means the cruel and unusual treatment or punishment prohibited by the Fifth, Eighth or Fourteenth Amendments to the Constitution of the United States'. The Human Rights Committee has ruled that these reservations are also 'incompatible with the object and purpose of the Covenant' and are therefore invalid. A similar situation arose with regard to the US government's ratification of the Convention against Torture and other Forms of Cruel, Inhuman or Degrading Treatment or Punishment. In its report to the UN Committee against Torture, the government claimed that it was not obliged to report on the use of the death penalty because the United States had made a condition of its ratification the proposition that the United States was only bound to Article 16 of the Convention to the extent that the definition of 'cruel,

---

[182] Anti-Terrorism and Effective Death Penalty Act of 1996, Public Law 104–132, Title VII.
[183] *New York Times*, 12 June 2001.

inhuman or degrading treatment or punishment' matches the 'cruel and unusual punishment' prohibited by the US Constitution as interpreted by the US Supreme Court. The United States also included an 'understanding' that the Convention did not limit 'any constitutional period of confinement prior to the imposition of the death penalty'.[184] In March 2000 Justice Sandra Day O'Connor of the US Supreme Court declared at a Conference on Democracy and the Rule of Law in a Changing World Order that '[The Court's] approach reflects the idea that in matters of domestic criminal law, the national sovereignty interests weigh more heavily in the balance than do international norms.'[185] What can better illustrate the reluctance of the United States to change its practices of capital punishment?[186]

In its reply to the United Nations Sixth Quinquennial Survey in 2000, the US government declared that:

The sanction of capital punishment continues to be the subject of strongly-held and publicly debated views in the United States. There are and have been, from time to time, legislative, policy, and other initiatives to limit and or abolish the death penalty. However, a majority of citizens have chosen through their freely elected state and federal officials to provide for the possibility of the death penalty for the most serious and aggravated crimes, under state law in a majority of the states (currently 38 of 50 states, plus the District of Columbia) and under federal law . . . Capital punishment is not prohibited by customary international law or by any treaty provision under which the United States is currently obligated. We recognize that many countries have abolished the death penalty under their domestic laws and that a number of countries have accepted treaty obligations to that effect, and we respect their decision to do so. However, we believe that in democratic societies the criminal justice system—including the punishment prescribed for the most serious and aggravated crimes—should reflect the will of the people freely expressed and appropriately implemented through their elected representatives.

Several hypotheses have been advanced as to why capital punishment has remained so strongly entrenched in the United States when it has disappeared from the penal armoury of those countries that share with it a common political heritage and culture. Some commentators have suggested that the nature of American Federalism, under which capital punishment in practice (at least until McVeigh's execution) was a matter mainly for state law and for state politics, has meant that the issue was isolated from international pressures.[187] Indeed, a mission to the United

---

[184] See AI, n. 178 above, p.13.   [185] Quoted *ibid.*, p. 55.

[186] Quoted from William A. Schabas, 'Invalid Reservations to the International Covenant of Civil and Political Rights: Is the United States Still a Party?', *Brooklyn Journal of International Law* 21 (1995), pp. 277–325 at 278–282. It should be noted, however, that Justice O'Connor has, on other occasions 'called upon U.S. judges to consult case law in foreign jurisdictions regarding the interpretation of international treaties and the relationship between national courts and international tribunals'. See Harold Hongju Koh, 'Paying "Decent Respect" to World Opinion on the Death Penalty', *UC Davis Law Review* 35 (2002), pp. 1085–1131, referring to Justice O'Connor's speech in 1997 to the American College of Trial Lawyers, at 1119 n. 141. She expressed similar views to a meeting of the American Law Institute in May 2002, but, according to Associated Press, stressed that while the Supreme Court had been urged to consider what people in other countries consider cruel and unusual punishment, to help US relations with those countries, the question for the Court is limited to whether there is a consensus in the United States that the executions are cruel.

[187] See L. J. Hoffmann, 'Justice Dando and the "Conservative" Argument for Abolition', *Indiana Law Review* 72 (1996), pp. 21–24.

States by the International Commission of Jurists in 1996 was dismayed to find 'a general lack of awareness among state officials, and even amongst judges, lawyers, and teachers, of the obligations under the international instruments that the country had ratified'.[188] That may have been changing since the European Union began its démarches to state governors (see Chapter 1 page 17).

Others have emphasized the degree to which issues that arise in one state have had little impact in others. And this is related to a third point, namely that the populist nature of American politics has meant, as Hugo Adam Bedau put it in 1996, that 'It is now widely assumed that no political candidate in the United States can hope to run for president, governor, or other high elective office if he or she can be selectively targeted as "soft on crime": the candidate's position of the death penalty is the litmus test.'[189] And it also appears clear that 'the politics surrounding the election and retention of state judges has made it more difficult for judges to overturn or refuse to impose death sentences without losing their judgeship'.[190]

There can be no doubt that support for capital punishment has been fuelled by some exceptionally brutal murders, such as the Oklahoma bombing by Timothy McVeigh, and by the discovery of appalling serial killers like Ted Bundy. Yet other countries have faced similar outrages without seeking to execute the perpetrators. Furthermore, when passions are aroused, as was shown in relation to persons accused of bombing atrocities in England, several wrongful convictions resulted (see page 26 above).

Other commentators have suggested that the opponents of the death penalty in America have followed the wrong strategy, through the courts rather than a direct attack through the democratic political process.[191] Indeed, several abolitionist supporters have come to the unhappy conclusion that by trying to narrow down the categories of person who may be executed, they have left the public with the belief that only the most egregious murderers, 'those who deserve to die', are in fact executed.

However, the abolitionist movement in the United States, which appeared to have very little political weight behind it—'too few members, too little money . . . and too little broad appeal in the message the movement has tried to deliver'[192]—

---

[188] International Commission of Jurists, *Administration of the Death Penalty in the United States* (1996).
[189] H. A. Bedau, 'The United States', in P. Hodgkinson and A. Rutherford (eds), *Capital Punishment: Global Issues and Prospects* (1996), pp. 45–76 at 50.
[190] See Leigh B. Bienen, 'The Quality of Justice in Capital Cases: Illinois as a Case Study', *Law and Contemporary Problems* 61 (1998), pp. 193–217 at 193.
[191] See A. Rutherford, 'Abolition: A Tale of Two Struggles', in P. Hodgkinson and A. Rutherford (eds), n. 189 above, pp. 261–277 at 269.
[192] For a first-class analysis of the reasons why the anti-death penalty movement was so weak, see Herbert H. Haines, *Against Capital Punishment. The Anti-Death Penalty Movement in America, 1972–1994* (1996). 'In a nation where policy advocacy has become a capital-intensive enterprise, death penalty opponents have little money. On an issue that is fought mostly at the state level, abolitionism consists primarily of eastern-based national organizations with weak state affiliates and few local ones. These two disadvantages are linked intimately to a third. In the cynical and angry climate that exists in America, abolitionists have trusted mostly in their ability to bring about not just a national change of *mind*, but a change of *heart*. What has remained undeveloped in the movement is a more pragmatic vocabulary, capable of doing more than just preaching to the choir', at p. 167.

has shown a remarkable revival in the last few years. Although not declaring a policy position on the death penalty per se, the American Bar Association (ABA) in 1997 adopted a resolution calling on all jurisdictions that impose capital punishment not to carry out executions until policies and procedures '(1) ensure that death penalty procedures are administered fairly and impartially, in accordance with due process, and (2) minimise the risk that innocent persons may be executed'.[193] And in July 2000 the incoming President of the ABA issued a fresh call to American lawyers to support a moratorium on executions, and, on leaving office a year later, urged both the Senate and House Judiciary Committees to support the National Death Penalty Moratorium Act.[194] Similarly, the American Psychiatric Association Assembly resolved to ask its Trustees to call for a moratorium.[195] Furthermore, the Catholic Church and Reform and Orthodox Jewish movements have joined forces recently to campaign against the death penalty alongside most (but not the fundamentalist) Protestant groups.[196]

This support for reform, even if not abolition, has been fuelled by the spectre that innocent persons may have been put to death. Particularly dramatic was the action taken by the Governor of Illinois in January 2000, when informed that a study by student investigative journalists had uncovered convincing evidence that Anthony Porter, who had earlier come within two days of execution, had been wrongfully convicted of a crime to which another man had confessed, that a further innocent man was awaiting execution on Illinois's death row and that a further 12 had been released because they were deemed to have been wrongfully convicted. In announcing an immediate moratorium on executions, pending the outcome of the review by a fourteen-member Commission of the administration of the death penalty, ordered in May 1999 by the Illinois House of Representatives, the Governor declared:

I have grave concerns about our state's shameful record of convicting innocent people and putting them on death row. And, I believe, many Illinois residents now feel that deep reservation. I cannot support a system which, in its administration, has proven to be so fraught with error, and has come so close to the ultimate nightmare, the state's taking of innocent life.

This had an immediate impact on public support for capital punishment. For

---

[193] See American Bar Association, *A Gathering Momentum: Continuing Impacts of the American Bar Association Call for a Moratorium on Executions*, ABA Section on Individual Rights and Responsibilities, Jan. 2000.

[194] For further developments, see American Bar Association, Section of Individual Rights and Responsibilities, *Towards Greater Awareness: The American Bar Association Call for a Moratorium on Executions Gains Ground. A Summary of Moratorium Resolution Impacts from January 2000 through July 2001* (Aug. 2001). See also for a wide-ranging review, Jeffrey L. Kirchmeier, 'Another Place Beyond Here: The Death Penalty Moratorium Movement in the United States', *University of Colorado Law Review* 73 (2002), pp. 2–116.

[195] See AI, *The Death Penalty Worldwide: Developments in 2000*, AI Index ACT 50/001/2001, p 7.

[196] See Ronald J. Tabak, Commentary, 'Finality without Fairness: Why we are Moving towards Moratoria on Executions, and the Potential Abolition of Capital Punishment', *Connecticut Law Review* 33 (2001), pp. 733–763 at 742. Also, Michael L. Radelet, 'The Role of Organized Religions in Changing Death Penalty Debates', *William and Mary Bill of Rights Journal* 9 (2000), pp. 201–214, quoting at 207 n. 43 the American Friends Service Committee's publication *The Death Penalty: The Religious Community Calls for Abolition* (1998).

example, a poll conducted by the *Chicago Tribune* in February 2000 found that 58 per cent of registered voters were in favour of it, compared to 63 per cent in the previous year and 76 per cent in 1994 (on public opinion more generally in the United States, see Chapter 8 below).

Similar concerns were voiced in Maryland, Massachusetts, Nebraska, Washington, and several other states. In April 2000 and again in January 2001 bills (the National Death Penalty Moratorium Act of 2000) were introduced in the US Senate to establish a National Commission to review the administration of the death penalty and to suspend executions under state and federal law until it had reported. In both New Hampshire[197] and New Mexico[198] bills to abolish the death penalty were narrowly defeated.

In the years 1999–2001 bills to restrict the use of the death penalty, and some to abolish it (although with little hope of success), were introduced in at least thirty retentionist states, and the Federal system[199] and attempts to introduce a moratorium to halt executions were under consideration in at least fifteen states and the Federal system.[200] An ABC News Poll in April 2001 found that 51 per cent of Americans favoured a moratorium on executions until a commission could report on whether the death penalty is being applied fairly, and in some states as many as 70 per cent of citizens supported a moratorium.[201] Ten jurisdictions had set up such Commissions by the end of 2001 (and another seven are considering doing so) to study the way in which the death penalty has been administered, with a view to ascertaining whether improvements can be made to eliminate the possibility of arbitrary or wrongful conviction.[202] Furthermore, in five states bills have been passed to ensure that capitally convicted persons have access to DNA testing and in a further nine states and the Federal system bills were introduced to that effect.[203]

---

[197] In May 2000 the New Hampshire Senate endorsed the State House of Representative's earlier decision to abolish the death penalty (which had not been imposed for many years) and to replace it with life imprisonment without parole. However, the Governor of the State, Jeanne Shaheen, vetoed the bill, and when it was reintroduced in April 2000 it was narrowly (by a 188–180 vote) defeated.

[198] A Senate bill to abolish capital punishment was lost by only one vote in February 2001. However, an execution took place later that year (at the defendant's own request), the first execution in New Mexico since 1960.

[199] Arizona, Arkansas, California, Connecticut, Florida, Georgia, Illinois, Indiana, Kansas, Kentucky, Louisiana, Maryland, Mississippi, Missouri, Montana, Nebraska, Nevada, New Hampshire, New Jersey, New Mexico, New York, North Carolina, Ohio, Oregon, Pennsylvania, South Carolina, South Dakota, Texas, Virginia, Washington, and the Federal system.

[200] Alabama, Connecticut, Kentucky, Louisiana, Maryland, Missouri, New Jersey, North Carolina, Ohio, Oklahoma, Pennsylvania, Tennessee, Texas, Virginia, Washington, and the Federal system. See Michael L. Radelet, 'More Trends toward Moratoria on Executions', *Connecticut Law Review* 33 (2001), pp. 845–860.

[201] Death Penalty Information Center, *Summaries of Recent Poll Findings*, www.deathpenaltyinfo.org/Polls.html. See also *San Francisco Chronicle*, 21 July 2000, reporting that 73% of citizens polled supported a moratorium in order to study the fairness of the state's capital punishment system.

[202] Arizona, Connecticut, Illinois, Indiana, Maryland, Nebraska, Nevada, North Carolina, Virginia, and the Federal system.

[203] In California, Florida, Maryland, Texas, and Virginia bills were passed, and in Idaho, Indiana, Louisiana, New Jersey, North Carolina, Ohio, Pennsylvania, Utah, Washington, and the Federal system bills were introduced.

Undoubtedly, the concern about wrongful executions—an issue never previously strongly to the fore of the abolitionist debate in the United States[204]—has become of much greater significance, perhaps indicating a greater appreciation that the system of capital punishment in the United States (although largely a matter for state law) bears on the nation's reputation as a whole. The Death Penalty Information Center and the Innocence Project, led by Professor Barry Scheck of Cardozo Law School, have played an important role in bringing to public attention the fact that as many as 101 persons have been freed from death row between 1973 and June 2002 on the grounds that they were innocent, and that the annual rate has been increasing. Of particular note is the high standard of proof provided in 12 of these cases through the use of DNA evidence.[205] Thus, Justice Sandra Day O'Connor, a staunch supporter of capital punishment, recently acknowledged the inadequacy of many defence lawyers in capital cases and expressed concern that 'the system may well be allowing some innocent defendants to be executed'.[206] Similarly, Judge Gerald Kogan, formerly Chief Justice of the State of Florida, announced his opposition to capital punishment after serving for twelve years as a Justice of Florida's Supreme Court, on the grounds that the court had 'certainly . . . executed those people who either didn't fit the criteria for execution in the state of Florida or who, in fact, were factually not guilty of the crime for which they were executed'.[207]

Further weight to these concerns was added by the publication in June 2000 of a study carried out at Columbia University which showed that about two-thirds of death sentences imposed between 1973 and 1995 had been reversed during the processes of state and federal reviews and appeals (see Chapter 5 pages 135–136). Far from convincing abolitionists that all errors were ultimately discovered, the opposite conclusion was drawn. Namely, that the system was so 'broken' that it was likely that some innocent persons had probably been executed.

As this book was about to go to press, the Commission set up by Governor Ryan of Illinois reported, after two years of deliberation. Its report was hailed as a blueprint for the way in which other states and the federal government should review the operation of capital punishment in their jurisdictions, to ensure that it is administered

---

[204] See Samuel Gross, 'Lost Lives: Miscarriages of Justice in Capital Cases', *Law and Contemporary Problems* 61 (1988), pp. 125–217 at 125. Also, writing in 1998, Michael Radelet and Hugo Adam Bedau had noted that, up to that time, 'The fact that innocent persons (in one or another sense of 'innocence') are executed seems to have had little if any real impact on opinion towards the death penalty.' See, 'The Execution of the Innocent', *ibid.*, pp. 105–124 at 118.

[205] See Barry Scheck, Peter Neufeld, and Jim Dwyer, *Actual Innocence: Five Days to Execution and other Dispatches from the Wrongfully Convicted* (2000), New York: Doubleday. Also www.deathpenaltyinfo.org/Innocentlist.html.

[206] Speech in Minneapolis to women lawyers on 2 July 2001, reported in AI, *Death Penalty News*, Sept. 2001, AI Index: ACT 53/004/2001.

[207] See report in *The Spectator*, Mar. 2001. In addition Justice Blackmun of the US Supreme Court a former supporter of the death penalty, had in 1994 announced his opposition to it (see page 187 below), and so has former Justice Powell, who had also while on the court favoured capital punishment (see n. 177 above, p. 64), both of them on the grounds that it could not be administered fairly. Other examples include former Chief Justice James Exum Jr. of the North Carolina Supreme Court, who in July 2000 castigated the death sentence which 'cheapens the rest of us; it brutalizes the rest of us; and we become a more violent society'. Quoted in Kirchmeier, n. 194 above, p. 32.

with due process, fairly, and equitably.[208] A slight majority of the members declared itself in favour of abolition of the death penalty in Illinois, but all agreed that if it were to continue as a legally sanctioned punishment ('because if appears to have the support of the majority of Illinois citizens'), there would have to be sweeping reforms of legal, administrative, and criminal justice procedures. Eighty-five recommendations were made: including, that its scope should be substantially reduced from the twenty factual circumstances which made a defendant eligible for a death sentence in Illinois to only five circumstances, regarded as the most egregious types of murder; that procedural protections for suspects under interrogation should be greatly enhanced; that certain types of evidence could not be used to support a capital conviction, such as that from a jailhouse informant or accomplice, or from a single eyewitness; that a state-wide panel would have to review prosecutor's decisions to seek the death penalty to avoid the great disparities that were found to exist; that there should be enhanced training for trial lawyers and judges in capital cases; that judges must concur with the jury before a death sentence is imposed; and that the state Supreme Court should conduct in every case a proportionality review. The fact that such protections had not been in place for those currently on death row (about 160) was regarded as a potent reason for considering whether many of these persons should be granted clemency.[209]

Of particular significance, given that the Commission believed that such reforms were essential if the system were to be made 'fair, just and accurate', was its statement that 'the death penalty itself is incredibly complex . . . there are few easy answers. The Commission was unanimous in the belief that no system, given human nature and frailties, could ever be devised or constructed that would work perfectly and guarantee absolutely that no innocent person is ever again sentenced to death.'[210] It remains to be seen what impact this Report will have both within Illinois and across America, but there can be no doubt that it does support the abolitionist's contention that any system of capital punishment will be seriously flawed and inevitably breach principles of human rights.

Meanwhile, it can be noted that the number of executions carried out each year in the United States as a whole has fallen sharply in the last three years: from 98 in the year 1999 to 66 in 2001, although in some cases they have gone ahead even when, as in the case of Gary Graham in Texas, doubts about the safeness of the conviction had been strongly expressed.

---

[208] Statement of Robert E. Hirshon, President of the American Bar Association, on the report of the Illinois Commission on Capital Punishment, 15 Apr. 2002.

[209] Illinois, *Report of the Governor's Commission on Capital Punishment. George H. Ryan Governor* (Apr. 2002), pp. i–iii.

[210] *Ibid.*, p. 207. In May 2002 Governor Ryan announced legislation to put into effect the Commission's recommendations, and the Governor of Maryland announced a moratorium on executions until a study of racial bias in the administration of the death penalty has been completed. In June 2002 the Report of the Nevada Assembly Subcommittee to Study the Death Penalty and DNA Testing called for a raft of reforms, including restricting the number of aggravating factors making defendants liable to the death penalty and the provision in all cases of proper legal representation.

There is little doubt that the position of the United States as a moral leader on issues of human rights and as a democracy based on justice for all has been weakened by its stand on capital punishment, as several leading former ambassadors recently testified in evidence to the Supreme Court in the *McCarver* and later the *Atkins* case, concerning the death penalty for mentally retarded offenders, backed up by the European Union. It was of considerable significance that the majority in *Atkins* v. *Virginia*, decided in June 2002, cited the worldwide condemnation of executing the mentally retarded among its reasons for deciding that it could now be declared 'cruel and unusual punishment' (see Chapter 4 pages 126–130). Recently Professor Harold Koh, who was US Assistant Secretary of State for Democracy, Human Rights, and Labor between 1998 and 2001, declared: 'From extensive personal experience, I can now testify that . . . this issue has placed America and Europe on a collision course in almost every multilateral human right forum . . . the death penalty has become our Achilles heel.'[211]

Nevertheless, in March 2001, General Colin Powell, the US Secretary of State, was reported to have told European Union foreign policy leaders that he did not believe that there would be any change in the American position as regards the death penalty in 'the foreseeable future'.[212] This seems even more likely after 11 September 2001.

It remains to be seen whether confidence in the integrity of the system of capital punishment will decline in the United States sufficiently to lead to abandonment of capital punishment in those states that have made the most use of it. The decision of Judge Rakoff in the Federal District court in Manhattan in June 2002 may prove to be more than a straw in the wind. He held that the Federal Death Penalty Act is unconstitutional because it 'not only deprives innocent people of a significant opportunity to prove their innocence, and thereby violates procedural due process, but also creates an undue risk of executing innocent people, and thereby violates substantive due process'.[213] Those who continue to support the death penalty obviously hope that the reforms emanating from the various State Commissions set up to examine the administration of capital punishment will tighten up the system sufficiently, so that citizens will come once again to believe that only the most egregious and clearly guilty cases are executed—especially if DNA evidence becomes statutorily available to inmates to help them establish their innocence, as proposed in the Innocence Protection Act, still before Congress in mid-2002. On the other hand, the numbers executed may dwindle to such an extent that any claims for capital punishment's deterrent effect would become so otiose that the system could no longer be supported.

What is certain is that calls for moratoriums are not sufficient to bring about abolition, as the ten-year moratorium between 1967 and 1977 demonstrated. It is one thing to establish commissions to try to find ways to impose the death penalty fairly and without error and to ban it for the mentally retarded. But it is quite

---

[211] See Harold Hongju Koh, 'Paying "Decent Respect" to World Opinion on the Death Penalty', *UC Davis Law Review* 35 (2002), pp. 1085–1131 at 1105.

[212] *Daily Telegraph*, 8 Mar. 2001.

[213] Reported in *New York Times*, 1 July 2002.

another to come to the conclusion that capital punishment should be abolished as a matter of principle on the grounds that its enforcement inevitably involves 'cruel and unusual punishment'. It remains open for the United States Supreme Court to make that judgment under its 'emerging standards of decency' doctrine.[214]

[214] See *Weems* v. *United States*, 217 U.S. 349, 378 (1910) and *Trop* v. *Dulles*, 356 U.S. 86, 101 (1958).

3

The Scope and Practice of Capital Punishment

This chapter reviews what is known about the range of offences that may be subject to capital punishment in various countries; the extent to which death sentences are imposed and carried out by execution; the method by which, and the circumstances in which, they are carried out; the controversy over the involvement of physicians in the administration of capital punishment; and the consequences for those who await execution on death row.

1. The Scope of the Death Penalty

Unfortunately it is impossible to provide, for all countries, accurate and up-to-date information on the range of crimes which are deemed to be capital offences for which offenders may be sentenced to death. This is because so few of them have provided such information to the United Nations (see the Introduction, page 2). We do know, however, that not all countries have responded positively to the United Nations call 'to progressively restrict the number of offences for which capital punishment might be imposed' as a stage towards eventual abolition. Indeed, as this chapter will show, the range of crimes for which the death penalty may be imposed in some countries is very wide, and in some countries has expanded rather than contracted. Furthermore, as will be discussed in Chapter 6 some countries still retain a mandatory death penalty for certain crimes.

(a) What are 'the Most Serious Crimes'?

Article 6 (2) of the International Covenant on Civil and Political Rights (ICCPR) states that

In countries which have not abolished the death penalty, sentence of death may only be imposed for the most serious crimes in accordance with the law in force at the time of the commission of the crime and not contrary to the provisions of the present Covenant and to the Convention on the Prevention and Punishment of the Crime of Genocide.

This provision was somewhat strengthened in 1984, when the Economic and Social Council of the United Nations adopted by resolution the Safeguards Guaranteeing

Protection of the Rights of those Facing the Death Penalty.[1] The first of these safe-guards specified that

capital punishment may be imposed only for the most serious crimes, it being understood that their scope should not go beyond intentional crimes with lethal or other extremely grave consequences.

The definition of 'most serious crimes' may, of course, vary in different social, cultural, religious, and political contexts, but the emphasis on *intention*, and on *lethal* or *other extremely grave consequences*, was intended to imply that the offences should have led to loss of life or be life-threatening, in the sense that death is a very likely consequence of the action. Indeed, the Human Rights Committee, established under the ICCPR, has laid it down that the concept of 'most serious crimes' employed in the Covenant (Article 6, paragraph 2) 'must be read restrictively to mean that the death penalty should be a *quite exceptional measure*'.

It appears, however, that the death penalty can be imposed in some countries for crimes in which intent to kill does not have to be proven, and in other countries when the offence may not be life-threatening, except in the broadest of interpretations of that term. Thus, in the Philippines the wide scope of the death penalty law has been based on the concept of 'heinous crimes', defined in extraordinarily vague terms as 'grievous, odious and hateful offences . . . which by reason of their inherent or manifest wickedness, viciousness, atrocity and perversity, are repugnant and outrageous to the common standards and norms of decency and morality in a just, civilized society'.[2]

Several attempts have been made to define more precisely what does constitute 'most serious crimes', usually by stating what should be excluded. Thus, Article 4 (4) of the American Convention on Human Rights stipulates that 'in no case shall capital punishment be inflicted for political offences or related common crimes', and the UN Commission on Human Rights at its 1999 session, in line with the view expressed by the Special Rapporteur on extra-judicial, summary, or arbitrary executions,[3] urged all states that still maintained the death penalty not to impose it for 'non-violent financial crimes, or non-violent religious practice or expression of conscience'.[4] At its fifty-eighth session in 2002 the Commission added to this list 'sexual relations between consenting adults'.[5] In a series of judgments the UN Human Rights Committee has extended this list to include offences such as 'evading military service several times' (Iraq), abetting suicide and drug-related offences (Sri Lanka), apostasy, committing a third homosexual act, illicit sex (Sudan), 'vague categories of offence relating to internal and external security' and terrorism (Kuwait and Egypt), 'a person whose life endangers or corrupts society' (Libya), and

---

[1] On this, more generally, see Chapters 4 and 5.

[2] Paragraph 2 of the Preamble to the Republic Act 7659.

[3] United Nations, *Report of the Special Rapporteur on Extrajudicial, Summary or Arbitrary Executions* (hereafter cited as Special Rapporteur's *Report*), submitted to the Commission on Human Rights, E/CN.4.1999/39, para. 63.

[4] E/CN.4/1999/L.9.

[5] E/CN.4/2002/L.104, para. 4c, 'Promotion and Protection of Human Rights'.

aggravated robbery where the use of firearms did not produce death or wounding of any person (Zambia).[6]

This is undoubtedly a step in the right direction, but it cannot be denied that the retention of the amorphous phrases 'other extremely grave consequences' and 'most serious crimes' has left this safeguard open to wide interpretation by a number of countries. The policy objective of this safeguard has been to lead retentionist countries along the path taken by many (but not all) abolitionist states: namely to the last stage where capital punishment is available solely for the most serious offences of murder. There is, in my opinion, a strong argument for the safeguard now to read:

In countries which have not abolished the death penalty, capital punishment may be imposed only for the most serious offences of culpable homicide (murder), but it may not be mandatory for such crimes.

(b) Non-Retroactive Enforcement

As mentioned above, Article 6 (2) of the ICCPR allows for the death penalty to be imposed only for crimes that were capital offences in law at the time that the offence was committed. The United Nations Safeguard No. 2 for the protection of the rights of those facing the death penalty added a further condition, namely of '*it being understood that if, subsequent to the commission of the crime, provision is made by law for the imposition of a lighter penalty, the offender shall benefit thereby*'.

Yet in recent years several countries have introduced the death penalty retroactively. Israel did so after the Second World War so as to make it possible to punish severely Nazis found guilty of perpetrating atrocities during the Holocaust. Adolf Eichmann was the first and so far only person to have been executed under this provision.[7] When Islamic law was introduced in Sudan in 1983, the death penalty was retroactively applied to adultery between married persons, and concern was expressed when the new Penal Code of 1991, also based on Islamic law, appeared to make it possible to sentence to death persons who had committed apostasy by renouncing Islam prior to 1991. In 1984 Nigeria extended the death penalty by decree retroactively to cover 19 offences: and two men are known to have been executed for drug offences committed before the decree was promulgated. Iraq also

---

[6] See Official Records of the General Assembly, 37th Session (1982), suppl. no. 40 (A/37/40), Annex V, para. 7. In recent years the Committee has expressed its concern about the wide scope of the death penalty in at least 15 countries: Algeria, Belarus, Cameroon, Egypt, Guatemala, India, Iraq, Japan, Kuwait, Libya, Morocco, Peru, Sri Lanka, Sudan, Zambia. See Martin Scheinin, 'Capital Punishment and the International Covenant on Civil and Political Rights: Some Issues of Interpretation in the Practice of the Human Rights Committee', Paper presented to the EU–China Human Rights Seminar, Beijing, 10–12 May 2001.

[7] In relation to atrocities and war crimes committed during the Nazi period. The official reply to the UN Fifth Survey stated: 'According to the Nazi and Nazi Collaborators (Punishment) Law 1950, crimes against the Jewish people and crimes against humanity are punishable if committed during the Nazi regime (30 Jan 1933–8 May 1945) and war crimes are punishable if committed during World War II (1 September 1939–14 August 1945).' See Report of the Secretary-General, *Capital Punishment and Implementation of the Safeguards Guaranteeing the Protection of the Rights of those Facing the Death Penalty*, E/1995/78, 8 June 1995, para. 62.

invoked the death penalty retroactively in 1980 for membership of outlawed political parties, and by Decree No. 115 of 1994 the death penalty could be applied retroactively to persons who had evaded military service for the third time. The Decree promulgated by the Algerian government in September 1992, which broadened the definition of 'terrorist and subversive acts', provided for the application of penalties which did not exist at the time of the offence,[8] as did the Acts of Terrorism Act introduced in the Maldives in 1990, although no one has yet been sentenced under that legislation. Thus it is clear that not all countries have adhered to the safeguard against non-retroactive enforcement of capital punishment, although it is true to say that there have not been many examples of its breach in more recent years.

In response to the UN quinquennial surveys, seven countries (Burundi, Chad, Chile, Guinea, Guyana, Lebanon, and South Korea) have stated that, if a crime became punishable by a lesser penalty than death, an offender under sentence would not be eligible to receive that lesser punishment, and thus not be protected under the safeguard. And in the United States four states which raised the minimum age limit for the sentence of death to 18 in 1987 did not apply this benefit retroactively to those already under sentence of death, contrary not only to Safeguard No. 2, but also to Article 15 (1) of the ICCPR, and Article 9 of the American Convention on Human Rights. The same situation occurred in Pakistan, although this has now been rectified (see page 115 below).

(c) Offences against the State and Public Order

At present, capital punishment is available in most (77 of the 105) retentionist countries for certain offences against the state. In some of them the death penalty is limited to offences of waging or attempting to wage war against the state, but in many others it can be imposed for a wide range of actions which can best be described as 'political offences'. These encompass: treason, espionage, attempting to seize power by unconstitutional means; heading or organizing an insurrectionist movement; acts of terrorism and sabotage, including destruction or damage to buildings, railways, and other state property; and attempts on the life of the head of state, other government officials, or members of foreign embassies. In some countries, such as Singapore, the death penalty is mandatory for treason. Obviously, many of these offences are broadly defined and subject to varying interpretations. Indeed, they may not actually involve death or even injury to any persons. In Zambia, for example, 59 men were sentenced to death following the attempted coup of October 1997, despite the fact that no persons were harmed,[9] and in 1998 six people were sentenced to death in Myanmar for planning to detonate bombs and assassinate government officials.[10]

---

[8] AI, *Report 1993*, p. 50.
[9] See AI, *Zambia: Time to Abolish the Death Penalty*, AI Index: AFR 63/004/2001, p. 14. As of July 2001 these 59 prisoners were still being held on death row.
[10] AI, *Report 1999*, p. 258.

It is significant that in the last thirty years at least 21 countries[11] (including nine since 1988[12]) have extended capital punishment variously to one or more of the following crimes: espionage, treason, terrorism, counter-revolutionary activities, or membership of revolutionary groups, threatening the geographical boundaries of the state (in Jordan the sale of occupied land to Israel), organizing or promoting the secession of any parts of the country, evading military service several times, meeting to seek territorial or administrative dismemberment of the state, or even more broadly framed 'crimes against the state'. In Saudi Arabia the law provides the death penalty for 'sabotage and corruption on earth' to a potentially very wide range of actions: 'Anyone proved to have carried out acts of sabotage and corruption on earth which undermines security by aggression against persons and private or public property such as the destruction of homes, mosques, schools, factories, bridges, ammunition dumps, water storage tanks, resources of the treasury such as oil pipelines, the hijacking and blowing up of airplanes, and so on . . .'.[13]

The Egyptian Penal Code was criticized by the United Nations Human Rights Committee, as long ago as 1993, for similarly defining too widely the range of acts covered by Article 86 on terrorism, which can be punished by the death penalty. This states that

terrorism means any use of force, violence, *threat or intimidation* perpetrated as part of an individual or collective plan aimed at *breaching public order*, or endangering *public safety* or security, if this leads to *harming* or terrorizing individuals or endangering their lives, *freedom or security*, *or causing damage* to the environment, means of transport or communications, public or private property or buildings, *or occupying or appropriating* any of these, *or preventing or obstructing the authorities, places of worship or educational establishments in the performance of their duties, or preventing the implementation of the Constitution, laws or regulations.* (my emphasis)

[11] Algeria, Bangladesh, Belarus, China, Dominica, Egypt, Ghana, Guatemala, Indonesia, Iraq, Japan, Jordan, Kenya, Liberia, Malaysia, the Maldives, Nigeria, Pakistan, the Philippines, the United States of America under Federal Law, and Vietnam.

[12] Algeria (a new anti-terrorist law was introduced in 1992 by decree; this broadened the definition of 'terrorist or subversive acts' to include offences liable to threaten state security, including reproducing and distributing 'subversive literature'); Bangladesh (under the Curbing of Terrorist Activities Act 1992, for a wide range of activities covered by the terms 'terrorism' or 'anarchy', including such offences as extorting money, obstructing and diverting traffic, and harassing and abducting women and children—see Special Rapporteur's *Report*, E/CN.4/1994/7, para. 136); China (for 'seriously endangering public security'— through various amendments to the Penal Code passed between 1982 and 1992 China added 29 further capital offences to those that had been laid down in the Criminal Code of 1979); Egypt (in 1992 the Penal Code was amended to increase the number of terrorist offences punishable by death); Iraq ('evading military service several times', decree of 1994); the Maldives (under the Prevention of Terrorism Act 1990); Nigeria (in response to civil disturbances in Ogonoland, through the Special Tribunal Edict of 1994); the Philippines (in 1994 for treason, having previously abolished the death penalty); and the United States of America (for attempting to assassinate the President, under the Federal Death Penalty Act 1994). In August 1988 Saudi Arabia's religious authorities promulgated an edict ruling that the death penalty should apply to various acts of sabotage including the destruction of homes, public buildings, water and oil resources, and aircraft—AI, *Death Penalty News*, Nov. 1988. Sri Lanka also introduced the death penalty for people who threaten others with death or bodily harm under its Public Security Ordinance issued in *Gazette of the DSR* of Sri Lanka, 9 Nov. 1988.

[13] AI, *Saudi Arabia: Defying World Trends: Saudi Arabia's Extensive Use of Capital Punishment*, AI Index: MDE 23/105/2001.

Clearly there are many acts so encompassed which would not appear to fall within the meaning of Safeguard No.1 or Article 6 (2) of the International Covenant.[14]

In respect of the maintenance of *public order*, at least 14 countries have made it a capital offence to use firearms or explosives, especially but not necessarily when their use results in death.[15] Singapore, for example, has extended capital punishment to the use of firearms to commit or attempt to commit any crime. Furthermore, in at least two of the former states of the USSR, it is a capital offence to attempt to murder a police officer.[16] And in China, Sri Lanka, and Uganda it is a capital offence to trade illegally in, or smuggle, arms.

A crime often associated with *terrorist activities* is the hijacking of aircraft. In the 1970s this became of great concern and several countries responded by introducing the death penalty, especially, but not solely, in circumstances where there was loss of life. It remains a capital offence in Armenia, Belarus, China (sabotage), Indonesia. Egypt, Japan (for causing an air crash and for killing a hostage), Kuwait, Tajikistan, Thailand, and the United States (federal law). The last country to add aircraft hijacking or sabotage to its list of capital offences was Bangladesh, as recently as 1997.

In retentionist countries the range of *military offences* for which capital punishment can be imposed on a serving soldier is very wide, including: mutiny, desertion, insubordination, refusal to execute an order, abandoning a post, especially by a sentry, and cowardice in the face of an enemy. But in many retentionist countries military law can also be enforced on civilians for such offences as: leading an insurrection, inducement of foreign aggression, assisting an enemy, arson of an inhabited structure, destruction by explosives, damage to an inhabited structure by means of flooding, and use of explosives. However, in nearly all retentionist countries these crimes would only be subject to the death penalty in time of war or in a combat situation.

As pointed out in Chapter 1, most of the countries that have abolished capital punishment for crimes committed in peacetime have also abolished it for military offences, even those committed in time of war. This is because they do not find it necessary or desirable to enforce military discipline through threats of execution. Thus, of 89 abolitionist countries in December 2001, only 14 had retained capital punishment for military or wartime offences.

(d) Trading in Illicit Drugs

Many countries in Asia, the Middle East, and North Africa, and in a few other parts of the world, have responded to international concern about the growth of illicit traf-

---

[14] See Carsten Jürgensen, 'Egypt: Death Penalty after Unfair Trials', Paper presented to the 1st World Congress against the Death Penalty, Strasbourg, 21–3 June 2001.

[15] Bangladesh, Cuba, Democratic Republic of Congo, Ghana, Grenada, India, Kuwait, Malaysia, Mali, Nigeria (including attacks on customs officers), Pakistan, Singapore, Sri Lanka, and the United States under the Anti-Terrorism Act 1996.

[16] Belarus and Kazakhstan. It is also still a capital offence in Armenia (signed Protocol No. 6 to the ECHR) and the Russian Federation, pending abolition.

ficking in drugs by introducing the death penalty for both importation and 'possession for sale' of certain amounts of drugs, or by making the death penalty mandatory for such offences where it was previously optional. According to a survey in 1979 the death penalty could be imposed for drug trafficking in 10 of 125 retentionist countries. Just six years later, in 1985, a United Nations survey revealed that such offences could be punished by death in 22 countries.[17] By the end of 1998 the number had increased to at least 34. With the exceptions of Cuba, the Democratic Republic of Congo, Guyana, and the United States of America (under federal law), these countries are in the Middle East, North Africa, Asia, and the Pacific region.[18] Notable has been the introduction of the death penalty into the federal law of the United States for those involved in large-scale drugs offences as part of 'a continuing criminal enterprise', even though no proof of ensuing death is called for.

In a few other countries the statute specifies that the death penalty will only apply if the trafficking or supplying of drugs results in the death of others. Sometimes, as in Kuwait, it applies to the murder or attempted murder of law enforcement officials concerned with drug offences, and in some American states (Pennsylvania, New Hampshire, Illinois, and South Carolina), drug trafficking—'a calculated criminal drug conspiracy'—is a statutorily defined aggravating circumstance in murder. In other countries (Guatemala and Guyana) the death penalty has been extended to embrace cases in which death results from either supplying or administering drugs. Yet, as mentioned above, in 34 countries it is solely the importation and supplying of drugs (and sometimes cultivation, possession, storage, and even purchase)[19] which carries the death penalty.

A number of these countries have made the death penalty mandatory, especially for recidivist drug offenders and trading on a large scale.[20] Others, such as Iran (1969), Thailand (1979), Singapore (1975, 1989, and in 1998 for trafficking in more than 250 grams of crystal methamphetamine),[21] and Malaysia (1983), have made capital punishment mandatory for possession of even relatively small amounts.[22] The Dangerous Drug Act of Malaysia 1952 (as amended in 1983) states that 'any person found, without authorization, in possession of 15 grams or more of heroin or morphine, 1,000 grams or more of opium or 200 grams or more of

---

[17] See Slawomir M. Redo, *United Nations Position on Drugs Crimes*, UNAFEI Resource Material no. 27 (1985).

[18] Bahrain, Bangladesh, Brunei Darussalam, China, Egypt, India (for a second conviction under the Narcotics Drugs and Psychotropic Substances Act 1985), Indonesia, Iran, Iraq, Jordan, Kuwait, Libya (introduced in 1996), Malaysia, Myanmar, Oman, Pakistan, Philippines, Qatar, Saudi Arabia, Singapore, South Korea, Sri Lanka, Sudan, Syria, Taiwan (Republic of China), Tajikistan, Thailand, United Arab Emirates, Uzbekistan, and Vietnam.

[19] For example, the Bangladesh Narcotics Control Act of 1990 gave discretion to the courts to impose the death sentence for offences regarding cultivation, producing, possession, carrying, sale, purchase, or storage of heroin and cocaine (if the amount exceeds 25 grams) and other dangerous drugs (if the amount exceeds 10 grams) and for cannabis and opium if the amount exceeds 2 kilograms.

[20] In 1992 Taiwan made the death penalty discretionary rather than mandatory. In Saudi Arabia the death penalty is mandatory for recidivist drug distributors and drug smugglers; see AI, *Defying World Trends: Saudi-Arabia's Extensive Use of the Death Penalty*, AI Index: MDE 23/015/2001.

[21] AI, *Death Penalty News*, June 1998, AI Index: ACT 53/03/98, pp. 4–5.

[22] Mauritius also passed such legislation in 1992 but in 1995 abolished the death penalty.

cannabis shall be presumed, until the contrary is proved, to be trafficking in the said drug' and thus sentenced to death. The amounts specified in the statutes of some countries, such as Iran (where many more drug offences were made subject to the death penalty under the Anti-Narcotic Drug Law of 1988) are even lower.[23] For example, in Brunei Darussalam the death penalty is mandatory for the unauthorized trafficking, import, or export of over 15 grams of morphine or heroin; possession of over 30 grams of morphine or heroin for the purpose of unauthorized trafficking; and unauthorized manufacture of morphine or heroin.[24] In Vietnam trading, possessing, or trafficking in more than 3½ ounces of heroin and 11 ounces of opium can be punishable by death.[25]

In all of these countries it has been argued that the death penalty is an indisputable deterrent to drug trafficking, but no evidence of a statistical kind has been forthcoming to support this contention. Nor is it likely that any such evidence could be gathered. The low rates of effectiveness of law enforcement, the relative immunity from the law of those who profit most from the trade in drugs, and the higher risks of violence and death they most probably run from others engaged in the drug racket, all make it seem implausible that the death penalty in itself will have a marginally stronger deterrent effect than long terms of imprisonment. However, the only country to abolish capital punishment for drugs offences in recent years was Turkey, in 1992.

(e) Economic and Property Offences

The death penalty is provided for various kinds of economic crime in at least 25 countries.[26] For example, bribery or corruption of public officials is a capital offence in at least five countries;[27] embezzlement of public funds or theft of public property in at least nine countries;[28] manufacturing and distributing counterfeit money or securities in at least three;[29] in two, currency speculation,[30] and in one, profiteering.[31] Fraud and forgery, habitual theft, or aggravated forms of theft are also capital

---

[23] See Ezzat Fattah, 'The Use of the Death Penalty for Drug Offences and for Economic Crime', *Revue Internationale de Droit Pénal* 58 (1987), pp. 723–736 at 732. In Singapore a discretionary death penalty is available for possession of more than 3 grams of morphine or more than 2 grams of diamorphine, which shall be presumed to be for the purpose of trafficking, unless proved to the contrary. Early in 1989 Iran introduced a new law which laid down a mandatory death sentence for anyone found in possession of more than 5 kilograms of hashish or opium, or more than 30 grams of heroin, morphine, codeine, or methadone. See also AI, *The Death Penalty: No Solution to Illicit Drugs*, AI Index: ACT 51/02/95.

[24] AI, *Against the Tide: The Death Penalty in Southeast Asia*, AI Index: ASA 03/01/97.

[25] Associated Press, 10 Jan. 2002.

[26] Algeria, Armenia, Bangladesh, Burkina Faso, Cameroon, China, Democratic Republic of Congo, Ethiopia, Iran, Iraq, Libya, Malawi, Malaysia, Mali, Niger, Nigeria, North Korea, Singapore, Somalia, South Korea, Sudan, Thailand, Togo, Uganda, and Vietnam.

[27] Armenia, Bangladesh, China, Iran (corruption on earth), and Vietnam (including private firms).

[28] China, Democratic Republic of Congo, Mali, Niger, Somalia, South Korea, Sudan, Uganda, and Vietnam.   [29] Algeria, Armenia, and China.

[30] Democratic Republic of Congo (sabotage of the Congolese franc) and Libya (speculation in foreign currency).

[31] Iraq in 1992 in the wake of the Gulf War and the imposition of international sanctions.

offences in at least seven countries,[32] and smuggling in two.[33] It was also reported that death sentences have been handed down and persons executed for theft and embezzlement in North Korea.[34]

The death penalty is also widely available for offences against property with violence, in particular banditry and 'gangsterism' (at least four countries),[35] and robbery with violence, where it is mandatory in two countries.[36] Furthermore, banditry and 'gangsterism' are punishable by death in Belarus and Kazakhstan, and the death penalty is applicable for aggravated robbery in at least another 23 jurisdictions.[37]

(f) Sexual Offences

Thirty countries, at the minimum, retain the death penalty for sexual offences, mostly for rape, especially aggravated rapes such as the kidnapping and rape of a child. For example, rape is among the list of capital crimes in Belarus (aggravated rape), China (in special circumstances, including unlawful sexual intercourse with girls under the age of 14), Egypt (abduction combined with rape), Iraq (rape and incest, by a decree of the Revolutionary Command Council in 2001), Kazakhstan, Kuwait, Kyrgyzstan, Lesotho, Malawi, Mongolia (aggravated rape or rape of a minor), Morocco, Pakistan (gang rape),[38] Saudi Arabia, South Korea, Syria (aggravated rape), Taiwan, Tajikistan, Thailand, Tunisia, Uganda (defilement of a female under the age of 18 and unlawful sexual intercourse with a prisoner), United Arab Emirates, Uzbekistan (rape of a female under the age of 14), and the death penalty is mandatory in Jordan where the victim is under 15 years of age. When the Philippines restored the death penalty under the Republic Act 7659 of 1994, it was made mandatory for rape in nine circumstances.[39]

Under the influence of Islamic law, several countries in the Middle East and North Africa have made adultery and sodomy capital offences: for example, Saudi

---

[32] Burkina Faso (aggravated theft causing bodily harm or death), Cameroon, China (theft of cultural relics or large sums), Niger, South Korea (habitual theft), Thailand (aggravated theft causing bodily harm), and Vietnam (fraud and forgery).

[33] China (including smuggling Giant Pandas) and Iraq.

[34] See Hands Off Cain, *Towards Abolition* (1998), p. 93, see also AI, *Democratic People's Republic of Korea: Public Executions: Converging Testimonies*, AI Index: ASA 24/001/1997.

[35] Belarus, China, Kazakhstan, and Tajikistan.

[36] Kenya and Saudi Arabia (where there is loss of life).

[37] Benin, China, Cuba (new law 1999), Democratic Republic of the Congo, Ghana, Guinea, India (dacoity with murder), Iran, Liberia, Malawi, Mali, Morocco, Nigeria, Philippines, Rwanda, Saudi Arabia, Sierra Leone, South Korea, Sudan, Uganda, United Arab Emirates, Zambia, and Zimbabwe.

[38] AI, *Death Penalty News*, Dec. 1997, AI Index: ACT 53/01/98, p. 3.

[39] When the victim goes insane; when on occasion of the rape a homicide is committed; when the victim is under 18 and the offender is a parent, blood relative, or guardian; when the victim is under the custody of police or the military; when the rape is committed in front of others, or the victim is under 7 years of age; when the offender knows that he has AIDS; when the rape is committed by a member of the armed forces of the Philippines or a law enforcement agency; and when the victim has suffered permanent physical mutilation.

Arabia, Pakistan, and Sudan,[40] and most recently Nigeria, where, over the last two years, a number of northern states in Nigeria have introduced new penal legislation for Muslims based on the principles of the Shari'a.[41] 'Homosexual acts with violence' may be subject to capital punishment in Cuba,[42] and in February 2001 it was reported that a court in the self-declared autonomous region of Puntland in northern Somalia had sentenced to death two women who had had a lesbian relationship, for being guilty of 'exercising unnatural behaviour'.[43] The revolutionary Command Council of Iraq also decreed homosexuality to be a capital offence in November 2001.[44]

Iranian law casts the shadow of the death penalty over a wide range of sexual offences: incest; sex between a non-Muslim male and a Muslim female; adultery by married people; sodomy; other homosexual acts after a fourth conviction. For example, a death sentence has been imposed on a woman for reportedly engaging in sexual relations outside of marriage.[45] It can also be imposed in Sudan for recidivist prostitution, 'illicit sex', and on conviction for the third time of a homosexual act.[46] When the Taliban ruled Afghanistan, it was a capital offence not solely to commit adultery but for a woman to associate with unrelated males. Prostitution—becoming 'a cause of moral corruption'—is a capital offence in Iraq and Saudi Arabia. Pimping or procurement for prostitution is also subject to the death penalty in Iraq and China.

In 1977, in *Coker* v. *Georgia*, the Supreme Court of the United States held that capital punishment was an excessive, disproportionate, penalty for the offence of rape. This was a decision of great importance given that prior to the *Furman* decision in 1972 a considerable number of men (almost all of them black) had been executed after being convicted of rape in southern states. Nevertheless, in 1995 the state of Louisiana passed a law making it a capital offence to rape a female under the age of 12, and the following year, in the case of *Louisiana* v. *Wilson*, the Louisiana Supreme Court ruled that the death penalty for this crime was not unconstitutional. It held that the *Coker* decision applied only to the rape of an adult woman and left open the question whether capital punishment for a non-homicidal rape of a child was excessive. Although prosecutors in Louisiana sought the death sentence in such a case in February 2000, the jury was unable to agree. As no one has yet been sentenced to death under this law, it has yet to be ruled upon by the US Supreme Court.

---

[40] In Sudan, under the new Penal Code of 1991, based upon an interpretation of the Shari'a, a third offence of sodomy is a capital offence.

[41] AI, *Death Penalty News*, Sept. 2001, AI Index: ACT 53/004/2001.

[42] See UN Report of the Secretary-General, *Status of the International Covenants on Human Rights: Question of the Death Penalty*, E/CN.4/1998/82, Appendix.

[43] Reported by BBC News, 23 Feb. 2001.

[44] Reported in AI, *Death Penalty News*, Dec. 2001, AI Index: ACT 53/001/2002, p. 4.

[45] See Special Rapporteur's *Report*, E/CN.4/1999/39/Add. 1, para. 103.

[46] See Special Rapporteur's *Report*, E/CN.4/1999/39/Add. 1, para. 230. *Also Report of the Human Rights Committee*, A 53/40, vol. 1 (1998), p. 33.

(g) Religious Dissent

Religious dissent in the form of blasphemy or apostasy can be punished with death in some Muslim countries: notably, Egypt, Iran, Libya, Pakistan, Saudi Arabia, Sudan,[47] and when the Taliban ruled Afghanistan.[48] In Pakistan capital punishment was made the mandatory penalty for 'defiling the sacred name of the prophet Mohammed' as recently as 1986. Although no one has yet been executed, a High Court in July 2001 upheld the death sentence of a Christian sentenced for blasphemy. At the end of the year an appeal to the Supreme Court of Pakistan was pending and the Ministry of the Interior had acknowledged that the blasphemy laws were in need of amendment.[49]

(h) Other Offences

No less than 14 countries provide the death penalty for kidnapping.[50] It is also a statutory aggravating circumstance to murder in several other countries, such as Morocco, Thailand, and the American state of Montana. The Philippines made arson punishable by death in 1994. In response to a number of notorious instances, India made assisting to commit *sati* (the burning of widows) a capital crime in 1987. And in 1999 the United Arab Emirates announced that it would now be a capital crime to import banned materials or nuclear waste and to dump or store them in the country.[51] Sri Lanka provides the death penalty for giving false or fabricated evidence where the alleged offence is punishable by death and an innocent person is convicted and executed, Belarus provides the death penalty for 'undermining the work of a prison', and Uzbekistan retains it for organizing a criminal conspiracy.

Perhaps the most extreme example of the application of the death penalty to activity that the state seeks to suppress is its introduction in Iran (1993) for dealing in 'obscene products' and producing and distributing pornographic audio or video material. These offences would appear, even on the broadest of interpretations, to be not life-threatening in the sense laid down by Article 6 (2) of the ICCPR and the first United Nations Safeguard. It is notable that China removed these offences from the list of capital crimes in the Penal Code of 1997.

---

[47] However, the Sudanese Code gives the convicted apostate time to renounce his heresy and return to Islam and no persons have been charged with this offence since 1985.

[48] Attempting to convert Muslims to Christianity and for an Afghan Muslim to convert to Christianity was made a capital offence. Until freed during the war in Afghanistan in November 2001, eight foreign aid workers had been awaiting trial for 'preaching Christianity' and senior Taliban officials had warned that they might be executed were they found guilty. See BBC News, 5 Sept. 2001.

[49] AI, *Pakistan: Blasphemy Laws should be Abolished.* AI Index: ASA 33/023/2001; see also AI, *Death Penalty News*, Sept. 2001, AI Index: ACT 53/004/2001; also *AI Welcomes Releases in Pakistan*, The Wire, Mar. 2002.

[50] Algeria, Bangladesh (kidnapping and trafficking in women and children in 1996, see AI, *Report 1996*, p. 90), China, Grenada, Guatemala (1995 for those who threaten to kill victims of kidnapping; see Special Rapporteur's *Report*, E/CN.4/1996/4/Corr.1, para. 210), Guinea, Iran, Pakistan, Philippines (in 1994 for kidnapping with torture and serious illegal detention), India (kidnapping for ransom), Singapore, Taiwan, the United Arab Emirates, and Yemen.

[51] AI, *Death Penalty News*, Dec. 1999, AI Index: ACT 53/005/1999.

(i) The Position in China

The scope of the death penalty in China has been so wide that it deserves separate discussion. When the People's Republic of China enacted, in 1979, a new Penal Code and Code of Penal Practice, the death penalty was provided as the maximum sentence in 15 articles, encompassing 28 criminal offences.[52] Nine of the articles were concerned with military crimes and offences relating to national security or of a counter-revolutionary nature, such as sabotage. Six of them dealt with common offences: setting fires, breaking dikes, etc. when leading to serious injuries or death; intentionally killing others; rape; robbery; theft, fraud, or forcible seizure; at the scene of a crime using violence to resist arrest; and corruption.

However, in 1982 and 1983, in response to 'the constant increase of the crimes that seriously endanger social security and economic order',[53] the Standing Committee of the Chinese National People's Congress promulgated two decrees, 'Decision of the Standing Committee of the National People's Congress Regarding the Severe Punishment of Criminals who Seriously Undermine the Economy' and 'Decision of the Standing Committee of the National People's Congress Regarding the Severe Punishment of Criminal Elements who Seriously Endanger Public Security'. Under these two decrees there were 14 new criminal laws for which the death penalty was the maximum sentence. Although Chinese legal scholars criticized these provisions,[54] the tentacles of the death penalty spread to embrace even more offences, including theft, sale of narcotics, being the ringleader of a criminal hooligan group, intentionally injuring others, causing a person serious injury or death, organizing reactionary superstitious sects and secret societies to carry out counter-revolutionary activities, forcing or luring women into prostitution, and 'imparting criminal methods' (a new crime). By the time the New Criminal Law was promulgated in 1997, 'there were more than 50 articles of death penalty in Chinese laws, and more than 70 capital crimes'.[55]

The New Criminal Law of 1997 abolished capital punishment for a few crimes, such as 'being a ringleader of hooliganism' and also for common theft, but despite the fact that Article 48 provided that the death penalty should be reserved 'for those criminal offenders who have committed extremely serious crimes' (as had the 1979 Code),[56] it still contained 51 articles stipulating the death penalty, but always at the discretion of the court, for at least 62 and possibly 68 crimes. It is important to bear in mind that most articles of the Code providing for the death penalty do so with the limitation that it should only be applied in certain, listed, circumstances or more

---

[52] See Hu Yunteng, 'On the Death Penalty at the Turning of the Century', in M. Nowak and Xin Chunying (eds), *EU–China Human Rights Dialogue* (2000), pp. 88–94 at 89.

[53] *Ibid.*

[54] See AI, *People's Republic of China: The Continuing Repression. The Death Penalty and Anti-Crime Campaigns* (Sept. 1990), AI Index: ASA 17/56/90, pp. 9–12.

[55] Hu, n. 52 above, p. 89.

[56] See Hans-Jörg Albrecht, 'The Death Penalty in China from a European Perspective', in M. Nowak and Xin Chunying (eds), *EU–China Human Rights Dialogue: Proceedings of the Second EU–China Legal Experts Seminar held in Beijing on 19 and 20 October 1998* (2000), pp. 95–118 at 96.

vaguely in 'especially serious circumstances'.[57] The offences include, besides murder: offences against state and public security; grave offences against the economic order including embezzlement, receiving bribes, corruption, racketeering, smuggling (from smuggling firearms and drugs to smuggling cultural relics and rare species of wildlife), tax and VAT evasion, counterfeiting, and theft from a banking institution and stealing precious cultural relics; violent offences including rape, robbery, and illegally manufacturing and trading in firearms; dereliction of duties; manufacturing and trading of drugs, but also providing drug manufacturers with the substances needed to manufacture drugs; kidnapping and abducting women and children, usually for sale; as well as many military offences codified in 11 articles. Also included in the long list of capital crimes is when a 'judicial officer who extorts confession from a criminal suspect or defendant by torture or extorts testimony from a witness by violence . . . if he causes injury, disability or death to the victim'.

In October 1998 the semi-official *Guangming Daily* outlined China's legislative Guarantees for Human Rights in the Judicial Field. It stated: 'China's principle in applying the death penalty has consistently been to kill only a few, not to kill when this is not absolutely necessary, and only to apply such a sentence for criminals who have committed particularly serious crimes of extremely profound subjective evil, when social order could not be maintained if they were not killed.' Nevertheless, Chinese practice reveals that the death penalty is imposed for some offences which by international standards do not fall under the scope of the most serious or heinous crimes. Offenders found guilty of corruption, embezzlement, VAT fraud, and other economic crimes continue to be sentenced to death and some of them executed.[58] And even where crimes of violence are concerned, it is apparent that not only those who commit the most atrocious acts are sentenced to death. For example, in April 2001 it was reported that two men who had robbed an American diplomat of a camera and a watch and $US50 at knife point were sentenced to death—probably because they had previous convictions for similar offences.

2. THE SCALE OF DEATH SENTENCES AND EXECUTIONS

Although so many countries have provided the death penalty in law as a threat to a wide range of behaviour, it is obviously of crucial importance to examine the extent to which persons convicted of such crimes have, in fact, been sentenced to death and executed. As the following facts reveal, the law is generally and consistently broader and more threatening than the practice.

The Secretary-General of the United Nations has attempted through a series of

---

[57] According to Hu Yunteng, the number is 62. But Chen Xinliang states that it is 68: see *The Death Penalty in the United Nations Standards and China's Legal System of Criminal Justice* (1998), p. 536.

[58] AI, *People's Republic of China: The Death Penalty in China: Breaking Records, Breaking Rules* (Aug. 1997); AI, *China: Death Penalty Log 1996*, pt. I (1997); AI, *People's Republic of China: The Death Penalty in 1997*, AI Index: ASA 17/28/98, with reports on death sentences and executions involving, for example, theft and resale of items worth $US2,400, theft of 61 cattle or the theft of 2 trucks, p. 3.

six postal surveys to gather information at five-yearly intervals between 1969 and 1998 on the status of capital punishment in all member states, including the number of persons sentenced to death and the number executed in all countries which retained capital punishment. The data received has unfortunately been of limited value. This is partly because some countries replied to one or more of the surveys but not to others, but, more importantly, because many countries, in particular those that are known from other sources to make the greatest use of executions, failed to reply to any of the surveys or, if they did reply, failed to provide any data on the number of persons executed annually. Indeed, among the countries that could have replied to all six surveys covering a thirty-year period, 43 did not reply to any of them.[59] It has therefore been necessary to rely on the returns made annually by the non-governmental organization Amnesty International, which does its best to monitor the number of death sentences and executions in every country. Table 3.1 shows the trends in death sentences and executions over the last twenty years, as far as Amnesty International has been able to ascertain.

The main trends revealed by Table 3.1 are:

1. The number of death sentences and executions has fluctuated a great deal over these twenty years. There was a dramatic rise from 1980 to 1981, followed by a gradual decline to a relatively low number in 1986–7. It was not until 1993 that the number of *recorded* death sentences per annum began regularly to exceed 3,000; and in the nine years since then the average number of *recorded* executions has been around 2,550, but again with very considerable yearly variations—ranging from 4,272 in 1996, down to 1,457 in 2000, and up to 3,048 in 2001.

2. These yearly fluctuations in the total number of death sentences and executions have largely been due to changes in the policy of the Chinese authorities, for between 70 and 80 per cent of known judicial executions take place in China. Indeed, it may be that the apparent worldwide increase in death sentences and executions since the 1980s (in contrast to the great increase in the number of abolitionist countries) is really a reflection of increased knowledge of what is going on in China. In any case, it is clear that the recent large fluctuations in the numbers of recorded executions have been the result of China's periodic adoption of 'Yanda' or 'strike hard against crime' campaigns. Thus, owing to the strike hard campaign of 1996, the number of executions soared to over 4,000. By 1998 the number of recorded executions had more than halved, reflecting, according to the Supreme People's Court of China, the revisions to the Criminal Law, which came into force in October 1997.[60] Yet, in April 2001 another strike hard campaign was set in train, and with such zeal that at least 1,781 people had been executed by the end of July 2001. Eighty-nine people were reported to have been executed in one day.[61] This

---

[59] Only eight of these 43 replied instead to the Secretary-General's request for information on the implementation of safeguards published in 1988 or to the annual supplementary reports submitted to the Commission on Human Rights in 1998 and 1999. Seven of these 43 non-responding states had become abolitionist by the end of December 2001.

[60] See AI, *People's Republic of China in 1998* (Summary), AI Index: ASA 17/66/99.corr.

[61] *Agence France Presse*, 12 Apr. 2001. See also AI, *China's Execution Frenzy*, The Wire, Sept. 2001.

TABLE 3.1
Number of death sentences and executions worldwide, 1980–2001

Year	Numbers reported and recorded		Number of countries concerned	
	Death sentences	Executions	Death sentences	Executions
1980	1,295	1,229	41	29
1981	3,209	3,278	52	34
1982	1,435	1,609	60	42
1983	1,160	1,399	63	39
1984	2,068	1,513	55	40
1985	1,435	1,125	61	44
1986	1,272	743	67	39
1987	1,185	796	62	39
1988	1,240	1,903	58	35
1989	2,826	2,229	62	34
1990	2,005	2,029	54	26
1991	2,703	2,086	62	32
1992	2,697	1,708	62	35
1993	3,760	1,831	61	32
1994	4,032	2,331	75	37
1995	4,165	3,276	79	41
1996	7,107	4,272	76	39
1997	3,707	2,607	69	40
1998	3,899	2,258	78	37
1999	3,857	1,813	63	31
2000	3,058	1,457	65	27
2001	5,265	3,048	68	31

Source: AI, *Death Penalty Developments* (2001).

was reflected in the total number of death sentences—5,265—and executions—3,048—for the whole year: the second largest number of death sentences and third largest number of executions in the last 21 years since 1980. Indeed, the number of known executions in 2001 was over twice that known in 2000. This was entirely due to the strike hard campaign in China, which dispatched at least 2,468 (81 per cent) of the 3,048 people known to Amnesty International to have been executed.[62] And, as Amnesty pointed out, the number executed in China in 2001 was greater than the total judicially executed in the rest of the world during the previous three years.[63]

3. Despite the marked increase in the number of abolitionist countries over the last twenty years, the number of retentionist countries that have imposed death

[62] AI, *Facts and Figures on the Death Penalty* (Apr. 2002), AI Index: ACT 50/004/2002, p. 2.
[63] AI, News Release, AI Index: ASA 17/022/2001.

sentences and carried out executions has not shown an overall steady decline. Indeed there have been marked fluctuations. Thus, in the year 2001 death sentences were recorded in 68 countries and 31 of them were known to have carried out executions, whereas in 1990 the corresponding figures had been 54 countries imposing the death penalty and 26 carrying out executions. Yet the figures for 2001 were considerably lower than that for 1995, when as many as 79 countries imposed the death penalty and 41 of them executed offenders.

4. In making comparisons between countries, it is necessary, of course, to bear in mind the relative size of their populations. And it would be better still if it were possible to relate executions to the number of recorded offences liable to capital punishment, and the number of persons convicted of those offences. But regrettably such data exist only for a few countries, and even for them they are hard to interpret.

Table 3.2 shows, as far as can be ascertained from the figures in Amnesty International's annual reports, the countries in which 20 or more executions were carried out in the five years 1996 to 2000. It also shows the estimated rate of executions per million of the population. These figures come with a serious 'health warning'. First, they mask quite large annual fluctuations, often associated with political upheavals or perceived threats to the stability of states associated with outbreaks of serious crime. For example, there was only one execution in the Democratic Republic of Congo in 1996 and 1997, but 235 during the following three years. Secondly, and more serious, the figures for several countries are likely to underestimate substantially the true number of persons judicially executed. For example, other observers have estimated that the number of executions in China has been four- to fivefold greater than those publicly reported in the press.[64] Similarly, it is widely believed that many more people have been executed in Iran and Iraq (neither of which publishes any statistics) than have been discovered by Amnesty International.[65] Iraq did respond to the Secretary-General's Sixth Survey, but ignored the section requesting data on the number of persons executed in each of the years 1993 to 1998. Indeed, there are probably other countries, such as Tajikistan, that should be in this list but have escaped inclusion because of the difficulties of gaining information on the number of persons executed in each of these five years.[66] And, thirdly, of course, judicial executions may pale into insignificance in some countries when compared with the number put to death extra-judicially by the police, armed forces, or militias.

As can be seen from Table 3.2, the largest number of reported executions was

---

[64] M. Palmer, 'The People's Republic of China', in P. Hodgkinson and A. Rutherford (eds), *Capital Punishment: Global Issues and Prospects* (1996), pp. 105–141.

[65] For example, Amnesty International recorded 139 executions in Iran in 2001, but added 'the true number was believed to be much higher'. *Worldwide Executions Doubled in 2001*. AI Index: ACT 50/005/2002—News Service no. 59 (10 Apr. 2002).

[66] Following a four-year moratorium, executions recommenced in 1999. Amnesty International reported that two executions had been carried out in Tajikistan that year, although the true number was thought to be far higher. In 2001 it was reported that a conference on the death penalty in Tajikistan had been informed that 'around 100 people' had been executed in 2001. If this were to continue, it would put Tajikistan at the top of the world's states in terms of executions per million population: 15.2 (compare with Table 3.2). See AI, *Death Penalty News*, Dec. 2001, AI Index: ACT 53/001/2002, p. 4.

carried out during these five years in China, followed by Iran, Saudi Arabia, the United States of America, Democratic Republic of Congo, Taiwan, Belarus, Egypt, and Singapore. Substantial numbers of executions also took place in Ukraine and Turkmenistan[67] before moratoriums were brought into effect.

Raw numbers can, of course, be misleading when countries vary so greatly in the size of their populations. Thus, China (known executions 1.65 per million population) did not have the highest rate of executions per capita among the countries listed in Table 3.2. Singapore had the highest rate of executions (6.40), down from an annual rate of 13.57 per million population for the years 1994–9, followed by Saudi Arabia (4.46), Belarus (2.48), Sierra Leone (2.36), Jordan (1.96), and then China. But, of course, as noted above, the figures for China might be far higher in reality: until they are no longer classified as a state secret no one will know.

Only three retentionist countries executed more persons than the United States, yet the United States had one of the lowest rates of executions (an annual average over the years 1996 to 2000 of 74 executions): 0.27 per million population. However, this is rather misleading because the annual number of executions in the United States had been, with a few fluctuations up and down, gradually increasing since they were resumed in 1977. In 1990, 23 persons were put to death, in 1995, 56, and by 1999 the number had reached 98. However, the number fell a little in 2000—to 85—and then much more sharply to 66 in 2001. It has yet to be seen whether this is the beginning of a real downward trend, but in any case it must be balanced against the fact that in 2001 the Federal government carried out its first execution for thirty-eight years.

Furthermore, the figure for the United States as a whole is misleading because executions are much more frequent in some states than others. Indeed, between 1977 and 2001 two-thirds (65 per cent) of the 749 executions in the United States were carried out in five of the 50 states, 38 of which now have the death penalty on their statute books. Thirty-five per cent were in Texas and 12 per cent in Virginia, which, on average, had the highest rate in relation to population—which was in fact nearly the same as China's known execution rate. In the year 2000 executions occurred in only 14 states, and half (40 out of 83) of them took place in Texas. The following year, 2001, executions were carried out in 16 states, but only a quarter (17 out of 66) of them took place in Texas. Oklahoma had the highest number of executions in that year with 18, and this made it by far the greatest per capita user of capital punishment in the United States in 2001, with a rate of 5.37 per million population.

But these rates of execution have not kept pace with the number of persons sentenced to death annually in the United States. Thus, the number on death row has risen inexorably from about 1,000 in 1983 to over 3,700 at the end of December

---

[67] Turkmenistan and Ukraine both executed a high number of people until 1997 (Turkmenistan 374 between 1993 and 1997, equivalent to an execution rate of 14.96 per million population; Ukraine 467 between 1993 and 1997, equivalent to an execution rate of 1.86 per million population) when both countries ceased executions. In 1999 both countries abolished the death penalty for all crimes.

TABLE 3.2

*Countries reported to have executed at least twenty persons in the period 1996–2000
and estimated annual rate per million population*

Country or territory	Estimated population, 1998	Total executions, 1996–2000	Estimated annual rate per million population
Afghanistan	19,000,000	52	0.55
Belarus	10,500,000	130	2.48
China	1,248,100,000	10,275	1.65
Democratic Republic of the Congo	48,000,000	236	0.98
Cuba	11,000,000	27	0.49
Egypt	61,500,000	124	0.40
Iran (Islamic Republic of)	63,500,000	559	1.76
Japan	126,000,000	24	0.04
Jordan	5,200,000	51	1.96
Kazakhstan[a]	17,000,000	47/115	0.55/1.35
Kyrgyzstan	5,000,000	39	1.56
Nigeria	121,000,000	56	0.09
Pakistan	130,600,000	47	0.07
Republic of Korea	46,000,000	23	0.10
Russian Federation (ceased 1996)	146,000,000	56	0.08
Rwanda	8,000,000	23	0.58
Saudi Arabia	20,000,000	446	4.46
Sierra Leone	5,000,000	59	2.36
Singapore	3,500,000[b]	112	6.40
Taiwan Province of China	21,871,000	133	1.22
Thailand	61,000,000	23	0.08
Uganda	21,500,000	31	0.29
United States of America[c]	271,645,000	370	0.27
Texas	20,044,141	135	1.35
Virginia	6,872,912	52	1.51
Missouri	5,468,338	29	1.06
Oklahoma	3,358,044	24	1.43
South Carolina	3,885,736	20	1.03
Vietnam	78,000,000	64	0.16
Yemen	16,000,000	70	0.88
Zimbabwe	12,000,000	21	0.35

Notes:
    [a] It is particularly hard to assess accurately the number of executions carried out in Kazakhstan. According to a report by Kazak Commercial Television of 8 Nov. 2000, between 40 and 60 executions were being carried out in the country every year. Seventeen people had reportedly been executed in Kazakhstan in the first ten months of 2000. The report also quoted official statistics from 1996 which

stated that 63 people had been executed that year. AI, *Concerns in Europe, January–June 2001*, AI Index: EUR 01/003/2001. Yet, according to the report of the Organization for Security and Cooperation in Europe in 1999, no executions had been reported—although it noted that 'Kazakhstan does not disclose statistics on capital punishment', in violation of paragraph 17.8 of the Copenhagen Document, which commits member states to do so. See OSCE, *The Death Penalty in the OSCE Area*, Office of Democratic Institutions and Human Rights, OD/HR Background Paper 1999/1 (1999), p. 16.

   b Calculated on the basis of the average annual number of executions. Where there were no reports, it had to be assumed that the number was zero, although this may not have been the case in several of these countries. Population figures for 1998 from Keesing's Worldwide, LLC, *The Annual Register: A Record of World Events 1999* (2000) Washington. The estimate of 3 million for Singapore in the Annual Register was too low in the light of the Singapore Census of Population 2000, which states that Singapore had reached a population of 4 million in 2000. Therefore, for 1998 the population of Singapore was estimated to be 3.5 million. See www.singstat.gov.sg/C2000/census.html.

   c The population figure for the United States is the *Annual Register*'s estimate for 1999 and figures for the American states are estimates from the US Census Bureau for 1999, http://quickfacts. census.gov/qfd/states/12000.html.

Source: Other data derived from reports issued by Amnesty International

2001.[68] About 600 occupy death row in California, 450 in Texas, nearly 400 in Florida, and over 200 each in Pennsylvania, North Carolina, and Ohio.

Substantial numbers of prisoners (but these are often only estimates) are known to remain under sentence of death in Algeria (hundreds), Bangladesh (160), Burundi (350), Ethiopia (100), Ghana (170), Japan (at least 110, about half of whom have had their sentences confirmed by the Supreme Court), Kenya (at least 1,000 but perhaps as many as 2,000), Morocco (100), Pakistan (4,000), Philippines (1,100), Thailand (320), Uganda (260), Yemen ('hundreds'), and Zambia (230). Altogether they swell the death row population of the world to probably at least 12,000. Some of the implications of this aspect of the death penalty are discussed below.

(a) Executions for Crimes Other than Murder

The trend to extend the death penalty to crimes other than murder needs to be related to the number of executions for such crimes. Unfortunately no accurate figures are available and those that have been obtained must be regarded as only approximate. Furthermore, executions for 'other' offences may take place only sporadically and therefore a report of such an execution in a particular country cannot be taken to indicate that it is a common pattern or even that it will be repeated.

In the last decade reports have been received of executions for sex-related offences from a number of countries: for adultery in Iran, Saudi Arabia, and Somalia; for rape, especially of a minor, in China, Egypt, Iran, Iraq, Jordan, Kuwait, Morocco, Pakistan, Philippines, Saudi Arabia, Somalia, South Korea, Syria, Uganda, United Arab Emirates; for sodomy in Iran and Saudi Arabia; for prostitution, organizing 'a vice ring', and for distributing pornography in China, and possibly also in Iran. As

---

[68] *Death Row, U.S.A.—A Quarterly Report by the Capital Punishment Project of the NAACP Legal Defence and Education Fund, Inc.*, www.deathpenaltyinfo.org/DeathRowUSA1.html.

recently as February 2001 two women convicted of prostitution were hanged publicly in a sports stadium in Afghanistan,[69] and in October 2001 a woman was sentenced to death by stoning in Nigeria for fornication and adultery.[70] She was, however, exonerated on appeal after an international outcry.

There have been reports of executions for armed robbery from 12 countries since 1990: China, Democratic Republic of Congo, Ghana, Iran, Malaysia, Nigeria, Saudi Arabia, Sierra Leone, South Korea, Taiwan, Uganda, and Yemen. According to Amnesty International, 'in the past several years' people have been executed for other 'economic crimes', such as corruption, embezzlement, and fraud, in five countries: China, Iran, Iraq, Sudan, and Vietnam.[71]

Persons convicted of trading in illicit drugs have been executed in China, Egypt, Indonesia (although not within the last five years), Iran (which between 1989 and 1999 executed as many as 2,000 drug offenders),[72] Malaysia, Saudi Arabia, Singapore, Sudan, Thailand, Taiwan, Thailand, and Vietnam. The latest statistics from Singapore show that as many as 76 per cent of the 306 persons executed in the years 1994 to 2000 had been convicted of possession of drugs with intent to supply, many of them citizens of other countries. Other crimes for which persons are reported to have been executed include: kidnapping (China, Iran, and Taiwan); smuggling (China, Iraq, and Syria); piracy (China); apostasy (Iran and Saudi Arabia); brewing and distilling alcohol, as well as sorcery, in Saudi Arabia;[73] for 'setting up centres of corruption' in Iran;[74] and 'political offences' (Belarus, Iran, and Iraq).[75]

As indicated by its appearance in most of these lists, China executes a wider range of offenders than any other nation. Thus, during its 'crackdown' on crime in 1996 those executed in China (according to Amnesty International's *Death Penalty Log*)[76] included persons convicted of publishing and selling obscene materials, smuggling forged money, tax- and VAT-related offences, public order offences, and trafficking in women and children. The New Criminal Law of 1997 attempted to restrict somewhat the scope of the death penalty, and Amnesty International's *Death Penalty Log* covering the year 1999[77] suggests that this may have had some effect. The majority of reports of executions relate to murder, often associated with robbery, the use of firearms, and rape. The variety of other offences for which offenders were executed, wide though it was, appears to be somewhat more restricted than in the past. Nevertheless, a substantial number were executed for armed robbery, robbery, intentional injury, and the manufacture of, or trading in, large quantities of illicit drugs,

[69] AI, *Death Penalty News*, Mar. 2001, AI Index: ACT 53/002/2001.
[70] AI, *Death Penalty News*, Sept. 2001, AI Index: ACT 53/004/2001.
[71] AI, 'Public Opinion and its Place in the Debate about Abolition of the Death Penalty', Paper presented to the EU–China Seminar on Human Rights, Beijing, 10–12 May 2001.
[72] AI, *Death Penalty News*. Mar. 1999, AI Index: ACT 53/002/1999.
[73] AI, *Death Penalty News*, Mar. 2000, AI Index: ACT 53/001/2000.
[74] In June 1996, 12 men were hanged for this offence. See AI, *Report 1997*, p. 186.
[75] For example, on Iran, see AI, *Report 1998*, p. 202; on Iraq, *Report 1999*, p. 203.
[76] AI, *People's Republic of China: The Death Penalty Log 1996*, AI Index: ASA 17/35/97.
[77] AI, *People's Republic of China: The Death Penalty Log 1999*, AI Index: ASA 17/49/00.

the latter largely taking place to mark International Drugs Day in June each year. Indeed, of the 221 executions for drug offences recorded by Amnesty International in 1999, 196 (89 per cent) took place in the last week of June (see Chapter 6 pages 177–178).

In 1999 (according to the *Death Penalty Log*) there were quite a few executions of sex offenders for sexual assaults on children, rape, and selling women. A smaller number of white-collar offenders were executed for involvement in large-scale tax evasion, frauds, corruption, accepting bribes, and smuggling large amounts of goods. Executions also took place for political crimes, such as separatist activities or armed activities to overthrow the state, but also for the crime of 'taking part in illegal religious terrorist activities' (eight were executed in March 1999). Three people were executed for offences of 'spying for Taiwan' in August 1999. And there were a handful of executions for digging up ancient tombs and the theft of national treasures. At least two people were executed for poisoning livestock with the intention to buy the poisoned meat for a cheap price. Of concern is the great number of executions where the offence of which the prisoners were convicted could not be specified: they account for 20 per cent of all executions known to have been carried out in 1999.

According to newspaper reports, executions of officials and traders involved in corruption, embezzlement, tax and VAT fraud, and other economic offences have continued to receive publicity in China, as have some executions for theft of cultural relics; organizing prostitution; spying and 'separatism'. During 2000–1 the authorities turned their attention to cracking down severely on both organized criminal gangs and corrupt officials. Not only have some high-ranking members of the Communist Party been executed (see Chapter 2 page 52), but so too have senior police officers, and customs and bank officials. In May 2001 four businessmen were executed in Guandong province for their involvement in VAT frauds amounting to some $US9.6 million. The Vice-President of the Supreme People's Court was reported in *China Daily* to have justified the executions on the ground that 'This kind of crime not only presents a serious threat to the market order and causes a great loss to national interests, but also badly affects economic development and social stability.'

Some of those executed on the mainland had committed the offences in the Chinese Special Autonomous regions of Macau or Hong Kong, neither of which have the death penalty, raising the issue of the validity of what is called 'rendition' rather than extradition to mainland China.[78]

(b) Non-Enforcement of the Death Penalty

The question arises why a substantial number of countries retain the death penalty and do not enforce it. There are 34 countries (plus six American states and the US Military Jurisdiction) that have not executed anyone for the last ten years or longer, and Amnesty International classes 22 of them as truly abolitionist de facto. Thus, the

---

[78] AI, *People's Republic of China: The Death Penalty in 1999*, AI Index: ASA 17/005/2001.

death penalty in many countries appears to have a far greater symbolic than practical significance. In maintaining the status quo, the perceived weight of public opinion; the enduring belief that the threat of death, even if not enforced, still has a deterrent power; the belief that it should remain available for the truly 'exceptional case'; and the political fear that abolition may be perceived as a 'sign of weakness', all play their part. Nevertheless, its dormant existence in law can readily be translated into a practical reality in response to a heightened fear of crime or to political instability, such that the practice of executing offenders can be revived after decades without use.

As has been shown above (Chapter 1 pages 12–13) the mere absence of executions, even over a long period of time, cannot guarantee that the abolitionist de facto status of a nation will become permanent.

(c) The Need for Accurate Information

It cannot be regarded as satisfactory that the United Nations quinquennial surveys of member states produce such inconsistent and incomplete information on the death penalty and executions, such that it is impossible accurately to portray international trends. Nor can it be regarded as satisfactory that reliance has to be placed on incomplete reports gathered by the media, or by specialists, or even by non-governmental organizations, which often do not have access to official figures. It is even more regrettable that several retentionist countries publish no data at all on the number of persons sentenced to death or executed. In this respect China, Iraq, and Iran stand out.

Governments have a duty to make sure that all their citizens have the opportunity to base their views about the death penalty on a rational appreciation of the facts. This cannot be done unless there is a commitment to publish all official data on capital crimes and the death penalty and also a commitment to encourage properly funded independent research on the operation of the system at all levels and upon its effects on capital crimes. For example, Article 212 of China's Criminal Procedure Law of 1997 provides for the publication of every execution of a death sentence, and all courts have to prepare written records of the execution, yet no statistics on capital punishment are published, being still considered a state secret.

Systems of criminal justice need to be accountable to the citizens on whose behalf they enforce the law. They therefore need to be patently transparent: the more so where the death penalty is concerned and the lives of human beings are at risk from misapplication of the law by criminal justice agencies and from judicial error. Without such transparency and accountability, capital punishment is likely to be regarded as a secretly administered system of social and political repression. Moreover, the lack of accurate and detailed information makes it impossible for anyone, official supporters or opponents of capital punishment, to debate the issue in relation to the realities of how capital punishment is administered and enforced.

In Resolution 1989/64 the Economic and Social Council of the United Nations urged member states 'to publish, for each category of offence for which the death penalty was authorized, and if possible on an annual basis, information on the use of the death penalty'. That information was to include the number of persons sentenced to death, the number of executions actually carried out, the number of persons under sentence of death, the number of death sentences reversed or commuted on appeal, and the number of instances in which clemency had been granted. The poor response to the Secretary-General's Sixth Survey, as well as the continuing absence of officially published statistics on the use of the death penalty in so many retentionist countries, has shown, once again, how important it is for member states to respond positively to this request.

THE INFLICTION OF CAPITAL PUNISHMENT

Safeguard No. 9 promulgated by the UN Economic and Social Council in 1984 for the protection of the rights of those facing the death penalty in countries that have yet to abolish capital punishment declared that '*Where capital punishment occurs it shall be carried out so as to inflict the minimum possible suffering.*' In 1996 the Economic and Social Council made it explicit that this also applied to those under sentence of death awaiting their fate. It urged those member states in which the death penalty may still be carried out '*to effectively apply the Standard Minimum Rules for the Treatment of Prisoners, in order to keep to a minimum the suffering of prisoners under sentence of death and to avoid any exacerbation of such suffering*'.

These safeguards raise questions about the method by which judicial executions are carried out, where and under what circumstances they take place, the role assigned to personnel in carrying them out, particularly physicians who have a duty to preserve life, as well as the conditions under which and the amount of time during which persons are kept under sentence of death prior to execution or until their fate is otherwise determined.

(a) The Method of Execution

The United Nations Fifth and Sixth Surveys explored whether consideration had been given to minimizing the suffering of the offender when determining the method of execution. Some mentioned that the last wishes of the condemned are fulfilled, that a cleric is allowed to administer to religious needs, that executions are properly superintended to ensure a speedy end, and that a doctor is available to certify death. But none made any claims for the comparative advantages of their own method of execution in minimizing suffering.

The method of execution in most of the countries that retain the death penalty is hanging or shooting—usually by firing squad, although in China by a bullet from a pistol in the back of the head. Some employ hanging for civilians and shooting for military offences. In Sudan and Iran death can be inflicted by hanging, stoning, or shooting, according to the type of offence. Several other countries in the Middle East punish adultery with stoning to death, while the common method of execution in Saudi Arabia and Yemen is beheading with a sword.[79]

Until Oklahoma became the first state to introduce lethal injection as the method of execution in 1977, the preferred mode in the United States had been the electric chair and the supposedly 'more humane' gas chamber, although hanging or shooting were employed by a few states.

The electric chair—'old sparky' as it was sometimes referred to—was for a long time in America regarded as a modern, more efficient and humane alternative to the hangman's rope (a view not shared by the British Royal Commission of 1949–53).[80] But in the last three decades of the twentieth century acute concern began to be expressed about whether it was an efficient and relatively painless way of dispatching criminals.[81] Reports began to circulate about dramatic instances of 'botched executions' where the equipment appears to have malfunctioned to such an extent that flames had shot from the prisoner's body. The American scholar Deborah Denno has summarized the effects as follows: 'charring of the skin and severe external burning, such as the burning away of the ear; exploding of the penis; defecation and micturition, which necessitate the condemned person wearing a diaper; drooling and vomiting; blood flowing from facial orifices; intense muscle spasms and contractions; odors resulting from the burning of the skin and the body; and extensive sweating and swelling of skin tissue'.[82] Although it is not of course possible to judge with any

---

[79] An extreme example of the methods that may still be ordered for executing an offender was the verdict of a Pakistan special court in March 2000, which ordered a man convicted of 'serial killing and mutilation of dozens of runaway children . . . to be publicly strangled, cut him into pieces and thrown into acid'. This was, however, declared 'un-Islamic' by the Council of Islamic Ideology and an appeal was launched. AI, *Report 2001*, p. 186.

[80] See United Kingdom, *Royal Commission on Capital Punishment 1949–1953, Report* (Cmd 8932, 1953), pp. 253–265 at para. 734: 'we cannot recommend that either electrocution or the gas-chamber should replace hanging as the method of judicial execution in this country. In the attributes we have called "humanity" and "certainty" the advantage lies on balance with hanging'. The Supreme Court of India has held that hanging by the neck is the least painful and the most scientific method of execution. *Shashi nayar* v. *UOI* [1992] 1SCC 96.

[81] See Howard Hillman, 'The Possible Pain Experienced during Executions by Different Methods', *Perception* 22 (1993), pp. 745–753. Hillman argues that 'with the certain exception of intravenous injection and the possible exception of shooting, all the procedures are likely to cause severe pain', at p. 750.

[82] Most notably at the execution of Jesse Joseph Tafero in Florida in 1990, Pedro Medina in 1997, Allen Lee Davis (1999)—and where death has not been instantaneous—for example, Horace Dunkins in Alabama in 1989 and Derick Lynn Peterson in Virginia in 1990. See Deborah W. Denno, 'Is Electrocution an Unconstitutional Method of Execution? The Engineering of Death over a Century', *William and Mary Law Review* 35 (1994), pp. 551–692 at 554–557, 668–670, 672; 'Getting to Death: Are Executions Constitutional?', *Iowa Law Review* 82 (1997), pp. 319–417 at 359; 'Adieu to Electrocution', *Ohio Northern University Law Review* 26 (2000), pp. 655–688 at 673. See, in particular, the list of 49 'botched executions' (18 by electrocution, 8 by lethal gas, and 23 by lethal injection) in Appendix 1: 'Botched Executions Following *Gregg* v. *Georgia* (1976)', in Deborah W. Denno, 'Execution and the Forgotten Eighth Amendment', in J. R. Acker, R. M. Bohm, and C. S. Lanier (eds), *America's Experiment with Capital Punishment* (1998), pp. 547–577 at 572–576. Also, L. J. Hoffman, Note, 'The Madness of the Method: The Use of Electrocution and the Death Penalty', *Texas Law Review* 70 (1992), pp. 1039–1062. For a description of an execution, see Robert Johnson, *Death Work: A Study of the Modern Execution Process* (1998), pp. 175–178; and on executions generally, see Stephen Trombley, *The Execution Protocol* (1993), *passim*. Also the account in Robert J. Lifton and Greg Mitchell, *Who Owns Death? Capital Punishment, the American Conscience, and the End of Executions* (2000), pp. 42–69.

finality whether or to what degree these prisoners remained sufficiently conscious to suffer extreme pain, this kind of spectacle has suggested that such executions could be interpreted as a violation of contemporary 'standards of decency', and therefore cruel and unusual punishment. Nevertheless, the majority of the Canadian Supreme Court in the *Kindler* extradition case in 1991 stated that 'As far as the method of execution, electrocution, is concerned, there is a certain horror involved in any execution and it is far from clear that there are more humane methods.'[83] The US Supreme Court has never given an opinion on the matter.[84]

Considerable controversy also surrounded the use of the gas chamber in the United States. Between 1983 and 2000 the number of states employing this method of execution fell from seven to four (all of whom offer the alternative of lethal injection).[85] When, in April 1992, Arizona used the gas chamber for the first time for nearly a decade, witnesses described the execution as 'gruesome' and, as a result, the state's Attorney-General announced that he would seek to substitute lethal injection as the method of execution.[86] Following this, lawyers for Robert Alton Harris and other prisoners on California's death row brought a class action claiming that death by lethal gas in California was unconstitutional, being cruel and unusual punishment. The Supreme Court held that Harris had brought this action too late and he was therefore executed on 21 April 1992.[87] Subsequently, in *Fierro* v. *Gomez* (1994) a Federal judge ruled that California's use of the gas chamber is unconstitutional on the grounds of the time that it took to render the prisoner unconscious: it had 'no place in a civilised society'.[88] Furthermore, while the UN Human Rights Committee, in reviewing the *Kindler* case in 1993, had nothing to say about the legality of electrocution, it did hold Canada to be in breach of the Convention for its extradition of another prisoner, Charles Ng, to California, because he would be

---

[83] *Criminal Reports* 8 C.R. (4th) (1991), p. 5.

[84] The US Supreme Court had granted certiorari, for the first time in a case concerning the means of execution, in *Bryan* v. *Moore* in order to consider Florida's use of the electric chair, 528 U.S. 960; 145 L.Ed.2d 306 (1999). In January 2000 the Court dismissed the case as moot citing Florida's recent legislation which changed its primary method of execution from electrocution to lethal injection, 528 U.S. 1133; 145 L.Ed.2d 927 (2000).

[85] Arizona, California, Missouri, and Wyoming.

[86] See 'Gruesome Death in Gas Chamber Pushes Arizona toward Injections', *New York Times*, 25 Apr. 1992, p. 9; and Peter S. Adolf, Note, 'Killing Me Softly: Is the Gas Chamber, or Any Other Method of Execution, "Cruel and Unusual Punishment"?', *Hastings Constitutional Law Quarterly* 22 (1995), pp. 815–866.

[87] For the controversy surrounding the Supreme Court's decision, see Judge Stephen Reinhardt, 'The Supreme Court, the Death Penalty, and the *Harris* Case', *Yale Law Journal* 102 (1992), pp. 205–223; E. Caminker and E. Chemerinsky, 'The Lawless Execution of Robert Alton Harris', *ibid.*, pp. 225–254. For an alternative view, supporting the Supreme Court's decision, S. G. Calabresi and G. Lawson, 'Equity and Hierarchy: Reflections on the Harris Execution', *ibid.*, pp. 255–279.

[88] *Fierro* v. *Gomez* (1994) 865 F.Supp. 1387 (N.D.Cal.). This was subsequently upheld by a Federal Court of Appeals. See *Fierro* v. *Gomez* 1996, 77 F.3d 301 (9th Cir. 1996). See also *The Independent*, 14 Feb. 1994, reporting that a federal judge in Baltimore had approved the videotaping and monitoring of the brain by electroencephalograph of a Maryland prisoner awaiting death in the gas chamber so that fellow inmates would have evidence on which to argue that the method constitutes cruel and unusual punishment. However, in *Campbell* v. *Wood* 18 F.3d 662 (1994) the 9th Circuit Court of Appeals held that hanging did not constitute cruel and unusual punishment. The United States Supreme Court refused to grant certiorari in order to review this judgment.

exposed to execution in the gas chamber: 'a technique which the Committee considered to be torture or inhumane treatment'.[89]

In the face of these objectionable methods, almost all the retentionist states in America, (as well as the Federal government) had, by the beginning of the twenty-first century, followed Oklahoma's lead (see page 98 above), the last states to do so being Georgia and Florida.[90] Although six states gave prisoners sentenced to death before the introduction of lethal injection a choice between the old and the new method,[91] Nebraska is now the only state to use the electric chair as its sole method of execution.[92] Indeed, between January and December 2001 all 66 executions were carried out by lethal injection.

Lethal injection is now being accepted in other countries: executions by this means have been carried out in the Philippines and (as yet on a small scale) in China. It is on the statute books as an alternative to shooting in Taiwan, but has yet to be used. The Ministry of Justice of Thailand has asked a government committee to draft a bill so that lethal injection can replace the firing squad as the method of execution in that country.

As Deborah Denno has pointed out, 'some proponents [of capital punishment] feel that [lethal] injection can save the death penalty from abolition while some opponents believe injection can save inmates from torture'.[93] Yet, even though it is generally agreed that the 'sanitized' method of lethal injection is less likely to produce severe pain than any other form of execution, there have been problems caused by difficulties in administering the drugs which prolonged the execution and probably caused the prisoner considerable distress.[94] Newspaper reports of the execution of Raymond Landry in Texas in 1988 revealed the following scene:

[89] See William A. Schabas, '*Soering*'s Legacy: The Human Rights Committee and the Judicial Committee of the Privy Council Take a Walk Down Death Row', *International and Comparative Law Quarterly* 43 (1994), pp. 913–923 at 916–917.

[90] American Bar Association, *A Gathering Momentum: Continuing Impacts of the American Bar Association Call for a Moratorium on Executions* (Jan. 2000), p. 14. The Georgia legislature in 2000 had made lethal injection the method of execution for all convicted after 1 May 2000, but left those sentenced prior to this under threat of execution by electrocution. But in September and October 2001, in the cases of *Dawson* v. *the State* [274 Ga. 327] and *Moore* v. *the State* (274 Ga. 229 and 552 S.E.2d. 832], the Georgia Supreme Court held (by 4 to 3) that use of the electric chair violated the state's constitution because it 'inflicts purposeless physical violence and needless mutilation that makes no measurable contribution to accepted goals of punishment'.

[91] Arizona, Arkansas, Delaware, Georgia, Kentucky, and Tennessee. Three states authorize other methods of execution in case one is held unconstitutional or cannot be given, and nine states offer a 'genuine' choice between two methods of execution. For details, see Bureau of Justice Statistics, *Capital Punishment 2000* (2001).

[92] See AI, *United States of America: Failing the Future—Death Penalty Developments, March 1998–March 2000*, AI Index: AMR 51/03/00. In April 2002 Alabama changed to lethal injection, from 1 July 2002, but condemned inmates will still be able to choose the electric chair.

[93] Deborah W. Denno, 'When Legislatures Delegate Death: The Troubling Paradox behind State Uses of Electrocution and Lethal Injection and what it Says about Us', *Ohio State Law Journal* 63 (2002), pp. 63–260 at 65–66.

[94] See Thomas O. Finks, 'Lethal Injection: An Uneasy Alliance of Law and Medicine', *Journal of Legal Medicine* 4 (1983), pp. 383–403; Ronald Bayer, 'Lethal Injections and Capital Punishment: Medicine in the Service of the State', *Journal of Prison and Jail Health* 4(1) (1984), pp. 7–15; W. J. Curran and W. Cascells, 'The Ethics of Medical Participation in Capital Punishment by Intravenous Drug Injection',

While Landry was strapped to a gurney, executioners in Texas 'repeatedly probed' his veins with syringes for forty minutes attempting to inject potassium chloride. Then two minutes after the execution began, the syringe came out of Landry's vein, 'spewing deadly chemicals towards startled witnesses'. What officials termed a 'blowout' resulted in the squirting of lethal injection liquid about two feet across the room . . . A plastic curtain was pulled so that witnesses could not see the execution team reinsert the catheter into Landry's vein. After 14 minutes, and after witnesses heard the sound of doors opening and closing, murmurs and at least one groan, the curtain was opened and Landry appeared motionless and unconscious. Landry was pronounced dead 24 minutes after the drugs were initially injected.[95]

Sixteen further instances of botched executions have been reported since Landry's execution, up until August 1996.[96] And the Death Penalty Information Center noted a further eight botched executions carried out by lethal injection until December 2001. This has intensified the debate about the ethics of the medical profession using their medical knowledge in the administration of death.

On 16 May 2001 Jay D. Scott was already strapped to the gurney with injection shunts in his arms and only three minutes away from execution when a stay was announced by the Federal Appeal Court Sixth Circuit. This was the second time that this had happened within a month. The Ohio state Attorney-General admitted that 'It's almost like torturing him two or three times before you put him to death.'[97] It is hardly surprising that opponents of the death penalty have denied that a lethal injection is any more likely, given the difficulties of administering it and what is known about the way that different humans react to different levels of drugs, to avoid 'unnecessary and wanton infliction of pain'. For this reason they claim that it too is cruel and unusual punishment and therefore unconstitutional.[98]

(b) Public Executions

Burundi, Comoros, Guinea[99] and Lebanon,[100] were the only countries responding to the United Nations Fifth and Sixth Surveys to say that executions could take place in public.[101] Yet according to other reports, executions in public, or executions broadcast on television, have taken place since 1994 in at least 18 countries or

---

New England Journal of Medicine 302 (1980), pp. 226–230; and W. Cascells *et al.*, 'Doctors, the Death Penalty and Lethal Injections', *New England Journal of Medicine* 307 (1982), pp. 1532–1533. See the report of the execution of John Wayne Gacy in Chicago in *The Times*, 11 May 1994.

[95] Quoted by Denno, 'Execution and the Forgotten Eighth Amendment', n. 82 above, p. 564.

[96] *Ibid.*, Appendix 1, pp. 575–576.

[97] Reported in *Amicus Journal* 3 (2001), p. 1. For a moving description of the final hours before execution and its aftermath, see Johnson, n. 82 above, pp. 142–191.

[98] Denno, n. 93 above, pp. 100–116.

[99] But only for certain of the offences subject to capital punishment.

[100] Lebanon stated that in one case, 'Due to the horrific nature of the crime, public execution was used as a deterrent.'

[101] Under Argentinian military law the condemned can be shot in public, but there have been no such executions in recent years.

territories.[102] Public executions have been condemned by the United Nations Human Rights Committee as 'incompatible with human dignity'.[103]

In some countries stoning to death (the person being executed being buried waist deep, or to above the breast if a woman) is allowed for certain offences, either in public or within a prison. Two cases occurred in the summer of 2001 in Iran. One woman was stoned to death for 'adultery and corruption on earth' (acting in a pornographic film) under Shari'a law, and another for adultery and the murder of her husband.[104] During the height of the Iranian revolution bodies were left hanging in public view, sometimes at the site of the crime. The practice has persisted. For example, in March 2001 it was reported that a 30-year-old woman had been hanged in public after being convicted for possession of illegal drugs,[105] and in August 2001 about a dozen people were hanged in public, including three men sentenced to death for armed robbery.[106] Under Taliban rule in Kabul, Afghanistan, men convicted of working with oppositional forces were hanged by ropes from cranes and left there all day in both September 2000 and August 2001.[107] It was reported that in May 2000 in Saudi Arabia the body of an Egyptian man was crucified following his execution for charges of murder.[108]

There have been reports of many beheadings in public in Saudi Arabia and of mass executions by firing squad before large crowds in Nigeria in the mid-1990s.[109] In China (1979), Gabon (1982), Libya (1984), Kazakhstan (1995), and Guatemala (2000) executions have been televised. In Thailand in April 2001 the Corrections

---

[102] Afghanistan, Chechnya in the Russian Federation, Democratic Republic of Congo, Equatorial Guinea, Guatemala (televised), Guinea, Iran, Libya (televised), Nigeria, Pakistan, Rwanda, Saudi Arabia, Sierra Leone, Somalia, Syria, Uganda, Yemen (AR). The last substantiated report of public executions in China was in June 1986, when the *South China Morning Post* (Hong Kong) reported on 26 June that 31 criminals had been shot in public. In July 1986 the People's Supreme Court issued a directive to Provincial High Courts outlawing public executions. For a discussion of the earlier practice, see Larry L. Tifft, 'Reflections on Capital Punishment and the 'Campaign against Crime' in the People's Republic of China', *Justice Quarterly* 2 (1985), pp. 127–137; and the vivid report 'Día de ejecuciones en Zhengzhou', *El País* 28 Feb. 1988 (referring to events in 1983).

[103] See UN doc. no. CCPR/C/79/Add.65, 24 July 1996, para. 16, referring to public executions in Nigeria.

[104] See Nick Roberts, 'Death Penalty Developments around the World', *Amicus Journal* 3 (2001), p. 5. Also, AI, *News Flash, Iran: Stonings should Stop*, MDE 13/024/2001. Article 119 of the Islamic Criminal Code of Iran states that 'stones must not be too large [to ensure] that the convicted person does not die from one or two blows; they must also not be so small that they cannot be called stones'; quoted in A. S. Mikhlin, *The Death Penalty in Russia* (1999), p. 150.

[105] AI, *Death Penalty News*, Mar. 2001, AI Index: ACT 53/002/2001, p. 2.

[106] AI, *Death Penalty News* Sept. 2001, AI Index: ACT 53/004/2001, p. 3.

[107] AI, *The Death Penalty Worldwide: Developments in 2000*, AI Index: ACT 50/001/2001, p. 19. See also AI, *Death Penalty News*, Sept. 2001, AI Index: ACT 53/004/2001. And in Kandahar in February 2001 two women convicted of prostitution and 'becoming a cause of moral corruption' were hanged in a sports stadium, reportedly watched by thousands of people, *Death Penalty News*, Mar. 2001, AI Index: ACT 53/002/2001, p. 2.

[108] AI, *Report 2001*, p. 207.

[109] See AI, 'Saudi Arabia: Upsurge in Public Executions', *Death Penalty News*, June 1993, and 'Nigeria: Public Executions', *Death Penalty News*, Sept. 1995, AI Index: ACT 53/03/95, which reported the execution of 43 prisoners before a crowd of a thousand people in July 1995. According to a report in *The Independent*, 13 Sept. 1995, 18 men were shot in public in Nigeria and a stray bullet killed the driver who had brought them to the place of execution.

Department for the first time allowed reporters and cameramen to witness the execution of five prisoners by firing squad. It was reported that dozens turned up and that it was partly shown on public television.[110]

Representatives of the public and the press witness executions in the United States, and access is given to the media to interview prisoners awaiting death. A large number of witnesses, including the families of victims and the press, watched the execution of the Oklahoma bomber Timothy McVeigh in June 2001, some of them through a television relay. The question of right of access, including televising of executions, has provoked considerable controversy.[111] Indeed, some advocates of abolition believe, just as abolitionists in Britain believed when the Capital Punishment within Prisons Act was passed in 1868, that it would speed the cause of abolition if the general public were to be allowed to witness what was being done in their name: the cold and deliberate judicial execution of an offender.[112] This view has recently received the imprimatur of a leading campaigner for abolition in the United States, Professor Austin Sarat. In his book *When the State Kills* (2001), he argues:

I suggest that the survival of capital punishment in America depends in part, on its relative invisibility . . . The exclusion of the public means the exclusion of the court of last resort; no longer can the people rise up to save the condemned; no longer is the people's judgment truly the last word in state killing . . . Making this shame and this zeal visible to a mass audience would be likely to reveal the sadism that is at the heart of the state's tenacious attachment to capital punishment as reveal and invite the 'bad taste' of its viewers. For me the possibility of the former is well worth the risk of the latter.[113]

But, as David Garland has pointed out, one cannot think of anywhere in the world where such shock tactics have worked. Indeed the process of abolition has, in most countries, been marked by its removal from the public gaze into a secretive and eventually marginalized activity of the criminal justice system, one that has generally brought shame, or at least no plaudits, for those who take part in it. It seems unlikely that by making 'theatre' out of executions the public would not be brutalized too.[114]

In several countries members of the public have been involved in carrying out the executions, mostly by stoning. In Saudi Arabia and Iran the guardian of the murdered victim has the right to perform the execution himself, or hire another person to do it, but there is no information about how often this occurs, if at all. While the 1997 Law of Criminal Procedure outlaws public executions in China,

[110] 'Civilised Society in the Firing Line', *Bangkok Post*, 20 Apr. 2001.

[111] See Note, 'The Executioner's Song: Is there a Right to Listen?', *Virginia Law Review* 69 (1983), pp. 373–401. In *KQED* v. *Vasquez* (1991) a Californian court denied a public television station's request to televise the execution of Robert Alton Harris. See Bernard Schwartz, 'Death TV? Is there a Press Right of Access to News that Allows Television of Executions?', *Tulsa Law Journal* 30 (1994), pp. 305–353; and Wendy Lesser, *Pictures at an Execution* (1993).

[112] See Joe Keating, 'Out of Sight, Out of Mind', *Amicus Journal* 3 (2001), pp. 15–19.

[113] Austin Sarat, *When the State Kills: Capital Punishment and the American Condition* (2001), pp. 189–208.

[114] See David Garland's review essay of Sarat's book, 'The Cultural Conditions of Capital Punishment', *Punishment and Society* 4 (2002).

reports of public rallies, some of them televised, where persons convicted of capital offences are paraded and humiliated, sometimes in full view of the public, prior to being taken to an execution ground, continue to be forthcoming.[115] An Amnesty International news release, dated 6 July 2001, reported in relation to the latest 'strike hard' campaign:

Not for many years have mass rallies and sentencing been seen on this scale . . . Most executions take place after sentencing rallies in front of massive crowds in sports stadiums and public squares. Prisoners are also paraded through the streets past thousands of people on the way to execution by firing squad in nearby fields or courtyards. One such rally in Yunnan province was reportedly broadcast live on state television. Rallies in Shaanxi in April and May were reportedly attended by 1,800,000 spectators.

A recent report (22 June 2001) in the British newspaper the *Daily Telegraph*, under the headline 'Criminals Shot to Frighten the Monkeys', described how a convoy of open lorries had paraded nine condemned trussed-up 'drug dealers' to the execution ground after they had been humiliated at a sentencing rally before a crowd of 10,000 invited spectators including 6 to 12-year-old schoolchildren wearing red Young Pioneer scarves, and a group of medical students in their white coats. 'The stadium was ringed inside and out, with paramilitary police in camouflage fatigues carrying submachine-guns. Inside, hundreds more grim-faced officers sat and stood in rows beneath a red banner reading "Strike Hard must be severe, so society will be stable".'

Clearly, the imposition of the death sentence in China is still sometimes used to create a public spectacle. It is and is meant to be humiliating to the condemned, and presumably a deterrent to onlookers, even if the public are not allowed to see the 'final moments'.

(c) The Role of Physicians

There remains much dispute about the proper role of doctors in the administration of the death penalty. The issue has become even more contentious since states turned in increasing numbers to execution by lethal injection, which necessitates medical assistance in establishing the intravenous portal through which the lethal preparation will pass, to monitor the execution procedure, and to pronounce on death.[116] A report, *Breach of Trust: Physician Participation in Executions in the United States*, found that in most American states physicians were, in practice, required to attend executions, a practice which the American Medical Association opposes.[117] The Council of the American College of Physicians in 1993 stated that participation contrary to medical ethics would include (but not be limited to): 'prescribing or administering tranquillisers and other psychotropic agents and medications that are

---

[115] See AI, *People's Republic of China: The Death Penalty in 1998*, AI Index: ASA 17/57/99, pp. 4–5.

[116] For example, the execution of Rickey Ray Rector in Arkansas in 1992 required a medical team to find a vein in which to insert the catheter: they were prepared to insert it surgically.

[117] *Breach of Trust* was published by the American College of Physicians, Human Rights Watch, the National Council to Abolish the Death Penalty, and Physicians for Human Rights (1994).

part of the execution procedure; monitoring vital signs on site or remotely (including monitoring electrocardiograms); attending or observing an execution as a physician; and rendering of technical advice regarding execution'. And in the case where the execution was to be by lethal injection, the following would be unethical conduct: selecting injection sites; starting intravenous lines as a port for a lethal injection device; prescribing, preparing, administering, or supervising injection drugs or their doses or types; inspecting, testing, or maintaining lethal injection devices; consulting with or supervising lethal injection personnel. But it would not be counted as participation to certify death, providing that the person had been declared dead by another person (otherwise the physician might have to decide whether or not the execution should continue), nor to relieve acute suffering of condemned persons, providing that they voluntarily request it.[118]

However, there have been attempts to bypass medical opposition to taking part in executions both by employing persons who are not fully trained doctors and by changing the law relating to the duties of physicians. Illinois took this latter path in March 1995 when it exempted doctors who assist in executions from both the legal and medical ethical requirements of the Medical Practices Act.[119] And in India the Supreme Court ruled in January 1995 that doctors employed in prisons had an obligation to participate in hangings by examining the body every few minutes after the drop to ensure that death has occurred.[120] The only American state so far to move in the opposite direction is Missouri, which in July 1995 abolished the statutory requirement that a qualified doctor should assist at executions.[121] The subject remains very controversial. Indeed, a recent postal survey of 1,000 medical practitioners in the United States, asking about their willingness to be involved in and attitudes towards capital punishment, found that 41 per cent of the 413 who responded 'indicated that they would perform at least one action disallowed by the AMA'. Nineteen per cent said they 'would be willing to actually give the lethal injection,

---

[118] For the position of the American Medical Association, see 'Council on Ethical and Judicial Affairs. American Medical Association: Physician Participation in Capital Punishment', *Journal of the American Medical Association* 270 (1993), pp. 365–368; see also British Medical Association, *Medicine Betrayed* (1992), pp. 111–116. It should be noted that not all doctors in the United States are opposed to some participation in executions. For example, Dr Richard Ikeda, chief medical consultant to the Medical Board of California, has said that he does not believe assistance in monitoring death to be unethical; reported in the *Oakland Tribune*, 18 Aug. 1993. See also the correspondence in the *New England Journal of Medicine* 330 (31 Mar. 1994), pp. 935–937 in response to an article by R. D. Truog and T. A. Brennan, 'Participation of Physicians in Capital Punishment', *ibid.*, 329 (28 Oct. 1993), pp. 1346–1349. See also Charles Patrick Ewing, ' "Above All Do No Harm": The Role of Health and Mental Health Professionals in the Capital Punishment Process', in Acker, Bohm, and Lanier (eds), n. 82 above, pp. 461–476. See also the chapter entitled 'What is Unethical About Physicians Helping at Executions?', in Michael Davis, *Justice in the Shadow of Death: Rethinking Capital and Lesser Punishments* (1996), pp. 65–94.

[119] See AI, *Death Penalty News*, June 1995, p. 4. and *Medical Death Penalty Newsletter*, 7(2) (1995).

[120] 'India: Supreme Court Judgement Violates Medical Ethics', AI, *Medical Death Penalty Newsletter*, 7(3) (1995), p. 1.

[121] AI, *Death Penalty News*, Sep.1995, p. 4; and Andrew A. Skolnick, Note, 'Physicians in Missouri (but not Illinois) Win Battle to Block Physician Participation in Executions', *Journal of the American Medical Association* 274(7) (1995), p. 524.

and 36 per cent said they would be willing to pronounce the prisoner dead'.[122] A real example was the action of a Chief Medical Officer who was alleged to have authorized, in November 2001, the acquisition and provision of the drugs to be used for the execution by lethal injection of the first death row prisoner in New Mexico for forty-one years, contrary both to the stance of the American Medical Association and the provisions of the New Mexico Practice Act.

There have been many reports of the involvement of physicians in the process in China. Where lethal injection is used, doctors are appointed by the court to administer the injections. There has been even more concern expressed about the role of doctors in removing (often at the site of death) organs for transplantation, from an estimated 2,000–3,000 executed persons a year: estimates that do seem to be rather high given the recorded scale of executions in China. The Chinese authorities have claimed that this has only occurred for medical use with the full consent of the condemned or their families and have denied that organs are sold for profit.[123] Nevertheless, there are widespread allegations that they have been removed frequently without such consent, or at least unforced consent, and sold.[124] This practice is regarded as not only counter to international standards of medical ethics, but also likely to stimulate the use of the death penalty.[125] The forty-sixth World Medical Association General Assembly at Stockholm in September 1994 deemed such behaviour to be in direct contravention of the guidelines enunciated by the World Medical Association in its Declaration on Human Organ Transplantation adopted in October 1987.[126] Indeed, the World Medical Association at its fifty-second meeting in 2000 '*Resolved*, that it is unethical for physicians to participate in capital punishment, in any way, or during any step of the execution process'.[127]

---

[122] Neil J. Farber, B. M. Aboff, J. Weiner, E. B. Davis, E. G. Boyer, and P. A. Ubel, 'Physicians' Willingness to Participate in the Process of Lethal Injection for Capital Punishment', *Annals of Internal Medicine* 135(10) (2001), pp. 884–888.

[123] The harvesting of organs is also legally permitted in Taiwan, with the agreement of the condemned, but not for private sale or use. The offenders are executed by a single bullet to the head or heart according to the condemned's wishes or decision as regards the donating of organs. At present (Spring 2002) there is a moratorium on the use of organs while doctors are considering their position with regard to its acceptability. I am grateful to Peter Hodgkinson, Director of the Centre for Capital Punishment Studies, University of Westminster, for this information.

[124] 'Execution in China, through a Brother's Eyes', *New York Times*, 11 Mar. 2001. Also 'China's Bitter Harvest Shakes a Doctor', *International Herald Tribune*, 28 June 2001, report of evidence given by a Chinese doctor seeking political asylum in the United States that 'he took part in removing corneas and harvesting skin from more than 100 executed prisoners, including one who had not yet died'. Reuters reported on 28 June 2001 the response to this 'vicious slander' by a Chinese Foreign Ministry spokeswoman.

[125] See Human Rights Watch/Asia, *Organ Procurement and Judicial Execution in China* 6(9) (1994). For further discussion, see Michael Radelet, 'Physician Participation', in P. Hodgkinson and A. Rutherford (eds), *Capital Punishment: Global Issues and Prospects* (1996), pp. 243–260 at 244–248.

[126] See also British Medical Association, n. 118 above, pp. 100–102.

[127] Reported in AI, *The Death Penalty Worldwide: Developments in 2000*, AI Index: ACT/50/001/2001, p. 29; see the WMA's policy on www.wma.net/e/policy/20-6-81_e.html.

(d) On Death Row

Article 10 of the International Covenant on Civil and Political Rights states that 'All persons deprived of their liberty shall be treated with humanity and with respect for the inherent dignity of the human person.' It should be self-evident that this should apply in particular to those undergoing confinement while facing the prospect of execution. Yet, it appears that such prisoners are, in many countries, treated with little humanity.

There can be no doubt that waiting to be executed, or wondering over a long period of time whether or not one will be successful in avoiding execution, must cause great stress. Indeed, it was argued twenty years ago that 'the death penalty in a legalistic society inevitably causes cruelty by the delay in carrying it out, and . . . capital punishment therefore cannot be reconciled with constitutional rights and so is per se unlawful'.[128] In the United States the new post-*Furman* death sentence laws have brought so much litigation in their train that the average length of time spent on death row rose from around thirteen months in 1976 to over seven years by the 1990s and by 2000 to eleven years and five months.[129] Some prisoners wait far longer. In June 2000 Gary Graham was executed for a crime he had committed when aged 17, after nineteen years on death row.

A number of socio-psychological studies have described the reactions of prisoners who have experienced a long period of uncertainty about their fate, as well as the problems posed for humane prison management. These reactions have been found to be similar to those of terminally ill hospital patients, but exacerbated by the physical conditions of cellular confinement for anything up to twenty-two hours a day, restricted visits, and, in many states, no access to prison jobs, educational classes, clubs, religious services, or recreational facilities or programmes. Such conditions of despair and loneliness have been described as 'an austere world in which condemned prisoners are treated as bodies kept alive to be killed'.[130] As Margaret Vandiver has so eloquently observed, it is not only condemned prisoners who suffer over this protracted period, but also their families, and sometimes the families of their victims too.[131]

[128] See David Pannick, *Judicial Review of the Death Penalty* (1982), p. 162.

[129] Bureau of Justice Statistics, *Capital Punishment 2000* (2001), p. 1, US Department of Justice. This was, on average, about six months less than those executed in 1999.

[130] See Robert Johnson and John L. Carroll, 'Litigating Death-Row Conditions, the Case for Reform', in Ira P. Robbins (ed), *Prisoners and the Law* (1985), pp. 8–15; Robert Johnson, 'Under Sentence of Death: The Psychology of Death Row Confinement', *Law and Psychology Review* 5 (1979), pp. 141–158; *Condemned to Die: Life under Sentence of Death* (1981); and 'Institutions and the Promotion of Violence', in Anne Campbell and John J. Gibbs (eds), *Violent Transactions* (1986), pp. 181–205 at 197–198; Doug Magee, *Slow Coming Dark: Interviews on Death Row* (1982); Bruce Jackson and Diane Christian, *Death Row* (1980). For the view of a correctional administrator, see Charlotte A. Nesbit, 'Managing Death Row', *Corrections Today* (July 1986), pp. 90–106; and for more personal and moving accounts, see Helen Prejean, *Dead Man Walking* (1993), Jan Arriens (ed), *Welcome to Hell: Letters and Other Writings by Prisoners on Death Row in the United States* (1991), and Marie Mulvey Roberts (ed), *Out of Night: Writings from Death Row* (1994).

[131] For a study of the deleterious impact on prisoners' families of such prolonged uncertainty, see Michael L. Radelet, Margaret Vandiver, and Felix M. Berardo, 'Families, Prisons, and Men with Death Sentences', *Journal of Family Issues* 4 (1983), pp. 593–612; and Margaret Vandiver, 'The Impact of the Death Penalty on the Families of Homicide Victims and of Condemned Prisoners', in Acker, Bohm, and Lanier (eds), n. 82 above, pp. 477–505.

In 1994 Amnesty International examined H-Unit, a new 'state of the art' maximum security unit within Oklahoma State Penitentiary, and declared the conditions on death row 'cruel, inhuman and degrading treatment'. Inmates were confined to their cells twenty-three hours a day during weekdays and twenty-four hours a day at weekends, and allowed a fifteen-minute shower three times a week.[132] It has elsewhere been described as 'a solitary and sterile, a cold, oppressive human wasteland in which prisoners are interred—confined underground—in utterly self-contained cell blocks replete with dimly lit and sparsely furnished concrete cages'.[133]

Only a few American states do not hold their prisoners separately on a death row. Most of them have only a handful of prisoners, but Missouri is an exception. All the state's condemned prisoners have, since 1991, been 'mainstreamed' into the general population of the prison in which they are held, the other prisoners nearly all being lifers convicted of similar crimes to those awaiting execution. It has been reported that this has 'humanized' the environment for 'capital offenders' by opening up to them normal prison facilities, and 'enhanced the ability of officials to justify current capital punishment inmate management practices'.[134] It may also be a means of legitimizing the long periods for which such prisoners are held waiting execution, without addressing the psychological impact of that very fact.

Since 1978 several prisoners in the United States have challenged their overall conditions of confinement on death row as an infringement of their rights under the Eighth Amendment of the Constitution not to suffer any 'cruel or unusual punishment'.[135] Limited improvement in their conditions has resulted from such litigation in several states, where the courts have recognized the special needs of the condemned and the psychological impact of unnecessarily harsh conditions. For example, in Texas, as a result of *Ruiz* v. *Estelle* (1982), a class action in which the Fifth Circuit Court of Appeals found that the vastly overcrowded conditions under which all Texan prisoners were held violated the Eighth Amendment, agreement was reached in 1986 to improve conditions for death row prisoners. They were classified, and those deemed 'work capable' (about 40 per cent of the inmates) were given jobs and granted all the privileges and freedom of movement enjoyed by ordinary prisoners. For the majority not considered to be capable of work (for security, physical, or psychological reasons) conditions were also somewhat improved. As a result they were guaranteed at least fifteen hours' a week out-of-cell recreation, although they were still housed separately.[136] Several other states have laid down minimum condi-

---

[132] AI, *USA: Conditions for Death Row Prisoners in H-Unit, Oklahoma State Penitentiary*, AI Index: AMR 51/34/94. In an article, 'The Living Dead: Living on Death Row', *South African Journal on Human Rights* 5(2) (1989), pp. 183–195, Lloyd Vogelman remarks 'living in the death "factory" [i.e. death row] is a traumatic experience whether or not it results in execution. While the condemned are there, they are the living dead. For those who survive it takes years to recover', pp. 183–195 at 195.

[133] Robert Johnson, 'Life under Sentence of Death: Historical and Contemporary Perspectives', in Acker, Bohm, and Lanier (eds), n. 82 above, pp. 507–529 at 519–524.

[134] See George Lombardi, Richard L. Sluder, and Donald Wallace, 'Mainstreaming Death-Sentenced Inmates: The Missouri Experience and its Legal Significance', *Federal Probation* 61(2) (1997), pp. 3–11.

[135] This litigation follows the landmark decision *Pugh* v. *Locke* (1977), which ruled that the overall conditions of the Alabama prison system violated the Eighth Amendment.

[136] See Johnson, n. 82 above, pp. 74–76.

tions for death row inmates, assuring them of stipulated hours of out-of-cell time, recreational facilities, and opportunities to work, dine, and attend religious services with the general prison population. Death row inmates in California who are classified Grade A are entitled to six hours' out-of-cell activity per day seven days a week. They may also dine outside their cells together and attend group religious services. Those not so classified may still receive twelve hours' outdoor exercise per week, at least six of which are designated for outdoor exercise with sports facilities provided.[137]

Nevertheless, observers have described these improvements as mere palliatives to what 'by its very nature remains a prison within a prison'.[138] Indeed, a survey by the National Institute of Justice and the American Correctional Association in 1989 revealed that those under sentence of death had limited access to programmes and that visitation policies and procedures varied widely. Despite legal cases promoting 'greater access to programming and more out of cell time . . . the trend in management practice in many institutions . . . seems to point toward greater security measures and reduction of program time'.[139] And, of course, where prisoners are regarded as security risks or as serious control problems, such as to require maximum security, conditions can be extremely restricted. An insight into this was given when, in May 1988, a death row inmate in Idaho's Maximum Security Institution filed a lawsuit alleging that inmates were held in solitary confinement in small concrete and steel cells with solid metal doors and a narrow slit for a window. They were allowed out on their own and handcuffed in a mesh pen measuring 7 feet by 15 feet for a maximum of one hour per day, excluding weekends. Thus they spent 163 of the 168 hours per week in solitary confinement: a fate the filer of the lawsuit claimed he had suffered for sixteen years.[140]

In the second, impressive and moving, edition of his book *Death Work: A Study of the Modern Execution Process*, published in 1998, Robert Johnson defines death row as a species of 'torturous confinement' and concludes that 'Aside from a smattering of essentially cosmetic reforms in a number of prisons—access to educational classes in some systems; the availability, on paper at least, of mental health counselling; modest increases of out-of-cell time and access to visitors; and, in a few states, the availability of part-time work—death rows today are essentially indistinguishable from their counterparts in earlier years.' Indeed he remains of the opinion that 'The death penalty, when preceded by long confinement and administered bureaucratically, dehumanises both the agents and recipients of this punishment and amounts to a form of torture.'[141] Johnson provides an eerie and haunting description of these regimes:

[137] See Nancy Holland, 'Death Row Conditions: Progression toward Constitutional Protections', *Akron Law Review* 2 (1985), pp. 293–310 at 300–310.

[138] Johnson, n. 82 above, p. 76.

[139] C. A. Nesbit, P. L. Howard, and S.M. Wallace, *Managing Death-Sentenced Inmates: A Survey of Practices* (1989), p. 55.

[140] See AI, *United States of America: Failing the Future—Death Penalty Developments, March 1998–March 2000*, AI Index: AMR 51/03/00, p. 17.

[141] Johnson, n. 82 above, pp. 71 and 218.

The peculiar silence of death row stems from the empty and ultimately lifeless regime imposed on the condemned. These offenders, seen as unfit to live in even the prison community, are relegated to this prison within a prison . . . Typical maximum security prisoners spend about eight to twelve hours a day in their cells; typically death row inmates spend twenty to twenty-two or twenty-three hours a day alone in theirs. Death row prisoners leave their cells to shower (often handcuffed) and to exercise (in a restricted area, sometimes fittingly called a 'recreation cage') . . . visits occur under heavy guard, are restricted in frequency and duration, and become increasingly rare as a prisoner's stay on death row continues . . . Deemed beyond correction, they typically are denied access to even meagre privileges, amenities, and services available to regular prisoners . . . With only rare exceptions, condemned prisoners are demoralised by their bleak confinement and defeated by the awesome prospect of death by execution. Worn down in small and almost imperceptible ways, they gradually become less than fully human. At the end, the prisoners are helpless pawns in the modern execution drill. They give in, they give up, and submit: yielding themselves to the execution team and the machinery of death.[142]

Johnson's analysis is summed up well by Willie Turner, who was seventeen years on Virginia's death row, and had experience of it as a reformed regime. Even under improved physical conditions, he described the psychological impact of waiting thus:

It's the unending, uninterrupted immersion in death that wears on you so much. It's the parade of friends and acquaintances who leave for the death house and never come back, while your own desperate and lonely time drains away. It's the boring routine of claustrophobic confinement, punctuated by eye-opening dates with death that you helplessly hope will be averted. It's watching yourself die over the years in the eyes of family and friends . . . I've spent over 5000 days on death row. Not a single waking hour of any of those days has gone by without me thinking about my date with the executioner . . . All that thinking about it is like a little dying, even if you're on the best death row on earth . . . nothing could have prepared me for the despair and the frustration, for the loneliness and the abuse, for the shame and sorrow, for the hopes raised and dashed, for the dreams and nightmares of my death that my seventeen years facing my own advancing demise have served up.[143]

Conditions on death row in several other countries are even more extreme. For example, prisoners under sentence of death in Japan have been subjected to very close confinement in manacles for considerable periods. Indeed the UN Human Rights Committee has expressed serious concern about the conditions as well as the restrictions placed on visits from families and lawyers.[144] In Zambia the section of the prison in Lusaka—originally built for 48 prisoners under sentence of death—housed, in the spring of 2001, more than 200. Some of the cells, approximately 3

---

[142] *Ibid.*, pp. 71 and 93. Johnson notes, however, that death row conditions for women are, in most states, much better: 'More often than not, condemned women are held in settings that are cosy and congenial, more like group homes or even private homes than like prisons or death rows.' However, he expects this to change if the execution of women begins to occur 'with any regularity', at pp. 86–87. See also Jane Officer (ed), *If I Should Die . . . A Death Row Correspondence* (1999).

[143] Johnson, n. 82 above, p. 85.

[144] AI, *Japan: Executions: Continuing the Secret and Cruel Practice*, AI Index: ASA 22/005/2001; see also AI, *Japan Complacent over Human Rights: Government Must Implement Human Rights Committee's Recommendations*, AI Index: ASA 22/014/1998; and AI, *Japan's Human Rights Record must be Challenged*, AI Index: ASA 22/013/1998.

metres by 2 metres, held up to six prisoners, and a recent Amnesty International report stated that there were cases of tuberculosis but virtually no access to medical treatment. The prisoners' uniforms 'in some cases consisted of rags of material crudely stitched together'.[145] Similarly overcrowded and fetid conditions have been reported from several Caribbean countries.[146] In China, where prisoners are not kept long under sentence of death prior to execution, they are, according to Amnesty International, 'usually kept handcuffed and some also have their feet shackled from the time they are sentenced to death until their execution', even though leg-irons and chains are prohibited as instruments of restraint under international prison standards.[147]

Prisoners in the United States are not the only ones to experience the agonizing delays in waiting for execution. In Japan men have been under sentence of death for over thirty years, and in 1997 one person was reported to have been executed after spending twenty-eight years on death row,[148] where conditions have been described by Amnesty International as inhuman and degrading.[149] And they are exacerbated by the fact that government policy is not to tell prisoners, their lawyers, or families when the execution will take place. In Belarus, too, relatives are not informed of the date of the execution nor informed of the place of burial.[150] And in Taiwan neither the family of the condemned person nor the victim are notified until after the execution has taken place, apparently 'in the interest of prison harmony'.

All but two of the 17 people executed by Indonesia in 1985–7 had been under sentence for more than fifteen years, and in Malaysia a man sentenced to death in 1988 was not executed until 2000. In Zambia there are apparently at least 30 prisoners who have been on death row between eight and twenty-five years, and in Swaziland some prisoners have served at least eighteen years on death row before being pardoned. Under Islamic law in Saudi Arabia offenders have sometimes had to wait for as long as fifteen years until the victim's son had reached maturity and was able to make the decision whether to exact retaliation (Qisas) or accept compensation (Diya),[151] and a prisoner may not be informed of whether or not an appeal has been successful until the day of the execution itself.

International norms have been developing on the question of the so-called 'death row phenomenon'. After considering the effects of the 'death row syndrome', the

[145] AI, *Zambia: Time to Abolish the Death Penalty*, AI Index: AFR 63/004/2001, p. 17.

[146] AI, *Caribbean: Unacceptably Limiting Human Rights Protection: An Update*, AI Index: AMR 05/001/2000.

[147] See AI, 'People's Republic of China: The Death Penalty: Killing Chickens to Scare Monkeys', Paper presented to the 1st World Congress against the Death Penalty, Strasbourg, 21–3 June 2001.

[148] AI, *Japan: Amnesty International Condemns Executions*, AI Index: ASA 22/006/1997.

[149] AI, *Japan: Resumption of Executions and Ill-Treatment of Prisoners on Death Row*, AI Index: ASA 22/09/93. See also 'Life in the Shadow of Death: Capital Punishment in Japan is Cloaked in Secrecy', *International Herald Tribune*, 4 May 2001.

[150] See OSCE, *The Death Penalty in the OSCE Area*. Office of Democratic Institutions and Human Rights, OD/HR Background Paper 1999/1 (1999), p. 13.

[151] It was reported that, owing to this, two men were executed in Saudi Arabia in 1983 for murders committed in 1966 and 1968. See Sandra Mackey, *The Saudis: Inside the Desert Kingdom* (1987), p. 270–271.

European Court of Human Rights decided in July 1989 in the case of *Soering* v. *UK* that it would be a breach of Article 3 of the European Convention on Human Rights for the United Kingdom to extradite the prisoner who would face the death sentence in Virginia, because his inevitably long wait on death row would amount to inhuman and degrading treatment and punishment.[152] The Judicial Committee of the Privy Council in London has gone some way to try to define what length of stay on death row is compatible with the human rights of the offender. Inmates had waited for up to twelve years in Jamaica and Trinidad and Tobago before being executed. Finding the conditions of confinement to be intolerable, the Privy Council ruled in 1993 in the cases of *Pratt and Morgan* v. *Attorney General for Jamaica* that it would amount to inhuman and degrading punishment to execute a prisoner after a wait of five years, and even held out hope that a wait of over two years might be arguably inhumane treatment. Lord Griffiths, delivering the judgment, said:

There is an instinctive revulsion against the prospect of hanging a man after he has been held under sentence of death for many years. What gives rise to this instinctive revulsion? The answer can only be our humanity; we regard it as an inhuman act to keep a man facing the agony of execution over a long extended period of time . . . To execute these men now after holding them in custody in an agony of suspense so many years would be inhuman punishment within the meaning of section 17(1) [of the Constitution of Jamaica].

This judgment applies to other Commonwealth countries in the Caribbean and to several more for whom the Judicial Committee of the Privy Council is the final court of appeal.[153]

However, not all courts have followed these judgments. Asked in 1991 to apply the test in *Soering*, the Supreme Court of Canada ruled that the extradition of *Kindler*, who was facing capital punishment in Pennsylvania, did not violate the Canadian Constitution. Having decided this, the majority declared that 'The death row phenomenon and the psychological stress inherent in it cannot be dismissed lightly, but it pales by comparison to the death penalty. Moreover a defendant is never required to pursue the delay of appellate remedies.'[154]

However, a decade later, in February 2001, the Canadian Supreme Court in *Burns* changed its mind and held that unconditional extradition to the state of Washington, without assurance that the death penalty will not be imposed, would violate Section 7 of the Canadian Charter of Rights and Freedom (see Chapter 1

---

[152] *Soering* v. *United Kingdom*, Federal Republic of Germany intervening, 161 *Eur. Ct. H.R.* (ser. A) 34 (1989).

[153] Pratt and Morgan had spent more than fourteen years on death row. The judgment affected 105 prisoners in Jamaica. *Pratt and Morgan* v. *Attorney General for Jamaica* [1993] 4 All E.R. 769 and 783 (PC). See William A. Schabas, 'Execution Delayed, Execution Denied', *Criminal Law Forum* 5 (1994), pp. 180–193. A similar judgment on the unconstitutionality of long waits on death row was decided by the Zimbabwean Supreme Court in June 1993 in *Catholic Commission for Justice and Peace in Zimbabwe* v. *Attorney General, Human Rights Law Journal* 14 (1993), p. 323. But William Schabas notes that a mere five months later a constitutional amendment negated this ruling, 'Execution Delayed, Execution Denied', 7 and 54 and accompanying text.

[154] *Kindler* v. *Canada (Minister of Justice)*, 1991 Criminal Reports 8 C.R. (4th), p. 5. See Schabas, n. 89 above, pp. 913–923.

page 22). In part, this decision reflected a different judgement about the significance of the 'death row phenomenon':

The finality of the death penalty, combined with the determination of the criminal justice system to try to satisfy itself that the conviction was not wrongful, inevitably produces lengthy delays, and the associated psychological trauma to death row inhabitants . . . The 'death row phenomenon' is not a controlling factor in s.7 [of the Canadian Charter of Rights and Freedoms] balance, but even many of those who regard its horrors as self-inflicted concede that it is a relevant consideration.

In a description of how the court weighed factors in the Section 7 balance the Court also stated: 'we regard it as an inhuman act to keep a man facing the agony of execution over a long extended period of time.'[155]

In the United States the issue remains an 'important undecided one', yet to be fully tested by the Supreme Court.[156] But fifteen years on death row was not regarded by a Federal Court of Appeals in 1998 as a situation that 'even begins to approach a constitutional violation' of cruel and unusual punishment prohibited by the Eighth Amendment.[157] In the cases of *Knight* v. *Florida* and *Moore* v. *Nebraska* the Court decided not to hear at this time (1999) an appeal from two death row inmates concerning the cruelty of the amount of time they had spent on death row. Justice Breyer dissenting stated: 'Both of these cases involve astonishingly long delays . . . The claim that time has rendered the execution inhuman is a particularly strong one.'[158] Similarly, when dissenting in the case of *Elledge* v. *Florida* in 1998, Justice Breyer wrote that a lengthy delay between sentencing and execution may be unconstitutional: 'After such a delay, an execution may well cease to serve the legitimate penological purposes that otherwise provide a necessary constitutional justification for the death penalty.'[159]

The suffering of prisoners, kept, often in very restricted circumstances and under conditions of mortal uncertainty, seems to me to violate the spirit of Safeguard No. 9.

---

[155] *United States* v. *Burns*, 2001 SCC 7. File No.: 26129. Once the state of Washington, which had sought the extradition, had given these assurances, the prisoner and his associate were surrendered to face trial in the United States.

[156] In *Lackey* v. *Texas* (1995) the Supreme Court denied the petition for a writ of certiorari to a prisoner who sought to raise the question whether spending seventeen years on death row violates the Eighth Amendment's prohibition against cruel and unusual punishment. Justice Stevens, in denying the writ, stated that this did not constitute a ruling on the merits but that 'a denial of certiorari on a novel issue will permit the state and federal courts to "serve as laboratories in which the issue receives further study before it is addressed by this Court" '.

[157] *Chambers* v. *Bowersox*, 157 F.3d 560 at p. 570 (8th Cir. 1998).

[158] *Knight* v. *Florida*; *Moore* v. *Nebraska*, 528 U.S. 990 (1999).

[159] *Elledge* v. *Florida*, 525 U.S. 944 (1998).

4

Protecting the Vulnerable from Capital Punishment

The United Nations has established safeguards to protect juveniles, the aged, pregnant women, and new mothers, the insane, and the mentally retarded from being executed. In 1984 Safeguard No. 3 established the norm that *'persons below 18 years of age at the time of the commission of the crime shall not be sentenced to death, nor shall the death sentence be carried out on pregnant women, or on new mothers, or on persons who have become insane'*. This was strengthened in 1989 by establishing that there should be *'a maximum age beyond which a person may not be sentenced to death or executed; and by eliminating the death penalty for persons suffering from mental retardation or extremely limited mental competence, whether at the stage of sentence or execution'*. This chapter reviews the extent to which these safeguards have been adhered to.

1. THE ISSUE OF JUVENILES

In addition to the force of the UN safeguards, states that are party to the International Covenant on Civil and Political Rights (ICCPR) (Article 6 (5)) and the American Convention on Human Rights (Article 4 (5)) are prohibited from imposing capital punishment for offences committed by persons below 18 years of age, unless of course they add a reservation to this effect—as the United States of America has done.[1] Moreover, this prohibition is embodied in the Convention on the Rights of the Child (Article 37a),[2] which has been ratified by every country except the United States and Somalia, although in May 2002 Somalia signed the Convention and stated its intention to ratify it in the near future. In recent years Yemen (1994), China (1997), and Sudan (1998) have passed legislation to prohibit the use of the death penalty for such 'juveniles', and in 2000 a bill banning the death penalty for people under 18 was introduced in Thailand.[3]

---

[1] See the discussion in Ch. 2 above at page 66. Also, William A. Schabas, 'Les Réserves des États-Unis d'Amérique au pacte international relatif aux droits civils et politiques en ce qui à trait a la peine de mort', *Revue Universelle des Droits de l'Homme* 6 (1994), pp. 137–150, an article inspired by the execution on 1 July 1993 of Curtis Paul Harris in Texas for a crime committed when he was a minor.

[2] Adopted by General Assembly Resolution 44/125 of 20 Nov. 1989, entered into force on 2 Sept. 1990, and currently ratified by 191 countries. Also in the Draft United Nations Standard Minimum Rules for the Administration of Juvenile Justice, which were adopted in 1984: known as the Beijing Rules, and adopted by General Assembly Resolution 40/33, 29 Nov. 1985.

[3] AI, *Report 2001*, p. 240.

In 1999 the UN Sub-Commission on the Promotion and Protection of Human Rights condemned 'unequivocally the imposition and execution of the death penalty on those aged under 18 at the time of commission of the offence' and called on all states to commit themselves to abolishing the death penalty for such persons.[4] However, at least 16 countries that are parties to the Convention on the Rights of the Child have not yet formally abolished the powers to sentence juveniles to death.[5] In several of these countries the minimum age is fixed as low as 16 and, in a few, death sentences may be imposed on even younger children, sometimes because (as under Malaysia's 1975 Internal Security Act) no distinction is drawn between adults and minors. In some of these countries youth is statutorily defined as a mitigating factor, but by no means in all. For example, in India the Supreme Court upheld the death sentence in May 2001 on a youth who had been convicted of murder at a time when he was suspected of being only 15 years of age, whereas under India's Juvenile Justice Act persons under the age of 16 cannot be sentenced to death.[6] The prisoner was, however, tried in an adult court, and the Supreme Court in twice reviewing the sentence has declared that 'the awarding of a lesser sentence only on the ground of the appellant being a youth at the time of occurrence cannot be considered as a mitigating circumstance'.[7] Pakistan, which ratified the Convention of the Rights of the Child in 1990, issued a Juvenile Justice System Ordinance in July 2000 prohibiting imposition of the death penalty on anyone under the age of 18 at the time of the offence.[8] However, it was not applied to those juveniles already under sentence of death (in breach of UN Safeguard No. 2), for in November 2001 it was reported that a young man was hanged for a murder he had allegedly committed when he was 13. It was only in December 2001 that the President of Pakistan, Pervez Musharraf, commuted the death sentences of all the 100 or so juveniles on death row to life imprisonment.[9]

---

[4] Resolution 1999/4. The vote was 14 in favour and 5 opposed with 5 abstentions. The UN Sub-Commission on the Promotion and Protection of Human Rights was previously the Sub-Commission on Prevention of Discrimination and Protection of Minorities. The resolution also requested the UN Secretary-General to report to the Sub-Commission at its next session on the number of executions of juvenile offenders and on the total number of executions worldwide.

[5] These 16 countries are: Afghanistan, Bangladesh, Burundi, Congo (formerly Zaire), Egypt, India, Indonesia, Iran, Iraq, Malaysia, Morocco, Myanmar, Nigeria (except in federal law), North Korea, Saudi Arabia, United Arab Emirates. In addition to these countries are 25 states in the United States of America. Also, under Argentinian military law there is no bar to sentencing offenders under 18 to death, although it is a mitigating factor. In Cyprus, where no death sentences have ever been imposed under the Military Criminal Code, the minimum age for imposing a death sentence is 16; youth is not a statutory mitigating factor but would be considered under case law. Several countries have adopted a higher exemption age than 18: it is age 20 in Bulgaria, Cuba, and Thailand.

[6] AI, *Death Penalty News*, June 2001, AI Index: ACT 53/003/2001.   [7] See *ibid*, p. 4.

[8] The Pakistan Penal Code and Code of Criminal Procedure do not establish an age limit below which the death penalty may not be imposed, but in 2000 the government of Pakistan restricted the use of the death penalty to adults when it issued the Juvenile Justice System Ordinance 2000, which prohibits the death penalty for anyone under the age of 18 at the time of committing the offence. AI, *Death Penalty News*, Dec. 2000, AI Index: ACT 53/001/2001, and AI, News Release, *Pakistan: Young Offenders Taken off Death Row*, AI Index: ASA 33/029/2001.

[9] Reported in AI, News Release, *Pakistan: Young Offenders Taken off Death Row*, AI Index: ASA 33/029/2001, and AI, *Death Penalty News*, Dec. 2001, AI Index: ACT 001/2002/, p. 2.

A further difficulty arises in those countries where the poor, especially 'street children', may have no legal proof of age. For instance, it has been noted in the Philippines that despite the law prohibiting the sentencing to death, of 'juveniles' 13 young people under the age of 18 at the time of the offence were sentenced to death and at the end of 2001 nine of them remained on death row.[10]

In the United States the law varies from state to state. In the case of *Thompson* v. *Oklahoma* (1988) the majority of the US Supreme Court ruled that it was unconstitutional to impose the death penalty on a person who had committed the offence when aged 15, but over this age it was a matter for state legislatures. One year later, in *Stanford* v. *Kentucky* and *Wilkins* v. *Missouri*, the Court held, by a five to four majority, that it was not unacceptable to the values of contemporary society and therefore did not violate the constitution to sentence to death persons who had committed murders when aged 16 and 17.[11] This was so, even though opinion polls have shown that the majority of the population questioned have been opposed to the use of capital punishment for juveniles.[12] Furthermore, it should be noted that since 1983 the American Bar Association has declared itself in principle opposed to the imposition of capital punishment upon any person who committed the offence under the age of 18.[13]

By March 2002 only 13 of the 38 retentionist states, as well as the federal jurisdiction, had set the minimum age at 18. In four it was age 17, in 12 states it was age 16, and in seven states the minimum age is not specified.[14] Thus 24 state legislatures do not adhere to, nor believe they are legally bound by, international conventions because the Federal government has refused to ratify any restrictions on the execution of persons which has not been defined as unconstitutional by the US Supreme Court. The only special protection provided in states where the lower age limit is 16

[10] See Free Legal Assistance Group (FLAG), 'Position Paper on the Death Penalty Bills, *Flag Newsletter*, Dec. 2001.

[11] See Kenneth E. Gewirth and Clifford K. Dorne, 'Imposing the Death Penalty on Juvenile Murderers: A Constitutional Assessment', *Judicature* 75(1) (1991), pp. 6–15. Also, Joan Kirkpatrick, 'The Relevance of Customary International Norms to the Death Penalty in the United States', *Georgia Journal of International and Comparative Law* 25 (1995), pp. 1–16. It should be noted that in *Thompson* v. *Oklahoma* the Court had accepted that international practice was relevant to its decision, yet in *Stanford* v. *Kentucky* the majority held that 'it is *American* conceptions of decency that is dispositive' not the juvenile sentencing practices of other countries. See Harold Hongju Koh, 'Paying "Decent Respect" to World Opinion on the Death Penalty', *UC Davis Law Review* 35 (2002), pp. 1085–1131 at 1100–1.

[12] It appears from at least one survey in a retentionist state (Ohio) that the majority (two-thirds) of the public questioned in a telephone survey were opposed to the death penalty for juveniles over the age of 14 convicted of murder. See S. E. Skovoron, J. E. Scott, and F. E. Cullen, 'The Death Penalty for Juveniles: An Assessment of Public Support', *Crime and Delinquency* 35 (1989), pp. 546–561. A Gallup Poll in 1994 had found that 61% said that 'teenagers should not be spared the death penalty on account of their age'; reported in Samuel R. Gross, 'Update: American Public Opinion on the Death Penalty— It's Getting Personal', *Cornell Law Review* 83 (1998), pp. 1448–1475 at 1466. But a poll taken in Arizona in July 2000 found that only 37% of respondents favoured the death penalty when the convicted murderer is a juvenile offender; www.deathpenaltyinfo.org/Polls.html.

[13] See Victor Streib, 'Moratorium on the Death Penalty for Juveniles', *Law and Contemporary Problems* 61 (1998), pp. 55–74 at 56.

[14] See Bureau of Justice Statistics, *Capital Punishment 2000* (2001). Indiana raised the age from 16 to 18 in March 2002.

or 17 is the ruling in *Eddings* v. *Oklahoma* (1982) that age, emotional upbringing, and childhood experiences should always be considered as mitigating factors. However, it is clear that courts do not always have before them, or give full consideration to, such mitigating factors.[15] On the other hand, it is of significance that the death penalty provisions introduced into federal law by the Violent Crime Control Act of 1994 did exempt persons who were less than 18 years of age at the time of the offence.

The arguments on both sides in the United States have been predictable. Those who oppose reform of the law have claimed that any 'bright line' fixing the minimum age of those who may be punished by death would prove to be arbitrary. Although they accept that youth should be a mitigating factor, they argue that there are some among those who commit murder below the age of 18 whose crimes are so heinous and who show such dangerous propensities that they should be treated as adults—each case should be judged on its own merits.[16] Those who oppose executing those who have committed the crime when still under age 18, argue that juveniles should a priori be treated, as a category, differently because they are less mature and therefore less culpable than adults: there should be no discretion, whatever the circumstances of the individual case. Not only do they believe that merciless retribution is an inappropriate response to any juvenile, they also point out that young persons who commit murder have often themselves been victims of abuse and that the state therefore has a duty to try to rehabilitate rather than eliminate them. Furthermore, any attempt to allow exceptions would most likely result in arbitrariness and error in the infliction of an irreversible penalty.[17]

There is a strong empirical basis for these claims. Most of the juveniles who have received the death sentence in the United States have been shown to have an unusually high incidence of neurological impairment, psychiatric disorders, low IQ, and histories of being seriously abused.[18] Furthermore, a study of all cases in the United States between 1973 and 1991 showed that most juveniles sentenced to death had been severely disadvantaged by the fact that mitigating factors had neither been properly investigated nor brought effectively forward at either trial or appeal hearings.[19]

In 1986 Victor Streib, a leading scholar in this field, expressed the hope that the seven juveniles who had been sentenced to death in that year, and the 28 then under

---

[15] See Dinah A. Robinson and Otis H. Stephens, 'Patterns of Mitigating Factors in Juvenile Death Penalty Cases', *Criminal Law Bulletin* 28 (1992), pp. 246–275.

[16] See, for example, Warren M. Kato, Note and Comment, 'The Juvenile Death Penalty', *Journal of Juvenile Law* 18 (1997), pp. 112–149.

[17] See, for example, Carol Steiker and Jordan Steiker, 'ABA's Proposed Moratorium. Defending Categorical Exemptions to the Death Penalty: Reflections on the ABA's Resolutions Concerning the Execution of Juveniles and Persons with Mental Retardation', *Law and Contemporary Problems* 61 (1998), pp. 89–104.

[18] See D. O. Lewis *et al.*, 'Neuropsychiatric, Psychoeducational, and Family Characteristics of 14 Juveniles Condemned to Death in the United States', *American Journal of Psychiatry* 145 (1988), pp. 584–589. Also D. O. Lewis, *Guilty by Reason of Insanity: A Psychiatrist Explores the Minds of Killers* (1999).

[19] See Robinson and Stephens, n. 15 above, pp. 246–275. Also see Victor L. Streib, *Death Penalty for Juveniles* (1987).

the death sentence in the United States, were 'simply the last examples of a fading practice'.[20] Although bills have been introduced in several states in recent years to raise the lower age limit to 18,[21] in the same or other states alternative bills have come forward to lower the age to 17 or 16.[22] By the end of 2001 there were still 'juveniles' on death row in 15 states, as many as 30 of them in Texas.[23] Of the 18 'juveniles' (they were of course much older by the time they were put to death) executed between 1976 and December 2001, 15 had met their fate since 1990.[24] Indeed, nine[25] of the 15 persons convicted as juveniles who have been executed anywhere in the world between 1997 and the end of 2001 were put to death in the United States.[26] Thus the trend has not been going the way predicted or hoped for by Professor Streib: there has been no sign of the practice 'fading'.

It is certainly arguable that the prohibition on the use of the death penalty for persons convicted when juveniles has become a principle of 'customary international

---

[20] Streib, 'Juvenile Death Penalties: The Beginning of the End of a Scandalous American Practice', Paper presented at the 1986 Annual Meeting, of the American Society of Criminology, Atlanta, Ga., and his 'Imposing the Death Penalty on Children', in Kenneth C. Haas and James A. Inciardi (eds), *Challenging Capital Punishment* (1988), pp. 245–267. For a historical perspective, see Robert L. Hale, *A Review of Juvenile Executions in America* (1997).

[21] Bills that unsuccessfully attempted to prevent the execution of juveniles were put before the legislature during 1998 and 1999 in Indiana, Iowa, Kentucky, South Dakota (exempting under 16s vetoed by governor but passed by the legislature), and Texas. Such bills were still pending in Pennsylvania, South Carolina, and South Dakota.

[22] During 1998–9 in California. Oregon, Wisconsin, and Texas to reduce the age to 16 and in New York to reduce it to 17.

[23] 14 in Alabama, 5 in Arizona, 4 in Florida, 4 in Georgia, 2 in Kentucky, 3 in Louisiana, 6 in Mississippi, 2 in Missouri, 2 in Nevada, 1 in North Carolina, 1 in Oklahoma, 3 in Pennsylvania, 5 in South Carolina, 30 in Texas (as counted from data available on the Texan death row, see www.tdcj.state. tx.us/stat/offendersondrow.htm), 2 in Virginia. See AI, *United States of America: Too Young to Vote, Old Enough to be Executed. Texas Set to Kill Another Child Offender*, AI Index: AMR 51/105/2001.

[24] The only person executed during this period who had been aged 16 at the time of the offence was Sean Sellers, by the state of Oklahoma on 4 Feb. 1999. It had been forty years since a person of this age at the time of committing the offence had been executed. He was Leonard Shockley, executed on 10 Apr. 1959. See Victor L. Streib, 'Executing Women, Children, and the Retarded: Second Class Citizens in Capital Punishment', in J. R. Acker, R. M. Bohm, and C. S. Lanier (eds), *America's Experiment with Capital Punishment* (1998), pp. 201–221 at 207.

[25] Of these nine, 5 were executed in Texas, 1 in Oklahoma, and 3 in Virginia.

[26] See AI, *United States of America: Failing the Future—Death Penalty Developments, March 1998–March 2000*, p. 37, AI Index: AMR 51/03/00. Also, AI, *Children and the Death Penalty: Executions Worldwide since 1990*, AI Index: ACT 50/10/00. Executions had also taken place in the Democratic Republic of the Congo, Iran, Nigeria, Pakistan, and Saudi Arabia. Despite a moratorium on executions announced in December 1999 by the Minister for Human Rights of the Democratic Republic of Congo, a 14-year-old child soldier was executed in January 2000 within thirty minutes of his trial. He and four other soldiers had been found guilty of murdering a driver. See AI, *Death Penalty News*, June 2000, AI Index: ACT 53/002/2000, p. 4. An item in *Death Penalty News*, Dec. 1999, stated that on 24 Oct. 1999 the Tehran newspaper *Keyhan* reported that a 17-year-old and an 18-year-old male had been hanged in Iran for murdering a man and his 16-year-old son; AI Index: ACT 53/05/99, p. 5. And in May 2001 another prisoner was hanged in Iran for committing a murder when he was just 16 years old, *Death Penalty News*, June 2001, AI Index: ACT 53/003/2001, p. 4. In relation to the execution of a 17-year-old male in Nigeria, see Special Rapporteur, *Report*, E/CN.4/1998/68, para. 91. For the report of the execution in Pakistan of a male who at the time of the offence was 14 years of age, see AI, *Report 1998*, p. 269. In May 2002 the State of Texas executed Napoleon Beazley, an African American aged 26, who had been convicted of a murder committed when he was 17.

law', binding on all countries regardless of whether or not they have ratified international treaties. Thus, the UN High Commissioner on Human Rights, when appealing to the US authorities in June 1999 to prevent the execution of Chris Thomas in Virginia, called upon them to 'reaffirm the customary international law ban on the use of the death penalty on juvenile offenders'.[27] Yet, in 1999 the US Solicitor General filed a brief in the US Supreme Court setting out the government's view that the United States is not obliged under customary international law or US treaty obligations to exempt children. It believes that it can continue to execute juveniles by virtue of its reservation to Article 6 (5) of the ICCPR.[28] The Supreme Court has stood aloof. But its decision in 2002 banning the execution of the mentally retarded (see pages 129–130), has given hope that—especially if a few more states were to prohibit the execution of juvenile offenders—the Supreme Court will before long rule it unconstitutional.

Of course, the discussion above does not tell the whole story. The number of 'juveniles' executed after conviction before a court of law is tiny compared with those who have been victims of extra-judicial executions and 'disappearances' in several countries during the last twenty years. In the 1990s Brazil, Colombia, and Guatemala in particular were indicted on this account,[29] and as recently as 2000 the United Nations Special Rapporteur on extra-judicial, summary, or arbitrary executions alleged that the right to life of children had been violated in Bolivia, Burundi, Colombia, Honduras, Israel, Myanmar, Nepal, the Russian Federation, Rwanda, and Sudan.

2. THE QUESTION OF THE AGED

The Economic and Social Council of the United Nations has urged all member states to establish a maximum age beyond which persons may not be sentenced to death or executed, but only a few countries have done so. No one over 70 years of age may be executed in the Philippines and Sudan; in Kazakhstan and the Russian Federation no one over age 65; and in Mongolia, Guatemala, and Mexico (for military offences) no person over 60.[30]

The reason why this safeguard is not more widely embraced is probably because the rationale for exempting persons on the basis of age per se is less easy to accept than the rationale for exempting the young on the grounds of their lesser responsibility. Of course, age can bring lesser responsibility when senility can be established,

---

[27] See AI, *United States of America: Failing the Future—Death Penalty Developments, March 1998–March 2000*, AI Index: AMR 51/03/00, p. 37.

[28] *Ibid.*, p. 41.

[29] United Nations, *Report of the Special Rapporteur on Extrajudicial, Summary or Arbitrary Executions* (hereafter cited as Special Rapporteur's, *Report*), submitted to the Commission on Human Rights, Resolution 1993/71, E/CN.4/1994/7, para. 722. And *Report* pursuant to Resolution 1994/82, E/CN.4/1995/61, para. 412.

[30] There are other exemptions. For example, in Sudan Islamic law exempts a father who kills his son or daughter.

but this can always be taken into account as an exculpating form of insanity or limited mental capacity.

Very little information is available on the ages of persons executed worldwide, but it is known, for example, that in Japan a man of 70 was executed in 1993 and another in 1995 and at least 13 persons aged over 60 were on death row, the oldest being aged 83. In December 2001 the oldest person on death row in the United States, still awaiting execution was 84, having been under sentence of death for twenty-nine years. This is yet another aspect of the 'death row phenomenon', which was discussed in Chapter 3.

3. THE EXEMPTION OF PREGNANT WOMEN

It is by no means universally the case that pregnant women are exempted from the death penalty by law, or that they are spared as 'new mothers' after having given birth. However, in recent years there have been no reports of pregnant women being executed, although a death sentence was imposed on one in the Democratic Republic of Congo in 1998.[31] It is not known whether any women with recently born children have been executed since 1994.

Once a woman has given birth, some countries (such as Kuwait) automatically commute the sentence to imprisonment for life. But the following countries have informed the United Nations that they would not invariably do so: Bahrain, Bangladesh, Barbados, Burundi, Cameroon, Egypt, Guatemala, Guinea, Japan, Jordan, Lebanon, Niger, Rwanda, South Korea, Togo, and Turkey. The laws of several countries specify no minimum period before a woman who has been delivered of a child may be executed; the execution is merely 'stayed' (Barbados, Cameroon, Japan, Lebanon, Niger, Rwanda, South Korea, Thailand, Togo, Turkey and the United Arab Emirates). But others set specific periods. In Indonesia the period is 40 days, in Egypt and Libya 2 months, in Jordan 3 months,[32] in the Philippines 1 year,[33] and in Yemen 2 years, provided that there is someone to support the child. In Antigua and Barbuda, Belarus, Indonesia, and now in China, the imposition of the death penalty is no longer allowed if a female offender is pregnant at the time of the trial.[34]

Although there is no international norm barring the sentencing to death and execution of women in general, they have been exempted altogether from capital punishment in a few countries, mainly those associated with the former Soviet

---

[31] See Special Rapporteur's *Report*, E/CN.4/1999/39/Add. 1, para. 68.

[32] Article 358 of the Penal Procedure Code of Jordan. However, Article 17 of the Penal Code stipulates that 'in the event that a woman under sentence of death proves to be pregnant, the death penalty shall be commuted to hard labour for life'.

[33] Republic Act No. 8177, amending Art. 81 of the Revised Penal Code, as amended by section 24 of Republic Act No. 7659.

[34] See Hans-Jörg Albrecht, 'The Death Penalty in China from a European Perspective', in M. Nowak and Xin Chunying (eds), *EU–China Human Rights Dialogue: Proceedings of the Second EU–China Legal Experts' Seminar Held in Beijing on 19 and 20 October 1998* (2000), pp. 95–118 at 97.

system: Belarus, Mongolia, Uzbekistan, and the Russian Federation. Nor has a woman been executed in Cuba since the revolution. Nevertheless, women are usually not categorically exempted, and indeed the case for exempting them as a matter of principle is not easy to establish.[35] Reports of women sentenced to death have come from many retentionist countries, including China, Congo, Indonesia, Iraq, Japan, Nigeria, Saudi Arabia, Thailand, and the United States. In the United States 54 women were on death row by the end of 2001.

In 1998, when the state of Texas executed a woman, it was the first such execution in the United States since 1984, but since then another six women (three of them in Oklahoma in 2001) have been executed.[36] Women have also been executed recently in Japan (a man and his wife in 1997), Botswana (2001), and more frequently in China (according to Amnesty International's *Death Penalty Log* at least 33 women were executed in 1999) and in Saudi Arabia, where at least nine women were executed between 1997 and 2000.

4. PROTECTION OF THE INSANE

It has already been established by both the Ancel (1962) and Morris Reports (1967) to the United Nations that in all retentionist countries there are provisions that, in one way or another, exclude the insane from liability to the death penalty.[37] But Marc Ancel's caveat is as pertinent today as it was when he raised it forty years ago: 'it would have been interesting to discover to what extent insanity or mental disturbance *in reality* barred death sentences' (my emphasis).

In the United States a number of the retentionist states and the US Federal government modified various features of the insanity defence in the wake of John Hinckley's acquittal in 1987, on grounds of insanity, for attempting to assassinate President Reagan. Notwithstanding these changes, all but three states and the federal government have retained the insanity defence as a ground of acquittal. Twelve states have also supplemented the insanity defence with an optional verdict of 'Guilty but Mentally Ill', which appears to preclude a death sentence. While the impact of the various changes in the insanity defence on the proportion of defendants in capital cases who are sentenced to death is hard to gauge,[38] there is no doubt that psychiatric evidence is of growing importance after a finding of guilt to a capital charge. This is because, before deciding on whether or not the defendant should be sentenced to death, the court (usually the jury) must consider the defendant's mental

---

[35] For an interesting discussion of this issue, see Jenny E. Carroll, Note, 'Images of Women and Capital Sentencing among Female Offenders: Exploring the Outer Limits of the Eighth Amendment and Articulated Theories of Justice', *Texas Law Review* 75 (1997), pp. 1413–1451.

[36] For a very thorough state-by-state study relating to the 175 women sentenced to death between 1900 and 1998, see Kathleen A. O'Shea, *Women and the Death Penalty in the United States, 1990–1998* (1999).

[37] In its response to the UN Sixth Quinquennial Survey in 1999 Togo (an abolitionist de facto country) indicated that the law would allow death sentences to be imposed on insane persons or those suffering from mental retardation. This may have been an error.

[38] See R. D. Mackay, 'Post-Hinckley Insanity in the USA', *Criminal Law Review* (1988), pp. 88–96.

state in relation to mitigating his or her culpability for the crime or, in some states, assessing the defendant's future dangerousness (see Chapter 6 pages 183–184).

Of course, where the line is drawn between mental incapacity, amounting to 'insanity' for the purpose of a defence to the crime, and mental abnormality, amounting to diminished responsibility for the crime, remains in many cases a mystery. It is dependent not only on the mental state of the person concerned at the time he or she is examined by a psychiatrist, but also on the sympathy of the jury, the heinousness of the crime, and the competence, authority, and persuasiveness of the psychiatrists before the court. It is made even more difficult to assess when psychiatrists appear for both prosecution and the defence, each with a different interpretation of the defendant's mental state. Where a psychiatrist is asked to assess not only those features of the defendant's mental state that might mitigate the penalty but also those that might indicate his potential as 'a continuing serious threat to society', the testimony can obviously have quite opposite effects on the decision whether or not to impose the death penalty. Thus, psychiatric testimony has become a two-edged sword, such that 'efforts to show diminished capacity' may be 'self-defeating'.[39]

Diminished mental responsibility is specifically listed as a mitigating factor in the capital sentencing statutes of most American states, and psychiatric evidence of this nature must be admitted and considered by the sentencing judge or jury under various constitutional rulings of the US Supreme Court, whether or not the factor is specified by statute. Typical formulations of the mitigating criteria refer to impairment of the defendant's capacity 'to appreciate the criminality of his conduct or to conform his conduct to the requirements of the law' or to the influence of 'extreme mental or emotional disturbance'. Nevertheless, in *Commonwealth* v. *Moser* (1988) the Pennsylvania Supreme Court upheld the death penalty for a man found by the sentencing panel to have been under the influence of extreme mental or emotional disturbance at the time of the offence and to have no prior criminal record. And in *Commonwealth* v. *Logan* (1988) it upheld the death penalty for a mentally ill man who instructed his attorney to present no mitigating evidence at the sentencing stage. Also in *Commonwealth* v. *Fahy* (1986) the court upheld a death sentence for the torture killing of a 12-year-old girl despite the fact that the jury found that the defendant 'was under the influence of extreme mental or emotional disturbance' and that 'the defendant's capacity to appreciate the criminality of his conduct or conform his conduct to the requirements of law was substantially impaired'.[40]

---

[39] See George E. Dix, 'Psychological Abnormality and Capital Sentencing: The New "Diminished Responsibility" ', *International Journal of Law and Psychiatry* 7 (1984), pp. 249–267 at 265. Also, W. J. Curran and S. M. Hyg, 'Psychiatric Evaluations and Mitigating Circumstances in Capital Punishment Sentencing', *New England Journal of Medicine* 307 (1982), pp. 1431–1432; C. Robert Showalter and Richard J. Bonnie, 'Psychiatrists and Capital Sentencing: Risks and Responsibilities in a Unique Legal Setting', *Bulletin of the American Academy of Psychiatry and Law* 12 (1984), pp. 153–167.

[40] See Bruce Ledewitz, 'Sources of Injustice in Death Penalty Practice: The Pennsylvania Experience', *Dickinson Law Review* 95 (1991), pp. 651–690 at 657–661, who also cites other cases. However, in Louisiana in 1990 a diagnosis of Multiple Personality Disorder was 'recognised as a potentially mitigat-

Where medical examinations are cursory, or carried out by psychiatrists who too rigidly interpret the law, as seems to have been the case, at least in the 1980s, in Zimbabwe for instance,[41] further medical examinations ordered by the court have often revealed that the offender was suffering from mental defect or illness. Thus, it has been accepted by the Judicial Committee of the Privy Council in London that the shortage of qualified forensic psychiatrists in certain Commonwealth Caribbean countries has meant that the mental health of defendants in murder cases is not routinely assessed, either on behalf of the state or by independent psychiatrists for the defence.[42] This must also be the case in other regions where there is a shortage of such experts, especially when combined with a shortage of financial resources available to the defence to obtain an independent mental assessment.

But it is a problem not confined to countries with few psychiatrists. A medical investigation in the 1980s of 15 death row inmates in the United States whose executions were imminent found that 'all had histories of severe head injuries, five had major neurological impairment and seven had other less serious neurological problems (e.g. blackouts, soft signs) . . . Six subjects had schizophreniform psychoses antedating incarceration and two others were manic depressive.'[43] This evidence speaks for itself and there is no reason to think that the situation has changed remarkably for the better in recent years.

There is no reliable information on the extent to which retentionist countries take account of the mental state of a person sentenced to death *after* conviction when deciding whether or not to proceed with the execution. It is clear that subsequent mental illness is no bar to eventual execution in many countries, although it appears that it is often the practice to delay the execution until the person has sufficiently recovered.[44] On the other hand, it has been alleged that a few prisoners who had shown distinct signs of mental illness have been executed in recent years in the United States. The case of Rickey Ray Rector, executed by the state of Arkansas in 1992, is often cited as an example,[45] but more recently Jeremy Vargas Sagastegui was

ing factor in a . . . granting of a new sentencing procedure for a man sentenced to death . . . and the subsequent commutation of his sentence'. *Wilson* v. *Smith* quoted in Dorothy Otnow Lewis and Jennifer S. Bard, 'Multiple Personality and Forensic Issues', *Psychiatric Clinics of North America* 41(3) (1991), pp. 741–756 at 747.

[41] See Mr Justice E. Dumbutshena (Chief Justice of Zimbabwe), 'The Death Penalty in Zimbabwe', *Revue Internationale de Droit Pénal* 58 (1987), pp. 521–532 at 532.

[42] See, for example, *Ramjattan* v. *Trinidad and Tobago, The Times*, 1 Apr. 1999, and *Campbell* v. *Trinidad and Tobago*, 21 July 1999, unreported.

[43] Dr Dorothy O. Lewis *et al.*, 'Psychiatric, Neurological, and Psycho-educational Characteristics of 15 Death Row Inmates in the United States', *American Journal of Psychiatry* 143 (1986), pp. 838–845. Also, Marilyn Feldman, Kathleen Mallouh, and Dorothy O. Lewis, 'Filicidal Abuse in the Histories of 15 Condemned Murderers', *Bulletin of the American Academy of Psychiatry and Law* 14 (1986), pp. 345–352. Eight had been victims of potential filicidal assaults and there was evidence of extraordinary abuse in 12 cases.

[44] Turkey was the only country specifically to state that persons can be executed after medical treatment.

[45] 'Rickey Ray Rector was a brain-damaged African-American who had been sentenced to death by an all-white jury. Rector had destroyed part of his brain when he turned his gun on himself after killing the police officer . . . Logs at the prison show that in the days leading to his execution, Rector was howling

executed in Washington state in 1998 having waived his right to appeal and having represented himself at trial. Three months before he committed the crime he was diagnosed as suffering from schizophrenia and manic depression.[46]

In November 2001 New Mexico resumed executions more than four decades after the last execution by putting to death an allegedly brain-damaged man who had given up his appeals after spending fourteen years on death row.[47] But whether in such cases (and there have been similar reports from Japan and Vietnam) the mental illness could be said to have been of a degree of seriousness amounting to a breach of the safeguard against executing the insane cannot be determined with precision. There is clearly a need for more detailed information to be gathered on this subject.

It is obvious that if persons are detained for long periods on death row awaiting execution, as they are in many countries, their mental states may seriously deteriorate. A survey, conducted in 1985, of the then 36 American states that authorized the death penalty, revealed that each of them had a statutory, common law, case law, or executive clemency provision to ensure that the incompetent should not be executed. Yet a study of the working of the Florida statute revealed that the criteria for incompetence (i.e. that the person is unable to understand the nature of the death penalty and its effects) were vague, as were the procedures for bringing cases to the attention of the governor and for the defendant to contest the validity of either the psychiatrist's or the governor's judgement. In 1986 the US Supreme Court in the case of *Ford* v. *Wainwright* ruled, as a matter of constitutional law, that a state may not execute an incompetent person, and that judicial procedures must be used to adjudicate the question. In *Perry* v. *Louisiana* (1990), where the state wanted to forcibly feed Mr Perry to render him competent for execution, the Supreme Court held that the rule laid down in *Washington* v. *Harper* (1990) should be applied, which stated that although an inmate could refuse psychotropic drugs, this was not an absolute right. This meant that forced medication would be permitted under the Due Process Clause when the state could show that the inmate was likely to be dangerous in the future and that the medication is in the prisoner's medical interest.[48] As a reflection of these serious concerns, the Texas legislature passed into law in 1999 a bill that exempted the 'incompetent' from the death penalty, defined as

and barking like a dog, dancing, singing and laughing inappropriately, and saying that he was going to vote for Clinton (who was Governor of Arkansas and running for the Presidency of the USA). After the execution, guards found that Rector had put aside his pie thinking that he was coming back to eat it after the execution.' Quoted from Stephen B. Bright, 'The Politics of Capital Punishment: The Sacrifice of Fairness for Executions', in Acker, Bohm, and Lanier (eds), n. 24 above, p. 120.

[46] See AI, *United States of America: Failing the Future: Death Penalty Developments, March 1998–March 2000*, AI Index: AMR 51/03/00, p. 18.

[47] AI, *Seven O'Clock Shadow: First New Mexico Execution since 1960 Due*, AI Index: AMR 51/160/2001.

[48] On the problem of finding an adequate terminology for the mentally incompetent, such as 'severe mental impairment', see Roberta M. Harding, ' "Endgame": Competency and the Execution of Condemned Inmates—A Proposal to Satisfy the Eighth Amendment's Prohibition against the Infliction of Cruel and Unusual Punishment', *Saint Louis University Public Law Review* 14 (1994), pp. 105–152. For discussions on 'synthetic sanity' and the competence to be executed, see G. Linn Evans, '*Perry* v. *Louisiana* (1990): Can a State Treat an Incompetent Prisoner to Ready him for Execution?', *Bulletin of*

'One who does not understand that s/he is to be executed and that the execution is imminent, and the reason that s/he is being executed'. But in 2000 only two states, Maryland and Montana, had determined to commute immediately and permanently a death sentence to life imprisonment without parole once a prisoner under sentence of death is certified to be insane.[49]

The assessment of 'mental competence to be executed' and the treatment of persons under sentence of death has placed psychiatrists in an acute ethical dilemma and aroused considerable controversy. Should a psychiatrist use professional skills to treat a mentally ill person who, upon recovery, may be executed? If not, is the person to be allowed to suffer the pains of acute mental illness? And on what scientific evidence are judgements of competency to be executed based? Are they not inevitably likely to be influenced by the psychiatrist's own views on the morality and efficacy of the death penalty? Indeed there is evidence in the United States that psychiatrists who are willing to make competency assessments are also more likely to favour the death penalty than those who refuse to make such judgements.[50] Nor is it clear in the United States that an indigent defendant has any remedy in due process if his psychiatrist turns out to be incompetent: i.e. there is no right to competent psychiatric assistance.[51]

---

the American Academy of Psychiatry and Law 19 (1991), pp. 249–270 at 256–258; and Keith A. Byers, 'Incompetency, Execution, and the Use of Antipsychotic Drugs', *Arkansas Law Review* 47 (1994), pp. 361–391. For another useful discussion, see Eric M. Kniskern, 'Does *Ford* v. *Wainwright*'s Denial of Executions of the Insane Prohibit the State from Carrying out its Criminal Justice System?', *Southern University Law Review* 26 (1999), pp. 171–195; and for a review of the relevant legislation, see James R. Acker and Charles S. Lanier, 'Unfit to Live, Unfit to Die: Incompetence for Execution under Modern Death Penalty Legislation', *Criminal Law Bulletin* 33 (1997), pp. 107–150.

[49] See Kniskern, n. 48 above, pp. 191–194; Md Code Ann. Art. 27 §75A (1997); Mont. Code Ann. §46–19–201 (1997).

[50] See R. J. Bonnie, 'Dilemmas in Administering the Death Penalty: Conscientious Abstention, Professional Ethics, and the Needs of the Legal System', *Law and Human Behavior* 14 (1990), pp. 67–90; Stanley L. Brodsky, 'Professional Ethics and Professional Morality in the Assessment of Competence for Execution: A Response to Bonnie', *ibid.*, pp. 91–97; R. J. Bonnie, 'Grounds for Professional Abstention in Capital Cases: A Reply to Brodsky', *ibid.*, pp. 99–102; M. A. Deitchman, W. A. Kennedy, and J. C. Beckham, 'Self-Selection Factors in the Participation of Mental Health Professionals in Competency for Execution Evaluations', *ibid.*, 15, pp. 287–303; and D. H. Wallace, 'The Need to Commute the Death Sentence: Competency for Execution and Ethical Dilemmas for Mental Health Professionals', *International Journal of Law and Psychiatry* 15 (1992), pp. 317–337. Also, British Medical Association, *Medicine Betrayed*, Report of a Working Party (1992), pp. 109 and 201. Mark A. Small and Randy K. Otto, 'Evaluations of Competency to be Executed: Legal Contours and Implications for Assessment', *Criminal Justice and Behavior* 18 (1991), pp. 146–158; and for another view, arguing that psychiatrists can ethically carry out this task, see Douglas Mossman, 'Assessing and Restoring Competency to be Executed: Should Psychiatrists Participate?', *Behavioral Sciences and the Law* 5 (1987), pp. 397–405, and his article 'The Psychiatrist and Execution Competency: Fording Murky Ethical Waters', *Case Western Law Review* 43 (1992), pp. 1–95. Also, Robert D. Miller, 'Evaluation of and Treatment to Competency to be Executed: A National Survey and an Analysis', *Journal of Psychiatry and Law* (1988), pp. 67–90. For a thorough study of the Ford case and its consequences, see Kent S. Miller and Michael L. Radelet, *Executing the Mentally Ill: The Criminal Justice System and the Case of Alvin Ford* (1993). See also Robert T. M. Phillips, 'Professionalism, Mental Disability, and the Death Penalty: The Psychiatrist as Evaluator: Conflicts and Conscience', *New York Law School Law Review* 41 (1996), pp. 189–199.

[51] See Gordon B. Burns, 'The Right to Effective Assistance of a Psychiatrist under *Ake* v. *Oklahoma*', *Criminal Law Bulletin* 30 (1994), pp. 429–457.

5. The Status of the Mentally Retarded

The Fifth UN Quinquennial Survey in 1995 asked for the first time whether the law eliminated the death penalty for persons suffering from mental retardation or extremely limited mental competence—a mental development disorder variously referred to in some countries as 'mental handicap' or 'learning disability'.[52] According to the replies from this and the Sixth Survey in 1999, there are no such legal provisions in Tonga, Trinidad and Tobago, or Tunisia.[53] It appears probable that in these and several other countries the mentally retarded are covered by the more general provisions relating to prisoners suffering from mental illness.[54]

Only in its most extreme forms is mental retardation likely to be grounds for acquittal or a verdict of guilty but insane. Rather, it is usually regarded as a factor to be considered in mitigation of sentence, on the grounds of diminished responsibility, as for example in the Thai Penal Code. But it is not merely that the mentally retarded have a lesser capacity to understand the meaning and consequences of their actions and are much less likely to be deterred by threats of punishment; they are also much more vulnerable when, as suspects, they fall into the hands of the criminal justice system. They are likely to be more suggestive, more ready to please by confessing, less knowledgeable about their right not to answer questions without the advice of a lawyer, and less adept at negotiating pleas: more likely therefore to be wrongly convicted.[55] A tragic example of this was the case of Earl Washington, a man with an IQ variously assessed as being between 57 and 69, who was convicted of rape and murder of a young woman in Culpepper, Virginia, in 1982 on the basis of a confession he made to the police. It is not clear that all members of the jury were aware of his degree of mental retardation and so they accepted that he had voluntarily waived his right to remain silent. Yet, sixteen years after he was sentenced to death—at one time he came within three days of execution—he was exonerated and pardoned when a DNA test proved that he was not guilty of the crime.[56] More recently, in the Philippines, a man who was a deaf mute with a mental age of 8 years 5 months had his death sentence for rape and homicide affirmed by the Supreme Court in 1997, and it took two further years before this was reversed after medical tests proved his non-competence.[57]

---

[52] See James Welsh, *Mental Retardation and the Death Penalty*, AI Index: ACT 75/002/2001.

[53] Tunisia, however, stated that in practice 'Courts do not impose the death sentence on mentally retarded persons.'

[54] For example, in Sri Lanka the mentally retarded probably fall under the general provisions relating to 'unsoundness of mind'. The Egyptian Penal Code 'provides that loss of senses and faculty of reasoning at time of commission of crime due either to insanity or mental ailment is considered preclusive of punishment in general'. Similarly, Guinea stated in its reply to the UN that 'such persons are treated in the same way as the cases of mentally ill persons, who are not responsible for their criminal actions'.

[55] See Human Rights Watch, *Beyond Reason: The Death Penalty and Offenders with Mental Retardation* (Mar. 2001), New York, pt. IV.

[56] *Ibid.*, Summary and Recommendations, p. 3. See also Raymond Bonner, 'Death Row Inmate is Freed after DNA Test Clears Him' (referring to Charles Fain freed after nearly eighteen years on death row in Ohio, when DNA analysis of hair which had been said to match his was found by DNA analysis to belong to some other person). *New York Times*, 24 Aug. 2001.

[57] See *FLAG Newsletter*, Dec. 2001.

The problem is that there appears to be no common agreement on how severe such retardation must be to lead to acquittal of the imposition of a lesser sentence than death. For instance, the reply from Belarus in 1995 stated: 'Only persons who have been declared sane (i.e. capable of understanding and controlling their actions) may be criminally prosecuted. If . . . mentally retarded persons or persons with limited mental faculties were aware of the significance of their actions and were able to control them, they are then liable in the manner provided for by the law in the same way as others.' Similarly, Article 18 of the Criminal Law of the People's Republic of China (1997) states that 'If a mental patient has not *completely* lost the ability of recognizing or controlling his own conduct . . . he shall bear criminal responsibility; however he *may* be given a lighter or mitigated punishment' (my emphasis). Presumably this refers not only to those of diminished responsibility due to mental illness but also to those who are not fully competent because of mental retardation. It does not, of course, absolutely bar the execution of those who have a degree of mental retardation, as the word 'may' signifies, and how it is interpreted in the practice of capital punishment is unknown owing to the official secrecy which surrounds the subject in China.[58] Given the speed with which cases are processed, especially during 'strike hard' campaigns, it is not difficult to imagine that there will not always have been a careful review of the accused's state of mental competence before an execution is carried out.

It is impossible, therefore, on a worldwide basis to gauge the extent to which the widespread prohibition on the execution of the mental retarded has in fact provided a safeguard for all those to whom it might apply in principle. This is mainly because in most countries there have been no studies of the mental abilities of prisoners facing the death sentence, there is a shortage of experts to make the assessments, and in any case there may be differences between cultures in defining the level of mental functioning that constitutes 'retardation' and no reliable means of distinguishing between those who are 'learning disabled' and those who simply have very little learning.

Until the Supreme Court of the United States handed down its judgment in *Atkins* v. *Virginia* in June 2002, there was no constitutional bar to sentencing to death mentally retarded persons convicted of murder in the United States. While the United States had not been entirely alone in continuing with this practice—there had been a report of one such execution in Japan[59] and another in Kyrgyzstan[60] in the mid-1990s—by the end of the twentieth century the USA was the only country officially continuing to execute such offenders.

In the late 1980s a groundswell of public opinion began in the United States that persuaded more and more legislatures to prohibit the execution of the mentally retarded.[61] In 1987 the Georgia Board of Pardons and Paroles refused clemency to James Bowden, a man with full-scale IQ of 65, on the grounds that they considered it high enough for him to know right from wrong. In the furore pending his execution, a statewide poll was conducted which found that two-thirds of respondents opposed

[58] See Albrecht, n. 34 above, pp. 97–98.
[59] See Special Rapporteur's *Report*, E/CN.4/1995/61 (Dec. 1994), para. 380.
[60] Special Rapporteur's *Report*, E/CN.4/1997/60 (Dec. 1996), para. 90.
[61] For the position up to 1992, see Miller and Radelet, n. 50 above, pp. 175–176.

the execution of the mentally retarded.[62] A year after Bowden was executed Georgia became the first state to pass a bill prohibiting the execution of the mentally retarded.

In *Penry* v. *Lynaugh* (1989) the Supreme Court had decided that mentally disordered offenders were not 'categorically' exempt from capital punishment and that the appellant, who was mentally retarded, with an IQ of 50–65, organic brain damage, and a history of considerable physical and emotional abuse as a child, should not be spared the death penalty—because although it diminished his blameworthiness, it was held also to increase the probability of dangerous behaviour in the future.[63] The Court held that there was at that time no consensus of opinion in the United States that the execution of the mentally retarded amounted to cruel and unusual punishment, because only two states at that time—Georgia and Maryland—had enacted statutes barring it. This decision, according to a national opinion poll was very unpopular: 71 per cent of those questioned believed that such retarded persons should not be executed.[64]

The controversy in the United States was fuelled by several high-profile cases.[65] It has been claimed that at least forty-four prisoners with 'mental retardation or significant organic brain damage' were executed between 1984 and March 2001—some with intelligence quotients as low as 59 and the lower 70s—equivalent to the mental age of 7- to 10-year-olds.[66] However, the number of the mentally retarded executed each year began to decline substantially: one in 1997, two in 1998, and one in August 2000, when Oliver Cruz, a man with an IQ rated between 64 and 76 depending on the test used, was executed in Texas for rape and murder, the prosecutor having argued that his not being 'very smart' made him 'more dangerous'.[67] Nevertheless, according to a report by Human Rights Watch in 2001, experts believed that there may have been 'two or three hundred' mentally retarded persons on death row in the United States at that time.[68]

By the beginning of the new millennium it had become clear that the time was ripe for a fresh constitutional assault on this practice. By December 2001 Georgia had been

---

[62] In a Gallup Poll taken in 2001 it was similarly found that two-thirds of a sample of the American public were opposed to executing people with mental retardation, and only 16% of those who otherwise supported capital punishment supported the execution of a person who is mentally retarded. Cited in *McCarver* v. *State of North Carolina*, brief of Amici Curiae Diplomats (No. 00–8727), 8 June 2001, p. 17.

[63] See, William A. Schabas, 'International Norms on Execution of the Insane and the Mentally Retarded', *Criminal Law Forum* 4 (1994), pp. 95–117 at 108–109. Penry's death sentence was overturned by the US Supreme Court for a second time in June 2001, but on grounds other than his mental retardation as such: namely, the jury had not been given adequate instructions on how to weigh his mental disabilities in mitigation against the severity of the crime.

[64] See Thomas R. Marshall, 'Public Opinion and the Rehnquist Court', *Judicature* 74 (6) (1991), pp. 322–329 at 324.

[65] See, for example, Special Rapporteur's *Report*, E/CN.4/2001/9 (2001), para. 82.

[66] See D. Keyes, W. Edwards, and R. Perske, 'People with Mental Retardation are Dying, Legally at least 44 have been Executed', *Journal of Mental Retardation* 40(3) (2002), pp. 243–244. Also William J. Edwards, 'Capital Punishment and Mental Disability: *Amici Curiae* Brief in *Penry* v. *Johnson*', *Criminal Law Forum* 12 (2001), pp. 267–276.

[67] Raymond Bonner and Sara Rimer, 'Executing the Mentally Retarded even as Laws Begin to Shift', *New York Times*, 7 Aug. 2000. For excellent summaries of the life histories of the cases cited in this section, as well as others, see Human Rights Watch, n. 55 above, pt. VIII.

[68] Human Rights Watch n. 55 above, Summary and Recommendations, p. 1.

joined by seventeen other states and the federal government, the District of Columbia, and Puerto Rico.[69] President George W. Bush had declared, perhaps in an off-guard moment, in June 2001 that 'we should never execute anybody who is mentally retarded': at least, one might say 'in principle'.[70] The issue was to be tested in the US Supreme Court in the case of *Ernest Paul McCarver* v. *State of North Carolina* (No. 00-8727, 2000), a man with an IQ of 67. In briefs to the court it was argued that the execution of the mentally retarded had become 'manifestly inconsistent with evolving international standards of decency'. This was backed up by the testimonies of distinguished foreign diplomats on the negative reaction of foreign countries to America's failure to ban the 'cruel and uncivilized practice' of executing the mentally retarded. It was argued that to execute McCarver would 'strain diplomatic relations with close American allies, provide diplomatic ammunition to countries with worse human rights records, increase US diplomatic isolation, and impair other United States foreign policy interests; furthermore, that the Supreme Court could not 'meaningfully evaluate 'evolving standards of decency that mark the progress of a maturing society'[71] without weighing international as well as domestic opinion.[72]

This effort became moot when North Carolina abolished capital punishment for the mentally retarded, and applied the act retrospectively to cover all such cases under sentence of death. But in June 2002 the Court held, by a majority of 6 to 3, in the case of *Atkins* v. *Virginia* (122 S.Ct. 2242 (2002)), a man with an IQ of 59 who had been convicted of kidnapping and murdering a 21-year-old airman when he was just 18, that 'evolving standards of decency' had now produced a 'national consensus' in opposition to the execution of the mentally retarded: a consensus that was backed by international condemnation of the practice. It was not just the fact that now twenty, rather than two, jurisdictions had abolished capital punishment of the mentally retarded, it was 'the consistency of the direction of change' that provided 'powerful evidence that today society views mentally retarded offenders as categorically less culpable than the average criminal'. Moreover, the fact that the majority gave weight to the overwhelming disapproval of the practice of sentencing the mentally retarded to death 'within the world community' was a significant shift away from the Supreme Court's previous stance on the relevance of international human rights opinion—despite the fact that the minority, as voiced by Justice Scalia, continued to 'fail to see . . . how the views of other countries regarding the punishment of their citizens provide any support for the Court's ultimate determination'.

The decision in *Atkins* did not, however, lay down how mental retardation should be defined. The majority quoted the definitions of the American Association of Mental Retardation (AAMR) and the American Psychiatric Association, both of which stressed

[69] See Death Penalty Information Center, *Mental Retardation and the Death Penalty*, www.essential.org/dpic/dpicmr.html.

[70] Raymond Bonner, 'President Says the Retarded Should Never be Executed', *New York Times*, 12 June 2001.

[71] *Trop* v. *Dulles*, 356 U.S. 101 (1958).

[72] See Harold Hongu Koh, 'Paying "Decent Respect" to World Opinion on the Death Penalty', *U.C. Davis Law Review* 35 (2002), pp. 1085–1131.

'significant subaverage intellectual functioning'[73] but came to the conclusion that 'we leave to the States the task of developing appropriate ways to enforce the constitutional restriction upon its execution of sentences'.

However, there is no common statutory definition among those states that had already passed laws abolishing capital punishment for the mentally retarded. Although some have an identified IQ threshold, others do not. some stipulate that the defendant's state of mental retardation must have been disclosed by age 18, others by age 22, and yet others have no age limit. 'Additionally, the state statutes contain varying weight of evidence and procedural standards.'[74] Thus, in July 2001, when Missouri banned execution of anyone convicted in future who is mentally retarded, the condition was defined as involving 'substantial limitations in general functioning characterised by significant sub-average intellectual functioning with . . . deficits and limitations in two or more adaptive behaviours such as communication, self-care, home living, or social skills . . . which conditions are manifested and documented before eighteen years of age'; no IQ level was specified.[75] Six American states stipulate that there is a rebuttable presumption that the person is mentally retarded when the tested IQ level is 70 or below,[76] but the Federal Criminal Code has no definition of mental retardation. It thus remains to be seen whether the Supreme Court ruling will be the end of the matter. While there is strong opposition to capital punishment in general, there is likely to be continuing disputes about who is and who is not 'sufficiently' mentally retarded to benefit from the constitutional ruling that to execute the mentally retarded is 'cruel and unusual punishment' prohibited by the Eighth Amendment. It is likely, therefore, that the focus will shift among abolitionists to broaden the definition of those who may benefit from this ruling.[77] It is ironic that, shortly after the *Atkins* decision was handed down, a Texas jury found John Paul Penry, at his third trial, not to be mentally retarded and sentenced him once again to death, despite the fact that he had never tested above an IQ level of 70.

---

[73] The AAMR denied mental retardation as 'substantial limitations in present functioning. It is characterized by significantly subaverage intellectual functioning, existing concurrently with related limitations in two or more of the following applicable adaptive skill areas: communication, self-care, home living, social skills, community use, self direction, health and safety, functional academics, leisure and work. Mental retardation manifests before 18.' The American Psychiatric Association's definition uses almost the same wording. It too stresses that the onset 'must occur' before age 18 years. Neither definition states an IQ level.

[74] See Victor L. Streib, 'Executing Women, Children, and the Retarded: Second Class Citizens in Capital Punishment', in J. R. Acker, R. M. Bohm, and C. S. Lanier (eds), *America's Experiment with Capital Punishment* (1998), pp. 201–221 at p. 215.

[75] See Missouri Legislation, Bill SB 267 (2001).

[76] Kentucky, Maryland, and Nebraska stipulate that an IQ of 70 or below is presumptive evidence of mental retardation; Tennessee and Washington set a 'required' level of IQ at 70 or below; South Dakota's statute states that an IQ level exceeding 70 is presumptive evidence that the defendant does *not* have significant sub-average general intellectual functioning. Arkansas has set an IQ of 65 or below as the standard for a rebuttable presumption of mental retardation.

[77] For example, Dalton Prejean, who was executed in 1990, was widely regarded as mentally retarded although he had a measured IQ of 76; this was seen as equivalent to the mental functioning of a 13½-year-old.

5

Protecting the Innocent

1. International Standards

UN Safeguard No. 4 for the protection of the rights of those facing the death penalty states that *'capital punishment may be imposed only when the guilt of the person charged is based on clear and convincing evidence leaving no room for an alternative explanation of the facts'*.

Furthermore Safeguard No. 5 states that *'capital punishment may only be carried out pursuant to final judgment rendered by a competent court after legal process which gives all possible safeguards to ensure a fair trial, at least equal to those contained in article 14 of the International Covenant on Civil and Political Rights, including the right of anyone suspected of or charged with a crime for which capital punishment may be imposed to adequate legal assistance at all stages of the proceedings'* (Article 14 is reproduced in Appendix 3).

In 1989 the Economic and Social Council added: *'Affording special protection to persons facing charges for which the death penalty is provided, by allowing time and facilities for the preparation of their defence, including the adequate assistance of counsel at every stage of the proceedings, above and beyond the protection afforded in non-capital cases.'*

As mentioned in the Introduction (see page 3 above), it is hardly surprising that nearly all retentionist countries which responded to the circular of 1987 on the provision of safeguards and/or to the Fifth and Sixth Quinquennial Surveys covering the years 1989–98 claimed, in effect, that their rules of criminal procedure or Constitutions required that the decision must only be based on evidence submitted during the course of the proceedings, tested in court, and subjected to cross-examination, the facts of the case against the defendant being established beyond reasonable doubt. The defendant is to be presumed innocent until proven guilty.[1] For

---

[1] In responding to the UN Fifth Survey Bahrain was the only country to say that there was no presumption of innocence. However, the answers to the question on whether a defendant facing the death penalty is not compelled to testify against him or herself or to confess guilt were hard to interpret. Bangladesh reported that defendants can be compelled to testify in the witness box and compelled to confess guilt. The Criminal Procedure Code requires that the accused be examined for the purpose of enabling him 'to explain any circumstances appearing against him', the object being 'to enable the accused to explain each and every circumstance in the evidence against him'. In other words, the burden of proof falls on the defendant not the prosecution. Similarly, in Guinea the practice is said to be that 'the accused and witnesses appear freely and testify, after due hearings of the parties, at a public hearing'. The only question in the Sixth Survey regarding the innocence of the defendant asked whether the death penalty could only be imposed when the guilt of the defendant was established on the basis of clear and convincing evidence. No questions regarding the presumption of innocence were asked.

example, in Egypt the test is 'certitude and certainty stemming from conclusive evidence attributable to the act of the accused' and, furthermore, 'The death penalty . . . must be passed by unanimous opinion, after having consulted the Mufti of the Republic [the official responsible for delivering legal opinions] on the legality of the sentence in accordance with the provisions of the Islamic Shari'a.' However, the replies from several countries were rather more vague. For example, in Chad and Madagascar, unless the law provides otherwise, 'any form of evidence may be brought to establish guilt' and 'the judges shall decide according to their own (deep-seated) inner convictions'.

The next section of this chapter therefore reviews the evidence on whether the protections offered are such that convictions for capital crimes have been free of error and that there is no, or only the very slightest, possibility that an innocent person could be executed.

2. EXECUTION OF THE INNOCENT?

The retentionist countries which replied to the UN Sixth Survey said that no cases of an innocent person being executed had come to light during the period 1994 to 1998. This is not surprising. For who is going to reply that persons have been executed where there was clear doubt about their guilt? It is more important to recognize that observing this safeguard in any country with the death penalty is an aspiration, rather than a statement of what is, in reality, achieved in all cases. The real issues are how the rules of procedure are operated in practice and whether the activities of police, prosecutors, judges, and juries are such as to endeavour scrupulously to avoid any possibility of wrongful conviction. That can only be assessed by careful independent academic empirical research or in-depth case studies.

According to an Amnesty International Report entitled *Fatal Flaws: Innocence and the Death Penalty in the USA*, published in 1998, there have been reports not only from the United States, but also from several other countries, of persons being released from prison, sometimes after many years in custody, on the grounds of their innocence. These reports have come from Belize, China, Japan, Malawi, Malaysia, Pakistan, Papua New Guinea, the Philippines, Trinidad and Tobago, and Turkey (which stated that this was not the case in its response to the survey). In Thailand a recent editorial in the *Bangkok Post* stated that 'Executing someone who has been wrongly convicted, a police scapegoat, is also a disturbingly real possibility in this country.'[2] Furthermore, convictions that had resulted in executions were posthumously overturned in the United Kingdom of Great Britain and Northern Ireland, Uzbekistan, and the Russian Federation.[3] Furthermore, the fact that miscarriages of

---

[2] *Bangkok Post*, 20 Apr. 2001.

[3] AI, *Fatal Flaws: Innocence and the Death Penalty in the USA*, AI Index: AMR 51/ 69/98. In Britain the Court of Appeal in February 1998 quashed the conviction of Mahmoud Hussein Mattan, a Somali national who had been hanged for murder in 1952 (*R* v. *Mattan*, transcript provided by Smith Bernal, *The Independent*, 4 Mar. 1998, or *The Times*, 5 Mar. 1998). And again in July 1998 the Court quashed

justice have continued to surface after abolition of the death penalty has reminded those who might favour restitution of capital punishment of the awful cost. Thus, in the United Kingdom in 1994 the Conservative Home Secretary, Michael Howard, a politician renowned for his tough policy on crime and his previous strong support for capital punishment, told Parliament that the failure of the appellate system to protect the 'Birmingham Six' from wrongful conviction for a terrible terrorist bombing, as well as other cases, had changed his mind: 'When we consider the plight of those who have been wrongly convicted, we cannot but be relieved that the death penalty was not available. We should not fail to consider the irreparable damage that would have been inflicted on the criminal justice system had innocent people been executed.'[4] In Canada, too, at least six prisoners convicted of first-degree murder have subsequently been released when evidence of their innocence was established, one of them after having spent ten years in custody.[5]

Miscarriages of justice are especially likely when there are 'crackdowns' on crime or when particularly heinous crimes lead to pressure on the police to produce 'an offender'. This may lead overzealous police to misinterpret or even fabricate evidence or to extract confessions by torture or other illegitimate methods. This may be exacerbated by poor legal defence and by an over-readiness of courts to convict. Thus, in China during the 'strike hard campaigns' of 1997 and 1998 there were several reports of wrongful convictions.[6] And in the Russian Federation Valerii Borshchev, the Chair of the President's Commission on Human Rights, estimated that when the President declared a 'war' on crime during 1995 and 1996, the proportion of those executed who were later found to be innocent increased from the already high rate of 15 per cent to 30 per cent.[7] There have been similar concerns in Bangladesh and the Philippines (especially aroused by the allegation of torture of the suspects in the

---

the conviction of Derek Bentley, an 18-year-old mentally retarded man who had been hanged for his part in the murder of a policeman in 1952, although he was under arrest at the time his 16-year-old accomplice, Christopher Craig, had fired the shot that killed the policeman. Craig had escaped the death penalty because he was under the age of 18. In quashing Bentley's conviction (it had been claimed that he had goaded Craig to fire by shouting 'let him have it Chris'), the then Lord Chief Justice of England, Lord Bingham, said: 'We cannot read these passages as other than a highly rhetorical and strongly worded denunciation of both defendants and their defences. The language used was not that of a judge but of an advocate (and it contrasted strongly with the appropriately restrained language of prosecuting counsel) . . . In our judgment, the summing-up in this case was such as to deny the appellant that fair trial which is the birthright of every British citizen', [2001] 1 Cr.App.R. 21.

[4] House of Commons Debates, 21 Feb. 1994, col. 45. Quoted in Gavin Drewry, 'The Politics of Capital Punishment', in G. Drewry and C. Blake (eds), *Law and the Spirit of Inquiry* (1999), pp. 137–159 at 154–155.

[5] Mark Warren, *The Death Penalty in Canada: Facts, Figures and Milestones* (2001).

[6] See Hans-Jörg Albrecht, 'The Death Penalty in China from a European Perspective', in M. Nowak and Xin Chunying (eds), *EU–China Human Rights Dialogue: Proceedings of the Second EU–China Legal Experts' Seminar Held in Beijing on 19 and 20 October 1998* (2000), pp. 95–118 at 116, referring to reports in *China Youth Daily*, 8 May 1998; *Oriental Daily*, 12 Sept. and 25 Sept. 1997; *Xinjiang Legal News*, 24 Oct. 1997; *Xinmin Evening News*, 17 Oct. 1997.

[7] Patrick Henry, 'Execution Foes Press for Moratorium', *Moscow Times*, Sept. 1997, quoted in D. Barry, and E. Williams, 'Russia's Death Penalty Dilemmas', *Criminal Law Forum* 8 (1997), pp. 231–258 at 253.

Rolando Abadilla murder)[8] where errors had been found in 70 per cent of the 511 cases involving 591 death-sentenced inmates that the Philippines Supreme Court had reviewed between 1994 and late in 2001.[9] In Israel the discovery of new evidence in the case of John Demjanjuk, who had been identified with such certainty as 'Ivan the Terrible', a camp guard responsible for mass murder of Jews during the Second World War, produced doubts where none hitherto had existed.[10] To take yet another example: in the Caribbean state of Belize over half of those sentenced to death in recent years have been successful on appeal, some of whom may have been innocent.[11]

There is a particular danger when suspects are rounded up by the authorities following attempted coups. Thus, in Zambia following a coup attempt in October 1997, 59 men were convicted and sentenced to death. An official inquiry ordered by the government following allegations made in court of the use of torture found that there had been beatings, burning, electric shocks, enforced painful postures, sexual harassment, mental torture—such as simulated execution—and other degradations. The Commission found that 'victims were both physically and mentally affected by these experiences to the extent that they had no choice but to make incriminating statements'. Amnesty International has therefore called for a retrial based on evidence untainted by torture.[12]

In the United States a report issued in 1993 by the Subcommittee on Civil and Constitutional Rights, Committee on the Judiciary of the US Congress, entitled *Innocence and the Death Penalty: Assessing the Danger of Mistaken Executions*, noted that

at least 48 people have been released from prison after serving time on death row since 1973 with significant evidence of their innocence. In 43 of these cases, the defendant was subsequently acquitted, pardoned, or charges were dropped . . . Some of these men were convicted on the basis of perjured testimony or because the prosecutor improperly withheld exculpatory evidence. In other cases racial prejudice was a determining factor. In yet others, defence counsel failed to conduct the necessary investigation that would have disclosed exculpatory information.[13]

Since that time the doubts have not been dispelled. Rather they have increased. The

---

[8] AI, *Philippines: The Rolando Abadilla Murder Inquiry—An Urgent Need for Effective Investigation of Torture*, AI Index: ASA 35/08/00.

[9] See Free Legal Assistance Group (FLAG), 'Position Paper on the Death Penalty Bills', *Flag Newsletter*, Dec. 2001.

[10] John Demjanjuk was sentenced to death on 18 April 1988. In July 1989 his sentence was overturned by the Supreme Court of Israel after the court examined exceptionally admitted newly discovered evidence at the appeals stage, and held that this created the possibility of a reasonable doubt as to the identification of John Demjanjuk as 'Ivan the Terrible'.

[11] See Saul Lehrfreund, 'The Death Penalty and the Continuing Role of the Privy Council', *New Law Journal* 149 (1999), pp. 1299–1301.

[12] See AI, *Zambia: Time to Abolish the Death Penalty*, AI Index: AFR 63/004/2001, p. 14.

[13] Death Penalty Information Center, *Innocence and the Death Penalty: Assessing the Danger of Mistaken Executions*, Staff Report by the Subcommittee on Civil and Constitutional Rights, Committee on the Judiciary, One Hundred and Third Congress, First Session (1993), pp. 2 and 8.

appeals procedures in the United States have led to a substantial number of persons being removed from death row. Between 1977 and 2000, 6,208 persons were received into US prisons under sentence of death and 2,312 of them were 'removed from under a death sentence by appellate court decisions and reviews, commutations or death'.[14] But, of course, a substantial proportion of those still under sentence of death had yet to exhaust all avenues of appeal.

The full scale of 'serious reversible error' found in death penalty convictions in the United States was revealed for the first time in June 2000 by a study carried out at the Columbia Law School by Professor James Liebman and colleagues. This study, of every capital conviction and appeal between 1973 and 1995, found that in 68 per cent of cases that had reached the final third stage of state and federal appeal during this period (a process that on average took nine years), an error had been found sufficient to overturn the original capital conviction. Ninety per cent of these prejudicial errors had been discovered during appeals to the state courts, but even where cases proceeded to the federal appeal courts, a high error rate was still apparent. This high rate of 'reversal' persisted over the entire period covered by the study and across most states: three-fifths of the states had an error rate of 70 per cent or higher. The most common causes of these errors, accounting for 76 per cent of the cases, were found to be: 'egregiously incompetent defense lawyers' who did not even look for—and *demonstrably missed*—important evidence that the defendant was innocent or did not deserve to die (37 per cent of cases); police and prosecutors who *did* discover that kind of evidence but *suppressed* it, again keeping it from the jury (19 per cent of cases); and faulty instructions to jurors (20 per cent of cases). Furthermore, 82 per cent of those who had their death sentences overturned were not sentenced to death when the errors were cured on a retrial, and 7 per cent were found to be innocent of the capital crime. Thus, only 11 per cent of those originally sentenced to death were judged to deserve such a sentence when the errors of the original trial were corrected.[15] Further analysis of this data revealed that the proportion of errors was greatest in those states and counties which most often sentenced offenders to death: in other words, the percentage of errors increased in proportion to the percentage of homicides which resulted in a death sentence, especially in relation to cases that were not highly aggravated. Furthermore, errors were greater in states and counties where the risk of a white being murdered came 'close to equalling or surpassing the risk to blacks'; in states where there was a relatively high proportion of black Afro-Americans in the population; in states where a relatively low rate of serious crimes resulted in the apprehension, conviction, and imprisonment of offenders; and where trial judges were subject to popular, partisan, elections. Professor Liebman and his colleagues hypothesized that all these variables are likely indicators of factors that increase fear of crime and put pressure on prosecutors and judges to seek the death

---

[14] See Tracy L. Snell, *Capital Punishment 2000* (2001), Washington: US Department of Justice, Bureau of Justice Statistics, 9.

[15] James S. Liebman, Jeffrey Fagan, Valerie West, and Jonathan Lloyd, 'Capital Attrition: Error Rates in Capital Cases, 1973–1995', *Texas Law Review* 78 (2000), pp. 1771–1803.

penalty in capital trials. And, of course, pressure to obtain 'a result' was more likely to lead to procedural or factual error. Thus, they concluded:

The lower the rate at which a state imposes death sentence—and the more it confines those verdicts to the worst—the less likely it is that serious error will be found. The fewer death verdicts a state imposes, the less overburdened its capital appeal system is, and the more likely it is to carry out the verdicts it imposes. The more often states succumb to pressures to inflict capital sentences in marginal cases, the higher is the risk of error and delay, the lower is the chance verdicts will be carried out, and the greater is the temptation to approved flawed verdicts on appeal. Among the disturbing sources of pressure to overuse the death penalty are political pressures on elected judges, well-founded doubts about the state's ability to convict serious criminals, and the race of the state's residents and homicide victims.[16]

In 1999 alone eight condemned prisoners were released from US death rows after evidence of their innocence emerged[17] and a further fifteen between January 2000 and June 2002, making a total of 101 since the reinstatement of the death penalty in 1976.[18] In Oklahoma Ronald Williamson was released after DNA evidence cleared him of the offence, having spent six years on death row, only five days before he was due to be executed. His trial lawyer had failed to investigate his extensive record of mental illness and the fact that another man had confessed to the crime. Another death row prisoner was released in Nevada after spending twenty years behind bars when a court decided that the police illegally withheld evidence that would have exculpated him.[19] In Illinois, where twelve prisoners had been released from death row since 1994 because of doubts about their guilt, a prisoner named Anthony Porter, who had a measured IQ of merely 51 and was only five days away from his execution date in 1999, was exonerated after students of journalism, under the guidance of their professor, had investigated his case. As a result, Governor Ryan of Illinois, a former strong supporter of capital punishment, announced a moratorium on executions until an inquiry into the administration of the death penalty in the state had reported on the state's 'shameful record of convicting innocent people and putting them on death row' (see Chapter 2 page 69).[20]

As if to emphasize his point, a few months later yet another innocent prisoner,

[16] See James S. Liebman, Jeffrey Fagan, Andrew Gelman, Valerie West, Gareth Davies, and Alexander Kiss, *A Broken System*, Pt. II: *Why is there So Much Error in Capital Cases, and What Can be Done About It?* (Feb. 2002), Columbia Law School Publications, www.law.columbia.edu/brokensystem2/ index2.html.

[17] See Death Penalty Information Center, *Innocence: Freed from Death Row*, www.essential.org/dpic/Innocentlist.html.

[18] American Bar Association, *Death Knell for the Death Penalty* (June 2000). See also AI, *Death Penalty News* Sept. 2001, AI Index: Act 53/004/2001. See 'Innocence: Freed from Death Row', Death Penalty Information Center, www.deathpenaltyinfo.org/Innocentlist.html. The average time between being sentenced to death and exoneration was eight years: 43 were black, 44 white, 12 Latino, one native American, and one other. Over a third of those released on grounds of innocence had been sentenced in Florida (22) and Illinois (13). Seven had been freed from Texas.

[19] *Las Vegas Review Journal,* Feb. 2000.

[20] See AI *United States of America: Failing the Future—Death Penalty Developments March 1998–March 2000,* AI Index: AMR 51/003/2000. Five of the 13 exonerations in Illinois were the result of DNA evidence. At least 8 of the 98 men and women who have been freed from death row nationwide since the 1970s owe their freedom to DNA evidence.

Steve Manning, was identified early in 2000.[21] If such a large number of legal and factual errors made at trials for capital offences are found by appeals courts in the United States of America, where the scope of capital punishment is narrowly drawn and the legal system is well developed, it is hard to believe that they will not occur also in many other retentionist countries.

The conservative response to all this evidence has been perhaps predictable, namely that it merely proves how thorough the American appeal process is in ensuring that innocent persons are not executed.[22] But the fact of the matter is that many of these cases have come to light not through the thoroughness of the state's review processes, but through the vagaries of luck, through confessions of other criminals, and by the hard effort of campaigners outside the official criminal justice system: 'In one way or another, virtually every case in which death row inmates are able to prove their innocence is a story of exceptional luck. Only when we realize how lucky the exonerated death row inmates have been can we realize how easy it is for fatal mistakes to go undetected.'[23] This is why many believe that some innocent persons must have been executed, for as in the case of Anthony Porter of Illinois, he only escaped the death penalty by the chance intervention of outsiders, rather than through any thorough investigation of his claims to innocence by the authorities. As Professor Hugo Adam Bedau, the leading campaigner against the death penalty, has put it: 'it is beyond reasonable doubt that innocent persons have been put to death, even if it cannot be proved'.[24] To some proponents of the death penalty, such as the American professor of philosophy the late Ernest van den Haag, the execution of some innocent persons is regarded as inevitable: because 'judges and juries are human and fallible we can minimize, but not altogether avoid such miscarriages'. He argued that 'there is a trade-off in minimizing them. To avoid convicting innocents we require so much evidence for conviction that many guilty persons escape punishment—which is no less unjust than convicting the innocent.' Furthermore, van den

[21] AI, *Death Penalty News*, Mar. 2000, AI Index: ACT 53/001/2000.

[22] In an article in *Wall Street Journal Europe*, 16 June 2000, Paul Cassell, Professor of Law at the University of Utah, argued that all the innocent people released from death row are merely proof that the criminal justice system is working efficiently: 'the 68% "error rate" in capital cases—might accordingly be viewed as a reassuring sign of the American judiciary's circumspection before imposing the ultimate sanction'.

[23] Michael Radelet and Hugo Adam Bedau, 'The Execution of the Innocent', *Law and Contemporary Problems* 61 (1998), pp. 105–217 at 118. Also, Samuel R. Gross, 'Lost Lives: Miscarriages of Justice in Capital Cases', *ibid.*, pp. 125–152.

[24] See Michael L. Radelet, Hugo Adam Bedau, and Constance E. Putnam, *In Spite of Innocence* (1992). For criticisms of this book, claiming that no proof had been forthcoming of innocent persons being executed, see Stephen J. Markman and Paul G. Cassell, 'Protecting the Innocent: A Response to the Bedau–Radelet Study', *Stanford Law Review* 41 (1988), pp. 121–160; and the reply by Hugo Adam Bedau and Michael L. Radelet, 'The Myth of Infallibility: A Reply to Markman and Cassell', *ibid.*, pp. 161–170. It should be noted that Markman and Cassell argued that, even if a few innocent persons had been executed, this was a loss justified by the gains of capital punishment in terms of its utility in controlling murder. Also, Kelli Hinson, 'Post-Conviction Determination of Innocence for Death Row Inmates', *SMU Law Review* 48 (1994), pp. 231–261 at 254. For strong support for Bedau and Radelet, see Lawrence C. Marshall, 'In Spite of Meese', *Journal of Criminal Law and Criminology* 85 (1994), pp. 261–280.

Haag argued, in true utilitarian vein, some innocent persons have to suffer in order that sufficient guilty persons can be convicted to provide the general deterrent effect that he believed executions provide, so saving many lives of yet unknown innocent victims (see Chapter 7).[25] Whatever else, this is not a 'human rights' argument.

It is difficult at present to estimate what the impact might be on the capital punishment debate of the widespread availability of genetic fingerprint DNA testing. There is a strong movement in the United States to make this statutorily available to defendants protesting their innocence in all retentionist states and the federal jurisdiction; and 17 states passed laws during 2001 to allow inmates access to post-conviction DNA testing.[26] DNA will not help of course in every case, but where it can, the belief that it can be used to confirm guilt with absolute confidence may well persuade advocates of capital punishment that only those who deserve to die are put to death and rob the opponents of capital punishment of one of their most powerful and emotive arguments against it. Yet, it could have another effect, as Austin Sarat has pointed out. By being able to demonstrate conclusively that mistakes can occur in the types of crime where DNA evidence is most likely to be available, people may come to see that the probability of mistake may be even greater for those types of crime where the only evidence is eyewitness or circumstantial.[27]

3. Ensuring Fair Trials

(a) Trial Procedures

In 1996 the Economic and Social Council further encouraged member states in which the death penalty has not been abolished:

'*to ensure that each defendant facing a possible death sentence is given all guarantees to ensure a fair trial, as contained in article 14 of the International Covenant on Civil and Political Rights, and bearing in mind the Basic Principles on the Independence of the Judiciary, the Basic Principles on the Role of Lawyers, the Guidelines on the Role of Prosecutors, the Body of Principles for the Protection of All Persons under Any Form of Detention or Imprisonment, and the Standard Minimum Rules for the Treatment of Prisoners*' and '*to ensure that defendants who do not sufficiently understand the language used in court are fully informed, by way of interpretation or translation, of all the charges against them and the content of the relevant evidence deliberated in court.*'

---

[25] Ernest van den Haag, 'Justice, Deterrence and the Death Penalty', in J. R. Acker, R. M. Bohm, and C. S. Lanier (eds), *America's Experiment with Capital Punishment* (1998), pp. 139–156 at 147. A similar view has been expressed by a Russian scholar: 'It must be said that errors are committed in all spheres of human activities [for example in medical operations] but this is not grounds to renounce such activity'; Alexander Mikhlin, *The Death Penalty in Russia* (1999), p. 167.

[26] Associated Press, 3 Jan. 2002. The Innocence Protection Act, to provide inmates with access to DNA testing, was still before Congress in mid-2002.

[27] Ronald J. Tabak, Commentary; 'Finality without Fairness: Why we are Moving towards Moratoria on Executions, and the Potential Abolition of Capital Punishment', *Connecticut Law Review* 33 (2001), pp. 733–763 at 751. See also the website of the Innocence Project at Cardozo Law School, which reviews cases where defendants say that they have been wrongfully convicted and, where appropriate, arranges for DNA tests to be carried out, at www.cardozo.yu.edu/innocence-project. Also the interview with Barry Scheck at www.pbs.org/wgbh/pages/frontline/shows/case/interviews/scheck.html.

The relatively small number of retentionist countries which responded to the Fifth and Sixth United Nations Surveys affirmed that the defendant is informed of the nature of the charge and the evidence against him or her, with adequate time and facilities to prepare his or her defence, to examine witnesses, and to obtain witnesses on his own behalf under the same conditions (including financial conditions) as the prosecution witnesses against him. They all stated that there had been no instances where persons were executed without and/or outside the judicial process.

But, of course, these assurances cannot be taken at face value in all countries, for there may be a wide gap between the aspirations of procedural law and the actual practices of the organs of criminal justice. This is probably even more likely to be the case in some of the larger number of retentionist countries which have never responded to the United Nation's requests for information. The reports of the Special Rapporteur on extra-judicial, summary, or arbitrary executions contain allegations that death sentences have been imposed in several countries following trials that did not conform to international standards. Many of these allegations concerned the trial of civilians and soldiers before special tribunals or military courts set up to deal with civil unrest (see page 154 below). In this respect, the following countries have been cited by the Special Rapporteur or by the UN Human Rights Committee: Algeria, the Democratic Republic of Congo, Egypt, Iraq, Kuwait, Nigeria, Pakistan, and Sierra Leone.[28] Other concerns have focused upon powers given to Islamic courts to impose death sentences under a kind of summary jurisdiction, as in Chechnya, Afghanistan, and in northern Nigeria, where many of the judges are said to be virtually untrained in law.[29] In Somalia local 'clan' courts have sentenced people to death.

Furthermore, it has been reported that in some countries trials have taken place where the defendant has had either no legal representation at all, inadequate legal representation, or representation provided too late to make it possible to mount an adequate legal defence. For example, in Saudi Arabia, 'the suspect is denied access to the outside world [including] legal assistance . . . until a confession is obtained'. And once this is obtained, the defendant is questioned by the judge or judges without a lawyer or legal expert being present to defend him or her. Neither are the press or any members of the public given access to hearings. It remains to be seen whether the adoption of a new code of criminal procedure will guarantee the right to be defended by a lawyer in conformity with international standards.[30] The Special

[28] For Algeria, E/CN.4/1995/61, paras. 45–48. For the Democratic Republic of Congo, E/CN.4/1999/39/Add. 1, para. 66. For Egypt, E/CN.4/1995/61, paras. 119 and 126, also E/CN.4/1998/68/Add. 1, paras. 146–153. For Iraq, *Report of the Human Rights Committee*, A/53/40, vol. 1 (1998), p. 30. For Kuwait, E/CN.4/1995/61, paras. 202–205, also E/CN.4/1996/4/Corr.1, para. 288. For Nigeria, E/CN.4/1996/4/Corr.1, paras. 338–353, also *Report of the Human Rights Committee*, A/51/40, vol. 1 (1997), para. 42. For Pakistan, see Special Rapporteur's *Report*, E/CN.4/1998/68/Add. 1, para. 303. And for Sierra Leone, E/CN.4/1999/39/Add. 1, para. 216.

[29] Special Rapporteur's *Report*, E/CN.4/1998/68, para. 85. Also, for example, in the Shari'a Courts in northern Nigeria, see AI, *BAOBAB for Women's Human Rights and Amnesty International Joint Statement on the Implementation of New Sharia-Based Penal Codes in Northern Nigeria*, AI Index: AFR 44/008/2002.

[30] Lamri Chirouf, 'Defying World Trends: Saudi Arabia's Extensive Use of Capital Punishment', Paper presented to the 1st World Congress against the Death Penalty, Strasbourg, 21–3 June 2001.

Rapporteur has expressed concern that trials have failed to conform to international standards of fairness in one or more of these respects in the following countries and territories: Afghanistan (under Taliban rule), China (at least prior to the reform of Criminal Procedure in 1997), the Palestinian Authority, Rwanda, Saudi Arabia, and Yemen.[31]

(b) Allowing Sufficient Time to Prepare a Defence

Several countries have enacted, sometimes by decree or under military law, legislation which is aimed to speed up the trial and expedite all processes of post-trial review. Thus, before the reform of the criminal law in 1997 there were many reports from China of executions occurring within six to eight days after arrest for the crime. And, since then, concern has been expressed about incidents such as the one which occurred in Shenzen in April 1998 when a large public sentencing rally was held for over 40 defendants. It was reported that 14 were sentenced to death and escorted to the execution ground straight after the rally to be shot.[32] When 'strike hard campaigns' are in progress, such as the one begun in the spring of 2001, police, prosecutors, and lawyers are urged to speed up the process of criminal trials even more, with the result that there is a great risk of wrongful convictions.

From Iran, also, there have been reports of summary trials for drug offenders before Revolutionary Courts, with no defence counsel or right of appeal, even though these courts can impose the death sentence. Both Ethiopia (in 1974) and Pakistan (in 1987) introduced 'speedy trial' courts and allowed only a short period for appeal to be lodged (seven days only in Pakistan). In Kenya, under the provisions of the 'Hanging Bill' of 1975 (which made robbery with violence subject to a mandatory death penalty on conviction), the defendant was not eligible for state legal aid and thus had difficulty in completing the legal formalities of appeal. At various times—in Bangladesh, India, Indonesia, Nigeria, South Korea, Taiwan, and Guatemala (although in neither of the last two in recent years), trials which resulted in the death penalty were held before military tribunals which afforded lesser rights than civilian courts. In India and Sri Lanka, for example, martial law placed the burden of proof on the defendant. The Special Rapporteur on extra-judicial, summary, or arbitrary executions expressed concern that, under the Curbing of Terrorist Activities Act 1992 in Bangladesh, investigations of such offences had to be completed within thirty (exceptionally forty-five) days and that the trial, held before a special tribunal, was to be completed within sixty (exceptionally ninety) days. Of course, such time limits might make it difficult to prepare an adequate defence.

---

[31] For Afghanistan, see Special Rapporteur's *Report*, E/CN.4/1999/39/Add. 1, para. 4–5, and E/CN.4/1998/68/Add. 1, paras. 442–443. For China E/CN.4/1997/60/Add. 1, paras. 100–114. For Palestinian Authority, E/CN.4/1998/68/Add. 1, para. 438. For Rwanda, E/CN.4/1999/39/Add. 1, paras. 101–111. For E/CN.4/1999/39/Add. 1, para. 205. For Saudi Arabia, E/CN.4/1999/39/Add. 1, para. 212. And for Yemen, E/CN.4/1998/68/Add. 1, para. 443.

[32] *Shenzen Legal Daily*, 25 Apr. 1998.

(c) Adequate Legal Representation?

To what extent do defendants charged with a capital offence have the right to communicate with a counsel of his or her own choosing and a right to legal assistance for trial and appeals, without payment if he or she does not have sufficient means to pay for it? In response to the Sixth UN Survey in 1999, Bahrain, Barbados, Comoros, Kazakhstan, Thailand, and Turkey stated that provision of counsel was above and beyond that which was afforded in non-capital cases. For example, Bahrain stated: 'if the defendant is unable to retain a lawyer, the Government will assign one to him, at the expense of the Ministry of Justice, to provide him with legal advice at all stages of the proceedings'. Article 20 of the Kyrgyzstan Code of Criminal Procedure makes the participation of defence counsel in court mandatory in capital cases and 'The head of the legal advice office or the Presidium of the Bar Association are obliged to provide a lawyer to defend the suspect, accused or defendant.'[33]

However, Japan, Lebanon, and Togo stated that this was not the practice, and they are clearly not the only countries that do not automatically provide counsel of high quality at public expense to those threatened with the death sentence. Thus, in Iran, if the accused does not have his own lawyer, the state, according to the 1980 Constitution, is supposed to provide counsel. However, this is not common practice, perhaps because of the expense involved. But even when defence lawyers are appointed, they cannot intervene in police or court investigations or interrogations without prior permission from the judge. In special jurisdictions like the Revolutionary Courts, Religious Courts, and Military Courts, the only lawyers allowed to defend the accused are those named by these courts, which of course may include some lawyers who are less likely to challenge the authority of the court.

Zambia employs only ten lawyers in its Department of Legal Aid, each of them having to cover up to 50 cases a year. This is apparently 'considered a very low status employment'. Amnesty International has noted that the Legal Aid Act of 2001 makes it possible for private lawyers to be paid on a case-by-case basis, but it is 'not clear whether this new system will ensure adequate legal representation for defendants in capital cases'.[34]

According to the Chinese Law of Criminal Procedure (1997), defence counsel has to be appointed in cases where an indigent defendant risks the imposition of the death sentence. Article 151 states that 'After the People's Court has decided to open a court session, it shall . . . deliver to the defendant a copy of the bill of prosecution of the People's Procuratorate not later than ten days before the opening of the court session. If the defendant has not appointed a defender, he shall be informed that he may appoint a defender or, when necessary, designate a lawyer that is obligated to provide legal aid to serve as a defender for him.' This article is to be read in conjunction with Article 34: 'If there is the possibility that the defendant may be sentenced

---

[33] Commission of Human Rights, CCPR/C/113/Add. 1, Dec. 1999, p. 50.
[34] AI, *Zambia: Time to Abolish the Death Penalty*, AI Index: AFR 63/004/2001, pp. 3–4.

to death and has not yet entrusted anybody to be his defender, the People's Court shall designate a lawyer that is obligated to provide legal aid to serve as a defender.' So no lawyer is available to the defendant during the crucial stages of questioning and investigation prior to the trial while the evidence is being assembled. Furthermore, while the defender is allowed to 'meet and correspond with the criminal suspect in custody' (Article 36), it is understood that, in practice, it is forbidden for the lawyer to disclose to the client the state's case against him or her, and so it is almost impossible for the lawyer to receive 'instructions' in the way expected in Western legal systems. These procedures particularly disadvantage those of 'low and precarious educational and socio-economic position', who make up the majority of those charged with capital offences.[35]

In a series of death penalty cases concerning Caribbean defendants, decided between 1987 and 1990, the UN Human Rights Committee declared that defendants have an absolute right to *effective* counsel, including legal aid, under Article 14 (3) (d) of the International Covenant on Civil and Political Rights.[36] Yet, according to one commentator, 'representation in capital cases [in Caribbean countries] is probably even of a lower quality than [it can be] in the southern states of the USA'.[37] Adrian King, a respected attorney-at-law in Barbados, complained at a Commonwealth Human Rights Seminar held in Belize in September 2000 that the legal aid provided for persons accused of murder in Barbados is so limited that 'the State is largely able to execute without being out of much expense in providing a fair trial for the accused'. In fact the Community Legal Services Act neither provides for access to an attorney during the investigation or any of the pre-preliminary trial procedures, nor for an appeal to the Judicial Committee of the Privy Council in London. Any lawyer on the Legal Aid List can be granted a Legal Aid Certificate, and 'so it is possible, and often the practice, for an accused person to be assigned a very junior member of the bar, who will be required to prepare the defence, usually without the aid of expert help, medical or otherwise'. Thus, defendants have to rely 'upon the inadequately rewarded services of attorneys and the *pro bono* services of solicitors and barristers in London'.[38] It is indisputable that many persons on death row in the Caribbean have been saved from execution by the intervention of lawyers in London, in particular since 1992 by Saul Lehrfreund and his colleagues at the Commonwealth Caribbean Death Penalty Project, supported by the firm of Simons

---

[35] See Albrecht, n. 6 above, pp. 98 and 115.

[36] *Robinson* v. *Jamaica*, UNHRC Communication no. 223/1987, decided 30 Mar. 1989; *Reid* v. *Jamaica*, decided July 1990; *Pinto* v. *Trinidad and Tobago*, decided July 1990; *Pratt and Morgan* v. *Jamaica*, decided Apr. 1989.

[37] See R. B. M. Antoine, 'International Law and the Right to Legal Representation in Capital Offence Cases—a Comparative Approach', *Oxford Journal of Legal Studies* 12 (1992), pp. 284–294. In Jamaica legal aid is not normally granted for appeals to the Judicial Committee of the Privy Council (it being done pro bono mainly by attorneys in the UK). Nor is there, apparently, any guarantee 'that legal aid will be allowed for the proposed Caribbean Court of Appeal nor that there will be any facility substituted for the present pro-bono programme'. *Ibid.*

[38] Adrian King, 'Legal Aid and Access to Justice', in Penal Reform International *et al.*, *Commonwealth Caribbean Human Rights Seminar*, 12–14 Sept. 2000 (2001), London, pp. 49–59 at 50–51.

Muirhead and Burton and Penal Reform International in London, and co-funded by the Commission of the European Community.

It is obvious that defendants who receive good advice from experienced counsel are more likely to have their case favourably considered at all levels of the decision-making process. In the United States, where a number of studies have been conducted, it has been found that a decision to go to trial, rather than plead guilty, for instance, appears greatly to increase the odds of receiving a death sentence.[39] Indeed, a study of first-degree murder indictments in 21 of Florida's 67 counties found that the single most powerful factor associated with whether the prosecutor committed the case for trial was whether or not the defendant was represented by a private attorney.[40] In both Florida and Georgia defendants who had a court-appointed, rather than a private, attorney were considerably more likely to be sentenced to death. Indeed, in Georgia, when all other relevant factors had been accounted for, the rate of death sentences in cases where the defendant had access only to a court-appointed defence counsel was 2.6 times higher.[41] These findings clearly indicate that indigent defendants are at a considerable disadvantage.

Despite the Supreme Court's judgment in *Strickland* v. *Washington* (1984) that defendants in capital cases are entitled to 'effective assistance of counsel' who are presumed to be competent and effective, it is well known that court-appointed lawyers are very poorly paid in comparison with privately appointed counsel. Virtually all the prisoners (99.5 per cent) on death row in America are indigent and most of them do not have attorneys. In many states the funds for the defence of these indigent defendants are provided by the relatively impecunious county governments, and even where the state government meets the cost, the provision is very variable and in some states grossly inadequate. According to Stephen B. Bright, the Director of the Southern Center for Human Rights, in 1991 'About the best an attorney [could] be paid in a capital case in the South today is $50 an hour. A rate of $30 for time spent in court and $20 for out of court is more likely'.[42] In a Texas case the

---

[39] See E. L. Murphy, 'Application of the Death Penalty in Cook County', *Illinois Bar Journal* (Oct. 1984), pp. 90–95 at 91. In Cook County, Illinois, only 2% of those who chose a bench trial by the judge and 3% of those who pleaded guilty received a death sentence as opposed to 16% of those who chose trial by jury (5 to 8 times as many).

[40] Linda A. Foley and Richard S. Powell, 'The Discretion of Prosecutors, Judges, and Juries in Capital Cases', *Criminal Justice Review* 7 (1982), pp. 10–22.

[41] W. J. Bowers, 'The Pervasiveness of Arbitrariness and Discrimination under Post-*Furman* Capital Statutes', *Journal of Criminal Law and Criminology* 74 (1983), pp. 1067–1110 at 1078–1083; and D. C. Baldus, G. Woodworth, and C. A. Pulaski, *Equal Justice and the Death Penalty* (1990), p. 158.

[42] Stephen B. Bright, 'Counsel for the Poor: The Death Sentence not for the Worst Crime, but the Worst Lawyer', *National Legal Aid and Defender Cornerstone* 13(3) (1991), at 8–10; a much fuller version of this article is to be found in the *Yale Law Journal* 103 (1994), pp. 1835–1883 at 1853–1857 and 1866–1870; also Bright, 'Death by Lottery—Procedural Bar of Constitutional Claims due to Inadequate Representation of Indigent Defendants', *West Virginia Law Review* 92 (1990), pp. 679–695—arguing that the rule in *Wainwright* v. *Sykes* (1977) that 'meritorious constitutional claims may be barred from federal review because of an attorney's failure to satisfy state procedural rules or the attorney's failure to anticipate changes in the law' is unfair to the indigent because of the low standard of legal counsel. Bright quotes on this: American Bar Association Task Force on Review of State Capital Cases, *Toward a More Just and Effective System of Review in State Death Penalty Cases* (1989), ch. 2, which concludes that inadequacy of

Federal Appeal Court for the Fifth Circuit stated in 1992: 'We are left with the firm conviction that [the defendant] was denied his constitutional right to adequate counsel in a capital case in which actual innocence was a close question. The state paid defence counsel $11.84 per hour. Unfortunately the justice system got only what it paid for.'[43]

Many other instances have been cited where court-appointed lawyers were evidently extremely ill equipped to handle the trial of a murder case. 'The case reporters and academic literature are filled with countless accounts of inadequate legal representation in capital cases, both at the trial and sentencing phases', declared Justice Brennan of the US Supreme Court in 1994. 'Notwithstanding the heroic efforts of resource centres and appellate projects throughout the country, the meagre hourly rates and expenditure caps that many states impose on appointed counsel in capital cases do not suggest that a solution to this crisis is imminent.'[44] At least 16 of those executed between 1985 and 2001 had been, according to Amnesty International, represented at trial by lawyers who were patently under-prepared or in other ways not competent, or who failed to mount an adequate case for the defence.[45] A senior official serving the federal courts pointed to a particularly ironic consequence in Virginia where, because of the very strict procedural default rules, 'inexperienced lawyering in state post-conviction proceedings has led to some capital petitioners losing the ability to obtain post-conviction review at all with respect to certain claims, as well as lengthy (and costly) litigation of procedural default questions in federal court by others'.[46]

Despite the fact that a few states, such as Alabama, Illinois, and Louisiana, have attempted to improve the amounts allowed to defence lawyers in capital cases, the situation in the United States has not markedly improved over the last decade, as the

counsel is one of 'the principal failings of the capital punishment process today'. See also, Stephen B. Bright, 'The Politics of Crime and the Death Penalty: Not "Soft on Crime", but Hard on the Bill of Rights', *Saint Louis University Law Journal* 39 (1995), pp. 479–503 at 492–495, discussing numerous instances where seemingly ineffective assistance was held to be 'effective'. Also, Stephen B. Bright, 'Casualties of the War on Crime: Fairness, Reliability and the Credibility of the Criminal Justice System', *University of Miami Law Review* 51 (1997), pp. 413–424.

[43] *Martinez-Macias* v. *Collins* (1992), quoted in Death Penalty Information Center, *The Future of the Death Penalty in the U.S.: A Texas-Sized Crisis* (May 1994), p. 17.

[44] Justice William J. Brennan Jr, 'Neither Victims nor Executioners', *Notre Dame Journal of Law, Ethics and Public Policy: Symposium on Capital Punishment* 8 (1994), pp. 1–9 at 3. See also, Vivian Berger, 'The Chiropractor as Brain Surgeon: Defense Lawyering in Capital Cases', *New York University Review of Law and Social Change* 18 (1990–1), pp. 245–254.

[45] AI, *United States of America: Arbitrary, Discriminatory or Cruel: An Aide Mémoire to 25 Years of Judicial Killing*, AI Index: AMR 51/003/2002. See also, Rosemary Butler, 'Dying for Counsel', *New Law Journal* 144 (1994), pp. 1743–1745. A survey by the *National Law Journal* (11 June 1990), p. 34, in Mississippi, Texas, Georgia, Alabama, Louisiana, and Florida of 100 trial papers showed that more than half of the defence counsel surveyed admitted that they were dealing with their first capital case when their client was convicted and sentenced to death.

[46] Memorandum dated 28 Dec 1994, from Steven G. Aslin, Deputy Chief, Defender Services Division, Administrative Office of the US Courts, to Chair and Members, Subcommittee on Death Penalty Representation, Committee on Defender Services of the United States Judicial Conference. But the author noted that in Florida, where a state-funded defender organization regularly provides representation in both state and federal post-conviction proceedings, no such problems were reported.

Columbia Study of errors in capital cases has shown (see page 135 above). According to an investigation by the *Chicago Tribune* of the 131 death row inmates executed during George Bush's tenure as Governor of Texas, 43 were represented by defence attorneys who had been publicly sanctioned for misconduct, 40 of them presented no evidence to the court or provided only one witness on their client's behalf, and 29 used psychiatric testimony condemned as untrustworthy by the American Psychiatric Association.[47] Several of them were known to have slept throughout significant periods of the trial of their clients.[48]

The most remarkable instance of this is the case of *Burdine* v. *Johnson*.[49] Burdine was convicted of capital murder in Texas after a trial lasting three days. It was established that Burdine's defence counsel had slept during parts of the thirteen hours that the trial had taken up (the lawyer claimed that he was only concentrating). Yet, the Federal Court of Appeal for the Fifth Circuit held, by a majority, that although counsel had slept, the appellant had failed to prove (and it was ten years after the trial) that the lawyer had slept during consequential parts of the trial and that there could therefore be a presumption of prejudice.[50] In August 2001 the Federal Court of Appeal for the Fifth Circuit considered the case again and decided that the defender's 'unconsciousness during Burdine's capital murder trial [did amount] to constructive denial of counsel for substantial periods of that trial'. The Court concluded that 'the Supreme Court's Sixth Amendment jurisprudence compels the presumption that counsel's unconsciousness prejudiced the defendant'.[51] As Stephen Bright has pointed out, the Burdine case is not unique. Another Texas prisoner, George McFarland, remains on death row having failed to get his death sentence quashed by the Texas Court of Criminal Appeals on the grounds that his counsel had repeatedly fallen asleep and snored during his trial.[52] Furthermore, the recent decision of the Eleventh Circuit of the US Court of Appeals in the case of David Ronald Chandler appears to have set a very low standard for 'competent counsel'. Chandler's attorney admitted that he had hardly prepared for the sentencing part of the death penalty trial. He had concentrated on trying to prove his client innocent and did 'basically not anything explicitly' to bring forward mitigating circumstances to persuade jurors not to sentence his client to death.[53] In 2001 Chandler was granted clemency by then US president Bill Clinton.

---

[47] AI, *United States of America: The Death Penalty in Texas: Lethal Injustice*, AI Index: AMR 51/010/1998.

[48] See Michael Mello and Paul J. Perkins, 'Closing the Circle: The Illusion of Lawyers for People Litigating for their Lives at the Fin de Siècle', in Acker, Bohm, and Lanier (eds), n. 25 above, p. 271.

[49] *Burdine* v. *Johnson*, (2000) 231 F.3d 950 (5th Cir. Texas).

[50] For a scathing comment on this judgment, see *Amicus Journal* 2 (2001), pp. 15–16.

[51] *Burdine* v. *Johnson* (2001) No. 99-21034 (United States Court of Appeal for the 5th Cir.).

[52] See Stephen N. Bright, 'Symposium.: Restructuring Federal Courts: Habeas: Elected Judges and the Death Penalty in Texas. Why Full Habeas Corpus Review by Independent Federal Judges is Indispensable to Protecting Constitutional Rights', *Texas Law Review* 78 (2000), pp. 1805–1837 at 1811–1812, and also R. Copeland, Comment, 'Getting it Right from the Beginning: A Critical Examination of Current Criminal Defense in Texas and Proposal for a Statewide Public Defender System', *St. Mary's Law Journal* 32 (2001), pp. 493–540 at 523.

[53] *Chandler* v. *United States of America* (2000) 218 F.3d 1305. See also for list of sixteen cases where

Concerned that inadequate legal aid made it impossible to ensure satisfactory legal representation, the American Bar Association in 1997 called for a national moratorium on executions. Three years later the Attorney General of the United States, Janet Reno, declared that defendants should not be prosecuted 'for a capital crime until they have a lawyer who can properly represent them, and . . . the resources necessary to properly investigate the charges'.[54]

The situation, which is now hardly contested yet still tolerated, has been well summed up by Carol and Jordan Steiker as follows:

Perhaps the most significant source of inequality in the administration of the death penalty is the unevenness of representation. [There should be] firm guidelines for representation in capital cases that would include, among other things, minimum standards of appointment, adequate compensation for both counsel and experts, and presumptions about certain fundamental aspects of death penalty preparation and presentation. Such presumptions might include investigation of both guilt–innocence and punishment phase defenses, consultation with appropriate experts regarding physical evidence and psychiatric issues, thorough cross-examination of state witnesses, and research and advocacy regarding potential inadequacies of the state capital punishment scheme, including on appeal. As it stands, it is commonplace for many trial counsel to fail to present any evidence or argument during the punishment phase of a capital trial. Attorneys on direct appeal also routinely fail to attend oral argument at the one post-trial hearing in which all state law issues are subject to review. Notwithstanding these sorts of practices, federal and state courts have consistently rejected ineffectiveness of counsel claims.[55]

With the exception of three states—Arizona, California, and North Carolina—there is no statutory right to payment for expert assistance, in addition to counsel, for assessing mitigating considerations relating to sentencing, the matter being left entirely to the discretion of the court. Whatever may be attempted by skilled and committed attorneys to seek remedies at the post-conviction stage, all may be lost if the initial defence fails to undertake its task effectively. It is therefore heartening to see that, at last, members of the United States Supreme Court are recognizing the seriousness of this issue, mainly of course because it undermines the legitimacy of capital punishment. Thus, in July 2001 Justice Sandra Day O'Connor was reported to have made a speech in which she declared: 'perhaps it is time to look at minimum standards for appointed counsel in death penalty cases and adequate compensation for appointed counsel when they are used'.[56]

the prisoner had been executed, despite poor legal representation, a list 'that could be much longer'; AI, *United States of America. Arbitrary Discriminatory, and Cruel: An Aide-Memoire to 25 Years of Judicial Killing*, AI Index: AMR 51/003/2002, pp. 13–14.

[54] Reported in *USA Today*, 21 June 2000; see Death Penalty Information Center, *What's New*, July 2000. See also the case of Exavious Lee Gibson, who through poverty had been forced to appear without legal representation at his post-conviction hearing in 1996. He had been sentenced to death in 1990 for a murder committed when he was 17 and has an IQ of between 76 and 82. In 1999 the US Supreme Court refused to consider his appeal. See AI, *United States of America: Failing the Future—Death Penalty Developments, March 1998–March 2000*, AI Index: AMR 51/03/00, p. 18.

[55] See Carol S. Steiker and Jordan M. Steiker, 'Judicial Developments in Capital Punishment Law', in Acker, Bohm, and Lanier (eds) n. 25 above, pp. 72–73.

[56] AI, *Death Penalty News*, Sept. 2001, AI Index: ACT 53/004/2001.

It is not only in the United States and the Caribbean countries that the level of defence competence in many capital cases leaves much room for improvement. There is a need for rules that lay down the minimum competence of persons who are allowed to represent defendants in life-or-death cases.[57]

(d) The Plight of Foreign Nationals

Another issue of importance is the position of foreigners accused of capital crimes who do not speak or understand the language used by those who interrogate them at the police station or cross-examine them in court. There have been disturbing reports that migrant workers in the Middle East and some other parts of the world have not been provided with adequate interpretation and translation at every stage of the legal process.[58] Apparently in Japan free assistance of an interpreter for persons who cannot understand or speak the language used in court is only available after a means test. For this reason ECOSOC added to its safeguards in 1996 an encouragement to Member States '*to ensure that defendants who do not sufficiently understand the language used in court are fully informed, by way of interpretation or translation, of all the charges against them and the content of the relevant evidence deliberated in court*'.

The disadvantage suffered by foreigners has also raised the question of ensuring that consular assistance is provided for foreign nationals accused of crimes, as laid down in Article 36 (1b) of the Vienna Convention on Consular Relations. It has come to light that foreign nationals have been executed in the United States without ever being informed of their right to consular assistance, despite that country having ratified the Vienna Convention in 1969.[59] The US Supreme Court did not halt the execution of a prisoner named Breard, a citizen of Paraguay, by the State of Virginia, in blatant disregard of an order to do so by the International Court of Justice (ICJ)— and despite the fact that a strongly worded appeal to stay the execution had been sent to the Governor of Virginia by the United States Secretary of State, Madeline Albright[60]—on the grounds that there was no constitutional remedy for the violation of Breard's right to be informed of consular assistance, because he had failed to raise the issue at an earlier stage of his appeals.[61] After receiving a comprehensive apology from the United States, Paraguay withdrew its case at the ICJ.

---

[57] For example, in Britain defendants in capital murder trials were always provided under legal aid with a Queen's Counsel (senior barrister).

[58] See, for example, AI, *The Death Penalty: No Solution to Illicit Drugs* (1995), AI Index: Act 51/02/95, pp. 11–12. This records a case in Mauritius (at the time when the death penalty was in force) in which the accused was unable to understand the proceedings against him. The Judicial Committee of the Privy Council in London quashed the conviction on appeal.

[59] Advisory Opinion of the Inter-American Court of Human Rights (OC-16/99 of 1 Oct. 1999).

[60] Secretary Albright had written, 'The immediate execution of Mr Breard in the face of the Court's April 9 action could be seen as a denial by the United States of the significance of international law and the Court's processes in its international relations and thereby limit our ability to ensure that Americans are protected when living or travelling abroad.' However, the US Solicitor General opposed the stay. Cited in Harold Hongju Koh, 'Paying "Decent Respect" to World Opinion on the Death Penalty', *UC Davis Law Review* 35 (2002), pp. 1085–1131 at 1112–13.

[61] He was denied certiorari by the Supreme Court 6–3. *Breard* v. *Greene* (1998) 140 L.Ed.2d 529 (Supreme Court of the United States).

But yet another high profile case soon surfaced. Two German citizens, the brothers Karl and Walter LaGrand (who had lived most of their lives in the United States), were convicted in 1984 of the murder of a bank manager in Arizona during an attempted robbery in 1982. They were not informed of their rights under the Vienna Convention and it was not until 1992 that they discovered that they had a right to consular assistance. Such was the delay that they were precluded under the doctrine of 'procedural default' from challenging their conviction and sentence on these grounds. After one of the brothers, Karl LaGrand, had been executed on 24 February 1999, and one day before Walter LaGrand was due to be executed on 3 March 1999, Germany brought the case to the ICJ. On 3 March 1999 the ICJ issued an Order (called a provisional measure but similar to an interim injunction) stating that the United States should take all measures at its disposal to ensure that Walter LaGrand was not executed pending a final decision of the ICJ. The US Solicitor General informed the US Supreme Court that 'an order of the International Court of Justice indicating provisional measures is not binding' and the Supreme Court refused to grant a stay of execution on the grounds of 'the tardiness of the pleas and the jurisdictional boundaries they implicate'. The Order from the ICJ was conveyed to the Governor of Arizona without comment. He ignored it, along with the recommendation of the Arizona Clemency Board for a stay of execution, and Walter LaGrand was executed on 3 March 1999.

On 27 June 2001 the ICJ held that (*a*) the United States had breached its obligations to Germany and the LaGrand brothers under Article 36 paragraph 1 of the Vienna Convention on Consular relations; (*b*) by applying the 'procedural default rule' to deny reconsideration of the convictions and sentences of the LaGrand brothers the United States had breached its obligations under paragraph 2 of Article 36; and (*c*) the United States should have taken all measures to stay execution pending a final decision of the ICJ, because the Court's Orders indicating provisional measures are binding. In responding to this litigation the United States made a commitment to implement measures that would ensure its future compliance with the Vienna Convention.[62]

According to the Special Rapporteur on extra-judicial, summary, or arbitrary executions, Saudi Arabia, which has executed many migrant workers from Nigeria, India, Pakistan, Sudan, Eritrea, Yemen, the Philippines, Ethiopia, Egypt, and Iraq, has also failed to abide by the Vienna Convention,[63] thus depriving many of these foreigners of adequate legal assistance.[64] Apparently

---

[62] LaGrand case, *Germany* v. *United States of America*—Judgment, International Court of Justice, Press Release 2001/16, 27 June 2001. General List case no. 104. See also AI, *United States of America: A Time for Action: Protecting the Consular Rights of Foreign Nationals Facing the Death Penalty*, AI Index: AMR 51/106/2001.

[63] E/CN.4/1999/39/Add. 1, para. 213.

[64] A number of other foreign nationals have been executed in China—including several from Hong Kong and Macao SAR, where the death penalty has been abolished. These have been justified by the Chinese authorities on the grounds that the crimes have been 'cross-border' or that crimes carried out in these SARs had been planned on the mainland. At present the question of whether persons resident in

more than half of those executed in Saudi Arabia in the last decade were foreign nationals.[65]

(e) An Unbiased Jury?

In some countries trial is by jury and the jury may also recommend or determine the sentence, but very little is known about how juries reach their decisions in capital cases. It is an area almost entirely closed to the immediate scrutiny of researchers, and what is known is usually based on retrospective views of jurors.[66] Nor has any information been elicited through the United Nations surveys on the qualifications required for jury service in capital cases.

In the United States most of the thirty-eight states that have retained capital punishment had left the decision as to whether the defendant qualified for the death sentence and whether he or she should in fact be sentenced to death to the jury; in eleven states, however, the judge could determine the sentence. The involvement of judges in five of these states in determining whether the crime had involved the aggravating circumstances to make it 'death-eligible' was ruled unconstitutional in June 2002 in *Ring* v. *Arizona* (122 S.Ct. 2428 (2002)). In giving judgment Justice Breyer stated that 'Even in jurisdictions where judges are selected directly by the people, the jury remains uniquely capable of determining whether, given the community's views, capital punishment is appropriate . . . not "cruel", "unusual" or otherwise unwarranted . . . in the particular case in hand.'

Studies of how the jury reach decisions are therefore exceptionally valuable in understanding the use of capital punishment in the United States. It is well known that the requirement that juries must be 'death-qualified' has produced much controversy. Prospective jurors are questioned by the judge and attorneys in order to identify and reject those whose views on the death penalty are regarded as incompatible with their duty to apply the law conscientiously and to consider the 'full range' of penalties available to the court. It has been claimed that this has led to juries which are 'conviction-prone', less solicitous of a defendant's due process rights, and also unrepresentative of all sectors of society, particularly of women and black people.[67] There is some evidence to suggest that potential white male jurors who are

---

Hong Kong and Macao can be sent to mainland China is under discussion—the process not being strictly one of extradition, but of 'rendition'. See *People's Republic of China: The Death Penalty in 1999* (2001), AI Index: ASA 17/05/2001, pp. 14–16.

[65] AI, *Saudi Arabia, Defying World Trends: Saudi Arabia's Extensive Use of Capital Punishment*, AI Index: MDE 23/015/2001.

[66] On the need for research in this area, see Mark Constanzo and Sally Constanzo, 'Jury Decision Making in the Capital Penalty Phase: Legal Assumptions, Empirical Findings, and a Research Agenda', *Law and Human Behavior* 16 (1992), pp. 185–201.

[67] The 'death-qualified jury case' decided by the Supreme Court was *Lockhart* v. *McCree* (1986). One commentator, Professor Welsh White, has remarked that the Court's decision in this case shows that it 'holds that maintaining the smooth functioning of our system of capital punishment is a higher priority than protecting the rights of capital defendants', *The Death Penalty in the Nineties* (1994), p. 207. Among the large literature on this subject, of particular importance are: Samuel R. Gross, 'Determining the Neutrality of Death Qualified Juries', *Law and Human Behavior* 8 (1984), pp. 7–29; Patrick J. Callans,

'death-qualified' were more likely to convict a sample case they were presented with than were black or Hispanic juror candidates, and about 1.5 times more likely to sentence them to death.[68] This has been confirmed by the Capital Jury Project. Professor Bowers and his team analysed decision-making by jurors in 340 capital cases and interviewed 1,155 of the jurors in 14 states. They found that the racial composition of the jury had a marked effect on whether or not the jury sentenced the defendant to death in cases where the defendant was black and the victim white. They isolated a 'white male dominance effect' and a 'black male presence effect' (blacks were almost always in a minority) although there was no such effect as regards women jurors. There was a 41 percentage points difference in the likelihood of a death sentence where there were four or fewer white males on the jury (30 per cent sentenced to death) than where there were five or more (70 per cent sentenced to death). Where there was no black member of the jury, 71.9 per cent of defendants in black-defendant–white-victim cases were sentenced to death, as opposed to 37.5 per cent in similar cases where there were one or more black male jurors. Significantly, these differences were not found in white–white and black–black cases.

By interviewing black and white male jurors from the same juries, the researchers discovered that, as the decision-making process progressed from stage to stage, the differences between the views of black and white male jurors on the appropriateness of imposing a death sentence grew wider, especially in the black-defendant–white-victim cases.

At the guilt phase [of the trial] whites were three times more likely than blacks to take a pro-death stand on punishment (42.3% vs. 14.7%), and after sentencing instructions [from the judge] they were four times more likely to do so (58.5% vs. 15.2%). By the first vote on punishment [when they were asked again by the researchers what they thought], the differential between white and black jurors on death reached more than seven to one (67.3% vs. 9.1%).

By questioning the jurors further it was revealed that black male jurors were much more likely than white male jurors to have 'lingering doubts' about the defendant's degree of responsibility for the crime and therefore whether the defendant was guilty of capital murder; to be much more sensitive to indications of remorse; and to be much less likely to take into account perceptions of future dangerousness in decid-

'Sixth Amendment: Assembling a Jury Willing to Impose the Death Penalty: A New Disregard for a Capital Defendant's Rights', *Journal of Criminal Law and Criminology* 76 (1985), pp. 1027–1050; Michael Finch and Mark Ferraro, 'The Empirical Challenge to Death Qualified Jurors: On Further Examination', *Nebraska Law Review* 65 (1986), pp. 21–74. See also, a discussion of whether the empirical evidence bears out the contention that death-qualified jurors are more likely than excluded jurors to convict in capital cases; Roger Elliott, 'Social Science Data and the APA (American Psychology Association): The *Lockhart* Brief as a Case in Point', *Law and Human Behavior* 15 (1991), pp. 59–76, and Phoebe C. Ellsworth, 'To Tell what we Know or Wait for Godot?', *ibid.*, pp. 77–90. Also, Marla Sandys, 'Stacking the Deck for Guilt and Death: The Failure of Death Qualification to Ensure Impartiality', in Acker, Bohm, and Lanier (eds), n. 25 above, pp. 295–298.

[68] See the study based on 2,000 holders of Texas drivers' licences by Frank P. Williams III and Marilyn D. McShane, 'Inclinations of Prospective Jurors in Capital Cases', *Sociology and Social Research* 74(2) (1990), pp. 85–94.

ing on the imposition of the death penalty in black-defendant–white-victim cases.[69] What is striking is that these findings related to cases nearly all of which were decided *after* the US Supreme Court, in the case of *Turner* (1986), had ruled that 'a capital defendant accused of an interracial crime is entitled to have prospective jurors informed of the race of the victim [specifically in Turner's case, a black defendant and white victim] and questioned on the issue of racial bias'.[70] As Bowers and his colleagues rightly assert, their evidence suggests that this would do little to safeguard a black defendant in a white-victim case from racial bias. Thus, their research confirmed that the racial composition of a jury matters enormously in respect of a defendant's prospect of being sentenced to death. The inference to be drawn is that arbitrariness and discrimination in the application of the death penalty in black-offender–white-victim cases is bound up with different perceptions of persons drawn from different racial groups about whether a defendant deserves to die. As they point out, this question is fundamentally one that involves subjective judgements. And such judgements are inevitably affected by experience and prejudice. It appears, therefore, that leaving the resolution of such issues to citizens acting as jurors in a racially divided and discriminatory society is a fundamental flaw in the administration of capital punishment in the United States, the subject of Chapter 6 pages 196–200.

Earlier findings from the Capital Jury Project had indicated some of the other biases that may occur: jurors who underestimated (usually very considerably) the length of time a defendant would spend in custody if not sentenced to death were more likely to vote for death and so were jurors concerned about danger; there were worrying instances of racial prejudice and stereotyping and such feelings of outrage about the nature of the murder that some jurors were simply unable to give proper

---

[69] William J. Bowers, Benjamin D. Steiner, and Marla Sandys, 'Death Sentencing in Black and White: An Empirical Analysis of the Role of Jurors' Race and Jury Racial Composition', *University of Pennsylvania Journal of Constitutional Law* 3 (2001), pp. 171–272. See also, William Bowers, Marla Sandys, and Benjamin D. Steiner, 'Foreclosed Impartiality in Capital Sentencing: Juror's Predispositions, Guilt-Trial Experience, and Premature Decision-Making', *Cornell Law Review* 83 (1998), pp. 1476–1556. This study showed that those jurors who favoured the death penalty rather than life imprisonment were more likely to have made up their mind during the guilt-finding phase of the trial and to stick to this decision during the penalty decision phase, whereas those who least favoured the death penalty were more likely to be affected by 'lingering doubts' when it came to sentencing. In Philadelphia Professor Baldus and his colleagues found that in the 110 death sentences imposed the jury had failed to find a single mitigating circumstance in 59 of them, and that this was particularly unfavourable to black defendants, even where the juries had a preponderance of black members. They concluded therefore that 'the principal source of the racial disparities in Philadelphia is jury, rather than prosecutorial, decision making' and that 'the race-of-defendant effects we see in jury weighing decisions may reflect a tendency for juries in black defendant cases to give less mitigative weight to the mitigators they find than they do in the non-black defendant cases'. Thus, 'penalty-trial death-sentencing rates for black and non-black defendants of .38 and .24 respectively, after adjustment for the relative culpability of the two groups of cases estimated with the salient factors measure of defendant culpability of the two groups of cases, was equivalent to 1.6 times greater (.38/.24)'. See David C. Baldus *et al.*, 'Racial Discrimination and the Death Penalty in the Post-*Furman* Era: An Empirical and Legal Overview, with Recent Findings from Philadelphia', *Cornell Law Review* 83 (1998), pp. 1638–1770 at 1680, table 3, 1715, 1721, and 1726.

[70] *Turner* v. *Murray, Director, Virginia Department of Corrections,* 476 U.S. 28 (1986).

consideration to mitigating factors.[71] Perhaps most worrying of all, there was a high level of misunderstanding of capital sentencing law, especially the factors which could be regarded as mitigating circumstances and the way in which they should be balanced against aggravating factors, such that for 'virtually three out of four jurors . . . sentencing instructions did not guide their decision-making on punishment but served instead as an after-the-fact façade for a decision made prior to hearing the instructions'.[72]

The Supreme Court of the United States has recently held that a judge who refused to explain the meaning of an instruction to a jury—he simply told them to go back and read it again—had not acted in a way that prejudiced the defendant, Lonnie Weeks. The jury in this case had asked 'whether they were *required* to sentence him to death if they believed his crime was heinous, or if they believed Weeks himself constituted a continuing threat to society'. The right answer, of course, was no, because there are no mandatory capital statutes in the United States. But an astute study by Stephen Garvey and colleagues, using a mock jury of college students, found that only (*sic*) 29 per cent incorrectly interpreted the law after being given instructions by the 'judge' compared with 49 per cent of those who were (as in the real case) sent back to read the printed instructions themselves.[73] What is more, all the factors discussed above have been shown to be more, rather than less, likely to increase the probability of jurors handing down a death sentence.[74]

Of particular concern to black defendants in American murder trials has been the prosecution's use of peremptory challenges to exclude 'otherwise qualified and unbiased persons from the petit jury' due to their race. This was forbidden by the Supreme Court in the case of *Batson* v. *Kentucky* in 1986,[75] which held that 'specious reasons have been upheld for striking black jurors off the list' and that a person's race is simply 'unrelated to his fitness as a juror'. In 1992 this prohibition was extended, in the case of *Georgia* v. *McCollum*, to defence counsel's use of peremptory chal-

---

[71] See A. Sarat, 'Violence, Representation, and Responsibility in Capital Trials: The View from the Jury', *Indiana Law Journal* 70 (1995), pp. 1103–1135.

[72] See William J. Bowers and Benjamin D. Steiner, 'Choosing Life or Death: Sentencing Dynamics in Capital Cases'. in Acker, Bohm, and Lanier (eds), n. 25 above, pp. 309–349 at 321–328. In the case *Weeks* v. *Angelone*, the US Supreme Court ruled that a judge presiding over a death penalty case was not obliged to clarify a sentencing instruction that, while constitutional, left the jury confused. See Death Penalty Information Center, *New from the US Supreme Court 1999–2000 Term*, www.essential.org/dpic/supremecourt.html.

[73] See Stephen P. Garvey, Sheri Lynn Johnson, and Paul Marcus, 'Correcting Deadly Confusion: Responding to Jury Inquiries in Capital Cases', *Cornell Law Review* 85 (2000), pp. 627–651 at 639 and 642.

[74] Dr James Luginbuhl's interviews with 49 jurors in North Carolina were reported in Margaret Vandiver, *Jurors in Capital Cases*, Evidence to a Commission of Inquiry into the Use of the Death Penalty in the United States of America, 7 Aug. 1993. Also, James Luginbuhl, 'Comprehension of Judge's Instructions in the Penalty Phase of a Capital Trial: Focus on Mitigating Circumstances', *Law and Human Behavior* 16 (1992), pp. 203–218 at 217. A report based on interviews with 83 jurors who served on North Carolina juries in capital trials between 1990 and 1994 confirmed these earlier findings and revealed, in particular, the extent to which jurors did not understand the instructions they received on capital sentencing law. James Luginbuhl and Julie Howe, 'Discretion in Capital Sentencing Instructions: Guided or Misguided?', *Indiana Law Journal* 70 (1995), pp. 1161–1181.

[75] *Batson* v. *Kentucky*, 476 U.S. 79 (1986).

lenges.[76] However, it would not, of course, be irrational for defence counsel to seek to obtain a jury that he or she believes would lessen the prospect of his client's conviction, and the same might be said with even more force about a prosecutor keen to ensure conviction.

It is not surprising, therefore, to find that mere exhortation did not have the effect that the Supreme Court intended. A recent study by David Baldus and colleagues of the use of peremptory challenges to remove jurors in murder trials in Pennsylvania between 1981 and 1997 has shown that 'discrimination in the use of peremptory challenges on the basis of race and gender by both prosecutors and defence counsel was widespread' and that the *Batson* judgment had only had a marginal effect. Such discrimination was based on stereotypes 'that reflect fundamental differences in how male and female, black and non-black jurors view issues of criminal responsibility, culpability and punishment'. The prosecutors rather than defence counsel were most successful in obtaining a jury of their choice, for they were 'more successful in striking life-prone black venire members than were defense counsel in striking death-prone non-black venire members'. Baldus and his colleagues concluded, 'the upshot of the [prosecutor's] comparative advantage in its use of peremptory strikes appears to be enhanced death-sentencing rates, particularly in cases involving black defendants'. This research had uncovered 'a significant source of injustice in the peremptory strike system, at least as used in Philadelphia capital trials' that could 'be justified neither legally or morally'.[77]

Some believe that the only effective remedy would be to ban peremptory challenges entirely so as to leave supervision of jury selection to the judge. That, of course, would require an assurance that judges were also not biased against black jurors.[78]

(f) Special Courts: Independent and Impartial Tribunals?

As Marc Ancel pointed out, it is extremely difficult to compare the status of the courts in different countries that are empowered to impose the death sentence in the first instance. In most jurisdictions, only the highest level of criminal court or the Supreme Court has the power to impose a death sentence. But in several countries

---

[76] *Georgia* v. *McCollum*, 505 U.S. 42 (1992).

[77] David C. Baldus, George Woodworth, David Zuckerman, Neil Alan Weiner, and Barbara Broffitt, 'The Use of Peremptory Challenges in Capital Murder Trials: A Legal and Empirical Analysis', Symposium: Race, Crime, and the Constitution, *University of Pennsylvania Journal of Constitutional Law* 3 (2001), pp. 3–170 at 124–128.

[78] In *Powers* v. *Ohio* (1991)—a white defendant who appealed against peremptory challenges against African American prospective jurors—the Court held that such challenges could not be used for the purpose of excluding 'otherwise qualified and unbiased persons from a petit jury' on grounds of their race. See Lawrence Elman Jr, Note, 'Peremptory Challenges under *Batson* v. *Kentucky*: Equal Protection under the Law or an Unequal Application of the Law', *Criminal and Civil Confinement* 20 (1994), pp. 481–538 at 538; and Susan N. Herman, 'Why the Court Loves *Batson*: Representation-Reinforcement, Colorblindness and the Jury', *Criminal and Civil Confinement* 20 (1994), pp. 1807–1853. And Bryan A. Stevenson and Ruth E. Friedman, 'Deliberate Indifference: Judicial Tolerance of Racial Bias in Criminal Justice', *Washington and Lee Law Review* 51 (1994), pp. 509–527 at 519–527.

they are described vaguely as 'Court of Justice', 'Divisional', 'Regional', 'District', or even 'Competent' courts. Where Islamic law has been adopted, the Shari'a Courts have power to impose the death sentence, and it has been claimed (as mentioned above) that the judges of these courts are not always fully trained in the law, nor are all procedural guarantees such as representation by a competent counsel guaranteed.[79]

Several countries, when under military rule, set up Military Tribunals or Special Courts to deal with what they regarded as politically motivated offences or in response to particular outbreaks of crime. For example, in Nigeria special military Armed Robbery and Firearms Tribunals as well as Civil Disturbances Special Tribunals, consisting of two judges and one military officer selected by the government, were, until Nigeria returned to civil rule in 1999, empowered to impose death sentences. So were the Public Tribunals in Ghana, made up largely of lay members, which dealt with certain cases of murder of public officials and conspiracies against the government between 1982 and 1993.[80]

'Special Emergency Courts' were established in Sudan in 2001, and they have summarily imposed death sentences for murder, armed robbery, and arms smuggling on offenders who, according to Human Rights Watch, are denied legal representation. And in March 2002 a military court in Uganda sentenced two soldiers to death for murder after a peremptory court martial lasting only two hours and thirty-six minutes. They were publicly executed by firing squad four days later, leading Amnesty International to condemn the procedures for their lack of fair procedures and independence.

In Turkey Courts of National Security, rather than the Assize Courts, deal with certain offences against the state where the death penalty could be imposed; and in Guatemala some cases which have led to execution were apparently dealt with by Special Military Tribunals, even though they had not been finally judged in a Court of Appeal or the Supreme Court of Justice. The Special Rapporteur on extra-judicial, summary, or arbitrary executions has reported that, in a number of cases in Egypt, 'defence lawyers had only limited access to their clients, and that the time allowed for preparation of the defence was not adequate'. Furthermore, he was concerned about 'the impartiality and independence of the Military Appeals Bureau and the lack of the effectiveness of this review procedure'.[81]

Similar concerns have been expressed that military tribunals in the Democratic Republic of Congo have sentenced many to death without proper due process. And, as mentioned above, the procedures in Iran's Revolutionary Courts do not meet

---

[79] For example, in the Shari'a Courts in Northern Nigeria where death sentences have been imposed. See AI, *BAOBAB for Women's Human Rights and Amnesty International Joint Statement on the Implementation of New Sharia-Based Penal Codes in Northern Nigeria*, AI Index: AFR 44/008/2002.

[80] See AI, *The Public Tribunals in Ghana* (July 1984), and on the procedures of the Civil Disturbances Special Tribunals in Nigeria, see Michael Birnbaum QC, *Nigeria: Fundamental Rights Denied: Report of the Trial of Ken Saro-Wiwa and Others*, A Report for the Bar Human Rights Committee of England and Wales, Law Society of England and Wales, and Article 19, the International Centre against Censorship (June 1995).

[81] E/CN.4/1994/7, paras. 255–256.

international standards in these regards. Following the attack on the United States on 11 September 2001, Spain decided not to extradite a group of Al-Qaeda suspects to the United States unless they received guarantees that the suspects would not face the death penalty. President George W. Bush then decided to authorize by executive order on 13 November 2001 the establishment of Military Tribunals, sitting either inside or outside the United States, to try non-US citizens accused of terrorism, and gave that tribunal power to impose the death penalty.[82] At the time this book went to press, it remained to be seen whether they will be used in the face of strong criticism from civil liberties groups, and, if so, what procedural protections they will accord to the accused.

(g) Circumventing the Law Altogether

Whatever the safeguards for a fair trial may be in law, they are of little value if the state allows any of its organs to bypass normal criminal procedure through the use of internment, summary trials, or simply by summary executions, 'disappearances', and politically motivated murders carried out by the police, the army, militias, or other organs of the state. The tendency to resort to executions without any legal process as a tool of repression appears particularly at times of political instability and perceived threat to national security by 'terrorists' or 'separatists'. It is often associated but by no means solely with the assumption of power by the military and by post-revolutionary anti-democratic governments. Under such circumstances an observation, made in relation to some countries of Latin America, appears to hold true in other regions of the world: 'application of the death penalty is reduced to the minimum, while replaced by the more serious reality of constant violations of human rights, principally the right to life and the judicial rights and guarantees inherent in these rights'.[83] There is a wealth of material about the extent of such extra-legal killings, which have occurred in countries that have abolished capital punishment de jure, as well as in those that retain it and sometimes, as in the former Yugoslavia and Rwanda, on a scale that can only be described as genocide. While the true extent of such executions worldwide cannot be verified, they cannot be ignored in the context of any discussion of the death penalty.

Alarming reports have continued to surface during the 1990s in the reports of the Special Rapporteur on extra-judicial, summary, or arbitrary executions to the United Nations Commission on Human Rights. These constitute a dreadful catalogue of non-judicially sanctioned killings in far too many countries of the world, certainly on a scale out of all proportion to executions carried out under the due process of law and sometimes amounting to genocide. For example, in 1994 the Special Rapporteur informed the Human Rights Committee that he had received reports that over 2,300 persons (including 49 minors) had been extra-judicially, summarily,

---

[82] Associated Press, 26 Nov. 2001.

[83] R. Ulate, 'The Death Penalty: Some Observations on Latin America', *United Nations Crime Prevention and Criminal Justice Newsletter* 12 and 13 (Nov. 1986), p. 30; see also, E. R. Zaffaroni, 'Executions without Due Process', *Revue Internationale de Droit Pénal* 58 (1987), pp. 785–795.

or arbitrarily executed in 51 different countries. And no one would claim that this is anywhere near the true total.[84] Among the countries mentioned were Bangladesh, Bosnia-Hercegovina, Egypt, Peru, and Ukraine.[85] In his report to the Secretary-General in 1995, the Special Rapporteur mentioned 700 individuals so executed in 45 different countries; in 1996 he noted an increase in extra-judicial, summary, or arbitrary executions, including the deaths of 45 minors. In 2000 the newly appointed Special Rapporteur, Miss Asma Jahangir, noted an increase of extra-judicial killings and transmitted allegations regarding the violations of the right to life of more than 700 individuals to 37 countries.[86] Amnesty International also frequently reports on suspected extra-judicial executions and recently alleged that unlawful executions had been carried out during 2000 in 61 countries, including for example only: Burundi, Colombia, Iraq, Israel, Mozambique, Namibia, the Russian Federation in Chechnya, the Philippines, St Lucia, and Thailand.[87]

The evidence reviewed in this section suggests that the legal safeguards promulgated by the United Nations are still, in many parts of the world, not being observed in the way that they should be. Although all states when replying to United Nations surveys claim that their systems of trial meet the safeguards, it is clear that many simply ignore certain of them, or circumvent them altogether. People are killed by organs of the state without a fair and public hearing; without being presumed innocent until proven guilty according to law; without adequate time and facilities for the preparation of their defence; without being informed clearly in an understandable language of the charges against them; without legal assistance or being able to call defence witnesses and cross-examine all witnesses for the prosecution; and without being free from pressures to confess their guilt.

4. The Right to Appeal

UN Safeguard No. 6, as amended in 1989, states that '*Anyone sentenced to death shall have the right to appeal to a court of higher jurisdiction . . . by providing for mandatory appeals . . . in all cases of capital offences. Anyone sentenced to death shall have the right to appeal to a court of higher jurisdiction, and steps should be taken to ensure that such appeals shall become mandatory.*' These mandatory provisions for appeal go beyond the '*right [of the convicted person] to his conviction and sentence being reviewed by a higher tribunal*', set out in Article 14 (5) of the ICCPR. Furthermore, in 1996 the Economic and Social Council called upon member states in which the death penalty

---

[84] *Report* by the Special Rapporteur, Mr Bacre Waly Ndiaye, Economic and Social Council, E/CN.4/1994/7.

[85] E/CN.4/1994/7, 7 Dec. 1993, para. 680, and E/CN.4/ 1995/61, 14 Dec. 1994, para. 376.

[86] E/CN.4/1995/61, para. 20; E/CN.4/1996/4, para. 594, 604; E/CN.4/1998/68, para. 3, p. 5; E/CN.4/2001/9, para. 14, p. 9.

[87] AI, *Report 2001*, on the Internet, Regional Summaries, web.amnesty.org/web/ar 2001.nsf/regSUM/ regSUM? Open Document.

may be carried out '*to allow adequate time for the preparation of appeals to a court of higher jurisdiction and for the completion of appeal proceedings, as well as petitions for clemency, in order to effectively apply rules 5 and 8 of the safeguards guaranteeing protection of the rights of those facing the death penalty*'. Those countries that have responded to United Nations surveys all said that (with a very few exceptions relating to military law, such as death sentences imposed by Emergency Supreme State Security Courts in Egypt[88]), they provided a right of appeal from a death sentence to a court of higher jurisdiction or alternatively an automatic review by an appeal court or its equivalent. None would allow the punishment to be carried out while an appeal was pending. However, it appears that this legal prescription has not always been followed in practice. There have been reported instances of executions before appeal in China (prior to the reform of the Law of Criminal Procedure in 1997), in Iran, Iraq, and Syria, and of death warrants being issued in Malaysia before all avenues of appeal had been exhausted. There is, in fact, no right of appeal from the Revolutionary Courts in Iran, Iraq, or Libya, nor from courts dealing with exceptional cases in Jordan, nor was there from the Armed Robbery and Firearms Tribunals or the Civil Disturbances Special Tribunals in Nigeria, as the conviction and execution in 1995 of the human rights activist Ken Saro-Wiwa and others testify.[89] In Egypt no appeal is allowed against sentence as such, except on consideration on points of law, not facts, by the Court of Cassation. But before pronouncing a death sentence the trial court has to submit case documents to the Mufti, the highest religious authority in the country, for his opinion. If he does not respond, in favour or against the death penalty, within ten days, the court is empowered to pronounce sentence of death. All that remains, other than appeal for cassation, is to seek clemency or a pardon from the President of the Republic.[90]

It is mandatory, according to official replies to the United Nations, for death sentences to be automatically reviewed by a court of appeal on questions of law, procedure, fact, and severity of penalty in Bahrain, Bangladesh, Bosnia-Hercegovina, Bulgaria (for mitigation of sentence), Guatemala, India, Jordan, Kazakhstan, Kenya, Peru, Qatar, Sierra Leone, Singapore, South Korea, Thailand, Trinidad and Tobago, Tunisia, Turkey, and Zimbabwe. But Lebanon and Togo provide an automatic right of appeal on grounds of law and procedure only. The new Chinese Criminal Law of 1997 has made it mandatory for all death sentences, except for those that according to law should be decided by the Supreme People's Court, to be submitted to the Supreme People's Court for 'verification and approval'. The time limit for an appeal against a judgment is ten days (Article 183). The Supreme People's Court has to approve all death sentences (Article 199) and after receiving an order from the Supreme People's Court . . . the sentence [shall] be executed within seven days'(Article 211). However, where public security is at risk, appeals from death

---

[88] See Carsten Jürgensen, 'Egypt: Death Penalty After Unfair Trials', Paper presented to the 1st World Congress against the Death Penalty, Strasbourg, 21–3 June 2001.

[89] See n. 80 above.

[90] See Jürgensen, n. 88 above.

sentences have, since 1983, been delegated down to the high courts, thus depriving the defendants in such cases of one tier of review.[91] Similarly, suspended death sentences (see Chapter 6 page 178) are reviewed and confirmed by a high court rather than by the Supreme Court.[92] In one recently publicized case in Hebei, three men have had their death sentences overturned on three occasions by the provincial People's High Court, but have remained in prison while the prosecution authorities continue to try to find grounds for their conviction.[93]

Appellate review is not automatic or mandatory in the following countries, where defendants have to exercise their right to initiate the process: Armenia, Barbados, Belarus, Burundi, Guinea, Japan, Morocco, Singapore, Sri Lanka (although in that country the prison authorities are obliged by law to assist all prisoners to lodge an appeal against their sentence) Tonga, Trinidad and Tobago,[94] and Zambia. In its communication to the Commission on Human Rights dated 23 December 1998 the Government of the Islamic Republic of Iran stated that anyone sentenced to death has the right to appeal to a court of higher jurisdiction including the Supreme Court, but that the sentence would be carried out: (*a*) if no protest or appeal has been made within the legal time limit of thirty days; (*b*) if the verdict is confirmed by the Supreme Court; or (*c*) where the request for appeal has been rejected or the appeal has been rejected in a final judgment.[95] Comoros, where capital cases are tried at a Special Court of Assize, had no provisions for appeal because the Court of Cassation was not operating, apparently because no judges had yet been appointed by the National Assembly. According to the UN Special Rapporteur, the law of the Islamic state of Oman does not allow people to appeal death sentences for premeditated murder.[96]

Appellate review of the death penalty is automatic in all but one of the retentionist American states, as well as under federal law,[97] and all but a few have statutes

---

[91] See Albrecht, n. 6 above, p. 117.

[92] *Ibid.*, p. 98. Both the accused and the prosecutor are able to appeal death penalty cases (Art. 180/181), this would be considered double jeopardy in the United States. However, according to Chinese law and beliefs this concept allows for justice to be served, no matter which side originally prevailed. See P.A. Seay, 'Law, Crime, and Punishment in the People's Republic of China: A Comparative Introduction to the Criminal Justice and Legal System of the People's Republic of China', *Indiana International and Comparative Law Review* 9 (1998), pp. 143–153 at 150.

[93] Quoted in Marina Svensson, 'State Coercion, Deterrence and the Death Penalty in the PRC', Paper presented to the Annual Meeting of the Association for Asian Studies, Chicago, 22–5 Mar. 2001.

[94] In practice, as in Barbados, final appeals are heard by the Judicial Committee of the Privy Council in London.

[95] *Status of the International Covenants on Human Rights, Question of the Death Penalty,* Report of the Secretary-General submitted pursuant to Commission Resolution 1998/8, Commission on Human Rights 55th Session, E/CN.4/1999/52/Add.1.

[96] *Civil and Political Rights Including the Questions of Disappearances and Summary Executions,* Report of the Special Rapporteur 2001, Addendum E/CN.4/2001/9/Add.1, p. 69.

[97] Arkansas is the only state that does not provide mandatory appellate review of the death penalty. In *Whitmore* v. *Arkansas* (1990) the Supreme Court did not consider the constitutionality of this issue because it refused to allow a petitioner, Jonas Whitmore, to bring the case as a 'next friend' to Ronald Gene Simmons, who had waived his right of appeal in Arkansas, on the ground that he did not have the requisite standing. See Carol A. Fitzsimmons, '*Whitmore* v. *Arkansas*: Execution of an Individual, without a Prior Mandatory Appellate Review, Denied Scrutiny', *Criminal and Civil Confinement* 18 (1992),

or rules of procedure that require a 'comparative proportionality review' of the sentence. It is not, however, a constitutional requirement,[98] and in some states (for example, Missouri and New Jersey) proportionality review is very limited, relying for its comparison pool on the small subgroup of cases that were actually sentenced to death, not all who were 'death-eligible'. Those who have studied this approach have asserted that 'The Court has not elected to use its available resources for a meaningful proportionality review process. Proportionality review as applied in this jurisdiction does little more than allow the reviewing court to justify a death sentence.'[99]

In most retentionist countries there is a mandatory waiting period between the time that a person is sentenced to death and the time of the imposition of the death penalty so that adequate time is available to prepare the case for appeal, with legal assistance provided. But the time allowed varies considerably. Some countries, such as Yugoslavia (Serbia and Montenegro), Mali, Madagascar, and Chad allow only three days; Armenia, Bangladesh, Belarus, and Turkey, only a week; China ten days, Guatemala, Japan, Morocco, Sri Lanka, and Tunisia, two weeks or less; only Bahrain, Burundi, Iran, Lesotho, Libya, Rwanda, Syria, Thailand, and Tonga allow thirty days or more. In Texas a defendant has only thirty days after his conviction to present new evidence. Sixteen other states of the United States require a new trial motion based on new evidence to be filed within sixty days of judgment. Eighteen US jurisdictions have time limits between one and three years, and only nine states have no time limits.[100] Thus, in general, the time allowed to lodge an appeal is short and in some countries very short indeed, especially when one recognizes that a successful appeal may have to rest upon the protracted process of uncovering new evidence. Furthermore, despite the existence of formal appeal procedures, it is apparent that in some countries persons have been executed within days of their conviction. Early in 2000 a 14-year-old soldier was executed, alongside four other soldiers, in the Democratic Republic of the Congo within thirty minutes of being found guilty by a Military Court: hardly time to lodge an appeal let alone for consideration of clemency.[101]

According to Amnesty International, executions in China can occur within weeks

---

pp. 203–229. According to US Department of Justice, *Capital Punishment 2000*, Bureau of Justice Statistics (2001), the only one of the 38 states not to provide automatic review of all death sentences regardless of the defendant's wishes is South Carolina, where the defendant has the right to waive the review.

[98] See Richard van Duizend, 'Comparative Proportionality Review in Death Sentence Cases', *State Court Journal* 8(3) (Summer 1984), pp. 9–13 and 21–3. And US Department of Justice, *Capital Punishment 1987*, Bureau of Justice Statistics (1988).

[99] See Donald H. Wallace and Jonathon R. Sorensen, 'Missouri Proportionality Review: An Assessment of a State Supreme Court's Procedures in Capital Cases', *Notre Dame Journal of Law, Ethics and Public Policy: Symposium on Capital Punishment* 8 (1994), pp. 281–315 at 313.

[100] See AI, *Fatal Flaws: Innocence and the Death Penalty in the USA*, AI Index: AMR 51/69/98, pp. 15–16. See also, for an argument advocating the repeal of all time limits, Vivian Berger, '*Herrera* v. *Collins*: The Gateway of Innocence for Death-Sentenced Prisoners Leads Nowhere', *William and Mary Law Review* 35 (1994), pp. 943–1023.

[101] AI, *The Death Penalty Worldwide: Developments in 2000*, AI Index: ACT 50/001/2001, p. 21.

of the alleged crime being prosecuted and 'within hours of final approval'.[102] Indeed, the executions usually take place the day after the mandatory one-month appeal period has expired.[103]

Another procedural aspect that gives cause for concern is the time taken for appeals to be decided. In the United States the system of state and federal appeals almost inevitably allows many years to pass—often spent on a separate death row (as discussed in Chapter 3) before execution. In some other countries, such as Indonesia and Japan, prisoners have also had to wait many years to learn of the outcome of their appeals.[104] In Jamaica the inordinately long time (in one case as long as seven years) that the Appeal Court had taken to deliver a written judgment[105] was found by the UN Human Rights Committee in *Pratt* v. *Jamaica* (1989) to be a violation of due process and also cruel and unusual punishment.[106] A recent review of cases in the Philippines showed that since the death penalty was reinstated in 1994, the Supreme Court had only 'disposed of 511 cases involving 591 of the 1,594 persons sentenced to death': 37 per cent over a span of six years. On average, 'death penalty inmates wait between 4 and 5 years before the final disposition of their cases'.[107]

Attempts have been made in the United States since the late 1980s to speed up executions: to avoid the constant burgeoning of death-rows, and to make executions more 'normal', more certain, rather than 'infrequent, conflict-laden and sporadic'. Thus it sought to avoid what it regards as excessive appeals being used as a delaying tactic by restricting the right to make habeas corpus petitions to federal courts.[108] In 1989 the Court ruled in *Teague* v. *Lane* that (with two narrow exceptions) federal habeas corpus petitioners would not be allowed to benefit from any new rules pertaining to the application of the death penalty unless they had been introduced prior to the defendant's conviction becoming final. In other words, new rules could

---

[102] AI, *People's Republic of China: The Death Penalty: Killing Chickens to Scare Monkeys*, Paper presented to the 1st World Congress against the Death Penalty, Strasbourg, 21–3 June 2001.

[103] A report, '10,000 Held in Strike Hard Drive', in the *South China Morning Post* (7 May 2001), noted that the *Lanzhou Morning Post* (Gansu province), announcing death sentences on eight persons convicted of violent crime and gang activities, had stated: 'The death sentences were expected to be carried out after appeals in 10 days'.

[104] AI, *Indonesia: The Application of the Death Penalty* (Nov. 1987), AI Index: ASA 21/27/87, p. 5.

[105] AI, *Jamaica: The Death Penalty* (1989), p. 13. There has since 1986 been an attempt to speed up this process.

[106] See R. M. B. Antoine, 'The Judicial Committee of the Privy Council—An Inadequate Remedy for Death Row Prisoners', *International and Comparative Law Quarterly* 41 (1992), pp. 179–190 at 180; and William A. Schabas, 'Execution Delayed, Execution Denied', *Criminal Law Forum* 5 (1994), pp. 180–193 at 181–182, citing *Pratt* v. *Jamaica*, Report of the Human Rights Committee, UN, GAOR, 44th Session, suppl. no. 40 at 222. UN doc. A/44/40 (1989).

[107] See FLAG, n. 9 above.

[108] See, for example, Raymond Bonner, 'Death Penalty', *Annual Survey of American Law* (1984), pp. 493–513 at 504–505; Robert Weisberg, 'Deregulating Death', *Supreme Court Review* (1983), pp. 305–395 at 343–344; Julia E. Boaz, 'Summary Processes and the Rule of Law: Expediting Death Penalty Cases in Federal Courts', *Yale Law Journal* 95 (1985), pp. 349–370; and Timothy J. Foley, 'The New Arbitrariness: Procedural Default in Federal Habeas Claims in Capital Cases', *Loyola Los Angeles Law Review* 23 (1989), pp. 193–212.

no longer be retroactively applied to benefit prisoners on death row.[109] Two years later the Court in *McCleskey* v. *Zant* held that federal courts would not henceforth entertain repetitive requests for writs of habeas corpus. Prisoners would be obliged to set forth all their legal arguments the first time round or show good cause why an argument had not been filed earlier. Furthermore, the Supreme Court required federal courts to reject all claims if the proper procedures had not been followed by the defendant in state courts. An example was Roger Coleman, who filed in error (his attorney's error) his appeal in Virginia three days late. A federal court (*Coleman* v. *Thompson* (1991)) decided that Coleman had thereby procedurally defaulted and refused to hear his constitutional claim before he was executed.[110]

The Anti-Terrorism and Effective Death Penalty Act of 1996 laid down specific time limits within which appeals in the United States have to be made, a one-year limit to apply for a writ of habeas corpus at a state court (section 101). This was criticized in 1998 by the UN Special Rapporteur, who expressed concern that the Act, by severely limiting the ability of the federal courts to remedy errors and abuses in state proceedings, had 'further jeopardized the implementation of the right to a fair trial as provided for in the ICCPR and other international instruments'.[111] Andrew Cantu was executed in 1999, after failing to obtain a further review of his case because he had not complied with this one-year deadline.[112]

Similarly, in an attempt to limit the delay that can be brought about by repeated appeals on different grounds, the Florida legislature passed a bill in 2000 entitled the Death Penalty Reform Act of 2000 limiting the right of appeal, the overall aim being to reduce the time spent between sentence and execution to five years.[113] In 2001

---

[109] See Steven M. Goldstein, 'Chipping away at the Great Writ: Will Death Sentenced Federal Habeas Corpus Petitioners be Able to Seek and Utilise Changes in the Law?', *New York University Review of Law and Social Change* 18 (1990–1), pp. 357–414; also, James S. Liebman, 'More than "Slightly Retro": The Rehnquist Court's Rout of Habeas Corpus Jurisdiction in *Teague* v. *Lane*', *ibid.*, pp. 537–635. In another article Richard Faust, Tina J. Rubinstein, and Larry W. Yackle ('The Great Writ in Action: Empirical Light on the Federal Habeas Corpus Debate', *ibid.*, pp. 637–710), state that *Teague* and its progeny may ultimately curb, and curb drastically, the substantive scope of federal habeas jurisdiction; p. 646. Also, White, n. 67 above, pp. 19–23. See also Anthony Amsterdam's condemnation of the Court for interpreting delays in executions as a conspiracy of a small group of defence lawyers, rather than recognizing that in 1976, when it held that capital punishment was consistent with contemporary standards of decency, 'the Justices got that standard wrong' in, 'Selling a Quick Fix for Boot Hill', in Austin Sarat (ed), *The Killing State: Capital Punishment in Law, Politics, and Culture* (1999), pp. 148–183 at 165.

[110] See AI, *Fatal Flaws*, n. 100 above, p. 7. See also, Richard J. Bonnie, 'Preserving Justice in Capital Cases while Streamlining the Process of Collateral Review', *University of Toledo Law Review* 23 (1991), pp. 99–116; Joan Biskupic, *The Supreme Court Yearbook 1990–1991* (1992), pp. 11, 21–23, 58–59, and *Supreme Court Yearbook 1991–1992* (1993), pp. 8, 53–54.

[111] See AI, *United States of America: Failing the Future—Death Penalty Developments, March 1998–March 2000*, AI Index: AMR 51/03/00, p. 30. See also, Larry W. Yackle, 'The American Bar Association and Federal Habeas Corpus', *Law and Contemporary Problems* 61 (1998), pp. 171–192.

[112] *Cantu-Tzin* v. *Johnson* (1998) 162 F.3d 295 (United States Court of Appeals for the 5th Cir.). In 1999 the Mississippi legislature amended the code of criminal procedure, setting a time limit of one year within which a defendant must apply for post-conviction relief. See US, Department of Justice, *Capital Punishment 2000* (2001), p. 3.

[113] American Bar Association, *A Gathering Momentum: Continuing Impacts of the American Bar Association Call for a Moratorium on Executions* (Jan. 2000), Appendix D. See also, Florida state legislation on www.leg.state.fl.us/welcome/index.cfm Bill HB 1-A.

the Supreme Court of Florida amended Florida's rules of criminal procedure slightly to improve the capital post-conviction process and 'balance the concerns of fairness and justice with the need for finality in post conviction proceedings in death penalty cases'. However, the Supreme Court has not changed the time limitations provided by the Death Penalty Reform Act of 2000.[114] There is serious concern about how much further the courts can go in this direction without, as Professor Franklin Zimring has put it, 're-imagining fundamental principles of fairness and criminal justice'.[115]

Another issue has been whether prisoners should be able to exercise a right to terminate their appeals so as to expedite their execution. The US Supreme Court has allowed them to do so in a number of cases, which has given rise to considerable controversy.[116] Ten of the 66 people executed in 2001 had volunteered not to challenge their sentences and were therefore executed before all possible legal safeguards had been investigated. According to Amnesty International, more than 90 prisoners in the United States have done so between 1977 and 2001.[117]

To what extent do prisoners once sentenced to death have recourse to adequate legal representation for their appeals? Although in the United States constitutional issues have been fought with great skill by lawyers, especially those from the Legal Defence and Educational Fund of the National Association for the Advancement of Colored People, the situation in many states has been such that many indigent prisoners have had very limited legal assistance in making their appeals. In June 1989 the US Supreme Court in *Murray* v. *Giarratano (a class action)* held that indigent prisoners sentenced to death were not entitled to state-appointed attorneys beyond their first appeal. The situation appeared to have improved by the Anti-Drug Abuse Act of 1988 which gave an indigent death-sentenced prisoner a right to the assignment of one or more lawyers to represent him in habeas proceedings.[118] Minimum standards were set for years of experience and admission to practice in the relevant court, and 'reasonably necessary' investigative, expert, or other services were provided and fee caps dispensed with. In the wake of the Act the US Judicial Conference issued guidelines for a pay scale of $US75–125 per hour, and money was appropriated to set up Death Penalty Resource Centers to recruit and assist private

[114] (2001) *Amendments to Florida Rules of Criminal Procedure 3.851, 3.852, and 3.993 and Florida Rule of Judicial Administration 2.050n1* Supreme Court of Florida, no. SC96646.

[115] Franklin E. Zimring, 'The Executioner's Dissonant Song: On Capital Punishment and American Legal Values', in Austin Sarat (ed), *The Killing State: Capital Punishment in Law, Politics and Culture* (1999), pp. 137–147.

[116] See David Pannick, *Judicial Review of the Death Penalty* (1982), pp. 159–166; Tim Kaine, 'Capital Punishment and the Waiver of Sentence Review', *Harvard Civil Rights–Civil Liberties Law Review* 18 (1983), pp. 483–524; Melvin L. Urofsky, 'A Right to Die: Termination of Appeal for Condemned Prisoners', *Journal of Criminal Law and Criminology* 75 (1984), pp. 553–582; and Welsh S. White, 'Defendants who Elect Execution', *University of Pittsburgh Law Review* 48 (1987), pp. 855–877 at 871.

[117] AI, *United States of America: Arbitrary, Discriminatory, and Cruel: An Aide-Mémoire to 25 Years of Judicial Killing*, AI Index: AMR 51/003/2002.

[118] In *McFarland* v. *Scott, Director, Texas Department of Criminal Justice, Institutional Division* (1994) the US Supreme Court held that federal judges must appoint a lawyer for a death row inmate who requests assistance in preparing a habeas corpus petition and can stay the execution until a petition is filed.

lawyers handling death penalty cases. Centres were established in 19 states. However, even this injection of resources could not meet the scale of the problem. The 16 attorneys at the Texas Resource Center found it impossible to cope with the burden of work, and it was estimated in early 1993 that 'more than 75 death row inmates in Texas had no representation, many of whom were scheduled for execution within 5 weeks'.

Another report concluded that the funds were exhausted so that none could be allocated for payment of counsel or litigation expenses at the state habeas level. Clearly, without the Resource Centers the situation in regard to making effective use of the right to appeal would be even more dire.[119] It was therefore particularly worrying when the centres (now to be called Post-Conviction Defender Organizations) lost their federal funding in October 1995 after they came under attack, because of their success, by the National Association of Attorneys General.[120] In Alabama 95 per cent of the almost 200 prisoners on death row in 2001 were indigent, yet 30 of them were facing the death penalty with no assistance from a lawyer.[121]

The crisis engendered by the revelations of wrongful convictions in Illinois and elsewhere in the United States has had, at last, some effect on this dismal situation. In June 2001 an increase in the hourly rate for private counsel defending federal criminal defendants was agreed under the Criminal Justice Act. At the same time the Texas Fair Defence Act was signed by Governor Perry facilitating the establishment of public defender offices. The Act explicitly states that 'counties must adopt and publish consistent county-wide indigent defence systems which meet basic minimum standards'. The Act also adopted state-wide minimum qualifications for attorneys handling capital cases.[122]

5. The Right to Seek a Pardon or Commutation of Sentence

Article 6(4) of the ICCPR and UN Safeguard No. 7 both stipulate in almost identical wording that '*Anyone sentenced to death shall have the right to seek pardon, or commutation of sentence. Amnesty, pardon or commutation of the sentence of death may be granted in all cases of capital punishment.*'[123]

The Economic and Social Council (ECOSOC) further strengthened Safeguard No. 7 in 1989 by '*providing for automatic . . . review with provisions for clemency or*

---

[119] Death Penalty Information Center, n. 43 above, p. 19. See also the report by the Spangenberg Group, *A Study of Representation of Capital Cases in Texas* (1993), p. ii.

[120] See Stephen B. Bright, 'The Politics of Capital Punishment: The Sacrifice of Fairness for Executions', in Acker, Bohm, and Lanier (eds), n. 25 above, p. 128.

[121] See *American Prospect* 12(8) (1 May 2001).

[122] See Texas Fair Defence Act of 2001, SB 7. It should be noted, however, that in January 2002 the Texas Court of Criminal Appeals had ruled that death row inmates had no right to capable counsel in their appeals, prompting dissenting Judge Price to remark that 'competent counsel' 'ought to require more than a human being with a law licence and a pulse'. Reported in the *Houston Chronicle*, 12 Jan. 2002.

[123] Amnesty is not mentioned in Safeguard no. 7.

pardon in all cases. Seven years later, in 1996, ECOSOC called upon member states in which the death penalty may be carried out '*to ensure that officials involved in decisions to carry out an execution are fully informed of the status of appeals and petitions for clemency of the prisoner in question*'.

Those retentionist countries that have replied to the United Nations surveys have said that in every case where a death sentence had been imposed the possibility existed for seeking a pardon or commutation or reprieve or act of clemency—the three latter terms being used interchangeably to mean the substitution of a lesser penalty than death. Sometimes there is a time limit. In Egypt, for example, the sentence is executed if no order for pardon or commutation is issued within fourteen days. It appears that in most retentionist countries clemency can be sought both while the various appeal and confirmation procedures are pending and after final judgment is announced. In Thailand sixty days are allowed after final judgment for an appeal of clemency to the King. And China, for example, allows the defendant to present a petition 'after final judgment is announced but before it is submitted to the Supreme People's Court for approval and an order to execute the sentence of death is issued, or within seven days before execution after receiving the order to execute the death sentence'.[124] However, continuing reports, right up to the 'crackdown' in May–June 2001, of 'sentencing rallies' at which death sentences were affirmed before large crowds and the defendants afterwards swiftly executed suggest that this safeguard guaranteeing time to present an appeal for clemency is not always observed, or even if observed, given cursory consideration.[125]

In the United States the Governor alone has the authority to decide clemency in 14 states, in a further 11 he has discretion to decide, but only after considering a recommendation from the Pardons Board or Advisory Group. In eight states the Governor cannot commute a death sentence unless it has been recommended by the Board, although he or she may decline to follow a positive recommendation for clemency: Texas is such a state. In five states a Board or Advisory Group is solely responsible for making the determination, although in two of them the Governor sits on the Clemency Board.[126] In many states the Pardons Board is appointed by the Governor or appointed by procedures which the Governor can influence. In respect of federal prisoners only the President of the United States can grant clemency, and the procedures applying to prisoners under sentence of death are specified in the Code of Federal Regulations: 'No petition for clemency should be filed before proceedings on direct appeal have terminated, the prisoner should file a petition not later than 30 days after receiving notification on the scheduled day of execution.'[127] The President is assisted in his decision to grant clemency by the Office of the Pardon Attorney.

---

[124] Reply to *UN Safeguards Survey, 1987.*
[125] Report in the *Daily Telegraph,* 22 June 2001.
[126] See James R. Acker and Charles S. Lanier, 'May God—or the Governor—Have Mercy: Executive Clemency and Executions in Modern Death-Penalty Systems', *Criminal Law Bulletin* 36 (2000), pp. 200–237.
[127] Title 28, Ch. 1, para. 1.10, revised 1 July 2001.

There is very little data available on the extent to which powers to pardon, commute, or reprieve are exercised in retentionist countries. In a few it appears to have been quite often granted. For example, in Russia in the period 1992–4, 98 per cent of those who appealed for pardon to, and were considered by, the Pardons Commission were granted it. However, the policy changed, and in 1995 only 9 per cent were pardoned.[128] In the years 1994 to 1998, 133 prisoners in Thailand sought a pardon (including commutation of the sentence), and 50 were successful. In addition, 75 prisoners under sentence of death benefited from an amnesty granted by the King in 1996, and in 2000 a further 30 prisoners had their death sentences reduced to life imprisonment as part of another Royal Amnesty. In 2000 President Yoweri Museveni commuted the sentences of 16 prisoners from death to life imprisonment in Uganda, and in Nigeria those prisoners awaiting execution for more than twenty years were pardoned and released and those under sentence of death between ten and twenty years had their sentence reduced to life imprisonment.[129] In Swaziland, in 2001, four murderers who had been on death row for between sixteen and eighteen years were pardoned by King Mswati, on the grounds that they had served sufficient time. In January 2001, on leaving office as President of the Philippines Joseph Estrada signed commutation orders for 103 death row prisoners,[130] and in March of that year the newly appointed President, Gloria Arroyo, commuted the death sentences of two prisoners whose executions were imminent. At the time she stated that she would not support the carrying out of executions during her time in office,[131] but has since announced that she has changed her mind.

In several retentionist countries pardons are rarely granted: they include Bahrain, Indonesia,[132] and Singapore, where, according to Amnesty International, the commutation of a death sentence by the President of Singapore in 1998 was only the fifth to be granted in thirty-five years.[133] No prisoners in Japan had sought a pardon or a reprieve and the only one who had sought commutation of sentence in the five years 1994–8 did not have it granted.

In the United States it had become exceptionally rare for the Governor of the State or a Board of Pardons to exercise clemency in favour of the prisoner: 'The prospect of clemency provides only the thinnest threads of hope and is certainly no guarantee against an execution of an innocent individual.'[134] Indeed, as Professor Bedau has shown, grants of clemency have become rarer: from about one in every four or five death row inmates in the 1970s to about one in 40 by the late 1980s. There were only 29 commutations of death sentences for humanitarian reasons in the twenty- year period 1973 to 1992,[135] and altogether only 40 between 1973 and

---

[128] See Mikhlin, n. 25 above, pp. 7 and 103–122.

[129] AI, *Report 2001*, Uganda at p. 252 and Nigeria at p. 183.

[130] *AI Report 2000*. In one case the President failed to get through on the telephone to the execution chamber in time to grant a last-minute reprieve, p. 193.

[131] AI, *Death Penalty News*, Mar. 2001, AI Index: ACT 53/002/2001.

[132] See Special Rapporteur's *Report*, E/CN.4/1996/4/Corr. 1, para. 244.

[133] AI, *Death Penalty News*, June 1998, AI Index: ACT 53/03/98, p. 4.

[134] Death Penalty Information Center, n. 13 above, p. 18.

[135] See Radelet and Bedau, n. 23 above, p. 119.

June 1999: a ratio of 13.8 executions to every one commutation, 'or roughly three to nine times greater than the comparable ratios [according to the state concerned] during the pre-*Furman* years'. Thirteen of these clemency decisions were in fact made by the Governors of New Mexico and Ohio—both of whom were opposed to the death penalty—as they left office.[136] But this was unusual: in Texas, for example, the single commutation recommended by the Pardons Board to the Governor in 1998 was the first for seventeen years.[137]

Yet, the aura of uncertainty that has begun to surround the death penalty since then may well have an effect on Governors, particularly given the support for moratoriums on executions until structural problems in death penalty procedures can (if they can) be sorted out. Thus, grants of executive clemency reached an all-time high for recent years in 1999, when one female and four male prisoners had their death sentences commuted to life imprisonment in five separate states. In 2001 President Bill Clinton commuted the death sentence of David Ronald Chandler, and in April 2001 the Governor of Oklahoma commuted the death sentence of a man who had been on death row for sixteen years because of doubts about his guilt. This was the first time that this had happened in that state for thirty-five years.

Furthermore, in the United States due process is absent from reviews of appeals for clemency, for the American courts have refused to recognize clemency proceedings as anything more than 'a right to ask for mercy'. Thus, in 1998 the US Supreme Court affirmed in the case of *Ohio Adult Parole Authority* v. *Woodward* that the 'heart of executive clemency [is] . . . to grant clemency as a matter of grace'.[138] In saying this, the Court relied on a 1981 judgment that commutation of sentence 'is simply a unilateral hope', not a due process right.[139] It is hardly surprising, therefore, that clemency proceedings have been stigmatized as 'standard-less in procedure, discretionary in exercise, and unreviewable in result',[140] and that there is increasing pressure to recognize the need for due process and detailed guidelines to govern the exercise of discretion in such proceedings.[141]

A breakthrough in the recognition that due process rights can be vital in clemency proceedings was made in 2000 in the case of *Lewis* v. *Attorney General of Jamaica*.[142] The Jamaican system, like that in other common law countries (such as Zambia[143]),

---

[136] See Acker and Lanier, n. 126 above, p. 215. Also, National Coalition to Abolish the Death Penalty, *Death Penalty Profile (1999 Wrap-Up)* (1999), Washington, www.ncadp.org/stats.html.

[137] See AI, *Killing without Mercy: Clemency Procedures in Texas*, AI Index: AMR 51/85/99, p. 6. Similarly, the pardoning of a mentally ill prisoner, who had committed the murder when aged 17, by the Georgia Board of Pardons and Paroles in February 2002, was the first such pardon granted by that body since 1994.

[138] *Ohio Adult Parole Authority* v. *Woodward*, 523 U.S. 272; 140 L.Ed. 2d 387 (1998).

[139] *Connecticut Board of Pardons* v. *Dumschat*, 452 U.S. 458 (1981).

[140] Hugo Adam Bedau, 'The Decline of Executive Clemency in Capital Cases', *New York University Review of Law and Social Change* 18 (1990–1), pp. 255–272 at 257. And Michael L. Radelet and Barbara A. Zsembik, 'Executive Clemency in Post-*Furman* Capital Cases', *University of Richmond Law Review* 27 (1993), pp. 289–314.

[141] See Daniel T. Kobil, 'The Evolving Role of Clemency in Capital Cases', in Acker, Bohm, and Lanier (eds), n. 25 above, pp. 541–544. Also, Acker and Lanier, n. 126 above, pp. 220–229.

[142] *Lewis* v. *Attorney General of Jamaica*, PC [2000] 3 W.L.R. 1785.

[143] See AI, *Zambia: Time to Abolish the Death Penalty*, AI Index: AFR 63/004/2001, pp. 15–16.

gives power to the head of state to consider a report from the trial judge and the views of an advisory committee (in this case the Jamaican Privy Council) on whether the prerogative of mercy should be exercised. The decision was entirely discretionary and gave no rights to defendants or their representatives to play an active part in the process. The Judicial Committee of the Privy Council in London (the highest appeal court for Commonwealth Caribbean countries) held, in this important judgment, that the procedures for clemency should conform to the standards required by judicial due process. In other words, the petitioner should be able to make representations, and be allowed to see all the documents placed before the Jamaican Privy Council: 'The act of clemency is to be seen as part of the whole constitutional process of conviction, sentence, and carrying out the sentence . . . the prerogative of mercy should be exercised by procedures which are fair and proper and to that end are subject to judicial review [to ensure that they are].' Furthermore, it was held that all proceedings relating to petitions to the Inter-American Commission for Human Rights must be completed before the Jamaican Privy Council deals with the question of the prerogative of mercy, and if the report of the international body was not accepted that Privy Council should explain why. This judgment applied to all Commonwealth Caribbean countries.

In countries where Islamic law prevails, the system of Diya operates in place of commutation where the offender has been convicted of murder (a Qisas offence, see Chapter 2 page 37). The relatives of the victim are given the choice between execution and reprieve of the offender, with or without receiving compensation. Executions may be postponed until the heirs are old enough to give their approval. Apparently these negotiations can go on right up until the point of execution, as apparently happened in Pakistan in October 1994,[144] in Iran in 2000, when a 17-year-old convicted of the kidnapping, rape, and murder of an 18-month-old child was forgiven by its father,[145] and in Saudi Arabia in June 2001, when the life of a 20-year-old Yemeni man was spared by the victim's father while the executioner was raising his sword to behead him in public in Riyadh.[146] But, of course, such pardons depend on the ability of the family of the condemned person to organize financial compensation or to mobilize the sympathy of the victim's family. It is not surprising, therefore, to find that foreign workers are rarely protected from execution by Diya. Apparently there is one pardon granted in relation to every six executed Saudi Arabian citizens, but only one in relation to every 84 executed foreign workers.[147]

---

[144] See AI, *Medical Death Penalty Newsletter* 7(2) (1995).
[145] See AI, *The Death Penalty Worldwide: Developments in 2000*, AI Index: ACT 50/001/2001, p. 21. And in November 2001 a man was cut down alive after hanging on a gallows for four minutes when he was pardoned by an aged relative of the victim. See AI, *Death Penalty News*, Dec. 2001, AI Index: ACT/001/2002, p. 3.
[146] Reported in 'Last-Second Reprieve from Execution Blade', *The Times*, 28 June 2001, p. 15.
[147] AI, *Saudi Arabia, Defying World Trends: Saudi Arabia's Extensive Use of Capital Punishment*, AI Index: MDE 23/015/2001.

6. Finality of Judgment: Awaiting the Outcome of Legal Proceedings

UN Safeguard No. 8 is aimed to ensure that no one is executed while any appeal is pending to any authorized body, national or international: '*Capital punishment shall not be carried out pending any appeal or other recourse procedure or other proceeding relating to a pardon or commutation of sentence.*'

Those retentionist states that have provided information to the United Nations claim that it is their practice invariably to delay executions until all appeal, recourse, pardon, and clemency proceedings have been exhausted and the outcome communicated to the defendant and his or her legal advisers. Executions can only be carried out by written authority following consideration of appeals and clemency. However, this provision may be rendered ineffective if the courts place a time limit on consideration of new evidence. Thus, in *Herrera* v. *Collins* (1993) the US Supreme Court upheld a Texas statute forbidding the appellate courts from considering newly discovered evidence supporting a claim of innocence in a capital case unless the evidence had been filed within thirty days of the conclusion of the trial. Herrera's family had come forward with the new evidence (that his deceased brother was the murderer) eight to ten years after the original trial, and the Court held that this could not be dealt with by way of appeal or the ordering of a new trial.[148] The only recourse was executive clemency. Notwithstanding the fact that Chief Justice Rehnquist had said that society could count on governors and parole boards to exercise clemency when the defendant's guilt is in doubt, Herrera was executed without receiving a full hearing by the Texas Board of Pardons and Parole.

There have been other disturbing cases of executions going ahead before all avenues of appeal or other proceedings before international bodies have been completed. For example, the Special Rapporteur on extra-judicial, summary, or arbitrary executions expressed 'his most profound concern at this clear violation of the right to life' when Glen Ashby was executed on 14 July 1994 in Trinidad and Tobago while 'appeal procedures were still pending'.[149] More recently, when Mariette Bosch was executed for murder in Botswana in April 2001, neither her family nor her lawyer was informed of the execution date, even though her lawyer had given notice of intention to petition for Presidential clemency following the rejection of her appeal.[150] In another case, Trinidad and Tobago carried out an execution in July 1999 while the prisoner's petition was still pending before the

---

[148] The Court noted that the procedural ban could not be set aside as a miscarriage of justice because Herrera's claims of innocence were not supported by any claim that there were constitutional errors at his trial. Nevertheless, it held that to execute an innocent person would be cruel and unusual punishment, violating the Eighth Amendment. Thus, in a more recent decision in *Schlup* v. *Delo* (1995), the appellant was not procedurally barred from consideration of his constitutional claims in federal court because the alleged constitutional errors that occurred in his trial 'probably' resulted in the conviction of one who is actually innocent.

[149] E/CN. 4/1995/61, para. 382.

[150] AI, *Botswana: Amnesty International Appalled by Secret Execution*, AI Index: AFR 15/002/2001.

Inter-American Commission on Human Rights.[151] Similarly, early in 2000 a man was executed in the Bahamas despite the fact that a petition was pending before the same body. Furthermore, three men were executed in the Philippines in 1999 despite the fact that the UN Human Rights Committee had asked the government not to do so while their cases were still under consideration relating to allegations of the violation of their right to counsel during a police line-up, their right not to be tortured, and their right to life.[152] Not surprisingly the Committee found the Philippines in breach of its international obligations. A similar situation is reported to have occurred in Tajikistan when a man was executed while his case was under review by the Committee.[153]

In the Caribbean, Trinidad and Tobago, Jamaica, and Guyana have expressed frustration with what they regarded as the excessive time taken for appeals to be heard and deliberated on by the UN Human Rights Committee and the Inter-American Commission on Human Rights: so long in fact that it barred them from enforcing the death penalty (see Chapter 2 page 62). So they took pre-emptive action. In May 1998 Trinidad and Tobago withdrew accession to the Optional Protocol to the ICCPR as well as the American Convention on Human Rights. The same day it reacceded to the ICCPR with reservations 'to the effect that the Human Rights Committee shall not be competent to receive and consider communications relating to any prisoner who is under sentence of death in respect of any matter relating to his prosecution, his detention, his trial, his conviction, his sentence or the carrying out of the death sentence on him and any manner connected therewith'.[154] However, the UN Human Rights Committee held in the case of *Rawle Kennedy*, an alleged victim of a human rights violation connected with the death penalty in Trinidad and Tobago, that it

Cannot accept a reservation which singles out a certain group of individuals for lesser protection than that which is enjoyed by the rest of the population . . . This constitutes a discrimination which runs counter to some of the basic principles embodied in the Covenant and its Protocols, and for this reason the reservation cannot be deemed compatible with the object and purpose of the Optional Protocol.[155]

While Jamaica continues to recognize the competence of the Inter-American Commission on Human Rights, it has unilaterally set a time limit of six months for the Commission to consider appeals against the death sentence once all domestic avenues of appeal and commutation have been exhausted. This is clearly contrary to

---

[151] Despite the fact that Trinidad and Tobago had withdrawn from the Inter-American Convention on Human Rights, the appellant had access to the Inter-American Commission on Human Rights by virtue of Trinidad and Tobago's membership of the Organization of American States.

[152] See FLAG, n. 9 above.

[153] See AI, *Concerns in Europe, January–June 2001*, AI Index: EUR 01/003/2001.

[154] Ministry of Foreign Affairs, Republic of Trinidad and Tobago, *Instrument of Accession to the Optional Protocol to the International Covenant on Civil and Political Rights with a Reservation Excluding the Competence of the Human Rights Committee to Receive and Consider Communications in Relation to the Imposition of the Death Penalty* (1998).

[155] Human Rights Committee, CPR/C/67/D/845/1999.

Resolution 1999/61 of the UN Commission on Human Rights that no one should be executed 'as long as any related legal procedure, at international or national level, is pending'.

7. THE QUESTION OF COST

If capital trials are to be conducted with full protections against wrongful convictions, appeals allowed for, with the best available legal assistance; and lengthy periods are spent in confinement, with only a small proportion of those convicted eventually executed, the costs of the system are bound to be high. Estimates made in the United States suggest that each execution costs the state somewhere between $2 million and $3.2 million. As one report says: 'The expansion of the death penalty is on a collision course with a shrinking budget for crime prevention.' It is possible that this heavy expenditure will inevitably lead to a shortening of the period allowed before execution of the sentence.[156] Indeed, the very high costs associated with the death penalty, when seen in the context of the small proportion of cases to whom it is eventually applied, was a reason why some members of the Illinois Commission which reported in April 2002 favoured abolition.[157]

8. CONCLUSIONS

This review of the evidence relating to the extent to which retentionist countries have abided (or perhaps it would be better to say, for some, have in practice been able to abide) by the safeguards established by the United Nations and the ICCPR for the provision of fair and impartial trials, the protection of the innocent, and the provision of effective appeals and clemency proceeding, shows how easy it is for abuses of human rights to occur when capital punishment is left on the statute book and put into effect.

Furthermore, very few retentionist countries appear to have put in place a systematic means for ensuring that all persons in the criminal justice system, including defendants and their legal representatives, are made familiar with the ECOSOC Safeguards and those provided by Articles 6 and 14 of the ICCPR. Most appear to assume that all concerned will be aware of the protections that are available under domestic law and procedure through the normal training they receive and that, as a

---

[156] See Death Penalty Information Center, *Millions Misspent: What Politicians don't Say about the High Cost of the Death Penalty* (rev. May 1994). Also, Philip J. Cook and Donna B. Slawson, *The Cost of Processing Murder Cases in North Carolina* (May 1993), Durham, NC: Terry Stanford Institute of Public Policy, Duke University. For a thorough analysis of the comparative costs of capital punishment and life imprisonment without parole, see Robert M. Bohm, 'The Economic Costs of Capital Punishment: Past, Present and Future', in Acker, Bohm, and Lanier (eds), n. 25 above, p. 458.

[157] *Report of the Governor's Commission on Capital Punishment. George H. Ryan Governor* (Apr. 2002), pp. 198–199.

matter of course, defendants will be made aware of safeguards by their counsel. Clearly, this is often not the case.

Yet while all must be done, where and while capital punishment persists, to make sure that the realities of criminal procedure match up to the international standards for the protection of those facing the sentence of death, it needs to be realized that many of the situations and practices reviewed in this chapter, and the next, arise by virtue of the very existence of the penalty of death and the emotions it arouses. Reform of procedures will simply not be sufficient to meet the human rights objections to capital punishment.

6

Questions of Equality and Fairness in the Administration of Capital Punishment

1. MANDATORY OR DISCRETIONARY?

Forty years ago Marc Ancel noted that 'in general the modern tendency is more and more to drop the mandatory character of the death penalty. It is provided as the ultimate punishment but replaceable by another penalty.'[1] The development of death penalty jurisprudence in the United States illustrates this well. In the 1960s 22 of the 42 American states had a mandatory death penalty. After the *Furman* decision in 1972 ruled all existing death penalty statutes to be unconstitutional, several states again enacted statutes which made death mandatory, but now for a narrower band of specifically defined categories of murder, such as the killing of a law enforcement officer, or killing while carrying out a robbery. However, in a series of cases, beginning with *Woodson* v. *North Carolina* and *Roberts* v. *Louisiana* in 1976, the Supreme Court struck down mandatory statutes of this kind. They were regarded as both too broad and too rigid. By not allowing the introduction of any mitigating circumstances they were liable both to invite juries to acquit, thereby reintroducing an undesirable element of arbitrariness into the system, and, where imposed, to be in some cases disproportionate to the circumstances of the case.[2] The Court had left the question open as to whether, in principle, a state could define a much more limited class of murder for which the death penalty might be applied mandatorily, and many commentators thought that this might be upheld for murder committed while serving a life sentence of imprisonment. However, the Nevada statute which provided

---

[1] United Nations, *Capital Punishment* (1962), para. 14, p. 11. It should be noted that this is hardly a modern trend. The movement to restrict capital punishment only to those instances of a capital crime where there were specific aggravations was a feature of law reform in England in the first half of the nineteenth century. See Leon Radzinowicz, *A History of English Criminal Law and its Administration*, vol. iv (1968), pp. 311–343.

[2] See *Columbia Law Review*, Note, 'Distinguishing among Murders when Assessing the Proportionality of the Death Penalty' 85 (1985), pp. 1786–1807 at 1790. And for an interesting study of the effects of a mandatory death penalty in the period prior to the *Furman* decision, see H. A. Bedau, 'Felony Murder Rape and the Mandatory Death Penalty: A Study in Discretionary Justice', *Suffolk University Law Review* 10 (1976), pp. 493–520. In David Pannick's view, the mandatory death sentence is 'neither fair nor reasonable, and lacks the procedural safeguards demanded by the rule of law and due process of law', *Judicial Review of the Death Penalty* (1982), p. 114.

for this was ruled unconstitutional in 1987 in the case of *Sumner* v. *Shuman*. Since then it has been widely accepted in the United States that no specific class of murder can be defined in statute for which it would be right, whatever the circumstances in which it had been committed, to impose the death penalty. It is also the case that although the death penalty may be imposed for many offences in China, the power to do so is always at the discretion of the court, as it is also in India.[3]

However, the optimism implicit in Ancel's statement, that mandatory death sentences would wither away, has not materialized. In at least 36 countries capital punishment is still mandatory for some crimes.[4] While it is usually only mandatory for 'capital murder', it is the only sentence available for armed robbery in several African countries, including Kenya and Nigeria, and in as many as 21 specific circumstances in the Philippines, including rape of a child. Furthermore, 12 of the 26 countries which introduced the death penalty for producing, or trading in, illicit drugs have made it mandatory on conviction of possessing quantities over certain prescribed (and sometimes relatively modest) amounts. This is the case in Brunei Darussalam, Egypt, Guyana, Iran, Jordan, Malaysia, Philippines, Qatar, Saudi Arabia, Singapore, Thailand, and the United Arab Emirates (see Chapter 3 pages 80–82). These laws have been supported by the governments concerned on the grounds that the threat of the imposition of capital punishment has, in all circumstances, a potent deterrent effect, and that to make exceptions would limit that effect. They have been strongly criticized by opponents of the death penalty for the arbitrariness of such laws—capital punishment quite often depending on the chance factor of how much of the drug the offender had in his or her possession or how much the police could trace, and quite often falling upon persons who had a relatively low involvement or peripheral role in the organization of trading, rather than those who were the 'kingpins'.[5]

Some countries have devised an attenuated form of mandatory death sentence by invoking the principle of 'exceptional circumstances'. In Africa several countries— Botswana, Lesotho, Swaziland, and Zimbabwe—have imported Roman–Dutch

---

[3] Murder committed by a life-sentenced convict was made subject to a mandatory penalty of death by section 303 of the Indian Penal Code. This was struck down as unconstitutional by the Supreme Court of India in *Mithu* v. *Punjab*, because it 'deprived the court of the use of its wise and beneficent discretion in a matter of life and death . . . So final, so irrevocable and so irresistible is the sentence of death that no law which provides for it without involvement of the judicial mind can be said to be fair, just and reasonable', *Supreme Court Reports* (1983) 2 S.C.R. at pp. 692–693.

[4] Barbados, Bahrain (for premeditated murder of a police officer), Belize, Brunei Darussalam, Comoros (for offences against the state, treason, and espionage), Egypt, Ghana, Grenada (murder), Guyana, Guatemala (rape of a child), Iran, Iraq, Jamaica, Jordan, Kenya, Kuwait (drugs offences), Lebanon (for treason and collaboration with the enemy), Malawi, Malaysia (drugs), Nigeria, Pakistan, Philippines (rape of a child, drugs, and other offences), Qatar, Saudi Arabia (for drug importers, smugglers, and recidivist distributors), Singapore, Taiwan (Republic of China) (drugs), Tanzania, Thailand, Togo (although no executions since 1979), Trinidad and Tobago, Turkey (for offences against the state), Uganda (for three offences, although President Museveni proposed in 2001 to abolish mandatory penalties), United Arab Emirates, Yemen, Zambia (for treason and armed aggravated robbery, and presumptive for murder), Zimbabwe (capital murder).

[5] See Ezzat Fattah, 'The Use of the Death Penalty for Drug Offences and Economic Crime', *Revue Internationale de Droit Pénal* 58 (1987), pp. 723–736 at 732–734.

common law with its concept of 'extenuating circumstances', sufficient proof of which gives the court the discretion to reduce a capital to a non-capital offence and impose a sentence other than death.[6] A similar provision exists also in Belize. Nevertheless, the failure of legislation to give any guidance as to what can constitute an extenuating circumstance means that there is a 'danger involved in making such a vital matter as extenuation depend upon the exercise of subjective moral judgement based on rather nebulous factors'.[7]

Elsewhere the approach has been to try to evade the objections to mandatory sentencing by defining only certain types of murder, regarded as particularly heinous, as 'capital murder'. This happened in Jamaica in 1992 (Offences Against the Person (Amendment) Act) after the Judicial Committee of the Privy Council in London had ruled in 1989 that the mandatory death penalty for murder in Jamaica was unconstitutional, as it had applied to far too wide a range of circumstances in which murder might be committed. Some (but not all) of the other Commonwealth countries of the Caribbean—the Bahamas, Barbados, Guyana, and Trinidad and Tobago—adopted the same mandatory provisions for 'capital murder'.

However, this approach has been widely contested. In a series of judgments concerning the Bahamas, Jamaica, and Trinidad and Tobago, as well as Grenada and St Vincent and the Grenadines,[8] the Inter-American Commission on Human Rights and the UN Human Rights Committee have held that a mandatory death penalty is in breach of the Convention: 'International and domestic authorities suggest that individualized sentencing or the exercise of guided discretion by sentencing authorities to consider potential mitigating circumstances of offenders and offences is a condition *sine qua non* for the non-arbitrary and humane imposition of capital punishment.'[9] As explained above (Chapter 2 page 61), the constitutional courts of Trinidad and Tobago, Jamaica, the Bahamas, and Barbados, because of the 'savings clause' in their Constitutions, cannot consider any legal challenge to the application of capital punishment as such.[10] However, in a landmark judgment in April 2001, the East Caribbean Court of Appeal held, in the case of *Spence and Hughes* v. *The Queen*, that the mandatory death penalty in St Vincent and the other island states covered by the Court[11] was an arbitrary deprivation of

[6] See E. Dumbutshena, 'The Death Penalty in Zimbabwe', *Revue Internationale de Droit Pénal* 58 (1987), pp. 521–532.

[7] See Geoffrey Feltoe, 'Extenuating Circumstances: A Life and Death Issue', *Zimbabwe Law Review* 4 (1987), pp. 60–87.

[8] *Hilaire* v. *Trinidad and Tobago*, Inter-American Commission Report 66/99 (1999); *Baptiste* v. *Grenada*, CR 38/00 (2000); *Rose and Others* v. *Jamaica*, CR 66/99 (1999), *Downer and Tracy* v. *Jamaica*, CR 41/00 (2000), *Edwards* v. *The Bahamas*, CR 48/01 (2001). Also the judgment of the UN Human Rights Committee in *Thompson* v. *Saint Vincent and the Grenadines* (2000), UN Doc. CCPR/C/70/D/906/1998, which held that the mandatory death penalty breached Article 6 (1) of the ICCPR (the right to life). [9] *Baptiste*, para. 59.

[10] See Saul Lehrfreund, 'The Commonwealth Caribbean and Evolving International Attitudes towards the Death Penalty', in Penal Reform International *et al.*, *Commonwealth Caribbean Human Rights Seminar*, Belize, 12–14 Sept. 2000 (2001), pp. 79–82.

[11] The countries covered by this judgment are: Anguilla, Antigua and Barbuda, the British Virgin Islands, Dominica, Grenada, Montserrat, St Lucia, St Kitts and Nevis, and St Vincent and the Grenadines.

the right to life that was not protected by the 'savings clause'. Justice J. Saunders, delivering judgment, said:

The mandatory death penalty robs those upon whom sentence is passed of any opportunity whatsoever to have the court consider mitigating circumstances even as an irrevocable punishment is meted out to them. The dignity of human life is reduced by a law that compels the court to impose death by hanging upon all convicted of murder, granting none an opportunity to have the individual circumstances of his case considered by the court that is to pronounce sentence.[12]

In March 2002 appeals on behalf of the Crown in the case of *Hughes* and also from St Christopher and Nevis (also affected by the judgment of the East Caribbean Court of Appeal) in the case of *Berthill Fox*, were dismissed by the Judicial Committee of the Privy Council, which held that the imposition of a mandatory sentence of death on conviction for murder was in contravention to the offender's constitutionally guaranteed right not to be subject to inhuman or degrading punishment or treatment at the hands of the state.[13]

At the same time the Privy Council decided the case of *Patrick Reyes* v. *The Queen*, which sought to clarify whether a mandatory death penalty was acceptable under the Constitution of Belize, because it was applied only to a specific class of capital murder and was always subject to review by the Board of Pardons. The Judicial Committee (in a judgment delivered by Lord Bingham of Cornhill, the senior Law Lord) declared that the fact that there existed a well-established Board of Pardons in Belize, which could mitigate the imposition of a mandatorily imposed death sentence, did not suffice. For while the act of clemency (see Chapter 5 pages 163–167) was a proper part of the 'constitutional process of conviction, sentence and the carrying out of the sentence', it was nevertheless 'an executive act' of mercy which could not be 'a substitute for the judicial determination of the appropriate sentence'. Furthermore, the Committee accepted the argument that even a mandatory sentence imposed for a restricted category of capital murder (the applicant had been sentenced on conviction of murder by shooting) 'precluded any consideration of the humanity of sentencing him to death', given the wide range of circumstances under which a shooting could occur. Therefore, the Committee concluded:

To deny the offender the opportunity, before sentence is passed, to seek to persuade the court that in all the circumstances to condemn him to death would be disproportionate and inappropriate is to treat him as no human being should be treated and thus to deny his basic humanity, the core of the right that [the constitutional provision barring inhuman or degrading treatment or punishment] exists to protect.[14]

The Judicial Committee of the Privy Council were not called upon to decide

---

[12] *Spence and Hughes* v. *The Queen*, Criminal Appeal No. 20 of 1998, East Caribbean Court of Appeal, Judgment (2 Apr. 2001). See Saul Lehrfreund, 'International Legal Trends and the "Mandatory" Death Penalty in the Commonwealth Caribbean', *Oxford University Commonwealth Law Journal* 1 (2001), pp. 171–194.

[13] *The Queen* v. *Peter Hughes* [2002] UKPC 12, para. 30. *Berthill Fox* v. *Queen* [2002] UKPC 13.

[14] *Patrick Reyes* v. *The Queen* [2002] UKPC 11, para. 43.

'whether it would ever be possible to draft a provision for a mandatory death sentence which was sufficiently discriminating to obviate any humanity in its operation'. Yet it is clear that the types of statute that impose a mandatory penalty of death on 'capital murder' in other Caribbean states, such as Jamaica, have the same flaws as the provisions in Belize. It is only a matter of time before they too will be declared unconstitutional.

These developments clearly indicate that international standards have become yet more firmly set against the mandatory imposition of capital punishment, and those countries which maintain such penalties are in breach of a widely accepted 'human rights norm'.

Yet the abolition of mandatory sentences has not, and will not, resolve the problem of inequity or disproportionality in the administration of capital punishment. For the paradox is that when the death penalty is *not* mandated for a crime, there is inevitably 'a large element of uncertainty and discretion into the selection of who will die'.[15] In other words, whether the death penalty is mandatory or discretionary, arbitrariness and discrimination still remain. The circumstances in which capital crimes are committed and the degree of culpability of their perpetrators varies so widely that truly equitable enforcement of the death penalty remains a chimera.

2. THE EXERCISE OF DISCRETION IN CAPITAL CASES

In many retentionist nations whether or not the death penalty is imposed for a capital offence is left to the discretion of the court and it is the judge who pronounces the sentence of death. But in the United States it has now been established, since the Supreme Court handed down its decision in *Ring* v. *Arizona* in June 2002, that it is the jury that must determine whether the aggravating factors have been proved which make a convicted murderer eligible for the death penalty.[16]

---

[15] See Bryan Stevenson, 'Capital Punishment in the United States', in Penal Reform International *et al.*, n. 10 above, 68.

[16] *Ring* v. *Arizona* (122 S.Ct. 2428 (2002)) ruled that the death-sentencing statutes of five states were unconstitutional: three states (Arizona, Idaho, and Montana), where a single judge determined whether the aggravating factors were present and made the decision to sentence to death, and two states (Nebraska and Colorado), where a panel of judges made the decision. There were 129 inmates on death row in Arizona and 39 in the other four states. The ruling also cast into doubt the death penalty provisions of four other states (Florida, Alabama, Indiana, and Delaware), where the jury makes the decision on aggravating circumstances but then makes an advisory recommendation to the judge as regards the sentence. It appears likely that the ruling will be held to apply to those cases where the judge has overruled a recommendation by the jury of life imprisonment and imposed instead a death sentence. According to the American Bar Association, in Alabama 'nearly three dozen of the 186 death row inmates received their death sentences from judges who overrode jury recommendations of life in prison without parole'. See American Bar Association, Section on Individual Rights and Responsibilities, *Towards Greater Awareness: The American Bar Association Call for a Moratorium on Execution Gains Ground* (Aug. 2001), p. 18. It is less clear whether the ruling will invalidate those death sentences where the judge sentenced the person to death in conformity with the jury's advisory verdict. Also, defendants whose appeals against conviction on the charge of murder are not successful will also probably face another jury hearing to determine the

Whoever is empowered to decide whether or not a death sentence is imposed, some mechanisms usually exist that aim to ensure that it is not inflicted on persons at random or in an obviously discriminatory fashion. It seems that, virtually everywhere, the number sentenced to death and, in particular, the number executed, is a relatively small proportion of all the potential candidates. As pointed out in Chapter 2 (page 49), India, through its Supreme Court, has restricted capital punishment to only 'the rarest of rare', the 'gravest cases of extreme culpability . . . where the alternative option is unquestionably foreclosed'.[17] Japan has a policy of only executing those who commit 'extremely heinous offences'.[18] The death penalty for murder in Egypt is said to be reserved for cases with 'certain aggravating circumstances', such as where the murder is premeditated or planned, as in poisoning.[19]

In China most crimes for which there is a discretionary death penalty stipulate the alternative sentence to be not less than ten years' imprisonment. But the use of this discretion is not restricted or guided except by the very general and vague statement in Article 61 of the 1997 Criminal Code that 'punishment shall be meted out on the basis of the facts, nature and circumstances of the crime, the degree of harm done to society and the relevant provisions of this Law'.[20] It is not surprising therefore that there appears to be considerable arbitrariness in the imposition of capital punishment in China. One only has to peruse Amnesty International's *Death Penalty Log*, listing cases reported in some of the Chinese press, to see that the number of executions reported varies enormously month by month. In 1999 there were four in October, 26 in November, 41 in March, 91 in August, 135 in January, and 381 in June. Indeed, of the 221 executions for drug offences recorded by Amnesty International in 1999, 196 (89 per cent) took place between 21 June and the end of that month, around International Anti-Drug Day on 26 June—and none were recorded in five months of the year. It is clear that the execution of drug offenders, or at least the reporting of such executions, around a 'drug awareness day' in June, is meant to signal a powerful deterrent, whereas in other months of the year drug offenders are much more likely to escape execution. The existence of 'strike hard campaigns' and the determination to make examples of various types of offender, inevitably means that certain individuals at certain times and in particular parts of

---

sentence, and some may yet again be sentenced to death. See 'Fewer Death Sentences Likely if Juries make Ultimate Decision, Experts Say', *New York Times*, 25 June 2002, p. A19.

[17] See *Bachan Singh* v. *State of Punjab* 2 SCJ [1980] 474 at 524 and *Bachan Singh* v. *State of Punjab* [1983] 1 SCR 145 at 252 and 256. Also Chiranjivi J. Nirmal, 'Setting an Agenda', in C. J. Nirmal (ed), *Human Rights in India* (2000), pp. 234–269 at 252.

[18] Japan, National Statement on *Crime Prevention for Freedom, Justice, Peace and Development* (1985), p. 139.

[19] N. Hosni, 'La Peine de mort en droit égyptien et en droit islamique', *Revue Internationale de Droit Pénal* 58 (1987), pp. 407–420 at 412.

[20] See *Criminal Law of the People's Republic of China* (1997), ch. 4, 'The Concrete Application of Punishments', China Procuratorial Press. Also, Hans-Jörg Albrecht, 'The Death Penalty in China from a European Perspective', in M. Nowak and Xin Chunying (eds), *EU–China Human Rights Dialogue: Proceedings of the Second EU–China Legal Experts' Seminar Held in Beijing on 19 and 20 October 1998* (2000), pp. 95–118 at 96.

[21] AI, *People's Republic of China: Death Penalty Log 1999*, AI Index: ASA 17/49/00.

the country are selected for execution for smuggling, fraud, running prostitution rackets, for robbery, corruption, tax evasion, and other offences. The relative rarity with which they appear among the lists of those executed suggest that they are the unfortunate ones. It may be said by the authorities that this is because these individuals have committed 'the most grave crimes' in that category. But an examination of the brief details given in Amnesty's *Log* suggests that this may not always be the case. There are examples of large-scale frauds where the culprit was apparently not executed, just as there are some similar frauds that were punished by death; there are examples of executions for murder where the offenders appear to have been members of ruthless robber gangs, but there are also examples of executions for murders which appear to be 'domestic', where the motive has probably sprung from pervasive human weaknesses: jealousy, anger, and uncontrollable emotional turmoil.[21] Furthermore, it has been suggested that the death penalty in China, despite a few examples to the contrary as far as corruption is concerned, is generally, as in most retentionist countries, enforced against the poorer and least well-educated members of society.[22]

Only when China permits a thorough study of its criminal justice system will scholars in China be able to shed light on the way in which capital punishment is enforced. Only then will it be possible to assess whether examples of the kind referred to above are the result of an unacceptable degree of arbitrariness in the infliction of the supreme penalty.

The Chinese courts also have the possibility of ordering that the sentence of death be suspended for a period of two years, subject to hard labour so as to give the offender an opportunity to repent. The authorities in the past have claimed that this power is used very frequently as a means of pursuing its policy of retaining the death penalty as a powerful deterrent, yet in practice 'killing only a few'. It has been claimed that over 90 per cent of those whose sentence has been suspended have their sentences commuted to life imprisonment or, for particularly meritorious service, to a sentence of between fifteen and twenty years. Immediate execution is said to be reserved for those convicted of murder, multiple rape, armed robbery, and certain other serious crimes such as kidnapping of women and children, as well as those identified as recidivists who had previously resisted the attempts of the state to reform them. A Chinese scholar, writing in the 1980s, listed the criteria for suspension as: 'the people's indignation versus the criminal is not too great'; 'the criminal admits his or her guilt and is reformable'; 'he or she is not the prime offender in a joint crime'; 'there are mitigating personal circumstances'—the example given being that of a deaf mute.[23] But again, until China publishes reliable statistical data, there

---

[22] See Marina Svensson, 'State Coercion, Deterrence, and the Death Penalty in the PRC', Paper presented to the Annual Meeting of the Association of Asian Studies, Chicago, 22–5 Mar. 2001.

[23] Gao Ming Xuan, 'A Brief Dissertation on the Death Penalty in the Criminal Law of the People's Republic of China', *Revue Internationale de Droit Pénal* 58 (1987), pp. 399–405 at 403–404; and Yu Shutong, 'Le Système de la peine capitale dans le droit pénal chinois', *ibid.*, pp. 689–695. I am indebted to Professor Xuan for sending me several useful articles, among which was G. Chen, 'On the System of Death Sentences with Two Year Suspension of Execution in China', *Study of Law* (Beijing, 1986), pp. 59–64.

is no means of knowing how often this power is used, nor how many of those who receive a suspended death sentence are eventually executed.

Thus, the issue that arises from this general development towards a more restrictive use of a discretionary death penalty is whether, in practice, this has made it possible to impose it in a sufficiently even-handed and non-discriminatory manner for it to be acceptable, either under the law or constitution of the country concerned or under the generally accepted principle of equitable treatment of persons convicted of offences of equivalent gravity. This concern for even-handedness is usually linked to a desire to ensure proportionality, i.e. that only those who have committed the most heinous crimes suffer the death penalty. Yet legal definitions of capital murder, let alone of other potentially capital crimes, such as economic corruption, are notoriously difficult to draw up in a way that would guarantee this. Even so, some countries seem to be sure that their system produces this result. For example, in 1987 the Japanese government informed the United Nations that 'there is no possibility whatsoever of the Japanese Courts imposing the death sentence arbitrarily, since very strict standards and practices with regard to the application of the death penalty have been established over many years'.[24] On the other hand, the experience of those American states that have retained the death penalty under new statutes, which aim to limit and guide the discretion of the court so as to make its imposition no longer arbitrary or discriminatory, casts considerable doubt on the ability of draughtsmen or criminal justice systems to achieve this aim. The American experience, which has been subject to critical legal as well as detailed empirical analysis to an extent unknown in other countries, is worth reviewing for the lessons it offers.

3. LEGAL ANALYSES: THE AMERICAN EXPERIENCE

As is well known, the US Supreme Court held by a majority in *Furman* v. *Georgia* (1972) that the death penalty statute of the state of Georgia was unconstitutional because it was being applied in an arbitrary and capricious fashion, and in a way that discriminated against the poor and especially African Americans. The death penalty was being inflicted more and more rarely, and the circumstances in which persons were sentenced to the supreme penalty were often indistinguishable from many others where the defendant received a lesser penalty. In the oft-quoted words of Justice Stewart, for anyone to be sentenced to death was such a freakish event that it was 'cruel and unusual in the same sense that being struck by lightning is cruel and unusual'. As a result, all the outstanding death sentences in the retentionist states were commuted to life imprisonment.

Although many believed that capital punishment would not be resurrected, 38 states and the Federal government subsequently passed new statutes aimed at meeting the requirements of the equal protection clause of the Fourteenth Amendment and the prohibition against cruel and unusual punishment of the Eighth

---

[24] Reply to *UN Safeguards Survey*, 1987.

Amendment of the US Constitution. As mentioned above, the Supreme Court refused to endorse any statutes that laid down a mandatory death penalty. Thus, the new statutes had to define the categories of persons who could be sentenced to death sufficiently narrowly and with such constraints as to avoid its arbitrary or discriminatory infliction, and yet, at the same time, sufficiently broadly to allow the discretion necessary to treat each case on its specific merits.

(a) The Reformed Statutes

The solution, which had been offered by the Model Penal Code, was to enumerate a specific list of aggravating and mitigating circumstances. The procedures, according to this 'blueprint', were to be as follows:

A capital sentence is excluded if the court is satisfied that none of the aggravating circumstances was established by the evidence at the trial or would be established on a further proceeding to determine sentence; that substantial mitigating circumstances calling for leniency were established at the trial; that the defendant was under eighteen years of age at the time of the crime; that his mental or physical condition calls for leniency; or that the evidence does not foreclose all doubt respecting the defendant's guilt. If no such finding is made, a further proceeding is initiated before the court or court and jury. Much scope is given to the evidence admissible in that proceeding. The court or jury is directed to take into account the enumerated aggravating and mitigating circumstances and any other facts considered relevant. Capital sentence is again excluded unless the tribunal finds that one of the aggravating circumstances and no mitigating circumstance sufficiently substantial to call for leniency are established. Apart from this, the sentence is discretionary but if the jurisdiction puts the issue to the jury, it must be unanimous for penalty of death and the court must concur in its opinion for the sentence to be passed.[25]

In 1976 the Supreme Court, in a series of cases, upheld the statutes of Georgia, Florida, and Texas, all of which in one way or another provided legislative guidelines for the exercise of the discretion of judge and jury and conformed to several features of the Model Penal Code's draft statute.[26] They all listed a number of specific aggravating circumstances, such as murder carried out during a felony and murder of law enforcement personnel; provided for a bifurcated trial, with a separate hearing before a jury to determine sentence; and ensured an automatic review by the State Supreme Court or Court of Criminal Appeals. Yet, in other important ways the statutes differed quite widely both in their objectives and specific form;[27] for example, 27

---

[25] Quoted from Herbert Wechsler, 'The Model Penal Code and the Codification of American Criminal Law', in R. Hood (ed), *Crime, Criminology, and Public Policy: Essays in Honour of Sir Leon Radzinowicz* (1974), pp. 419–468 at 452–453.

[26] *Gregg* v. *Georgia; Proffitt* v. *Florida; Jurek* v. *Texas.* For a more detailed discussion of the way in which these statutes differed from the Model Penal Code, see F. E. Zimring and G. Hawkins, *Capital Punishment and the American Agenda* (1986), pp. 77–92. It should be recalled that the Supreme Court did not uphold the principle that the defendant should be under 18 years of age at the time of the crime. See Ch. 4 page 116.

[27] See, for example, James A. Acker and Elizabeth R. Walsh, 'Challenging the Death Penalty under State Constitutions', *Vanderbilt Law Review* 42 (1989), pp. 1299–1363 at 1362. And James R. Acker and

states, including Georgia and Florida, provided that the appellate review should include what is known as a 'proportionality review' to assess 'whether the death sentence is excessive or disproportionate to the penalty imposed in similar cases, considering both the crime and the defendant'. Four states included no such legal obligation but have nevertheless carried out such reviews, and seven states, including Texas, have no provisions for a proportionality review. Florida listed in the statute seven mitigating circumstances (as did some other states such as Kentucky). Georgia, Ohio, and three other states did not, leaving the range of mitigating factors completely unspecified.[28] The Georgia statute (and the Florida statute in similar terms) included within its list of specified aggravating circumstances whether the crime was committed by a person involved in one or more contemporaneous offences, such as a rape or an armed robbery, and whether the crime was 'outrageously or wantonly vile, horrible or inhuman in that it involved torture, depravity of mind, or an aggravated battery of the victim'.

Under the Supreme Court ruling in *Payne* v. *Tennessee* (1991), prosecutors were allowed, for the first time, to introduce evidence that the victim was 'an individual whose death represents a unique loss to society', thus making it possible to present to the court a 'victim-impact statement'.[29] Austin Sarat has called this the 'legitimation of revenge'.[30]

These provisions reflect retributive and denunciatory considerations, but the capital statutes of 21 states also include a defendant's potential for future violence among the aggravating factors that jurors *may* take into account if invited to do so. In Texas and Oregon, however, juries must unanimously agree that there is 'a probability that the defendant would commit criminal acts of violence that would constitute a continuing threat to society' before they may impose a death sentence. And in Virginia the jury must make a finding *either* of future dangerousness *or* that the crime was 'outrageously or wantonly vile, horrible, or inhuman in that it involved torture, depravity of mind or an aggravated battery to the victim'. In other words, juries are required to predict the likelihood of future serious violence.[31]

(b) Academic Critiques

These statutes have been subjected to critical scrutiny by many legal scholars, most of whom have concluded that they 'represent only the most modest advance towards

Charles S. Lanier, 'Matters of Life and Death: The Sentencing Provisions of the Capital Punishment Statutes', *Criminal Law Bulletin* 31 (1995), pp. 19–60.

[28] See J. A. Acker and C. S. Lanier, 'In Fairness and Mercy: Statutory Mitigating Factors in Capital Punishment Laws', *Criminal Law Bulletin* 30 (1994), pp. 299–345.

[29] *Payne* v. *Tennessee*, 501 U.S. 808. See Michael Vitiello, '*Payne* v. *Tennessee*: A "Stunning *Ipse Dixit*"', *Notre Dame Journal of Law, Ethics and Public Policy* 8 (1994), pp. 165–280 at 167.

[30] Austin Sarat, *When the State Kills* (2001), pp. 36–59 at 36.

[31] See Jonathan R. Sorenson and Rocky L. Pilgrim, 'An Actuarial Risk Assessment of Violence Posed by Capital Murder Defendants', *Journal of Criminal Law and Criminology* 90 (2000), pp. 1251–1270 at 1252.

formality over the old pre-Furman statute(s)'.[32] They have noted that in 23 states (or three-fifths of those with the death penalty) capital punishment can be imposed in cases of felony murder, even though the offender had himself or herself no intention to kill.[33] In a few jurisdictions a death sentence *must* be imposed if the sentencer finds that aggravating circumstances outweigh mitigating factors, or if it is found that one or more aggravating factors exist but no mitigating features have been established, as in Pennsylvania.[34] In 1990 the US Supreme Court ruled in *Blystone* v. *Pennsylvania* that this did not violate the ruling against a mandatory death penalty so long as the jury was allowed to review all mitigating factors.[35] It is obvious that if avoiding the death penalty is based on finding at least one mitigating factor, there must be much room for subjective assessment of the circumstances in which murders are carried out—which in Pennsylvania can be anything pertaining to the circumstances of the crime or the character and record of the defendant.

In most jurisdictions, however, the jury or judge (until the decision in *Ring* v. *Arizona* in June 2002; see page 149 above) 'weighs' the aggravating against the mitigating factors in deciding whether a death sentence should be imposed. And again there is much room for different perceptions, subjective judgements, and theories of crime causation to influence the interpretation of events on which a life-or-death decision rests.[36] This is particularly so where the jury or judge is required to consider as an aggravating factor whether the murder was 'heinous, atrocious or cruel' or some similar test.[37] 'Far from ensuring that the class of the "death-eligible" is meaningfully narrowed, factors that focus on whether an intentional murder was "especially heinous" or manifested an "utter disregard for human life" invite an affirmative answer in every case.'[38]

Critics have pointed to cases where death sentences were passed and upheld after appellate review which were by no stretch of the imagination the most egregious.[39] John Spinkellink, the first person to be executed by Florida under the constitutionally approved statute, was, according to the Assistant Attorney General who repre-

---

[32] See, for example, Robert Weisberg, 'Deregulating Death', *Supreme Court Review* (1983), pp. 305–395 at 321; and R. A. Bonner, 'Death Penalty', *Annual Survey of American Law* (1984), pp. 493–513 at 498–499.

[33] J. A. Acker and C. S. Lanier, 'The Dimensions of Capital Murder', *Criminal Law Bulletin* 29 (1993), pp. 379–417 at 385.

[34] Acker and Lanier, n. 27 above, p. 27.

[35] See Joan Biskupic, *The Supreme Court Yearbook, 1989–1990* (1991), p. 39. This is the case also under Arizona Law. See *Walton* v. *Arizona, ibid.,* p. 40. Also, Acker and Lanier, n. 27 above, pp. 29–30.

[36] For an interesting analysis of mitigating circumstances, see Deborah W. Denno, 'Testing *Penry* and its Progeny', *American Journal of Criminal Law* 22 (1994), pp. 1–75.

[37] J. A. Acker and C. S. Lanier, ' "Parsing this Lexicon of Death", Aggravating Factors in Capital Sentencing Statutes', *Criminal Law Bulletin* 30 (1994), pp. 107–152 at 124–130.

[38] See Carol S. Steiker and Jordan M. Steiker, 'Judicial Developments in Capital Punishment Law', in J. A. Acker, R. M. Bohm, and C. S. Lanier (eds), *America's Experiment with Capital Punishment* (1998), pp. 47–75 at 58.

[39] See, for example, B. L. Ledewitz, 'The New Role of Statutory Aggravating Circumstances in American Death Penalty Law', *Duquesne Law Review* 22 (1984), pp. 317–396 at 391–392, discussing the case of *Godfrey* v. *Georgia*; and *American University Law Review*, Note, 'The Death Penalty in Georgia: An Aggravating Circumstance' 30 (1981), pp. 835–861 at 853–854.

sented the state, 'the least obnoxious person on death row in terms of the crime he committed'.[40] Perhaps the former Chief Justice of Florida's Supreme Court had such a case in mind when he conceded that 'We certainly have executed those people who ... didn't fit the criteria for execution in the state of Florida ...'.[41]

Statutes which make an assessment of the convicted murderer's future dangerousness relevant to consideration of the death penalty have also been severely criticized. A Working Party set up by the British Medical Association expressed the view in 1992 that presenting evidence on future dangerousness is 'fraught with risks and the dangerousness element of death penalty legislation is a poor basis for making life and death decisions'.[42] Psychiatrists are called upon in these circumstances to say whether or not the prisoner will commit further homicides, yet all the evidence suggests that, despite their apparent certainty in individual cases, they are much more often wrong than correct. For example, a comparison was made between 92 death-sentenced but commuted Texan prisoners (who had been found to be very likely to commit criminal acts of violence that would constitute a continuing threat to society) and a group of life-sentenced prisoners convicted in capital murder trials. This comparison showed that the former 'dangerous murderers' had no higher incidence of prison violence: only one committed a gang murder in prison. Of 12 such 'dangerous murderers' who were released, one did commit a further murder but 11 did not. This is a very high rate of false positives (that is, persons predicted to be dangerous who turned out not to be so) and other studies have produced similar findings.[43] There is no doubt that jurors when asked to estimate the dangerousness of persons convicted of capital murder greatly overestimate the likelihood that they will commit further violent acts.[44]

[40] Quoted in J. Greenberg, 'Capital Punishment as a System', *Yale Law Journal* 91 (1982), pp. 908–936 at 926–927; see also, J. Kaplan, 'Administering Capital Punishment', *University Florida Law Review* 36 (1984), pp. 177–192 at 186–187.

[41] Reported in *The Spectator*, 21 Mar. 2001.

[42] British Medical Association, *Medicine Betrayed* (1992), p. 108.

[43] See James W. Marquart, Sheldon Ekland-Olson, and Jonathan R. Sorensen, 'Gazing into the Crystal Ball: Can Jurors Accurately Predict Dangerousness in Capital Cases?', *Law and Society Review* 23 (1989), pp. 449–468; J. W. Marquart and J. R. Sorensen, 'Institutional and Postrelease Behavior of *Furman*-Commuted Inmates in Texas', *Criminology* 26 (1988), pp. 677–693, which found a ratio of true to false positives among those regarded as dangerous of 1 : 20; and Marquart, Ekland-Olson, and Sorensen, *The Rope, the Chair, and the Needle: Capital Punishment in Texas, 1923–1990* (1994), pp. 175–184. See also, G. F. Vito, P. Koester, and D. G. Wilson, 'Return of the Dead: An Update on the Status of *Furman*-Commuted Death Row Inmates', in R. M. Bohm (ed), *The Death Penalty in America: Current Research* (1991), pp. 89–99, D. G. Wilson, and E. J. Latessa and G. F. Vito, 'Comparison of the Dead', *ibid.*, pp. 101–111; and Charles P. Ewing, 'Preventive Detention and Execution: The Constitutionality of Punishing Future Crimes', *Law and Human Behavior* 15 (1991), pp. 139–163, which recommends that psychiatrists and psychologists should abjure their role as expert witnesses because it gives credibility to the view that dangerousness can be predicted in individual cases.

[44] See Sorensen and Pilgrim, n. 31 above. Sorensen and Pilgrim estimated that the likelihood of a life-sentenced capital murderer repeating a murder over a forty-year term of life imprisonment was approximately 0.2%, while jurors in Texas believe that those they sentence to death have a likelihood of committing another homicide of about 50%. However, Sorensen and Pilgrim were able to show that a group of offenders under the age of 21, with certain personal and criminal career characteristics such as gang membership and multiple victims, had a probability of committing another murder as high as 54.6% over a forty-year period, pp. 1267–1269.

A bizarre application of 'categorical' rather than clinical risk assessment was made as recently as 1996 in a Texas capital murder case. The jury was asked to assess the defendant's risk of violence. The statutory question was whether the defendant, if not executed, 'would commit criminal acts of violence that would constitute a continuing threat to society'. The Attorney General of Texas introduced as an expert witness a psychologist who found that the defendant, Victor Saldano, possessed many risk factors for violence, including Hispanic ethnicity (based on the over-representation of Hispanics in the prison population), which the witness testified was 'a factor weighing in favor of future dangerousness'. The jury subsequently sentenced Saldano to death. The Texas Court of Criminal Appeals upheld the sentence, one of the judges stating: 'I am convinced that, the reference by [the witness] to the fact that Hispanics and African-Americans are incarcerated at a rate greater than their percentage of the general population of this country did not harm [the] appellant'. He nevertheless did not deny that 'The danger that such testimony could be interpreted by a jury in a particular case as evidence that minorities are more violent than non-minorities is real . . .'. The defendant petitioned for certiorari to the US Supreme Court, and at the hearing in 2000 the Texas Attorney General conceded that 'because the use of race in Saldano's sentencing seriously undermined the fairness, integrity, or public reputation of the judicial process, Texas confesses error and agrees that Saldano is entitled to a new sentencing hearing'.[45] As a result, an amendment to the Texas Code of Criminal Procedure, effective from 1 September 2001, laid down that 'Evidence may not be offered by the state to estab-lish that the race or ethnicity of the defendant makes it likely that the defendant will engage in future criminal conduct.'

Also to be considered is the constitutional propriety of making the death penalty dependent upon uncertain future actions which may fall short of causing death and thus are not, in themselves, liable to the death penalty, or dependent on judgements of future dangerousness based on past actions which were not at the time considered dangerous. Thus in the case of Steve Roach, executed in Virginia in January 2000 for shooting Mary Ann Hughes, assessment of his future dangerousness was based in part on a parole violation for possessing a shotgun, despite the fact that no adult, including the police, had seen fit to remove it from him.[46]

Furthermore, judgements might be based merely on the prisoner's 'record', as in the case of Thomas Barefoot, whose death sentence was upheld by the US Supreme Court in 1983 even though the psychiatric evidence of dangerousness was given by two practitioners who had not personally examined the defendant.[47]

---

[45] *Saldano* v. *Texas* 530 U.S. 1212 (2000). For a description of the case, see *Texas Lawyer*, 12 June 2000, 13 Nov. 2000, and 5 Mar. 2001.

[46] AI, *Death Penalty Developments March 1998–March 2000*, AI Index: AMR 51/03/00.

[47] Among the many articles which discuss *Barefoot* v. *Estelle* (1983) and other cases such as *Spaziano* v. *Florida* (1984), which allowed the judge to override the jury's non-capital sentence, are: S. Gillers, 'The Quality of Mercy: Constitutional Accuracy at the Selection Stage of Capital Sentencing', *University of California, Davis, Law Review* 18 (1985), pp. 1037–111 at 1039 and 1097–1101; and Daniel S. Goodman, 'Demographic Evidence in Capital Sentencing', *Stanford Law Review* 39 (1987), pp. 499–543. Also, C. R. Showalter and R. J. Bonnie, 'Psychiatrists and Capital Sentencing: Risks and

Another factor that has come to the fore is the extent to which jurors are able to make informed judgements between a death sentence or life imprisonment based on their knowledge of the real effects of being sentenced to life without parole or to a specific minimum period before consideration of parole. In an important judgment, *Simmons* v. *South Carolina* in 1994, the Supreme Court ruled that the jury must be told about the possibility of sentencing a defendant to prison for life without parole *if* the prosecution uses the defendant's dangerousness as an argument for the death penalty, so that a choice can be made between death and lifetime incarceration.[48] This has apparently been narrowly interpreted, especially in Texas, but a recent decision of the Supreme Court in *Shafer* v. *South Carolina*[49] has affirmed that whenever dangerousness is an 'issue' at the sentencing stage, due process requires that, under the sentencing statutes of that state, the jury must be informed that a life sentence carries no possibilities of parole.[50] Despite these rulings, in *Brown* v. *Texas*, decided in 1997, the Supreme Court denied certiorari by a majority of 5–4 in a case where the jury was denied information about how long the defendant would serve in prison if not sentenced to death. More recently, in *Weeks* v. *Angelone* (2000), the Supreme Court upheld a death sentence despite the fact that the jury had not understood that it was entitled to sentence the defendant to life imprisonment.[51]

Yet, an empirical study of jurors (as part of the Capital Jury Project) found that 'most jurors believed that capital murders would be back on the street even before they [could] become eligible for parole' and that the more the alternative to the death penalty was underestimated, the greater the likelihood that jurors would vote for the death penalty as the case came to be considered in the sentencing phase of the trial. This was true whether or not the defendant was alleged by the prosecutor to be dangerous. Professor Bowers and his team thus concluded that

Jurors' mistaken beliefs about the death penalty are a substantial influence on their sentencing decisions, and that it was just as important for jurors to know 'when' as it was to know 'if' the convicted murderer would be released. The fact that most jurors did not know or believe that in their state Life without Parole existed and was enforced was therefore a potent factor affecting their judgment that an accused should be sentenced to death.[52]

Responsibilities in a Unique Legal Setting', *Bulletin of the American Academy of Psychiatry and Law* 12 (1984), pp. 159–67; Paul S. Appelbaum, 'Hypotheticals, Psychiatric Testimony, and Death Sentence', *ibid.*, pp. 169–177; G. E. Dix, 'Expert Prediction Testimony in Capital Sentencing: Evidentiary and Constitutional Questions', *American Criminal Law Review* 19 (1981), pp. 1–48; Murray Levine, 'The Adversarial Process and Social Science in the Courts: Barefoot v. Estelle', *Journal of Psychiatry and Law* 12 (1984), pp. 147–181; Charles P. Ewing, ' "Dr Death" and the Case for an Ethical Ban on Psychiatric and Psychological Predictions of Dangerousness in Capital Sentencing Proceedings', *American Journal of Law and Medicine* 8 (1983), pp. 407–428. And Acker and Lanier, n. 37 above, pp. 118–121.

[48] See *Simmons* v. *South Carolina*, 114 S.Ct. 2187 (1994). Also, *The Supreme Court Yearbook, 1993–1994* (1995), p. 74.

[49] *Shafer* v. *South Carolina*, 121 S.Ct. 1263 (2001).

[50] See Julian Killingley, 'Note on *Shafer* v. *South Carolina*', *Amicus Journal* 3 (2001), pp. 20–21.

[51] *Weeks* v. *Angelone*, 528 U.S. 225 (2000).

[52] See William J. Bowers and Benjamin D. Steiner, 'Death by Default: An Empirical Demonstration of False and Forced Choices in Capital Sentencing', *Texas Law Review* 77 (1999), pp. 605–717, esp. 645–671.

Furthermore, a recent study based on interviews with jurors in South Carolina demonstrated that even when the prosecution did not emphasize in any way the question of future dangerousness, as many as two-thirds said that the jury's discussion had nevertheless focused at least 'a fair amount' on 'the need to prevent him [the offender] from killing again'. The authors concluded, with good reason, that the Supreme Court had not been correct in assuming, as it had done in *Simmons* v. *South Carolina*, that it was only necessary to instruct the jury on the length of time that the defendant would spend in prison if not sentenced to death in cases where the prosecution had raised this as an 'issue': in other words, they should be informed in all cases (on this see also Chapter 8 pages 237–238).[53]

Many legal scholars have also pointed out that the US Supreme Court, over the last twenty years, has endorsed statutes which, in certain ways, appear likely to loosen the constraints on the discretion of judges and juries and so once more give them wide, maybe too wide, discretionary scope. It decided (in *Lockett* v. *Ohio* (1978) and other cases) that all mitigating factors should be considered and weighed in the balance, even if they are not among those specifically listed in the statute. Under the law of several states, such as Florida, only statutory aggravating factors may be taken into account by the jury, but this is not required constitutionally, for in *Zant* v. *Stephens* (1983) the Court declared that all aggravating circumstances could be considered regardless of whether they related to the aggravating circumstance which had brought the defendant within the scope of the death penalty provisions of the statute. The argument was that the statutory aggravating factor merely acted to narrow the class of persons eligible for the death sentence, and that once such narrowing had taken place, all factors of aggravation and mitigation should be considered. It is not surprising that this has been regarded as undermining the policy of controlling the degree of discretion to impose a death sentence.[54] In addition, in *Pulley* v. *Harris* (1984), a Californian case, the Supreme Court confirmed that there was no constitutional requirement for the appeal court to compare the sentence of death with sentences imposed in similar cases: it was an additional safeguard but not a critical one.[55] Furthermore, the Court held that in Louisiana, where a proportionality review was mandatory, it was sufficient for the appeal court to compare the death sentence with cases from the same narrow judicial district rather than make a state-wide comparison with other cases (*Maggio* v. *Williams* (1983)).[56]

---

[53] John H. Blume, Stephen P. Garvey, and Sheri Lynn Johnson, 'Future Dangerousness in Capital Cases: Always "at Issue" ', *Cornell Law Review* 86 (2001), pp. 397–410 at 406–407.

[54] Bonner, n. 32 above, pp. 498–499. And for a succinct and up-to-date summary of the law, Bowers and Steiner, n. 52 above, pp. 608–625.

[55] It had, in effect, decided this when upholding the Texas statute, which does not provide proportionality review, in the case of *Jurek* v. *Texas* in 1976.

[56] See Bonner, n. 32 above, pp. 493–494; Barry Nakell and Kenneth A. Hardy, *The Arbitrariness of the Death Penalty* (1987), p. 66; and *Howard Law Journal* Note, 'Safeguarding Eighth Amendment Rights with a Comparative Proportionality Review in the Imposition of the Death Penalty, *Pulley* v. *Harris*' 28 (1985), pp. 331–333.

The Supreme Court has declared that it is 'unwilling to say that there is any one right way for a State to set up its capital sentencing scheme'.[57] Nevertheless, the conclusion reached by legal scholars is that the attempts made by the various states and the decisions reached by the Supreme Court have nowhere produced a system that reduces the scope of discretion to a level where arbitrariness will not result. In this they echo the conclusion of the British Royal Commission on Capital Punishment of 1953 that 'it is impracticable to frame a statutory definition of murder which would effectively limit the scope of capital punishment and would not have over-riding disadvantages in other respects'. The Royal Commission concluded that the 'quest is chimerical and that it must be abandoned'.[58]

In 1994, in the case of *Callins* v. *Collins*, Justice Blackmun, a former strong supporter of the death penalty, came to a similar conclusion about the efforts since *Gregg* in 1976 to fashion 'legal formulas and procedures that would sufficiently control arbitrariness in the infliction of the death penalty by capital juries'. He said:

The death penalty remains fraught with arbitrariness, discrimination, caprice, and mistake . . . Experience has taught us that the constitutional goal of eliminating arbitrariness and discrimination from the administration of death . . . can never be achieved without compromising an equally essential component of fundamental fairness—individualized sentencing . . . It is virtually self-evident to me now that no combination of procedural rules or substantive regulations can ever save the death penalty from its inherent constitutional deficiencies. The basic question—does the system accurately and consistently determine which defendants 'deserve' to die?—cannot be answered in the affirmative . . . The problem is that the inevitability of factual, legal, and moral error gives us a system that fails to deliver the fair, consistent, and reliable sentences of death required by the Constitution.[59]

In an oft-quoted passage Blackmun further declared:

From this day forward, I no longer shall tinker with the machinery of death . . . to continue to coddle the Court's delusion that the desired level of fairness has been achieved and the need for regulation eviscerated, I feel morally and intellectually obligated simply to concede that the death penalty experiment has failed.[60]

It is a conclusion that many academic lawyers believe has been borne out by experience over the last twenty years. In numerous books and articles they have emphasized the impossibility of concurrently maximizing both flexibility and non-arbitrariness; or of encapsulating in legal rules decisions that ultimately rest upon the subjective moral evaluations of prosecutors, juries, and judges.[61] At a

---

[57] Gillers, n. 47 above, p. 1111, quoting the judgment in *Spaziano* v. *Florida* (1984).

[58] United Kingdom, *Royal Commission on Capital Punishment 1949–1953, Report* (Cmd 8932, 1953), para. 483, p. 167, and Conclusion 39, p. 278; also para. 534, p. 189. See also J. R. Acker, and C. S. Lanier, 'Beyond Human Ability?', in Acker, Bohm, and Lanier (eds), n. 38 above, 81.

[59] *Callins* v. *Collins* 114 S.Ct. 1127 (1994), pp. 1129–1130. For a discussion of the importance of Blackmun's statement on what he calls the 'new abolitionism', see Sarat, n. 30 above, pp. 251–254.

[60] *Callins* v. *Collins*, p. 1130.

[61] See Zimring and Hawkins, n. 26 above, p. 90; L. S. Sheleff, *Ultimate Penalties: Capital Punishment, Life Imprisonment, Physical Torture* (1987), pp. 83–116, 372; Welsh W. White, *The Death Penalty in the Nineties* (1994); Margaret J. Radin, 'Cruel Punishment and Respect for Persons: Super Due Process for

meeting of distinguished American lawyers in 1980, three-quarters of those who voted adopted the following resolution: 'Proponents of capital punishment laws have the burden of providing that criminal justice systems in which these laws operate will be free of ethnic or racial discrimination and substantially free of caprice and the risk of mistake. They have not carried this burden and in our judgement are not likely to do so.'[62]

On the other hand, it has been argued that the apparently restrictive death penalty laws enacted in the United States in response to *Furman* have, in fact, 'legit-imated capital punishment' by creating 'a false aura of rationality', thereby giving the *impression* that 'the imposition of the death penalty is highly regulated and care-fully monitored, even when it is not'. 'The Court's death penalty law thus leaves sentencing judges and juries with a false sense that their power is safely circum-scribed.'[63] Yet, in his 1998 report on the death penalty in the United States, the UN Special Rapporteur on extra-judicial, summary, or arbitrary executions wrote that laws increasing the number of crimes which are eligible for the death penalty contravened the restrictive intent of Article 6 (2) of the ICCPR. For the truth is that aggravating factors, widening the potential scope of capital punishment, continue to be added to statutes across the United States. They include victims of 'hate crimes', children under 12, people over the age of 65, medical technicians, defence witnesses, mentally or physically vulnerable persons, 'peace officers' includ-ing parole officers and government investigators, as well as murders committed during car hijackings, drive-by-shootings, and by street gangs. Jonathan Simon and Christina Spaulding have called these often 'symbolic' additions to the list of aggra-vators 'tokens of our esteem . . . that legislators could use to serve constituencies interested in capital punishment'.[64]

Between 1998 and 2000 some further aggravating factors have been included in state death penalty statutes, such as: murder of two or more persons in the course of one 'scheme' and murder that was one of a series committed by the defendant (Alabama); murder 'because of the victim's race, color, ancestry, religion, or national origin' and 'use of a weapon during a Class 1 felony when use of the weapon itself constituted a felony under State or Federal Law' (Colorado); 'murder of a person in retaliation for providing court testimony' (Delaware); 'murder of conservation offi-

Death', *Southern California Law Review* 53 (1980), pp. 1143–1185; Stephen Nathanson, 'Does it Matter if the Death Penalty is Arbitrarily Administered?', *Philosophy and Public Affairs* 14 (1985), pp. 149–164; Weisberg, n. 32 above, pp. 305–395.

[62] *The Penalty of Death*, Final Report, Annual Chief Justice Earl Warren Conference on Advocacy in the United States, The Roscoe Pound—American Trial Lawyers Foundation (1980).

[63] See Steiker and Steiker, n. 38 above: 'Thus, the impulse to abolish or reform the death penalty has produced a body of law that may contribute substantially to the stabilization and perpetuation of capital punishment as a continuing social practice', pp. 67–68 at 70. See also Roger Hood, 'Capital Punishment', in M. Tonry (ed), *The Handbook of Criminology* (1998), pp. 739–776 at 767–768.

[64] Jonathan Simon and Christina Spaulding, 'Tokens of our Esteem: Aggravating Factors in the Era of Deregulated Death Penalties', in Austin Sarat (ed), *The Killing State: Capital Punishment in Law, Politics, and Culture* (1999), pp. 81–136.

cers' (Georgia and Mississippi); 'murder committed on school property or in any venue related to a school-sponsored activity when the perpetrator intended to cause death or substantial bodily harm to more than one person by means of a weapon, device or course of action that would normally be hazardous to the lives of more than one person' (Nevada); 'any murder where the victim had a domestic violence restraining order filed against the defendant' (New Jersey); 'killing a pregnant woman' (Indiana), 'intentional killing of an under 14 year old boy by an over 21 year old' (Virginia); 'where the victim was a peace officer at a state Hospital' (California); and 'murder in the commission of abuse against a child under 16 years of age' (Wyoming).[65] Simon and Spaulding conclude that when all these new aggravating circumstances are taken into account, some 80 to 90 per cent of defendants who were death-eligible before the *Furman* decision were still death-eligible.[66] Enacted on 18 September 2001, New York's Anti-Terrorism Act amended the state's death penalty statute to allow the death penalty to be imposed on persons who commit murder in furtherance of terrorist activities.[67]

This movement to extend the categories of persons and situations for which the death penalty may be imposed was, however, seriously challenged by the Report of Governor Ryan's Commission to investigate the use of capital punishment in Illinois. The Report, published in April 2002, recommended that 'the current list of 20 factual circumstances under which a defendant is eligible for a death sentence should be eliminated in favor of a simpler and narrower group of eligibility criteria'. In doing this, the majority of the Commission boldly advocated the abolition of the felony-murder category altogether, so that the death penalty could only be applied in five types of case: 'where the defendant has murdered two or more persons, or where the victim was either a police officer or a firefighter; or an officer or inmate of a correctional institution; or was murdered to obstruct the justice system; or was tortured in the course of the murder'. This selection of crimes was, it seems, chosen because those who wished to retain capital punishment believed that 'it retains an important role in . . . expressing on behalf of the community, the strongest condemnation of a small number of the most heinous crimes'.[68] While any abolitionist

---

[65] See AI, *United States of America: Failing the Future—Death Penalty Developments, March 1998–March 2000*, AI Index: AMR 51/03/00, p. 9. Also, US Department of Justice, *Capital Punishment 1999* (2000), p. 2, and *Capital Punishment 2000* (2001), pp. 2–3. The following legislative attempts failed: California (1998, murder of victim under 14 or murder by arson or kidnapping); 1999, murder of a victim protected by restraining order, or during rape or/molestation of child), Connecticut (murder with torture), Florida (murder of a victim protected by restraining order), Georgia (death caused by distribution etc. of drugs), Maryland (murder of a victim protected by court order, murder involving drug trafficking), Missouri (murder of child under 13), Texas (murder where victim protected by court order, where victim tortured), Washington (1999, murder where victim was pregnant).

[66] Simon and Spaulding, n. 64 above, p. 87.

[67] *New York Law Journal*, 18 Sept. 2001: 'State legislature approves tough anti-terrorism laws'. Washington was also seeking to 'expand' the state's death penalty for terrorist acts that result in death. See *Seattle Post-Intelligencer*, 26 Nov. 2001.

[68] *Report of the Governor's Commission on Capital Punishment: George H. Ryan Governor* (Apr. 2002), pp. ii, iii, and 65–67.

would welcome, as a step in the right direction, the reduction in the categories of crime to which capital punishment can apply, there is nevertheless no reason to believe that the selection of crimes chosen by the Commission is any more defensible, in terms of morality or social policy, than a list that would include other crimes. Nor will it avoid unsupportable anomalies—for example, it will not be obvious why killing a firefighter is intrinsically worse than killing an ambulance worker, or why killing a prison inmate is worse than killing a child.

4. CRIMINOLOGICAL INVESTIGATIONS

(a) Methodological Considerations

The validity of the legal case-based criticisms discussed above have, to some extent, been put to the test of empirical inquiry. Many such endeavours have been made in recent years to examine the extent to which the new laws in the United States have avoided being applied in an arbitrary and discriminatory manner. However, the problem that arises in any study that seeks to compare those sentenced to death with those who are not is to find a way of matching cases that are truly alike. While it is true to say that each crime has its own particular configuration of ingredients and each offender his or her own prior history, motivations, and personality, it is nevertheless possible to devise ways of controlling for those factors that are of legal relevance in weighing the aggravating and mitigating circumstances of each particular case. There are several ways of doing this, each with advantages and disadvantages. The following are the main approaches taken.

* Some of the earlier studies controlled for a relatively small number of variables such as whether the crime involved a stranger, or an accompanying felony.[69]

* Another method used in the 1980s was to develop a more descriptive classification of cases along three dimensions: the degree of certainty that the defendant was a deliberate killer; the status of the victim, whether a stranger or known to the defendant; and the 'heinousness' of the killing, which was assessed according to whether the offence arose out of 'self-defence', whether it had no peculiar features, or whether it involved multiple victims, was preceded by psychological torture or sexual abuse, or involved bizarre weapons or mutilation. These dimensions, when combined in all variations, produced a classification of 18 possible types of murder.[70]

---

[69] See, for example, Michael L. Radelet, 'Racial Characteristics and the Imposition of the Death Penalty', *American Sociological Review* 46 (1981), pp. 918–927; J. E. Jacoby and R. Paternoster, 'Sentencing Disparity and Jury Packing: Further Challenges to the Death Penalty', *Journal of Criminal Law and Criminology* 73 (1982), pp. 379–387; and discussion in R. Paternoster, 'Prosecutorial Discretion in Requesting the Death Penalty: A Case of Victim-Based Racial Discrimination', *Law and Society Review* 18 (1984), pp. 437–478 at 440–441.

[70] See Arnold Barnett, 'Some Distribution Patterns for the Georgia Death Sentence', *University of California, Davis, Law Review* 18 (1985), pp. 1327–1363.

* Yet another approach has compared, on a case-by-case basis and in great detail, those sentenced to death with those in which the situations were factually similar, yet the death penalty has not been applied.[71]
* Other studies have classified cases according to those factors thought to be most legally relevant or most likely to show discrimination; the number of aggravating circumstances they display, whether they involved a 'felony circumstance', the relationship of the offender to the victim, the sex of the victim, the weapon used, and part played in the event by both defendant and victim. The effects of these variables have been analysed both separately and in various combinations, and the overall contribution of variables to the odds that an offender will receive the death sentence has been calculated through the use of multiple regression analysis.[72]

Nevertheless, even these latter studies have been criticized for not including a sufficient number of variables and for not assessing the varying strength of the evidence of each aggravating circumstance or the particular weight given to a wide variety of mitigating circumstances.[73]

In an imaginative and sophisticated attempt to overcome the objection that 'matching' has been based on too few factors to be able to prove conclusively that the different rates of death penalty observed were due to arbitrariness or discrimination, Professors Baldus, Woodworth, and Pulaski embarked in the late 1970s and early 1980s on a major study of the imposition of the death penalty in Georgia—a state that had executed more offenders than any other in the previous thirty years and whose practice had been the subject of close scrutiny and rejected as in violation of the Constitution of the United States in *Furman* v. *Georgia* in 1972. Baldus and his colleagues compared the practice of the Georgia criminal justice system with regard to the imposition of the death penalty under the pre-*Furman* statute with its imposition under the post-*Furman* statute, which was approved by the Supreme Court in 1976 in the case of *Gregg* v. *Georgia*.

They recognized that it would be impossible, given the relatively small number of cases, to match each with another on more than three or four salient factors, and they therefore chose to develop a regression analysis, based on the 20–30 most statistically significant legitimate variables (out of 150 used in the initial analysis), in order to produce a 'culpability index'. Six groups of cases were identified by statistical analysis, within each of which the cases had a similar rate of death sentences, ranging from

---

[71] See S. D. Arkin, 'Discrimination and Arbitrariness in Capital Punishment: An Analysis of Post-*Furman* Murder Cases in Dade County, Florida, 1973–76', *Stanford Law Review* 33 (1980), pp. 75–101.

[72] For the best example of a study of this kind, see Samuel R. Gross and Robert Mauro, 'Patterns of Death: An Analysis of Racial Disparities in Capital Sentencing and Homicide Victimization', *Stanford Law Review* 37 (1984), pp. 27–153, and their book *Death and Discrimination: Racial Disparities in Capital Sentencing* (1989).

[73] See, for example, Stanley Rothman and Stephen Powers, 'Execution by Quota?', *Public Interest* (1994), pp. 3–17 at 11 and 13. Also, Alfred B. Heilbrun Jr., Alison Foster, and Jill Golden, 'The Death Sentence in Georgia 1947–1987: Criminal Justice or Racial Injustice', *Criminal Justice and Behavior* 16 (1989), pp. 139–153. For a cogent critique of this article, see Coramae Richey Mann, *Unequal Justice: A Question of Color* (1993), pp. 206–207.

a group among whom less than one in ten were predicted to get the death sentence to a group in which all were predicted to be sentenced to death. The cases in each group were therefore not necessarily factually similar but were similarly 'culpable' in the sense that a particular combination of aggravating and mitigating circumstances produced a similar probability—for example, whether low, medium, or high—of them being sentenced to death. On this basis it was possible to assess the extent to which the new legislation has reduced the incidence of arbitrary and discriminatory death sentences among cases of similar culpability.[74]

It should be noted that some of the published studies relied necessarily upon data collected in the 'interregnum' between *Furman* and *Gregg* when the long moratorium on executions had still not been broken. It was possible, therefore, that death sentencing in this period had followed a somewhat different pattern to that which it has taken since executions resumed in 1977 after the constitutional position of the death penalty had been clarified by the Supreme Court. Also, with only a few exceptions, the earlier studies concentrated upon those southern states where the incidence of death sentences and executions had been highest. What had been found in the southern states obviously may or may not have been true everywhere.[75] Furthermore, it was possible, as time went by, that practices would change: that what had been acceptable at one time in relation to the treatment of racial minorities in the south would become less and less so.

These studies inevitably raise the question: what degree of variation in the infliction of the death sentence, when various legally relevant factors are accounted for, is evidence of *unacceptable* arbitrariness or discrimination? For example, Baldus, Woodworth, and Pulaski, in their Georgia study, made the judgement that it would be presumptively 'excessive' if a death sentence were imposed on an offender when not more than 0.35 (35 per cent) of like cases were sentenced to death; and that it would only be 'presumptively even-handed' to sentence someone to death if the death-sentencing rate among similar cases was 0.8 (80 per cent) and over. This, like many other issues concerning the death penalty, is ultimately a matter for moral and political judgement.

It has also to be recognized that findings relating to disparities in the rate of death sentencing do not in themselves provide evidence of disparities in the rate of executions. It is necessary to study the entire post-conviction process, from appeal to clemency, in order to establish whether at the end of the day whatever arbitrariness may have existed at the time of sentence in the court of first instance still remains.

Bearing in mind these methodological issues, the striking fact remains that the evidence as a whole, although collected in a variety of different ways, points in the same direction. This is why it is so significant that more recent studies have, by and large, confirmed the earlier findings—if not in all respects, at least as regards the most important defects of capital sentencing. Nevertheless, it would still be wise to

---

[74] See David Baldus, George Woodworth, and Charles A. Pulaski Jr., *Equal Justice and the Death Penalty: A Legal and Empirical Analysis* (1990).

[75] See Gary Kleck, 'Racial Discrimination in Criminal Sentencing', *American Sociological Review* 46 (1981), pp. 783–805 at 793.

heed Professor Baldus's warning, in 1998, that 'The small number of systematic studies of any kind encourages scepticism about sweeping claims concerning the level of racial discrimination, especially in jurisdictions in which no one has conducted systematic studies.'[76]

(b) Probabilities of being Sentenced to Death

As already shown, there is no doubt that the new capital statutes have drawn the bounds of eligibility to include a far greater number of cases than prosecutors, judges, or juries are willing to see sentenced to death. Although death-sentencing rates vary considerably between states and between counties in the same state so that 'the most powerful predictor of differential imposition of the death penalty is . . . not substantive law, but rather geographical region', they are not high even in those areas that make most use of the death penalty.[77] A number of studies in different jurisdictions have charted what has happened to those cases that appeared, on the facts, to be legally eligible for the death sentence.

The first stage is, of course, dependent on prosecutorial discretion. A study in Cook County, Illinois, for example, showed that 438 death-eligible defendants were originally charged with murder, of whom 230 were found guilty with one or more of the statutory aggravating circumstances. But only 18 of these defendants were sentenced to death—only 8 per cent of all those originally found guilty. A more recent study for the Governor of Illinois's Commission, which reported in April 2002, showed marked variations in the proportion of cases charged as first-degree murder that resulted in a death sentence in the years 1988 through 1997, ranging from 8.4 per cent in rural counties, 3.4 per cent in urban counties, to only 1.5 per cent of cases in Cook County, which includes Chicago.[78] In Colorado the prosecutors accepted a guilty plea to a lesser charge or waived the death penalty in 104 of 171 cases (61 per cent) where defendants were initially charged with capital murder: only 11 were eventually committed for a penalty trial, and four of these were sentenced to death.[79] Prosecutors in South Carolina and New Jersey sought the death penalty in only one-third of cases which had at least one aggravating factor.[80]

---

[76] Baldus, Woodworth, and Pulaski, n. 74 above, p. 1658.

[77] Zimring and Hawkins, n. 26 above, p. 89. See also, Leigh B. Bienen, N. A. Weiner, P. D. Allison, and D. L. Mills, 'The Reimposition of Capital Punishment in New Jersey: Felony Murder Cases', *Albany Law Review* 54 (1990), pp. 709–817 at 780–781; and Leigh B. Bienen, 'A Good Murder', *Fordham Urban Law Journal* 20 (1993), pp. 585–607.

[78] Elizabeth L. Murphy, 'Application of the Death Penalty in Cook County', *Illinois Bar Journal* (Oct. 1984), pp. 90–95; Illinois, *Report of the Governor's Commission on Capital Punishment: George H. Ryan Governor* (Apr. 2002), p. 196.

[79] David Baldus, George Woodworth, and Charles A. Pulaski Jr., 'Arbitrariness and Discrimination in the Administration of the Death Penalty: A Challenge to State Supreme Courts', *Stetson Law Review* 15 (1986), pp. 133–261 at 147–148.

[80] See Raymond Paternoster, 'Race of Victim and Location of Crime: The Decision to Seek the Death Penalty in South Carolina', *Journal of Criminal Law and Criminology* 74 (1983), pp. 754–785 at 768; and L. B. Bienen, N. Weiner, D. W. Denno, P. A. Allison, and D. L. Mills, 'The Re-imposition of Capital Punishment in New Jersey: The Role of Prosecutorial Discretion', *Rutgers Law Review* 41 (1988), pp. 27–372 at 287.

Furthermore, in a study in New Jersey of felony-murders with at least one statutory aggravating factor (the most likely group to receive a death sentence), the county prosecutor decided not to serve notice of any aggravating factor to the defence in half the cases, thus removing them from threat of capital punishment. At the end of the process only 41 of 134 death-eligible cases were actually convicted of capital murder and only 15 of these (just over a third) were sentenced to death. In other words only 11 per cent of those originally indicted with a death-eligible murder received the death penalty.[81] Similarly, in Georgia, only 23 per cent of eligible defendants convicted of murder after trial were sentenced to death and no more than 37 per cent of those who had been convicted of murder along with a contemporary felony. This is because the prosecutors sought the death penalty in over half the eligible cases only if three or more statutory aggravating factors were present.[82] Similarly, in their recent study of the Philadelphia jurisdiction, Baldus's team found that only 110 of the 770 death-eligible cases studied were actually sentenced to death, and in Nebraska only 29 of the 175 death-eligible cases.

Baldus and his colleagues estimated that, from a pool of between 2,000 and 4,000 death-eligible cases processed annually in the United States, only 250 to 300 death sentences result: a rate of 6 to 15 per cent.[83] Taking a slightly wider category, a study conducted by Glenn Pierce and Michael Radelet for the Illinois Commission, which reported in April 2002, showed that during the years 1988 to 1997 only 115—2 per cent—of the 5,310 cases in which a defendant was convicted of first-degree murder resulted in the imposition of a death sentence.[84] The chances of being executed were, of course, even lower. For example, in North Carolina, only one of 319 defendants originally indicted with first-degree murder was eventually executed.[85]

All these studies suggest that prosecutors 'weed out' the less serious cases and proceed only to pursue the death penalty for the more egregious types of murder. To what extent, then, is there evidence that prosecutors and courts have been even-handed in their judgments and confined death sentences to those who have committed the gravest of crimes?

(c) Who is Selected for Death?

Only one study, that of Baldus *et al.*, has collected comparative data which throws light on whether the post-*Furman* statutes have led to a more homogeneous selection of the most egregious cases for the death sentence. They compared the 'culpa-

---

[81] Bienen *et al.*, n. 77 above, p. 744. See also, Bienen, n. 77 above, pp. 585–607.

[82] Baldus *et al.*, n. 74 above, p. 107.

[83] Baldus *et al.*, n. 79 above, pp. 146–156. A comparison between Georgia and California, for instance, shows that in the former state 40% of persons indicted for murder who had no prior record, who killed one person, and who killed the person in the commission of a serious contemporary felony were sentenced to death, yet in California no case of this kind received the death penalty. Quoted in G. M. Stein, 'Distinguishing among Murders when Assessing the Proportionality of the Death Sentence', *Columbia Law Review* 85 (1985), pp. 1786–1807 at 1806.

[84] Illinois, n. 78 above, p. 188.

[85] Nakell and Hardy, n. 56 above, pp. 108–109.

bility scores' (see page 192 above) of those sentenced both to death and to life imprisonment in pre- and post-*Furman* samples. The death sentence rate had, in fact, under the new law, increased by over a half, from 15 per cent of eligible convicted cases to 23 per cent. But the large overlap between death and 'life' cases which had existed prior to *Furman* had decreased: 'only 29 per cent of the post-*Furman* death sentence cases possessed culpability scores equal to or less than the culpability score of the 95th percentile life-sentence case, a decline from the pre-*Furman* figure of 61 percent'. In other words, post-*Furman*, seven out of 10 death-sentenced cases were more serious than all but the 5 per cent of most serious life-sentenced cases.[86] Furthermore, while pre-*Furman* 40 per cent of sentences were judged to be presumptively 'excessive' (in the sense that fewer than 35 per cent in that category were sentenced to death), after *Furman* only 13 per cent were 'excessive', although a further third of the death-sentenced cases had characteristics that put them in a category where between 35 and 70 per cent of 'like' offenders were sentenced to death.[87] And while pre-*Furman* only 23 per cent were 'even-handed' (at least 80 per cent in that category being sentenced to death), after *Furman* the proportion was 51 per cent. They therefore concluded that the reform of the capital statutes had created a more selective and less arbitrary system,[88] although half of those who received a death sentence were still not in the category where the expectation of getting such a sentence was at least 80 per cent.

Another study of the Georgia experience, using a rather different methodology, revealed that, in nearly two-thirds of cases, less than a quarter of 'like' offenders were sentenced to death—resembling 'strikes of lightning'—while, at the other end of the spectrum, there was a relatively small group of especially egregious cases (but only 13 per cent of the total) where over eight out of 10 received the death penalty.[89] Detailed comparisons of those sentenced to death with those who were spared revealed the same pattern. The case of Warren McCleskey, a black man sentenced to death for shooting a white policeman during a robbery (whose case, according to Baldus, was in a 'culpability' band where the probability of a death sentence was 31 per cent), was compared with 16 other cases of police killings in the same county in Georgia. None of the defendants in these cases had been sentenced to death and only one of them had advanced to a penalty trial.[90]

In one county in Florida 10 cases that had resulted in a death sentence were compared on a case-by-case basis with 44 felony murder cases in which the defendant had been convicted of first-degree murder but had received a life sentence. Among the 44 were six very grave cases which the researcher, Stephen Arkin, found 'no legitimate basis' for distinguishing from those who had been sentenced to death. Thus the probability of the most egregious cases being sentenced to death was 10 in

[86] Baldus *et al.*, n. 74 above, p. 91.

[87] Baldus *et al.*, n. 74 above, p. 92. Over a quarter of cases fell into a category with a predicted death-sentencing rate of 0.38 or lower.

[88] Baldus *et al.*, n. 74 above, p. 131.   [89] Barnett, n. 70 above, p. 1342.

[90] Baldus *et al.*, n. 74 above, pp. 334–335.

16 or 63 per cent—one in three being spared the ultimate penalty.[91] In their most recent study of capital sentencing in Nebraska, Baldus and colleagues found that disparities in death sentences were less marked than has been found elsewhere. Nevertheless,

When the comparative proportionality analysis is expanded to embrace death sentencing among all death-eligible cases (not merely those sent for penalty-trial) . . . in only 17% (5/29) of the Nebraska death-sentenced cases were death sentences imposed in cases in which the defendant's near neighbors (similar fact cases) were sentenced to death more than 70% of the time. And in 52% (15/29) of death-sentenced cases, a death sentence was imposed on the defendant's near neighbors less than 50% of the time. However, only one death sentence was imposed in a case in which the death-sentencing rate among the death-sentenced defendant's near neighbors was less than the .16 [16 per cent], which is the average death sentencing rate among all death eligible offenders.[92]

(d) Is there Evidence of Racial Discrimination?

A number of studies have noted the large discrepancy between the proportion of cases sentenced to death according to whether the defendant or victim was white or black. It has been recently pointed out that 80 per cent of the prisoners executed in the United States since 1977 were convicted of killing a white victim,[93] although whites account for only about a half of all homicide victims.[94] Furthermore, of 749 persons executed in the United States between 1977 and the end of December 2001, only 11 involved white defendants who had killed black victims.[95] A study in Texas, for example, in the mid-1980s noted that where the murder victim was black, the proportion of defendants sentenced to death was very low, whether the killer was black or white (2.5 and 2.4 per cent respectively). In comparison, 9.5 per cent of whites who killed whites and 13.2 per cent of blacks who killed whites were sentenced to death.[96]

But, of course, the differences in the types of murder which are intra-racial and those committed across racial boundaries have to be taken into account. For example, it appears that a considerably higher proportion of black-defendant–white-

---

[91] Arkin, n. 71 above, p. 94. It should be noted that there were 14 other cases where the distinction between them and those sentenced to death was 'debatable'. If these had been taken into account, the probability of receiving a death sentence would have been 10–30, or only 33%.

[92] Baldus *et al.*, n. 74 above, pp. 20–21 of Ms.

[93] *Death Row, U.S.A.* (1 Jan. 2002) NAACP Legal Defense and Educational Fund Inc.

[94] See AI, *United States of America* (1995), p. 4.

[95] These figures are taken from NAACP Legal Defense and Educational Fund Inc. *Death Row, U.S.A.* (1 Jan. 2002).

[96] 'Killers of Dallas Blacks Escape the Death Penalty', *Dallas Times Herald*, 17 Nov. 1985, quoted in R. J. Tabak, 'The Death of Fairness: The Arbitrary and Capricious Imposition of the Death Penalty in the 1980's', *New York University Review of Law and Social Change* 14 (1986), pp. 797–848 at 826. The differences found in Florida in the 1970s were even greater. Where the victim was white 83 of the 268 convicted of felony murder were sentenced to death, but only 1 of the 110 where the victim was black. See Hans Zeisel, 'Race Bias in the Administration of the Death Penalty: The Florida Experience', *Harvard Law Review* 95 (1981), pp. 456–468 at 459.

victim cases are committed in circumstances (such as murders in the course of committing a felony) that make them death-eligible (75 per cent) than white-defendant–black-victim cases (30 per cent). In comparison, white–white and black–black cases are only capital murders in 20 and 9 per cent of instances respectively.[97] When this and other factors are taken into account, the question still remains: to what extent do racial factors play a part in determining the odds of receiving a death sentence?

In a sample of pre-*Furman* Georgia cases, Baldus *et al.* found that the odds of a black defendant receiving the death penalty were 12 times that of a comparable white defendant. Yet the post-*Furman* sample revealed no state-wide race-of-defendant effect at all. This was confirmed by Gross and Mauro's study of post-*Furman* cases from Georgia, Florida, and Illinois, where the race-of-defendant differences disappeared once the number of aggravating factors was controlled for.[98]

However, many inquiries have found a race-of-victim effect. Those who kill white persons are considerably more likely to be sentenced to death than those who kill blacks, regardless of the race of the defendant. This effect has been found in the decisions of prosecutors as well as juries. There is some evidence to suggest that the race of the victim has played a lesser role under the post-*Furman* statutes. This was noted in Florida, where the proportion of defendants on death row who have killed only black victims has increased.[99] In Georgia Baldus *et al.* found that prior to *Furman* the gap between the death sentence rate of white defendants–white victims and black defendants–white victims, which had been 23 percentage points (8 per cent v. 31 per cent), had narrowed after *Furman* to 13 percentage points (22 per cent v. 35 per cent). Furthermore, in the earlier period knowledge of the race of the victim had improved predictive accuracy of the likelihood of a death sentence being imposed by 21 percentage points (from 43 to 64 per cent), whereas under the new statutes it only added 8 percentage points to predictive accuracy (72 to 80 per cent). Both of these findings were strong indicators of a lessening of the race-of-victim effect. But there has been evidence forthcoming to show that it is still not an insignificant factor.

It seems that prosecutors have required a significantly higher threshold of aggravation to be reached in cases with black victims before they sought the death penalty.[100] They may also be more prone to 'upgrade' white victim cases to felony-

---

[97] See Paternoster, n. 80 above, p. 767.

[98] There was some evidence of a race-of-defendant effect in Illinois which showed up in a regression analysis, but none for Georgia and Florida; Gross and Mauro, n. 72 above, p. 82. Similarly, studies of prosecution decisions to seek the death penalty in Florida or South Carolina have found no race-of-defendant discrimination once the type of case is controlled for. See Radelet, n. 69 above, pp. 918–927. It should be noted that Radelet seemed to view this result with some scepticism, p. 925; also Paternoster, n. 69 above, p. 450. Nakell and Hardy found that in North Carolina the odds of a non-white defendant's case being submitted to the jury as a case of first-degree murder was higher than for a white, but no race-of-defendant differences were found at either the verdict or penalty stages; Nakell and Hardy, n. 56 above, pp. 143–146.

[99] See Zeisel, n. 96 above, p. 465. Also M. Radelet and M. Vandiver, 'Race and Capital Punishment: An Overview of the Issue', *Crime and Social Justice* 25 (1986), pp. 94–113 at 105.

[100] Paternoster, n. 69 above, p. 473. In South Carolina the proportion of cases in which the death penalty was sought by prosecutors was found to be between 2.5 and 5 times higher in white-victim cases

murder, especially where the defendant is black.[101] Some studies have suggested that these differences may be somewhat less when cases move to the sentencing stage,[102] but the most sophisticated inquiries have nevertheless revealed that death sentences have been imposed between three and seven times more often in cases involving white victims than in those involving black victims.[103] Both Barnett and Baldus *et al.* calculated that the overall difference between the death sentence rate for white- and black-victim cases that had resulted in a murder conviction after trial in Georgia was 7 to 9 percentage points even after adjustment had been made for numerous legitimate characteristics of the cases. This may not convey the impression of a large effect, but given the low rate of death sentences, even a 6 percentage points difference is equivalent to a rate three times higher (i.e. 9 v. 3 per cent). Furthermore, both studies found that the disparity was greatest in the cases of medium gravity where the general probability of being sentenced to death was about 50–50. Here, the difference was as high as 20 to 36 percentage points: the odds of a death sentence for white-victim cases being 61 per cent and for black-victim cases only 25 per cent.[104] Baldus *et al.* estimated that 80 per cent of the presumptively 'excessive' sentences involved white victims and three out of 10 of these 'appear(ed) to be the product of race-of-victim discrimination'. Indeed, they calculated that a third of all the death sentences on white victims may result from this strong tendency to treat white-victim cases so much more seriously.[105]

A review of 28 studies by the US General Accounting Office published in 1990

---

than in cases involving black victims, and 4.5 times higher where the accused was black and the victim white than where both victim and the accused were black. Paternoster, n. 80 above, pp. 754–785. For a black defendant who killed a white victim in a rural area the rate was 11 times higher than for a black defendant who killed a black victim in an urban area; p. 783. See also, R. Paternoster, 'Prosecutorial Discretion and Capital Sentencing in North and South Carolina', in R. M. Bohm (ed), *The Death Penalty in America: Current Research* (1991), pp. 39–52 at 51; also Thomas J. Keil and Gennaro F. Vito, 'Kentucky Prosecutor's Decision to Seek the Death Penalty: A LISREL Approach', *ibid.*, pp. 53–68, who argue that race inevitably enters into calculations of seriousness because it is involved in the interpretation of the seriousness of interracial felony crimes.

[101] See Michael Radelet and Glenn Pierce, 'Race and Prosecutorial Discretion in Homicide Cases', *Law and Society Review* 19 (1985), pp. 587–621.

[102] See Radelet, n. 69 above, and W. J. Bowers, 'The Pervasiveness of Arbitrariness and Discrimination under Post-*Furman* Capital Statutes', *Journal of Criminal Law and Criminology* 74 (1983), pp. 1067–1110 at 1085.

[103] See Gross and Mauro, n. 72 above, who estimated, after regression analysis, that the odds in Georgia of receiving a death sentence for killing a white was 7.2 times greater than the odds of receiving the death sentence for killing a black—and 4.3 times greater in Florida. Nakell and Hardy found the rate to be 6 times higher in North Carolina, n. 85 above, pp. 147–148; Murphy, found it to be 4 times higher in Cook County, Ill., n. 78 above, p. 94.

[104] Baldus *et al.*, n. 74 above; these figures are extracted from table 32, p. 154. See also, Barnett, n. 70 above; Barnett noted that in the class of cases where there was a felony murder of medium gravity of a stranger 5.5 times more white-victim cases were sentenced to death than black-victim cases (10–20 v. 1–11); p. 1351. See also, Gross and Mauro, n. 72 above, pp. 74–75. On prosecutorial discretion, see also, Jonathan R. Sorensen and James W. Marquart, 'Prosecutorial and Jury Decision-Making in Post-*Furman* Texas Capital Cases', *New York University Review of Law and Social Change* 18 (1990–1), pp. 743–776.

[105] Baldus *et al.*, n. 74 above, pp. 140–197 at 155 and 160. In a separate study based on all cases charged with homicide in Georgia, the authors calculated the odds of a defendant in a white-victim case being sentenced to death as 4.3 times that of a defendant in a black-victim case.

concluded that 'in 82 per cent of the studies, race-of-victim [white] was found to influence the likelihood of being charged with capital murder or receiving the death penalty . . . This finding was remarkably consistent across data sets, states, data collection methods, and analytical techniques . . . [However] . . . the race of offender influence is not so clear cut . . .'.[106] The race-of-victim effect, therefore, can be correctly characterized as 'a real and robust phenomenon'.[107]

In 1998 Baldus and his colleagues published a review of all the research conducted since 1973. This showed that in 37 of the 55 studies where race-of-defendant effects could be calculated, none were found; in 13 of them race-of-defendant effects were found (five unfavourable to white defendants), although they did not reach a sufficient level of statistical significance; and in five studies the race-of-defendant effects were statistically significant (although in two cases they were unfavourable to whites rather than blacks). As regards race-of-victim effects: they were *not* found in only five of the 55 studies; they were close to being significant in 13 studies (and only in the unpredicted direction in one of them); and statistically significant in 37—all showing that killers of white victims were more likely to receive a death sentence.[108] It is important to recognize that all the 'racial disparities were *stronger* in well-controlled studies than in the less-well-controlled studies'.[109]

Professor Baldus and his team have published studies relating to New Jersey (1982–96) and Philadelphia (1983–93) and recently completed an analysis of capital sentencing in the state of Nebraska (1973–99).[110] The New Jersey study revealed race-of-victim effects in prosecutorial decision-making, but less pronounced than in studies carried out in southern states. Yet, this study, in contrast to those in the south, 'revealed substantial disparate treatment of black defendants by penalty-trial juries'. These effects were equivalent to an average 8 percentage points difference

---

[106] *Death Penalty Sentencing: Research Indicates Pattern of Racial Disparities*, US General Accounting Office, (1990), GAO/GDD-90-57, at 6.

[107] Gross and Mauro, n. 72 above, pp. 105–106. See also, Samuel R. Gross, 'Race and Death: The Judicial Evaluation of Evidence of Discrimination in Capital Sentencing', *University of California, Davis, Law Review* 18 (1985), pp. 1275–1325 at 1279.

[108] David C. Baldus, G. Woodworth, D. Zuckermann, N.A. Weiner, and B. Broffitt, 'Racial Discrimination and the Death Penalty in the Post-*Furman* Era: An Empirical and Legal Overview, with Recent Findings from Philadelphia', *Cornell Law Review* 83 (1998), pp. 1638–1770, Appendix B at 1742–1745. In another review they stated: 'In 89% (25/28) of these states, there is some evidence of race-of-victim disparities, and in 36% (10/28) of these states, there is some evidence of race-of-defendant disparities.' David C. Baldus and George Woodworth, 'Race Discrimination and the Death Penalty: An Empirical and Legal Overview', in Acker, Bohm, and Lanier (eds), n. 38 above, pp. 399–400. Similarly, a recently published meta-analysis, carried out by Sorenson, Wallace, and Pilgrim, of the findings from 15 well-conducted studies conducted in 11 states between 1977 and 1998, concluded: 'racial disparities are widespread in the capital punishment process. The most common type of racial disparity is victim-based, occurring most often from prosecutorial decisions made during the pre-trial stages of the case processing. The evidence of a race-of-defendant effect is more tenuous.' Jon Sorenson, Donald H. Wallace and Rocky L. Pilgrim, 'Empirical Studies on Race and Death Penalty Sentencing: A Decade after the GAO Report', *Criminal Law Bulletin* 36 (2001), pp. 395–408 at 403.

[109] Baldus *et al.*, n. 108 above, p. 1661.

[110] *Ibid.*, pp. 1638–1770. Also David C. Baldus, G. Woodworth, G. L. Young and A. M. Christ, *The Disposition of Nebraska Capital and Non-Capital Homicide Cases (1973–1999): A Legal and Empirical Analysis*, Final report (amended) (10 Oct. 2001). I am indebted to Professor Baldus for sending me this as yet unpublished manuscript, which will appear in the *Nebraska Law Review* in 2002.

between black and non-black defendants after controlling for the defendants' culpability that was estimated by the regression analysis. But they were much wider in the 'mid-range' of cases, where the average disparity between the rate of being sentenced to death was 30 percentage points (52 per cent for black defendants and 22 per cent for white defendants), a difference which was statistically significant.[111] The findings in Philadelphia were similar:

> Among the unanimously decided cases, the race-of-defendant effects were substantial, consistent, and statistically significant, or nearly so, in both the overall models of jury death-sentencing and in the analyses of jury weighing decisions . . . Because of the independent basis of our four measures of defendant culpability—logistic regression, the number of aggravating and mitigating circumstances found by the jury, the salient factors of the cases, and the case rankings from the murder severity study—we are particularly impressed with the consistency of the estimated race-of-defendant effects . . . The race-of-victim results are also substantial and statistically significant, or nearly so, across a range of analyses, but they are somewhat weaker than the race-of-defendant effects . . . In the light of these results and of our methodology, we consider it implausible that the estimated disparities are either a product of chance or reflect a failure to control for important omitted case characteristics.[112]

The latest study to be published, by Glenn Pierce and Michael Radelet, was carried out for the Illinois Commission set up by Governor Ryan. After analysing all first-degree murder convictions in Illinois between 1988 and 1997 they too found a robust race-of-victim effect even after aggravating factors, such as previous criminal history, were controlled for, but no statistically significant evidence of race-of-defendant effects once the same sort of factors had been taken into account.[113]

(e) The Effectiveness of Proportionality Review

To what extent has 'proportionality review' by state Supreme Courts cured any deficiencies as regards arbitrariness or racial differences post death-sentencing by trial courts? Detailed analysis by David Baldus and colleagues of the way in which proportionality review had been conducted by the Georgia Supreme Court revealed that between 20 and 25 per cent of death sentences were vacated, nearly always on procedural grounds, and only in very rare instances because they were deemed to be 'excessive and disproportionate'. Indeed, in a study of Supreme Court proportionality reviews in five states, it was found that the death penalty had been considered to be comparatively excessive in only one case, and similarly, in a ten-year period, the Missouri Supreme Court reversed only one of 70 cases on grounds of disproportionality.[114] Baldus *et al.* concluded that proportionality review had not eliminated

---

[111] At the $p < 0.006$ level. See Baldus *et al.*, n 108 above, pp. 1663 and 1664 n. 79.

[112] *Ibid.*, pp. 1713–1715.

[113] Illinois, n. 78 above, p. 196, and Appendix by Glenn R. Pierce and Michael L. Radelet, 'Race, Region, and Death Sentencing in Illinois, 1988–1997', p. 18.

[114] See George E. Dix, 'Appellate Review of the Decision to Impose Death', *Georgetown Law Journal* 68 (1979), pp. 97–161 at 111. Dix states that the Florida Supreme Court had 'Except in cases in which juries recommended life imprisonment (and the judge imposed the death sentence) . . . shown little will-

disparities: 17–25 per cent of the death sentences affirmed were in the presumptively 'excessive' category (less than 35 per cent probability) and nearly half were in the mid-category of culpability. Thus, only 20–30 per cent were in the 'presumptively even-handed' category (80 per cent or higher probability).[115]

Several inquiries have suggested that proportionality review has done nothing to correct race-of-victim disparities.[116] Killing a white victim still increased the odds of receiving a death penalty in Illinois, Florida, and Georgia, even after proportionality review. And over the thirteen years 1973 to 1986 the Georgia Supreme Court did not vacate a single sentence on the grounds of racial discrimination. Although reversal of cases on procedural grounds had reduced the race-of-victim difference by 35 per cent, it still remained a substantial factor affecting death sentences.[117]

All the research so far conducted has attributed the failure of proportionality review to remedy both arbitrariness and discrimination to the fact that comparisons have been made with only a narrow range of cases: the smaller 'the pool' the less likely is the Court to find aberrant cases. Thus, in comparing the case under review with other cases, State Supreme Courts have either searched for similar cases among those in which the death penalty had been imposed (eight states), or 'first degree murder convictions in which the death sentence was an issue, whether or not the sentence was imposed' (14 states). This, of course, excludes all those cases that were death-eligible under the statute, but where a guilty plea to a lesser charge was accepted. For this reason, the National Center for States Courts project on comparative proportionality review recommended that 'the pool of eligible cases . . . should contain, as a minimum, all cases in which the indictment included a death-eligible charge, and a homicide conviction was obtained (including manslaughter)'.[118] Professor Baldus and his colleagues found that the Georgia Supreme Court's procedures were 'biased in favor of findings that death sentences are not excessive or disproportionate' and that, as a consequence, 'it has never vacated a death sentence because of the infrequency with which death sentences occur in other similar cases'. Excessive sentences were only reversed as a side-wind of procedural argument not as

ingness to reduce death sentences'; p. 141. Also, M. Spreger, Note, 'A Critical Evaluation of State Supreme Court Proportionality Review in Death Sentencing Cases', *Iowa Law Review* 73 (1988), pp. 719–741; and Donald H. Wallace and Jonathan R. Sorensen, 'Missouri Proportionality Review: An Assessment of a State Supreme Court's Procedures in Capital Cases', *Notre Dame Journal of Law, Ethics and Public Policy* 8 (1994), pp. 281–315 at 286.

[115] For a less sophisticated but instructive study, which weighed aggravating and mitigating circumstances and found that cases were upheld after proportionality review, even though few were 'presumptively even-handed', see Wallace and Sorenson, n. 114 above, pp. 304–310.

[116] See Radelet and Vandiver, n. 99 above, p. 106; Gross and Mauro, n. 72 above, pp. 83–92.

[117] Baldus *et al.*, n. 74 above, p. 216. Their post-conviction follow-up study revealed that 7 out of 10 of the 100 death sentences imposed in Georgia between 1973 and 1978 had been permanently vacated by 1986 through habeas corpus proceedings in federal courts with no risk of their being reimposed. Of the 30% which had not succeeded, none were in the very least culpable range (less than 10% probability) and 65% were in the most culpable (80% or greater). However, 35% were still in the mid-range (10–79% probability). By the spring of 1987, 7 had been executed—all white-victim cases, 6 of the defendants being black.

[118] See Richard van Duizend, 'Comparative Proportionality Review in Death Sentence Cases', *State Court Journal* 8(3) (1984), pp. 9–23 at 11.

a result of comparative proportionality review. Nevertheless, they argued that if state Supreme Courts were to approach the task in a more systematic and empirically based manner, with or without the help of quantitative methods, it might be possible for them, when conducting proportionality reviews, to produce an even-handed result.[119]

The evidence so far available suggests that there is more reason to be sceptical whether proportionality review alone can ever eliminate all traces of arbitrariness and capriciousness in the choice of the very few who are eventually put to death. Baldus and his colleagues conclude their recent study by suggesting that 'the empirical findings from Philadelphia and New Jersey . . . indicate that the problem of arbitrariness and discrimination in the administration of the death penalty is a matter of continuing concern and is not confined to southern jurisdictions'.[120]

(f) Concerns at the Federal Level

All the data so far reviewed about arbitrariness in the imposition of capital punishment in the United States has referred to the practice of certain states. More recently, however, the question has been raised whether similar variations exist within the federal system. Former President Clinton, when in office, declared:

I am concerned also at the federal level related more to the disturbing racial composition of those who've been convicted. And the apparent fact that almost all the convictions are coming out of just a handful of states. Which raises the question whether, even though there's a uniform law across the country, what your prosecution may determine, may turn solely on where you committed the crimes.[121]

The review that he ordered the Department of Justice to carry out did, in fact, reveal marked geographical and racial disparities. Of 21 inmates facing the federal death penalty in September 2000 only three were white. Indeed, of all offenders for whom federal prosecutors sought the death penalty, three-quarters were from ethnic minorities. Furthermore, nearly a quarter of the death sentences imposed since 1995 had been prosecuted in the federal judicial districts covering Missouri, Puerto Rico, and Virginia, whereas in nearly half the 94 federal districts prosecutors had never sought the death penalty.[122] However, when the findings of the completed study were made public in June 2001, the Attorney General of the United States in President George W. Bush's administration, John D. Ashcroft, insisted that they revealed no racial bias.[123]

---

[119] D. C. Baldus, C. A. Pulaski, Jr, G. Woodworth and F. D. Kyle, 'Identifying Comparatively Excessive Sentences of Death: A Quantitative Approach', *Stanford Law Review* 33 (1980), pp. 1–74 at 68, and Baldus *et al.*, n. 74 above, pp. 404 and 408–419.

[120] Baldus *et al.*, n. 108 above, p. 1738. On the other hand it should be noted that their analysis of 175 death-eligible homicide cases in Nebraska, resulting in 29 death-sentenced defendants, found no significant differences in treatment based on the race of the defendant or the race of the victim (awaiting publication in the *Nebraska Law Review*).

[121] *New York Times*, 29 June 2000.

[122] See AI, *The Death Penalty Worldwide: Developments in 2000*, AI Index: ACT 50/001/2001, at p. 33.

[123] Reported in the *Washington Post*, 10 June 2001.

Since 1995 United States attorneys have been required to submit for review to the Department of Justice all cases in which the defendant is charged with a capital-eligible offence, whether or not the attorney would personally wish to seek the death penalty or not. Under this 'death penalty protocol' a Review Committee on Capital Cases makes an independent recommendation to the Attorney General. A more detailed study showed that, under this system, the Attorney General (previously Janet Reno) had decided to seek the death penalty for a higher *proportion* of white (38 per cent) than black (25 per cent) or Hispanic (20 per cent) defendants (although she had done so for 46 per cent of the 'other' ethnicity group). This certainly appeared to show that there had not been an unfavourable bias against ethnic minorities at this stage of the decision-making process. But the fact remained that 80 per cent (548) of the 682 cases reviewed by the Justice Department involved ethnic-minority defendants. In other words, there may well have been a bias at the charging stage of the criminal process, which brought a higher proportion of ethnic minorities into the 'life or death' review system.[124]

A decision was therefore made to expand the research. A group of experts advised that only a study that sought detailed information about all 'potentially capital' cases, and followed them through the process to examine the impact of race at all points in the decision-making process, could provide valid evidence from which inferences (not 'definitive answers') regarding racial bias could be made. The Department of Justice was unwilling to wait for such a study to be completed and instead decided to ask federal prosecutors to provide information on all cases in their offices 'in which the facts would have supported a capital charge'. This was, of course, a more subjective method. It showed that of the 973 defendants 83 per cent were from ethnic minorities, and that federal prosecutors had decided to seek a capital charge in a slightly higher proportion of cases with a white defendant (81 per cent) than black (79 per cent) or Hispanic (56 per cent) defendants. Again the Attorney General ultimately sought the death penalty for 27 per cent of the white defendants in this larger sample of 'potential' capital cases than black (17 per cent) or Hispanic (9 per cent) defendants. The Justice Department regarded these findings as conclusive evidence that the federal death penalty system operated without racial bias, affirming that its prosecutors were all 'professionals' who would never take such extraneous and legally irrelevant factors into account, and that the much higher proportion of ethnic minorities found among federal capital cases, and variations between federal prosecutorial districts, was due to the nature of the crime (such as drug-related murder) in which ethnic-minority defendants were more often involved than were whites.[125]

Needless to say, there has been profound academic scepticism, voiced especially by Professor Baldus, that such a research method has provided data adequate to refute the charge of racial bias, especially because no study was made of how cases were selected for federal prosecution from the pool of cases that could be eligible, nor

---

[124] US Department of Justice, *The Federal Death Penalty System: A Statistical Survey (1988–2000)* (12 Sept. 2000), Washington.
[125] US Department of Justice, *The Federal Death Penalty System: Supplementary Data, Analysis and Revised Protocols for Capital Case Review* (6 June 2001).

did the research design take into account the race-of-victim effect as an explanation of why the death sentence was sought more often for white defendants, whose victims were likely to be predominantly white.[126]

(g) Policy Implications

The US Supreme Court by a majority of 5–4 affirmed the death sentence in *McCleskey* v. *Kemp* (1987) despite the evidence of institutionalized race-of-victim bias provided by the Baldus research. The majority held that an appellant sentenced to death would have to prove that intentional discrimination had occurred in his or her specific case. Obviously, a statistical association could never provide such a standard of proof. According to Justice Powell, *McCleskey* 'cannot prove a constitutional violation by demonstrating that other defendants who may be similarly situated did not receive the death penalty'. Yet, the 'systemic' statistical evidence presented in *McCleskey* was precisely the sort of evidence that has been accepted by the Supreme Court as providing sufficient proof of discrimination in other fields. As Baldus and Woodworth point out, this means 'that equal protection claims of purposeful race discrimination in death penalty cases are now subject to a far heavier burden of proof than is applied to evaluate claims in ordinary jury and employment discrimination cases'.[127]

The issue has continued to arouse controversy. Some have argued that the fact that the death penalty is not administered fairly in relation to the race of the victim is not a reason to abolish capital punishment. They interpret the findings as indicating that capital punishment is not used enough in black-victim cases because black lives are not prized as highly as white lives. So they would like to see an 'evening up' of the scales of justice.[128]

On the other hand, it seemed to abolitionists unreasonable that the majority of the US Supreme Court would not accept that the evidence presented, which went unchallenged, was sufficient to show an inherent and systemic racial bias in the death penalty system as a whole. The majority of the Court was reluctant to admit this, because they feared that to concede this argument in relation to capital punishment would open up a challenge to discretionary decision-making throughout the criminal justice system.[129] There can be no doubt that the failure of the Court to uphold, under the equal protection clause, a class-wide claim of racial discrimination, based on uncontested social science research, was a setback for abolitionists. They had,

---

[126] See www.deathpenaltyinfo.org/Baldus statement.html (11 June 2001).

[127] However, the New Jersey Supreme Court in *State* v. *Marshall* (1992) ruled that under the equal protection clause of the New Jersey Constitution, claims of race-of-victim and race-of-defendant discrimination are cognizable. However, no remedies were discussed because in this case the court did not find evidence of unconstitutional racial discrimination. See Baldus and Woodworth, n. 108 above, pp. 407 and 411–412.

[128] See John C. Adams, 'Racial Disparity and the Death Penalty', *Law and Contemporary Problems* 61 (1998), pp. 153–170. Also, Ashutosh Bhagwat, 'The McCleskey Puzzle: Remedying Prosecutorial Discrimination against Black Victims in Capital Sentencing', in D. J. Hutchinson, D. A. Strauss, and G. R. Stone (eds), *1998 The Supreme Court Review* (1999), pp. 145–192 at 149.

[129] *McCleskey* v. *Kemp* (1987). On the Supreme Court's attitude towards empirical research, see James R. Acker, 'Research on the Death Penalty: A Different Agenda: The Supreme Court, Empirical Research

after all, relied in the past upon such evidence as a means of combating capital punishment, most notably in the famous *Furman* judgment. It appears, moreover, that since *McCleskey*, courts have routinely 'summarily dismissed . . . contentions [based on statistical evidence of differential treatment on the grounds of race] on the grounds that the Supreme Court . . . had precluded this type of challenge to a death sentence' altogether. This appears to be a very narrow interpretation, and it reinforces the claim that unrealistic demands for 'statistical proof' have been made, of a kind not called for in other areas of discrimination law.[130] It appears that the courts have simply not wanted to confront the issue. Indeed, in concluding the majority opinion in *McCleskey* v. *Kemp*, Justice Powell held that arguments about systemic discrimination were 'best presented to the legislative bodies'.[131]

Since 1988 the United States Congress has considered two very similar measures to allow defendants to challenge their death sentence (although not convictions) on the grounds of racial bias: the Fairness in Death Sentencing Act and the Racial Justice Act, the latter being incorporated in 1994 into the Violent Crime Control and Law Enforcement Act of 1994 as Title IX 'Racially Discriminatory Capital Sentencing'. The objective was to allow courts 'to consider evidence showing a consistent pattern of racially discriminatory death sentences in the sentencing jurisdiction, taking into account the nature of the cases being compared, the prior records of the offenders, and other statutorily appropriate non-racial characteristics'. The appellant would have had to show statistically that the disparity was significant and that his particular case fitted the pattern of racially discriminatory sentencing, and the prosecution would have been able to rebut the evidence and the inferences drawn from it.[132] This would have been a tough test for defendants to respond to. Nevertheless, the threat it was believed to pose to the operation of the death penalty was such that this Title was thrown out of the 1994 Violent Crime Control Act as it passed through the Senate.

Some, like Professor Baldus and his colleagues, believe that the mechanisms do exist to make the infliction of the death penalty fair:[133] 'the problems of discrimination in

Evidence, and Capital Punishment Decisions, 1986–1989', *Law and Society Review* 27 (1993), pp. 65–87, and Franklin E. Zimring, 'Research on the Death Penalty: The Liberating Virtues of Irrelevance', *ibid.*, pp. 9–17.

[130] For a valuable discussion of this issue, see John H. Blume, Theodore Eisenberg and Sheri Lynn Johnson, 'Post-*McCleskey* Racial Discrimination Claims in Capital Cases', *Cornell Law Review* 83 (1998), pp. 1771–1810 at 1798–1806.

[131] See Baldus *et al.*, n. 74 above, p. 415; F. J. Bendremer, G. Bramnick, J. C. Jones, and S. C. Lippman, '*McCleskey* v. *Kemp*: Constitutional Tolerance for Racially Disparate Capital Sentencing', *University of Miami Law Review* 41 (1986), pp. 295–355; Keith A. Green, 'Statistics and the Death Penalty: A Break with Tradition', *Creighton Law Review* 21 (1987), pp. 265–301.

[132] 103rd Congress, 2nd Session, House Report, pp. 103–458, *Racial Justice Act* (24 Mar. 1994), mimeo. And Ronald J. Tabak, 'Is Racism Irrelevant? Or should the Fairness in Death Sentencing Act be Enacted to Substantially Diminish Racial Discrimination in Capital Sentencing?', *New York University Review of Law and Social Change* 18 (1990–1), pp. 777–806.

[133] See D. C. Baldus, G. C. Woodworth and C. A. Pulaski, 'Reflections on the "Inevitability" of Racial Discrimination in Capital Sentencing and the "Impossibility" of its Prevention, Detection and Correction', *Washington and Lee Law Review* 51 (1994), pp. 359–430. Also, David C. Baldus, 'The Death Penalty Dialogue between Law and Social Science', *Indiana Law Journal* 70 (1995), pp. 1033–1041.

the use of the death penalty are as susceptible to identification, adjudication, and correction as are the practices of discrimination in other areas of American life that the civil rights movement has already addressed'.[134] Yet, others believe that capital punishment will probably remain a 'lottery' in which the system selects a few cases for execution on unacceptable social and moral criteria.[135] Indeed, in a recent review and summing up of the experiences under the post-*Furman* capital statutes, James Acker and Charles Lanier concluded that because they had failed to eliminate 'problems of race discrimination, erroneous convictions, and unequal justice' they may signal 'the beginning of the end of capital punishment in America'.[136]

It remains debatable whether any legislative formula or judicial practice can be devised that can satisfactorily eliminate the objectionable features of discrimination or other forms of arbitrariness from the enforcement of capital punishment without undermining the whole institution of the death penalty. Indeed, it is the belief that it is impossible to eliminate these problems 'in a manner that is compatible with our [American] legal system's fundamental commitment to fair and equal treatment' that underlines what has been dubbed 'the new abolitionism' in America.[137]

Those who have the power to shape policy must face the fact that in any discretionary system, even one with statutory guidelines, some persons will be sentenced to death whose cases it is impossible to distinguish from some of those who escape it. What degree of even-handedness is expected and what degree of capriciousness will be tolerated? Is it sufficient that 'even when viewed in the most favourable light, only 50 per cent to 60 per cent of the death sentences in [Georgia were] presumptively even-handed; and approximately one-quarter appear[ed] to be excessive'?[138] Or will it be agreed that 'a capital punishment system that provides arbitrary leniency for some defendants by definition is responsible for arbitrary execution of others',[139] and that this is neither morally nor politically acceptable? As Professor Baldus and his colleagues have put it:

Many consider it insensitive and unseemly, if not immoral, for a country with our historical record on slavery and racial discrimination to persist in using a punishment that whites almost exclusively administer and control, that serves no demonstrated penological function, and has a profound adverse impact—physically, psychologically, and symbolically—on its black citizens.[140]

---

[134] Baldus and Woodworth, n. 108 above, pp. 412–413. And the conclusion to Baldus *et al.*, n. 108 above, p. 1738.

[135] See, for example, the debate on the extent to which the death penalty might be regarded as a form of lottery: Richard A. Berk, Jack Boger, and Robert Weiss, 'Research on the Death Penalty: Chance and the Death Penalty', *Law and Society Review* 27 (1993), pp. 89–110; the response from Raymond Paternoster, 'Assessing Capriciousness in Capital Cases', *ibid.*, pp. 111–123; and 'Rejoinder' by Berk, Boger, and Weiss, pp. 125–127. See also, Bienen, n. 77 above, p. 607.

[136] See J. R. Acker and C. S. Lanier, 'Introduction: America's Experiment with Capital Punishment', in Acker, Bohm, and Lanier (eds), n. 38 above, p. 9.

[137] Sarat, n. 30 above, p. 251.

[138] Baldus *et al.*, n. 74 above, p. 400.

[139] Nakell and Hardy, n. 56 above, p. 161.

[140] Baldus *et al.*, n. 108 above, p. 1651.

The evidence reviewed in this chapter clearly illustrates the great value of empirical criminological inquiry in shedding light on the actual administration of death penalty statutes. Several retentionist countries have, in the past, informed the United Nations that they are carrying out research on the death penalty, but none, as far as can be determined, have done so. It behoves them to make available the funds, and provide the access to the data, that are necessary to carry out inquiries into the realities of how the death penalty is administered.

7

The Question of Deterrence

WHAT IS GENERAL DETERRENCE?

(a) Reliance on the Deterrent Justification

To many laymen the threat of death is self-evidently a more effective deterrent than the threat of life imprisonment. As the Victorian English judge Sir James Fitzjames Stephen put it: 'The plain truth is that statistics are no guide at all . . . the question as to the effect of capital punishment on crime must always be referred, not to statistics, but to the general principles of human nature.'[1] This 'gut reaction' is still widely shared and appears to lie behind the scepticism expressed towards social science data on the relationship between capital punishment and the rate of murder by those who currently support capital punishment.[2]

But although it must undoubtedly be the case that there have been instances when people have refrained from murder, in particular circumstances, for fear of execution, this in itself is an insufficient basis on which to conclude that the existence of the death penalty on the statute book, plus the (often remote) threat of execution, will lead to a lower rate of murder per head of population than would be the case without the threat of this ultimate penalty. In other words, the issue is not whether the death penalty deters some—if only a few—people but whether, when all the circumstances surrounding the use of capital punishment are taken into account, it is associated with a marginally lower rate of the kind of murders for which it has been appointed. The reason why one must take account of, and weigh, all its effects is that capital punishment has several drawbacks to counter its supposed 'obvious' advantages. For example, an offender threatened with death could have an added incentive to kill witnesses to his crime. Furthermore, capital punishment at the hands of the state is not the only threat that the offender faces: the police may intervene with deadly force, the intended victim may successfully strike back, or associates of the victim may seek swift revenge, as can happen in 'drug wars'.

---

[1] J. F. Stephen, 'Capital Punishments', *Fraser's Magazine* 69 (1864), pp. 753–772 at 753 and 759. See on this Leon Radzinowicz and Roger Hood, *A History of English Criminal Law*, vol. v, *The Emergence of Penal Policy* (1986), pp. 674–676.

[2] See Louis P. Pojman and Jeffrey Reiman, *The Death Penalty, For and Against* (1998). Views 'for' of Louis P. Pojman, pp. 44–51, and 'against' by Jeffrey Reiman, pp. 139–140. Also Michael Davis, *Justice in the Shadow of Death: Rethinking Capital and Lesser Punishments* (1996), pp. 9–31; and Gary Wills, 'The Dramaturgy of Death', *New York Review of Books* (21 June 2001), quoting William Weld, Governor of Massachusetts, 'My gut is that . . . capital punishment is a deterrent', and Bob Graham, former Governor of Florida, 'This is an issue that is inherently beyond what empirical research can validate.'

It must be recognized that it would be very difficult, if not impossible, to find empirical data relating to the deterrent effects of the threat of capital punishment that would utterly convince a committed proponent of the death penalty to change his or her mind. Indeed, as far as some crimes threatened by capital punishment in several countries are concerned, such as importing or trading in illegal drugs, there simply is no reliable evidence relating to the deterrent effects of executions. What can be done, however, with regard to the crime of murder is to weigh all the evidence carefully and attempt to reach a balanced conclusion. And that is the purpose of this chapter. But in doing so, it must be remembered that the utilitarian justification of deterrence is only one factor to weigh in the balance. Issues of proportionality, desert, humanity, respect for human rights, of arbitrariness and discrimination, and the dangers of wrongful convictions must all be weighed against whatever claims might be made in the name of general deterrence. Indeed, as the discussion on public opinion and the death penalty shows (see Chapter 8), the number of supporters of capital punishment in the United States who say that they favour it because of its deterrent effect is remarkably low (see page 241 below).

Even though some states may justify their use of the death penalty on simple retributive grounds, the most common justification is the belief that it has a unique general deterrent capacity to save further innocent lives or reduce significantly other capital offences.[3] If it does not have such a utility—or if it does not control crime through incapacitation of the criminal beyond what can be achieved by life imprisonment—it would be, in the words of the US Supreme Court in *Coker* v. *Georgia*, 'nothing more than the purposeless and needless imposition of pain and suffering', and thus an unconstitutional punishment.[4]

As Peterson and Bailey note: 'During the past 25 years a number of justices of the United States Supreme Court have emphasized the fundamental importance of the deterrent question to the constitutionality of capital punishment.' For example, in the 1984 case of *Spaziano* v. *Florida* Justice White stated that 'a majority of the Court has concluded that the general deterrence rationale adequately justifies the imposition of capital punishment at least for certain classes of offences for which the legislature may reasonably conclude that the death penalty has a deterrent effect'.[5]

The deterrent justification has also been voiced by many retentionist countries—by China, Japan, Malaysia, Singapore, by those countries of the former USSR that have yet to abolish capital punishment, by many nations in the Middle East and some in Africa. The Chinese authorities, for example, have held strongly to the opin-

---

[3] See, for example, George E. Pataki (Governor of New York State), 'The Death Penalty as a Deterrent', in David L. Bender *et al.* (eds), *Does Capital Punishment Deter Crime?* (1998), pp. 10–13. Also A. S. Mikhlin, *Capital Punishment in Russia* (1999), 'the deterrent effect of the death penalty is greater than that of any other punishments'; pp. 159–166 at 166.

[4] *Coker* v. *Georgia*, quoted in *Thompson* v. *Oklahoma* (29 June 1988), No. 86–6169, 108, *Supreme Court Reporter*, pp. 2687–2700 at 2700.

[5] Ruth D. Peterson and William C. Bailey, 'Is Capital Punishment an Effective Deterrent for Murder? An Examination of Social Science Research', in J. R. Acker, R. M. Bohm, and C. S. Lanier (eds), *America's Experiment with Capital Punishment* (1998), pp. 157–182 at 175; quoting Justice White in *Spaziano* v *Florida*, 468 U.S. 447 (1984).

ion that the use of the death penalty, by 'striking severely at the grave crimes', has increased public security and was, at least in part, responsible for the decline in the rate of recorded crime from 8.9 crimes per 10,000 of population in 1981 to 5 per 10,000 in 1987.[6] Similarly, it has been claimed that the imposition of Islamic law, including the death penalty, has been an essential factor in the transformation of Saudi Arabia into a society with a high degree of public order and low rate of crime.[7]

No empirical studies have investigated the impact of the death penalty or executions on the incidence of drugs offences, economic crimes, politically motivated violence, or any of the other offences to which the threat of capital punishment has recently been extended (see Chapter 3). Nor have there been any such studies on the effect of the death penalty as an exemplary punishment in law and order campaigns, such as have occurred in China[8] and Iran. The only exception is an interesting, but inevitably, given the available data, rather rudimentary, study of armed robbery carried out in Nigeria several years ago (see page 216 below). Consequently, all almost all the studies available for review are concerned with the deterrent effect of capital punishment on the rate of murder in the United States.

(b) Conceptual Issues: The Need for Clarification

It is necessary to distinguish between two different, although often related, conceptions of general deterrence. The usual sense in which it is used in discussions of the death penalty implies that the threat of the capital sanction, or to be more precise the perceived risk of being executed, causes those who are about to commit a capital offence to desist in more cases than would the alternative sanction of life imprisonment. It is therefore hypothesized that there will be an observable and regular relationship between the risk of execution (i.e. the probability of being executed following conviction) and the rate of capital offending. The second sense in which the concept of deterrence has emerged implies that the existence of the death penalty for a crime has a 'moralizing' influence on people's perceptions of the gravity of that crime, and therefore reinforces their inhibitions against committing it. This has been called 'general prevention' or 'long-term deterrence'.[9] Thus, it is argued that if the

---

[6] Personal communication from Professor Cheng Weique of the Law Department, China University of Politics and Law, Beijing.

[7] See Farouk Abdul Rahman Mourad, 'Effect of the Implementation of the Islamic Legislation on Crime Prevention in the Kingdom of Saudi Arabia: A Field Research', in UNSDRI, *The Effects of Islamic Legislation in Crime Prevention in Saudi Arabia* (1980), pp. 494–567. This study was based on the testimony of 22 aged persons about the state of crime before and after the establishment of the Saudi Kingdom. It made no attempt to disentangle the supposed influence of the death penalty from the influence of other changes in law enforcement and in social, economic, and political conditions over this period.

[8] It has been claimed that the 'war waged on criminal elements' in China in 1983 (when many executions took place) led to a drop of 36% in criminal offences. There is no means of knowing, however, what the effect of so many executions was on the willingness of citizens to report crime. See Yao Zaohiu, *New Crimes Emerging in the Process of China's Development and the Strategic Policies and Measures to be Taken.* UNAFEI Resource Material Series no. 30 (1986).

[9] See J. Andenaes, *Punishment and Deterrence* (1974), esp. ch. 2; Nigel Walker, 'The Efficacy and

death penalty for a type of crime were to be abolished, this would lower perceptions of the seriousness of that crime (say murder) and thus, over a period of some time (not necessarily in the short term), the incidence of that crime would rise. Indeed, the fact that some countries retain the death penalty but rarely, if ever, execute offenders is testimony to their belief in the symbolic power of the death penalty to repress the incidence of murder.

The alternative hypothesis, which has, in recent years, gained a number of adherents, is that capital crimes (here specifically homicide) may be stimulated, not suppressed, by the execution of offenders. This has been called the 'brutalization' hypothesis.[10] Like general deterrence, the theory might work on two levels. In the short term executions would stimulate the would-be killer by releasing inhibitions because he or she would be able to identify with the state as an 'enforcer' and 'executioner' seeking lethal vengeance.[11] It has also been suggested that the drama surrounding executions stimulates certain people to seek such notoriety or to see this as an alternative to suicide. If any of these effects were evident, one would find that in the aftermath of executions there would be an increase, rather than a decrease, in murders. In its other sense brutalization theory implies that the message given by executions stimulates, rather than inhibits, violence, and specifically condones killing as vengeance. It is common to quote Cesare Beccaria's dictum: 'the death penalty cannot be useful because of the example of barbarity it gives men . . . It seems to me absurd that the laws, which are an expression of the public will, which detest and punish homicide, should themselves commit it'.[12] It follows that those jurisdictions that retain the death penalty and use it would be expected, other things being equal, to have higher homicide rates than those that do not, and that a general increase in executions would be followed at some later date by an increase in homicides. Thus, while a general deterrent effect would be supported by negative correlations between executions and the homicide rates, brutalization would be supported by positive correlations. It is, of course, possible that both effects work on different segments of the 'threatened population', and that what will be measured is the marginal impact of one against the other, or perhaps a 'balancing out' of these contrary effects.

Deterrent or brutalizing effects are not the only possible consequences of executions. The existence of the death penalty, as has been shown (see Chapter 5 above), may have effects upon the practice of plea bargaining, on the willingness of prosecutors to seek convictions for capital murder, of juries to convict, and of courts and clemency authorities to impose the sanction. All of these may have an impact on the perceived certainty of punishment, and on the moral message imparted.

Morality of Deterrence', *Criminal Law Review* (1979), pp. 125–144; and Deryck Beyleveld, 'Identifying, Explaining and Predicting Deterrence', *British Journal of Criminology* 19 (1979), pp. 205–224.

[10] See in particular, William J. Bowers, with G. L. Pierce and J. F. McDevitt, *Legal Homicide: Death as Punishment in America, 1864–1982* (1984), pp. 271–335; and W. J. Bowers, 'The Effect of Executions is Brutalization, not Deterrence', in K. C. Haas and J. A. Inciardi (eds), *Challenging Capital Punishment* (1989), pp. 49–89.

[11] Bowers, 'The Effect of Executions is Brutalization, not Deterrence', n. 10 above, pp. 53–54.

[12] Cesare Beccaria, *On Crimes and Punishment* (1764), trans. Henry Paolucci (1963), p. 50.

2. GENERAL DETERRENCE IN CONTEXT

Virtually all studies of general deterrence have assumed that whatever the general preventive effects of the death penalty may be, they will not be sustained in the longer term if no executions take place. Most empirical studies have therefore concentrated on estimating the effect of changes in the probability of being executed on the incidence of homicide. Intuition suggests that the policy of deterrence is only likely to have any impact if it is enforced with a sufficient degree of certainty against persons who, in the course of their conduct, calculate the probable penal consequences.[13]

It has to be recognized that in the United States the probability of being executed if charged with a culpable homicide is very low—around 1 in 1,000. Even restricting the calculation to those murders that are statutorily 'death-eligible' the probability of being sentenced to death is only about 1 in 10 and of being executed between 0.6 and 1.25 per 100. Indeed, of the 6,588 persons who went into prison under sentence of death in the United States between 1976 (when the Supreme Court reaffirmed the death penalty) and the end of 2000, only about 10 per cent had been executed and a third had had the death sentence removed and received 'other dispositions' (see also the discussion in Chapter 6 pages 193–194 above).[14] In fact, low probabilities of execution have been found even in those countries that use capital punishment the most. South Africa was a good example when it had the death penalty: in 1978–9, just over two in every 100 alleged murders resulted in an execution.[15]

For any rational calculation of these probabilities to affect the offender's decision whether or not to commit the offence he or she must know whether the act is likely to be classed as a capital offence, whether or not the prosecutor will place it in that limited class which is likely to attract the death penalty, and whether he or she will be among that tiny group of offenders who eventually will be put to death.

The assumption upon which guided discretionary statutes rest is that the death sentence will be applied only to those from whom society needs the greatest protection.

---

[13] See T. Sellin, *The Penalty of Death* (1980), p. 100. It must be recognized that in reaching a decision people may take into account grave consequences even when the probability of them occurring is very low. There is a large literature on this phenomenon. None of it, however, relates to the question of capital punishment. See Daniel Kahneman, Paul Slovic and Amos Tversky (eds), *Judgment under Uncertainty: Heuristics and Biases* (1982). As mentioned before, it has frequently been pointed out that these consequences are often far more remote than being killed by a potential victim, a rival criminal, or the police.

[14] See US Department of Justice, *Capital Punishment 2000* (2001). This confirms an earlier estimate that it was unlikely in the longer term that more than 10% would be executed. See C. A. Nesbit, P. L. Howard, and S. M. Wallace, *Managing Death-Sentenced Inmates: A Survey of Practices* (1989), p. 26. In Illinois only 12 persons were executed between 1977 and 2002, although over 5,300 were convicted of first-degree murder between 1988 and 1997 alone, of whom 115 were sentenced to death. See Illinois, *Report of the Governor's Commission on Capital Punishment: George H. Ryan Governor* (Apr. 2002), p. 188.

[15] See M. C. J. Olmesdahl, 'Predicting the Death Sentence', *South African Journal of Criminal Law and Criminology* 6 (1982), pp. 201–218 at 202. Mr Delroy Chuck's report to the Fraser Committee in Jamaica noted that 'the 93 men whom we have hanged since 1958 . . . represent less than four per cent of the killers since then' (1981), mimeo, p. 120.

Thus, the prime aggravating circumstance which leads to a death sentence is that the murder was committed during the commission of another felony, the assumption being that these are the actions of rational 'calculating criminals', not those that have arisen from emotional outbursts among the ordinary population. Any study of deterrence should seek to test this specific hypothesis because the threat of death is not made to the generality of potential murderers. Furthermore, several of the aggravating circumstances that make a person liable for the death penalty in many jurisdictions relate to crimes that intuitively do not appear likely to be affected by rational calculation of the marginally increased probability of execution. The murders that are described as 'especially heinous, atrocious, or cruel'[16] are likely to be carried out by psychopathic personalities or persons who have lost control of their normal inhibitions. Those who are judged to be seriously at risk of repeating murder might be incapacitated, but those who have yet to commit a murder belong by definition to a category of offenders who have such poor control that they are very unlikely to be deterred by vague threats of death.

Thus, the restrictive policies now being pursued by most nations have made the intuitive arguments in favour of the deterrent impact of the death penalty less plausible, and made it more necessary than ever to seek to test its assumptions through empirical research. Yet this does not mean that if countries returned to past practices of using capital punishment more frequently, a deterrent effect would be found. At whatever period studies have been carried over the past seventy years or so, no convincing evidence has been forthcoming that capital punishment is marginally more effective as a deterrent to murder than long-term imprisonment.[17]

In 1967 Norval Morris observed:

There are three standard methods by which the deterrent effect of the death penalty may be tested. First, the commission of capital crimes such as murder may be measured in a given jurisdiction before and after the abolition or reintroduction of capital punishment. Secondly, the rate of crime of two or more jurisdictions—similar except that at least one has abolished the death penalty—may be compared. Thirdly, the commission of a crime such as murder within a single jurisdiction may be measured before and after widely publicised executions of murderers.[18]

Since the mid-1970s a further method has been introduced, namely the sophisticated statistical theory and techniques of econometric analysis. This has been employed to calculate over time and/or across jurisdictions the association between the rate of executions and the rate of homicides, once other factors that may affect both those rates have been controlled for through the use of multiple regression analysis.

---

[16] It is for murders of this class that many supporters of the death penalty have been seeking the reintroduction of the death penalty in the United Kingdom.

[17] See Peterson and Bailey, n. 5 above, pp. 157–182 at 177.

[18] United Nations, *Capital Punishment, Developments 1961 to 1965* (1967), pp. 40–41.

3. ASSESSING CRIME TRENDS

Both Marc Ancel and Norval Morris discussed, at length, what Ancel called 'the criminality curve' as a means of assessing whether a reduction in the use of capital punishment, or its complete abolition, appeared prima facie to produce a rise in the rate of murder or, conversely, whether the introduction of the death penalty had reduced it. It is obvious, however, that any change in the use of the death penalty may itself be associated with social changes and changes in penal practice that affect the rate of crime, and that unless these are taken into account no definite conclusions can be drawn about the impact of the death penalty alone. Nevertheless, although a rise in homicide might not necessarily be caused by the removal of the deterrent, one would not expect there to be a consistent fall in homicides if it were true that executions of those guilty of murder has a unique power as a restraint on committing homicides or those kinds of murder classed as 'capital'.

The fact that the statistics, cited below, continues to point in the same direction is persuasive evidence that countries need not fear sudden and serious changes in the curve of crime if they reduce their reliance upon the death penalty. In Australia, for example, where the last executions occurred in the mid-1960s, the reported homicide rate per 100,000 of the population has fallen, and the murder rate (those homicides resulting in a conviction for murder) has changed very little.[19] Although there was an increase in murder and manslaughter convictions in South Australia in the five years after abolition in comparison with the previous five years, a more long-term analysis revealed 'that abolition of the death penalty had no effect on homicide trends in that state'.[20] In 1999, twenty-three years after the abolition of the death penalty, the Canadian homicide rate was 1.76 per 100,000 population, 43 per cent lower than it had been in 1975 (3.02 per 100,000), the year before abolition.[21] Indeed, the murder rate had been increasing (from 1.25 per 100,000 population in 1961 to 3.02 in 1975, a rise of 142 per cent) prior to abolition. Thus, its sharp decline following abolition was a potent argument used by the Canadian Prime Minister in 1987 when opposing the reintroduction of capital punishment.[22]

Yet, if there are social factors creating an increase in violence as a whole in society, one would expect the rate of murder to rise irrespective of capital punishment. And if the removal of the threat of executions reduced the 'cost' of committing murder in relation to the 'costs' of committing other kinds of violent crime, one would expect murders to rise at a rate equivalent to, or more steeply than, other

---

[19] This may be because without the death penalty juries are more willing to convict for murder rather than a lesser homicide. For further evidence of this, see p. 223 below.

[20] See Ivan Potas and John Walker, *Capital Punishment* (1987), p. 3; also, Australian Law Reform Commission, *Sentencing Penalties*, Paper no. 30 (1987), para. 7.

[21] See AI, *Facts and Figures on the Death Penalty* (2001), AI Index: ACT 50/002/2001, p. 3. See also, Canada, *A Graphical Overview of Crime and the Administration of Criminal Justice in Canada 1998* (2000).

[22] Speech in the Canadian House of Commons, 22 June 1987, by the Rt. Hon. Brian Mulroney, Prime Minister of Canada, *Commons Debates*, p. 7477.

violent crimes.[23] I have not come across an example where this has been the case. In Jamaica the homicide rate hardly changed during the moratorium on executions between 1976 and 1982,[24] and the substantial increase in murders in recent years appears to be part of a more general breakdown of law and order, mainly in the capital, Kingston, where, in attempting to restore order, 21 people were killed by security forces in July 2001. The loss of control and the breakdown of law and order have been 'confirmed' by the recent decision of the Jamaican Prime Minister to pass police powers onto the army.[25]

While the number of recorded homicides per million population has risen by about 70 per cent in England and Wales since the abolition of the death penalty—from around an average of 7.1 in the years 1966 to 1970 to about 12 per million in the years 1996 to 1999/2000—the increase has been far less than the increase in serious violent offences, which over the same period rose almost 10 times. Furthermore, while the number of persons convicted of *murder* has risen more than threefold over these years, from around 70 to almost 250, the number convicted of all homicides has barely doubled, from about 250 to less than 500.[26] The reason for this, as noted below, is that without capital punishment an increasing proportion of those prosecuted for homicide have been convicted of the more serious charge of murder. In other abolitionist countries which have been experiencing a rise in crime, homicide rates have also lagged a long way behind increases in violent offences in general.[27]

In the United States the homicide (murder and non-negligent manslaughter) rate surged from 4.8 per 100,000 in 1960 to 8.8 per 100,000 in 1977, when the first execution took place after a ten-year moratorium. It continued to rise to a peak of 10.2 per 100,000 in 1980, after which it fell to 7.9 by 1985, only to rise again to 9.8 in 1991. Since then the rate declined sharply, to 5.7 per 100,000 by 1999.[28] Moreover, there had been no clear relationship between the number of executions in one year and the rate of murder and non-negligent manslaughter in the following

---

[23] See Bowers, with Pierce and McDevitt, n. 10 above, pp. 113–114.

[24] See AI, *Jamaica: The Death Penalty* (1984), pp. 35–36.

[25] AI, *Jamaica: The Culture of Violence Must Stop* (2001),. AI Index: AMR 38/017/2001.

[26] See Sir Leon Radzinowicz's authoritative statement on the dangers of using statistics of crime trends as evidence in favour of either abolition or retention: US Senate, *Hearings to Abolish the Death Penalty*, before the Sub-Committee on Criminal Laws and Procedures of the Committee on the Judiciary, United States Senate, 19th Congress, 2nd Session, on s. 1760 (20, 21 March, and 2 July 1968) (1970), Washington, pp. 55–68 at 62–66. Also see, *Criminal Statistics, England and Wales, 1993* (1995), table 2.15, p. 50.

[27] A study of crime trends in 12 of the countries (and 2 of their major cities) which had abolished capital punishment de jure revealed that, in general, the homicide rate in the longer term was more likely to fall than to rise relative to other non-capital crimes. See D. Archer and R. Gartner, *Violence and Crime in Cross-National Perspective* (1994), p. 136. For a similar finding, see also, E. A. Fattah, *A Study of the Deterrent Effects of Capital Punishment with Special Reference to the Canadian Situation* (1972). There have been very few attempts to assess the effects of capital punishment on the rate of other felonies. For an interesting example, which found no instances of a negative relationship between the use of capital punishment and felony rates, see William C. Bailey, 'The General Preventive Effect of Capital Punishment on Non-Capital Felonies', in R. M. Bohm (ed), *The Death Penalty in America: Current Research* (1991), pp. 21–38.

[28] US Department of Justice, *Homicide Trends in the U.S.—Long Term Trends and Patterns*, www.ojp.usdoj.gov/bjs/

year.[29] A perusal of the figures for the average number of murders and non-negligible manslaughters in the retentionist and abolitionist states over the years 1980 to 1995 showed that 'Contrary to the deterrent hypothesis, for each of the 16 years, rates are higher for states that prescribe capital punishment for murder. Indeed murder rates ranged from 1.39 (1989) to 1.83 (1995) times higher for retentionist jurisdictions over the period.'[30] A similar analysis conducted by the *New York Times* in 2000 also showed that 10 of the 12 states without the death penalty had lower homicide rates than the national average, while half the states with the death penalty had homicide rates above the national average. Indeed over the past twenty years states with the death penalty had homicide rates varying between 48 and 101 per cent higher than those states without capital punishment.[31] According to the Illinois Coalition to Abolish the Death Penalty, states without the death penalty had an average homicide rate of 4.9 per 100,000, which is a third lower than the rate of 7.4 homicides per 100,000 population in states with the death penalty. But, of course, to a convinced retentionist such comparisons would not mean much in themselves: they would only go to show that where murder rates were highest the need for capital punishment as a deterrent was greatest.

A state-by-state analysis also revealed that there is no pattern that would suggest that those states which have executed offenders have experienced any greater decline in their homicide rates than have states which have no death penalty at all. For example, between 1980 and 1985 the homicide rate fell by 21 per cent in Florida and 25 per cent in Georgia, both of them jurisdictions with relatively high rates of execution at the time; but over the same period the homicide rate in New York, a state without the death penalty, also fell by 26 per cent.

A study in Nigeria published in 1987 (the only recent inquiry into the deterrent effects of capital punishment outside the United States) found no consistent pattern in the relationship between the average number of executions carried out and the incidence of either murder or armed robbery. In some periods an increase in executions was matched by an increase in crime, in other periods by a decline. Furthermore, the introduction of the death penalty for armed robbery in 1970 was followed by an increase rather than a decrease in armed robberies. The author, Professor A. A. Adeyemi, concluded therefore that there was no evidence to support the general deterrent efficacy of the death penalty in Nigeria.[32]

Such studies provide valuable indicators, but they cannot of course settle the question in a way that would convince a staunch retentionist because they provide no means of controlling for those variables (other than the rate of executions) which may cause fluctuations in the rate of crime. It is this problem that researchers, particularly in the United States, have attempted to tackle.

---

[29] For information on recorded homicides in the USA see the annual publication *Crime in the United States*, Washington DC: U.S. Department of Justice.   [30] Peterson and Bailey, n. 5 above, p. 160.

[31] See Raymond Bonner and Ford Fessenden, *States with no Death Penalty Share Lower Homicide Rates* (22 Sept. 2000), Moratorium Campaign at www.moratorium2000.org.

[32] A. A. Adeyemi, 'Death Penalty: Criminological Perspectives. The Nigerian Situation', *Revue Internationale de Droit Pénal* 58 (1987), pp. 485–502 at 490–494.

4. THE COMPARATIVE METHOD

The renowned early studies by Professor Thorsten Sellin attempted to control for such factors by comparing the rates of wilful homicides in five groups of three contiguous states: three groups in the Mid-West, and two in New England. The states were chosen so that the three in each group resembled each other as closely as possible in 'social organization, composition of population, economic and social conditions, etc.', but differed in that at least one of the three states had the death penalty. The results showed unambiguously that the average annual rate of homicide in these states for the years 1940 to 1955 bore no relationship to whether or not death was the maximum penalty for murder.[33] A later review of such comparisons carried out between 1919 and 1969 showed that, in the majority of cases, abolitionist states had lower rates of homicide than their retentionist neighbours and that states that abolished the death penalty generally tended to have a smaller increase in homicides than did retentionist neighbouring states.[34]

Sellin's conclusions were criticized on two grounds. First, that his method was far too crude to take into account, and attach the appropriate weight to, the wide range of social factors and law enforcement and penal practices that might influence the homicide rates of the neighbouring states. And of course in some parts of the United States, notably the south, West Virginia is the only abolitionist state to compare with retentionist states. Secondly, that comparing states in relation to whether or not death was the maximum penalty was too weak a test to ascertain whether the perceived risk of execution affected the conduct of those contemplating murder. This could only be done by taking into account the execution rates. Nevertheless, a well-conducted study by Richard Lempert of the same neighbouring states, which correlated differences in the number of executions with differences in the murder rate, also found 'no linear relationship between a state's willingness to execute and the number of lives that a state loses to homicides'.[35] The most recent analyses of the homicide rates in groups of contiguous states for the years 1980 to 1995 has confirmed that 'for most of the six groupings, the evidence is contrary to the deterrent hypothesis'.[36]

Attempts have also been made, using the comparative method, to test whether the availability of the death penalty better protects the police and leads to fewer instances where they have to resort to deadly force for self-protection. Thorsten Sellin claimed that this was not so, and indeed that the opposite was true: police, slayers, and suspects were all more likely to be killed in retentionist than in abolitionist states.[37] But this, again, provided no convincing proof that without the death penalty the

---

[33] Thorsten Sellin (ed), *The Death Penalty* (1959), pp. 22–8. See also his contribution to *The Death Penalty: Retribution or Deterrence?*, UNAFEI Resource Material Series no. 13 (1977), pp. 41–52.

[34] Bowers, with Pierce and McDevitt, n. 10 above, pp. 279–80 n. 11.

[35] Richard Lempert, 'The Effect of Executions on Homicides: A New Look in an Old Light', *Crime and Delinquency* 29 (1983), pp. 88–115 at 100–101.

[36] See Peterson and Bailey, n. 5 above, pp. 161–164.

[37] Sellin, n. 13 above, pp. 89–102.

rates would not have been higher in the retentionist states. In two more sophisticated analyses of 50 states, for the period 1961 to 1971, 1973 to 1984, William C. Bailey noted that there had been a decline in the number of policemen killed. He used regression analysis to partial out the effects of a wide range of social variables on the level of those serious crimes that might be associated with police deaths, and also to control for the time-lag between police killings and a possible death sentence. This revealed no evidence that police killings were lower in those jurisdictions that provided for capital punishment than in those that did not, or in those that had a relatively high level of executions as opposed to a low rate.[38]

Yet another study by Peterson and Bailey, which analysed police killings in the United States over the years 1976 to 1989, 'found no evidence that overall and specific types of police killings were responsive to the provision of capital punishment, execution rates or television news coverage devoted to executions'. They concluded: 'Capital punishment does not appear to provide police officers with an added measure of protection against being murdered.'[39]

Sellin's comparative analysis had also found that the rate of homicides of persons in custody, either inmates or officers, was no higher in abolitionist than retentionist states. Some more recent comparisons have confirmed this still to be the case. In 1980 there were no differences in prison homicides between the 16 abolitionist and 36 retentionist states once the size of their prison populations were taken into account.[40]

All of these studies have undoubted methodological shortcomings. They cannot provide 'proof' of the absence of a deterrent effect. Nevertheless, their strength lies 'not in individual studies but on the work taken as a whole'.[41] Several different methods and data sources have been employed, all of which have produced results that fail to support the hypothesis that the death penalty is a marginally more effective deterrent than lengthy imprisonment. This has been seen, by those who believe that this rather crude methodology need not be abandoned, as 'a recognition of the complexity of the problem lacking in some sophisticated later work'.[42]

[38] William C. Bailey and Ruth D. Peterson, 'Police Killings and Capital Punishment: The Post-*Furman* Period', *Criminology* 25 (1987), pp. 1–25. And W. C. Bailey, 'Capital Punishments and Lethal Assaults against Police', *Criminology* 19 (1982), pp. 608–625; W. C. Bailey and Ruth D. Peterson, 'Murder, Capital Punishment and Deterrence: A Review of the Evidence and an Examination of Police Killings', *Journal of Social Issues* 50(2) (Summer 1994), pp. 53–74.

[39] See Peterson and Bailey, n. 5 above, pp. 172–173.

[40] See James A. Acker, 'Mandatory Capital Punishment for the Life Term Inmate who Commits Murder: Judgments of Fact and Value in Law and Social Sciences', *Criminal and Civil Confinement* 11–12 (1985), pp. 267–327 at 295 n. 53.

[41] Richard Lempert, 'Desert and Deterrence: An Assessment of the Moral Bases of the Case for Capital Punishment', *Michigan Law Review* 79 (1981), pp. 1177–1231 at 1205.

[42] Franklin E. Zimring and Gordon Hawkins, *Capital Punishment and the American Agenda* (1986), pp. 172–174.

5. SHORT-TERM EFFECTS

Since the mid-1930s attempts have been made to see whether it could be shown that an execution, particularly in a well-publicized and notorious case, had an impact on the subsequent number of homicides. The usual method has been to compare the number of reported cases in the week(s) before and after the execution. The early studies showed no decline, but rather an increase in homicides. However, they had too many flaws for much confidence to be placed in them.[43] More recent attempts to improve the methodology have not been entirely successful, producing conflicting findings and stirring up considerable controversy. In a study published in 1980 David Phillips analysed the effects on the weekly murder rate in London of 22 notorious executions listed in *The Times* newspaper between 1858 and 1921. He compared the number of homicides in the week before the execution took place with those in the week of the execution and in the weeks afterwards, and came to the conclusion that the execution had a marked effect in reducing the number of homicides both in the week of the execution and in the two weeks following. After that, the decline in numbers was cancelled out by an equivalent increase in the following few weeks.[44]

The most that can be said for this finding is that publicized executions 'defer' homicides, but do not, over the longer term, reduce them. Phillips's study of executions in London was vigorously criticized on a number of grounds, particularly for not specifying precisely the period over which the execution was expected to have an impact as well as for failing to control for seasonal and other factors. William Bowers therefore extended the number of reported homicides to ten weeks either side of the week of execution and reanalysed the data. This produced a substantial increase in the number of post-execution over pre-execution homicides, suggesting that each execution was associated with an average increase of 2.4 homicides. The increase was at least twice as high after the most publicized cases (measured by news space) as after the less publicized cases. There was no evidence that this was due to an 'anticipatory deterrent effect' producing a lower than normal level of homicides prior to the execution. Bowers interpreted this data as clearly consistent with the 'brutalization' hypothesis, specifically over the shorter-term period.[45] These findings appear to confirm an earlier study of the monthly execution rates and monthly rates of homicides in New York State between 1906 and 1963 which came to the conclusion that each execution had the effect of increasing the number of homicides by two in the first month after the execution.[46]

[43] Bowers, 'The Effect of Executions is Brutalization, not Deterrence', n. 10 above, pp. 66–67.

[44] David P. Phillips, 'The Deterrent Effect of Capital Punishment: New Evidence on an Old Controversy', *American Journal of Sociology* 86 (1980), pp. 139–148; Hans Zeisel, Comment, *ibid.*, at 168–169. See also, David P. Phillips, 'Strong and Weak Research Designs for Detecting the Impact of Capital Punishment on Homicide', *Rutgers Law Review* 33 (1981), pp. 790–798 at 797.

[45] Bowers, 'The Effect of Executions is Brutalization, not Deterrence', n. 10 above. See also the criticisms in Larry Tifft, 'Capital Punishment Research, Policy and Ethics: Defining Murder and Placing Murderers', *Crime and Social Justice* 21 (Summer 1982), pp. 61–68 at 63–64.

[46] Bowers, with Pierce and McDevitt, n. 10 above, p. 299.

In a later study Phillips and Hensley showed that in the United States between 1973 and 1979 highly publicized news stories of death sentences passed on persons who had killed whites led to a decline in the number of white-victim murders in the four-day period after the story. But again the effect was very short-lived. More significantly, there was no evidence that life sentences had a weaker deterrent effect than either death sentences or executions.[47] Yet claims of substantial deterrent effects from highly publicized executions have been made. Steven Stack calculated that as many as 480 innocent lives had been saved due to the impact of 16 such executions between the years 1950 and 1980. However, a careful and sophisticated time-series analysis of his and other data 'provided no indication that national media attention to executions had the hypothesised deterrent effect on homicides during 1940–1986 . . . For periods ranging through one year after executions, the overall effect of executions on homicide rates was essentially zero'.[48]

It might be thought that there would be a strong impact when a jurisdiction returned to capital punishment after a long period of suspension. Thus, an assessment was made of the effects on the homicide rate of the first four executions to take place in the United States after the ten-year moratorium was ended in 1977. This showed that in only one instance, the notorious execution of Gary Gilmore, did the national homicide rate subsequently decline in the following two weeks. However, further analysis revealed that no effect could be found in Utah (where the execution took place) or in other western states. The decline appears to have been mostly in the north-eastern and south-eastern states, which were immobilized by one of the worst ever blizzards. This is an instructive reminder of how variables not normally taken into account in studies of this sort can bias the findings.[49] A more recent study of the impact of Oklahoma's first execution for twenty-five years in 1990 came to the conclusion that it had had no effect on felony-murders but had produced an abrupt increase in the number of homicides in which a stranger was killed. The authors interpreted this as support for the brutalizing effect of the death penalty, through lowering inhibitions against killing.[50] On the other hand, Godfrey and Shiraldi showed a mixed outcome relating to murder rates before and after the widely publicized executions of Robert Alton Harris and David Mason in California (the first such executions in California for eighteen years). The comparative murder rates per month in the four months prior to and following Harris's execution in 1992 were

[47] David P. Phillips and John E. Hensley, 'When Violence is Rewarded or Punished: The Impact of Mass Media Stories on Homicide', *Journal of Communications* (1984), pp. 101–116.

[48] William C. Bailey and Ruth D. Peterson, 'Murder and Capital Punishment: A Monthly Time-Series Analysis of Execution Publicity', *American Sociological Review* 54 (1989), pp. 722–743 at 739. This study was undertaken in response to Steven Stack's article 'Publicized Executions and Homicide', *American Sociological Review* 52 (1987), pp. 532–540.

[49] Sam G. McFarland, 'Is Capital Punishment a Short-Term Deterrent to Homicide? A Study of the Effects of Four Recent American Executions', *Journal of Criminal Law and Criminology* 74 (1983), pp. 1014–1032 at 1025 and 1032.

[50] John K. Cochran, Mitchell B. Chamlin, and Mark Seth, 'Deterrence or Brutalization? An Impact Assessment of Oklahoma's Return to Capital Punishment', *Criminology* 32 (1994), pp. 107–134.

306 and 333. This suggested a 'brutalization effect'. The comparative figures for Mason's execution a year later were 362 prior to and 348 following his death. This would suggest a deterrent effect if the same logic were followed, or alternatively that homicide rates are, in fact, unaffected one way or another by an execution.[51]

This review has demonstrated one thing at least. None of these researchers were able to overcome the formidable methodological problems of relating executions to homicides over such a short time-span within a longer time-series, so as to be able to prove the existence of a 'brutalization' or a deterrent effect. Certainly, evidence from such short-term studies should not be used to sustain the contention that executions either raise or depress the rate of homicide in the longer run. And, indeed, the findings have not impressed the leading American academic experts. A survey of all living former Presidents of the American Society of Criminology, the Academy of Criminal Justice Sciences, and the Law and Society Association, published in 1995, found that 88 per cent of the 67 respondents believed (on the basis of their knowledge of the literature and research) that the death penalty does not *lower* the murder rate and 80 per cent of them believed that a significant increase in the number or speed of executions would not deter more homicides. On the other hand, two-thirds of them disagreed or strongly disagreed with the statement that 'overall the presence of the death penalty tends to *increase* a state's murder rate rather than to *decrease* it'. It appears therefore that most of these experts believe that capital punishment has a neutral effect on such crime, and that politicians who argue that capital punishment is a unique deterrent are really 'support[ing] the death penalty as a symbolic way to show they are tough on crime'.[52]

6. ATTEMPTS TO UNRAVEL THE DETERRENT EFFECT

In recent years two methods have been employed in order to try to assess what effect executions have upon homicides. Both have the same goal, namely 'to use multiple regression analysis to isolate through a process of mathematical purification, the effect of one variable upon the other, under conditions that exclude the interference of all other variables'.[53] One method is to analyse the fluctuations over time in the rates of executions and homicides and various 'control' variables. Such *time-series* may cover one jurisdiction only, but more commonly have aggregated all jurisdictions in order to obtain sufficient data upon which a reliable analysis can be based. The other method is to analyse the variations between states in executions and homicides over various time periods. Such *cross-sectional* studies set out to test whether the variations in homicide rates are explained by the different patterns of executions or by other factors.

[51] See Michael J. Godfrey and Vincent Shiraldi, 'The Death Penalty may Increase Homicide Rates', repr. in David L. Bender *et al.* (eds), *Does Capital Punishment Deter Crime?* (1999), pp. 47–52.
[52] See Michael L. Radelet and Ronald L. Akers, 'Deterrence and the Death Penalty: The Views of Experts', *Journal of Criminal Law and Criminology* 87(1) (1996), pp. 1–11.
[53] Hans Zeisel, 'The Deterrent Effects of the Death Penalty: Facts v. Faith', *Supreme Court Review* (1976), pp. 317–43 at 332–332.

These studies have produced conflicting results with at least as many estimates of negative effects (consistent with deterrence) as positive effects (consistent with 'brutalization'). A fierce controversy continues. So I shall first summarize the major findings of this research and then attempt to reach a balanced judgement on the methodological strengths and weaknesses of this attempt to isolate the 'general deterrent effect'.

Isaac Ehrlich's well-known study of the relationship between the homicide rate and the rate of executions in the United States over the period 1935 to 1969 produced a large negative correlation: in other words, the higher the rate of executions the lower the homicide rate. It led him to estimate that 'an additional execution per year over the period in question may have resulted, on average, in seven or eight fewer murders'.[54] He also suggested that the decline in the risk of execution between 1960 and 1967 may have accounted for about 25 per cent of the increase in the murder rate during that period. In a later study Ehrlich employed a cross-sectional rather than a time-series method. Instead of aggregating the data from all states over a long period, he computed the homicide rates for each state separately for two different years 1940 and 1950, distinguishing those states that executed offenders from those that did not. In addition to the probability of conviction, and the probability of execution given conviction, Ehrlich included a number of control variables that might explain the 'supply' of murders: the percentage of families with incomes below half the medium income for the state; the percentage of non-whites in the population; the percentages of the population aged 15–24 and 25–34; and the percentage living in urban areas.

Ehrlich found that this cross-sectional analysis corroborated his earlier time-series study. There was 'a statistically significant difference between the mean rates of murder in executing and non-executing states after the effect of the other variables [entering] the equation had been accounted for'. But, he added, 'this does not mean, necessarily, that the mean rate of murder in non-executing states is lower than the rate in executing states where the level [of executions] (the proportion executed of the number convicted) is lowest'. He concluded therefore that executions per se did not necessarily produce the lower rates of murder; it depended on the size of the risk of being executed once convicted. More precisely, it probably depended on the *perceived* risk of execution, which of course a study of this kind was unable to measure.

This finding and interpretation is particularly relevant to the discussion (see page 212 above) of the low risk of execution under modern constitutionally acceptable statutes. Ehrlich also concluded, by analysing separately the data for executing states,

[54] Isaac Ehrlich, 'The Deterrent Effect of Capital Punishment: A Question of Life and Death', *American Economic Review* 65 (1975), pp. 397–417. Ehrlich found that the coefficients for the murder rate and two different measures of the execution risk were –0.06 and –0.065 respectively. This means that a 0.06% decrease in the homicide rate was associated with a 1% increase in execution risk. Thus over the 35-year period 1933–67, when there was a yearly average of 8.965 murders and 75 executions, the marginal trade-offs were approximately 8,965 divided by 75 × 0.06 = 7.17 or 8,965 divided by 75 × 0.065 = 7.77. In some years, for example 1959 and 1966, he found the coefficients produced a trade-off of one execution for 17 fewer murders. See Ehrlich, 'Deterrence: Evidence and Inference', *Yale Law Journal* 85 (1975), pp. 209–227.

that the death penalty had a restraining effect on the frequency not only of murder but 'possibly of robbery as well'. Furthermore, this cross-sectional analysis led him to the '*tentative estimates*' of a 'trade-off' in executing states of between 20 to 24 fewer murders for each execution.[55]

Some other studies using the same methodology have come to similar conclusions. An analysis of homicides in England and Wales over the period 1929 to 1968 by Kenneth Wolpin estimated that 'with no adaptations by the police, juries or potential offenders which alter other deterrent variables, executing an additional convicted murderer . . . would reduce the number of homicides by . . . 4.08 potential victims'. However, he noted that increasing the proportion of homicides cleared as murder, rather than manslaughter, reduced the number of homicides, and 'such a change far exceeds that of any other "deterrent" variable'.[56] This finding has an added significance in light of the fact that in England and Wales, since abolition of the death penalty in 1965, it appears to have been easier to convict persons charged with homicide or murder, which carries with it a mandatory sentence to life imprisonment, rather than manslaughter, which does not. In fact, the proportion convicted of murder among all those convicted of a homicide increased from 28 per cent in 1965 to 49 per cent in 1998–9.[57] The same has been true in Canada, where the conviction rate for first-degree murder, rather than second-degree murder or a lesser charge, has doubled from under 10 per cent, when execution would result, to about 20 per cent, 'now they [juries] are not compelled to make life-and-death decisions'.[58]

In 1986 Stephen Layson published his replication of Ehrlich's time-series analysis, using the homicide figures from both the US Vital Statistics and the FBI, first for the period 1936–77,[59] and later for 1934–84 (to include the period when executions had resumed after the moratorium of 1968–76).[60] Both studies found a negative and statistically significant relationship between the homicide rate and the probabilities of arrest, of conviction, and of execution given a conviction. In other words, increases in the probabilities of these punishment variables were associated with decreases in the homicide rate. Again, the effect was greatest for the probability of conviction, and least powerful for the probability of execution once convicted. Nevertheless, Layson estimated that the trade-off was larger than the seven or eight

---

[55] Isaac Ehrlich, 'Capital Punishment and Deterrence: Some Further Thoughts and Additional Evidence', *Journal of Political Economy* 85 (1977), pp. 741–788 at 757–758 and 778–779.

[56] Kenneth A. Wolpin, 'Capital Punishment and Homicide in England: A Summary of Results', *American Economic Review* 68 (1978), pp. 422–427 at 426. Wolpin controlled for the proportion of males aged 20–9; the UK unemployment rate net of temporary lay-offs; the proportion of the population in rural areas; the real gross domestic product per capita for the UK; and dummy variables to distinguish prior and post the Second World War, prior and post the Homicide Act 1957, and a continuous time trend corresponding to the years 1929–68, exclusive of the years of the Second World War. Because the author did not provide all the data it is impossible to gauge the validity of the findings.

[57] UK Home Office, *Criminal Statistics England and Wales 1999* (Cm 5001, 2000), table 4.7, p. 86.

[58] See Mark Warren, *The Death Penalty in Canada: Facts, Figures and Milestones* (2001).

[59] Stephen A. Layson, 'Homicide and Deterrence: A Re-examination of the United States Time-Series Evidence', *Southern Economic Journal* 52 (1985), pp. 68–69.

[60] Stephen A. Layson, 'United States Time-Series Homicide Regressions with Adaptive Expectations', *Bulletin of the New York Academy of Medicine* 62 (1986), pp. 589–600.

homicides found in Ehrlich's time-series—varying from 8.5 to as many as 28 fewer homicides for each execution. In addition, he claimed that his data indicated 'no evidence in favour of the hypothesis that the probability of execution has a negative effect on the probability of conviction'.[61] This, until recently, was undoubtedly the strongest and most uncompromisingly presented evidence of a possible deterrent effect of the death penalty. In early 2002 news of two other American studies, both claiming substantial deterrent effects, emerged in the press. As yet they have not been published in peer-reviewed journals and so no authoritative comments can be made upon them. But using techniques similar to those employed by Ehrlich and Layson, H. Naci Mocan and R. Kaj Gittings, two economists at the University of Colorado, claim to have found 'statistically significant relationships between executions, pardons and homicide. Specifically each execution reduces homicides by 5 to 6, and three additional pardons generate 1 to 1.5 additional murders.'[62] Another team of economists at Emory University in Georgia, led by Paul Rubin, have also carried out an analysis based on homicide and execution rates for over 3,000 counties in the United States for the period 1977 to 1996. Claiming to have used more sophisticated statistical controls than either Ehrlich or his critics, Rubin and his colleagues state that 'The most conservative estimate (that is the one with the smallest effect) was that each execution led to an average of eighteen fewer murders.'[63]

Other studies, however, have failed to find such an effect. William Bowers and Glenn Pierce repeated Ehrlich's time-series analysis and found that when the last five years of his series (from 1964 onwards) were excluded, during which there were very few executions and a sharply rising homicide rate, 'all empirical support for the deterrent effect of executions disappears'. Indeed, there were more positive than negative coefficients of the relationship between executions and homicide for the years 1935 to 1964 when executions were at their most frequent.[64] Both Passell,[65] and Black and Orsagh, using cross-sectional designs for the years 1950 and 1960 (the latter differentiating between southern and northern states), were unable to find a consistent relationship between sanctions and homicide. This was a period when very few executions were carried out—less than 2 per cent of those convicted of first-degree homicide in

[61] Layson, n. 59 above, p. 80. In his study covering the later years up to 1984 Layson estimated a trade-off of 15 murders for each execution. However, he does sound a note of caution because 'there is always the possibility that some important variable has been omitted from the analysis'. The relative trade-off of 15 should therefore be treated as 'a rough estimate'. Layson, n. 60 above, p. 599.

[62] H. Naci Mocan and R. Kaj Gittings, 'Pardons, Executions and Homicide', unpub. paper, University of Colorado at Denver, Oct. 2001. I am grateful to Professors Michael Radelet and Jeffrey Fagan for some helpful comments on this unpublished work, as far as it can yet be judged, as well as to Dr Andrew Roddam, statistical consultant to the University of Oxford Centre for Criminological Research.

[63] Paul H. Rubin, 'The Death Penalty and Deterrence', *Phi Kappa Phi Forum* 82(1) (2002), pp. 10–12.

[64] See W. L. Bowers and G. L. Pierce, 'The Illusion of Deterrence in Isaac Ehrlich's Research on Capital Punishment', *Yale Law Journal* 85 (1975), pp. 187–208; and Bowers, with Pierce and McDevitt, n. 10 above, pp. 320–322.

[65] P. Passell, 'The Deterrent Effect of the Death Penalty: A Statistical Test', *Stanford Law Review* 28 (1975), pp. 61–80 at 80.

1960. They concluded, therefore, 'that a similar policy of executing a very small percentage of persons convicted of first-degree homicide should again have no appreciable effect on the homicide rate'.[66] William Bailey also used the cross-sectional method to study homicide rates in 39 states over 28 selected years between 1910 and 1962 and found only small negative correlations between executions and homicide rates. He concluded that socio-demographic indicators and the length of imprisonment were both better determinants of the murder rates than were executions.[67]

Brian Forst used a different test. He employed a cross-sectional approach combined with a time-series analysis in 32 states, in order to see whether those states in which the execution rate declined the most between 1960 and 1970 also had the largest increases in the homicide rate. Forst included in his regression analysis social and demographic factors and also other punishment variables—the rate of conviction for murder and the average prison term served by convicted murderers. This produced no evidence that 'those states in which the actual use of capital punishment ceased during the 1960s experienced (any) greater increase in the murder rate than did those states that did not use capital punishment in the first place'. The inference drawn was that the upsurge in the rate of homicide of 53 per cent during this period was coincidental with the moratorium on capital punishment, not caused by it, the most significant factor being the rate of conviction and the rate of imprisonment for homicide. The data is thus consistent with the deterrent hypothesis, but really supports the view that certainty of punishment is the factor that has the greatest impact, not the severe sanction of execution.[68]

Although not employing econometric theory or the most advanced techniques, valuable studies have been carried out of the execution and homicide rates over long periods in individual states, thus avoiding the problems associated with aggregating data from different states. These time-series studies have been carried out by William Bailey in six states: California, New York, North Carolina, Ohio, Oregon, and Utah. Using regression analysis they have attempted to partial out the effects of various socio-demographic variables, such as: the proportion of the population that is male, the proportion 20–40 years of age, the proportion non-white, the proportion in urban areas, and the percentage unemployed.[69] In some instances, the execution rates were found to be negatively correlated with the homicide rates, but not significantly so. For example, the largest correlation found in a time-series analysis of Utah

[66] Theodore Black and Thomas Orsagh, 'New Evidence on the Efficacy of Sanctions as a Deterrent to Homicide', *Social Science Quarterly* 58 (1978), pp. 616–630 at 629.

[67] William Bailey, 'A Multivariate Cross-Sectional Analysis of the Deterrent Effect of the Death Penalty', *Sociology and Social Research* 64 (1980), pp. 183–207.

[68] Brian E. Forst, 'The Deterrent Effect of Capital Punishment: Cross-Sectional Analysis of the 1960s', *Minnesota Law Review* 61 (1977), pp. 743–767 at 754–764.

[69] W. C. Bailey, 'The Deterrent Effect of the Death Penalty for Murder in California', *Southern California Law Review* 52 (1979), pp. 743–764; 'Murder and Capital Punishment in the Nation's Capital', *Justice Quarterly* 1–2 (1984), pp. 211–223; 'An Analysis of the Deterrent Effect of the Death Penalty in North Carolina', *North Carolina Central Law Journal* 10 (1978), pp. 29–51; 'The Deterrent Effect of the Death Penalty for Murder in Ohio', *Cleveland State Law Review* 28 (1979), pp. 51–81; 'Deterrence and the Death Penalty for Murder in Oregon', *Williamette Law Review* 16 (1979), pp. 67–85; 'Deterrence and the Death Penalty for Murder in Utah', *Journal of Contemporary Law* 5 (1978), pp. 1–20.

covering the years 1910–62 suggested that 'a one percent increase in the certainty of the death penalty is associated with an approximate reduction in homicides of only eight hundredths of a person per 100,000 population'. In other words, a doubling of the execution rate would reduce the homicide rate by only eight-tenths of a person.[70] Such studies, however, have been inconclusive for three reasons. First, they have controlled for very few of the variables that might explain the 'supply' of murders: in particular they have generally included no other law enforcement variables than the execution rate. Secondly, their level of statistical sophistication cannot account for all the possible interrelationships between variables. Thirdly, the execution rate in most states has been very low for many years, and this has made statistical tests rather suspect.

7. Questions of Validity

It has been common for abolitionist writers to say that Ehrlich's work and studies using similar data and techniques have been discredited. It is nevertheless essential to assess the extent to which the findings provide a sound basis for any policy decisions. This is because their results have been frequently employed to support the arguments for the death penalty. For example, Ehrlich's first time-series study was cited by the Solicitor General of the United States in a pro-death penalty brief before the Supreme Court,[71] and his findings have been accepted uncritically by some scholars as 'proof' or 'vindication' of deterrence.[72] Layson's study was referred to by two senior members of the US Department of Justice as providing 'clear support for the proposition that the death penalty deters murder'.[73]

The best of these studies have used the most up-to-date 'state of the art' techniques.[74] While criticisms have not been directed at the technical skills of those who have used regression analysis and, more specifically, the models of econometric research, the appropriateness of applying such a methodology to the issue of capital punishment has generated great controversy.[75] The criticisms have been aimed at five broad issues, namely:

See also, Scott H. Decker and Carol W. Kohfeld, 'A Deterrence Study of the Death Penalty in Illinois, 1933–1980', *Journal of Criminal Justice* 12 (1984), pp. 367–377.

[70] Bailey, 'Deterrence and the Death Penalty for Murder in Utah', n. 69 above, p. 15.

[71] In the case of *Fowler* v. *North Carolina* (1975) and then *Gregg* v. *Georgia* (1977), see Lempert, n. 41 above, p. 1206.

[72] For example, by Ernest van den Haag, in E. van den Haag and John Conrad, *The Death Penalty: A Debate* (1983), p. 128, and E. J. Mishan, 'The Lingering Debate on Capital Punishment', *Encounter* (Feb. 1988), pp. 61–75 at 70–71.

[73] William F. Weld and Paul Cassell, *Report to the Deputy Attorney-General on Capital Punishments and the Sentencing Commission* (1987), mimeo.

[74] I am especially indebted to Timothy Besley, Professor of Economics at the London School of Economics, for a technical assessment of this area of research, conducted when I was preparing the first edition in 1989.

[75] See Professor James A. Fox's testimony to the Subcommittee on Criminal Justice, Committee on the Judiciary, US House of Representatives, on 7 May 1986, entitled 'Persistent Flaws in Econometric

First: Is the theory of rational choice upon which the econometric model is based an appropriate one for studying the relationships between the act of murder and the existence of a threat of execution?

Abolitionists have commonly rejected the deterrence argument on the grounds that most murders are not committed for large gains by professional or calculating criminals, but are the outcome of innumerable woes: the murderers are 'characteristically uneducated, impoverished social misfits whose crimes appear to be the stupid or senseless manifestations of anger or fear'.[76] The inference drawn is that the fear of capital punishment rather than long imprisonment will not restrain those who are apt to commit murder, because murder usually arises from an explosion of temper or loss of control, from mental illness or defective personality, or from panic when faced with imminent capture. The alternative interpretation of these undeniable facts has commonly been that the low number of well-adjusted persons among known murderers proves that such persons calculate the odds and draw back for fear of suffering death.

Ehrlich's theoretical model rests upon the premiss that human beings respond to incentives and disincentives. He has stated that he finds

no compelling reason to expect perpetrators of crimes of passion necessarily to be less responsive to incentives than perpetrators of crimes involving material gains only. Those with a great proclivity or 'taste' for violence are indeed more likely to commit assault or murder than others, given the same objective motives and equal prospects of punishment. However they need not be less responsive to changes in these factors . . . Being emotional does not preclude the ability to make self-serving choices . . . the prospect of punishment . . . still may prevail upon individuals to avoid situations in which 'loss of control' is likely to occur.[77]

Critics have denied that the theory of 'utility maximization' is the correct model for estimating perceived probabilities of execution in all the variety of situations in which homicides most commonly take place. They argue that, whatever the predictive power of the model may be, no *causal* inferences of deterrence can be drawn because the social and psychological mechanisms involved in murders of different types are far too complex to be explained by *correlations* obtained from aggregated data. The same criticisms apply to the, as yet, unpublished work of Mocan and Rubin, especially Mocan and Gillings' claim that a very small number of pardons (by which, as Michael Radelet has pointed out to me, he really means executive commutations of sentence) could 'cause' murders to be carried out. The issue is not likely to be resolved further until better specifications of the dynamics of capital murders are presented in ways that are empirically testable.

Studies of the Death Penalty: A Discussion of Layson's Findings', mimeo: 'None of my criticisms here should suggest any deficiency in Professor Layson's skill. Even the most expert econometrician could not derive reliable estimates of the deterrent effect of capital punishment with these data and with this approach', at p. 8. Fox's criticisms have since been published: James Alan Fox and Michael L. Radelet, 'Persistent Flaws in Econometric Studies of the Deterrent Effect of the Death Penalty', *Loyola of Los Angeles Law Review* 23 (1989), pp. 29–44.

[76] Bowers, with Pierce and McDevitt, n. 10 above, p. 273.

[77] Ehrlich, n. 55 above, pp. 742–743. See also, I. Ehrlich, 'On Positive Methodology, Ethics, and Polemics in Deterrence Research', *British Journal of Criminology* 22 (1982), pp. 124–139 at 124.

Second: Are the data upon which the estimates of both homicide and execution are based appropriate and reliable?

The data on homicides in the United States assembled by the FBI are notorious for not having been collected in a uniform series from across the country as a whole until recent years. Time-series which have included data going back as far as the early 1930s have therefore been criticized for providing a discontinuous data set. The proportion of jurisdictions reporting homicides has varied and there is no sure way of knowing what biases might have been introduced. It has been suggested, there-fore, that a different picture would emerge if the more reliable homicide data from the Vital Statistics were used.[78] This argument has been to some extent undermined by Layson, who employed the Vital Statistics and found that the negative coefficients were even larger than when using the FBI data: in other words they offered more, not less, support to the deterrent hypothesis.[79]

A more seriously damaging criticism is that all these studies have used as the dependent variable, the aggregate of all homicides and non-negligent manslaughters, whether they were subject to the death penalty or not. This appears also to be the case in Mocan and Gittings and Rubin's studies. If there is a different motivation for capital and non-capital murders and other types of homicide—or for the different types of capital murder—such an aggregation would bias the econometric analysis. Yet without any specific tests having been made it is not possible to say whether the aggregation bias would support or reject the deterrent hypothesis.

The execution rate is, of course, computed as a proportion of the homicide rate, or the arrest or conviction rate. And as executions are relatively rare even a small error in these rates may produce 'unusually strong spurious appearances of a deterrent effect'.[80] Furthermore, the inclusion of non-capital cases in the numerator of the homicide rate (i.e. number of homicides per 100,000 population) and in the denom-inator of the execution rate (i.e. number executed/number of homicides) will, as Professor Fox has pointed out, tend to push the deterrent effect towards the negative direction, unless the ratio of capital to non-capital crimes remains constant over time, which of course it has not.[81] Mocan and Gittings calculated the execution rate as the ratio of executions to the number of death row inmates, but given the length of time which inmates in the United States spend on death row and the number of cases which are successful on appeal (see pages 165–166 above) this appears to be a very suspect measure of the probability of being executed once convicted.

The aggregation of all data from different states in the time-series analyses makes

---

[78] See, for example, the criticisms of Fox and Radelet, n. 75 above; David Cantor and Lawrence E. Cohen, 'Comparing Measures of Homicide Trends: Methodological and Substantive Differences in the Vital Statistics and Uniform Crime Report Time-Series (1933–1975)', *Social Science Research* 9 (1980), pp. 121–145; Bowers and Pierce, n. 64 above, pp. 188–189. The FBI data used by Ehrlich and Layson was dropped by the FBI in 1978 because it was regarded as too unreliable for use in the national Uniform Crime Reports.

[79] Layson, n. 59 above, p. 73; and n. 60 above, pp. 591–593.

[80] See L. R. Klein, B. Forst, and V. Filatov, 'The Deterrent Effect of Capital Punishment: An Assessment of the Evidence', in A. Blumstein, J. Cohen, and D. Nagin (eds), *Deterrence and Incapacitation* (1978), pp. 336–360.   [81] Fox and Radelet, n. 75 above, pp. 38–39.

the assumption that an execution in an executing state is affecting homicides in the following year (the usual time-lag specified by these studies), whether they occur in the executing state or not. Clearly this is an unsatisfactory test of the deterrent hypothesis. Indeed the failure to pay sufficient attention to the dynamics of the period over which executions may be expected to have an effect on homicide rates, through changes in perceived risk over time, is also problematic. There is a large econometric literature which shows that if the assumption made about the temporal relationship between the dependent variable (here homicide) and the hypothesized causal variable (here executions) is wrong, spurious coefficients result. Although it would be possible, of course, to disaggregate the data and deal with separate time-series for each state, as Bailey has done (see page 225 above), the number of executions is generally so low that econometric tests would not be valid. It is therefore doubtful whether this technique when used over long time-series and aggregated over jurisdictions can overcome these problems.

Third: Is the observed relationship sufficiently stable between different samples and over different time periods for reliable conclusions to be drawn?

A major criticism directed at Ehrlich's time-series analysis was that it obscured different and contrary findings over shorter time-series. In particular it was found that if the period after 1964 was excluded, positive, *not* negative, correlations were found between murder and the execution rate for the years 1935 to 1964.[82] This is a matter of much dispute because Layson, using the homicide data from Vital Statistics, found 'reasonably stable' regressions over 21 different thirty-year periods beginning with 1934–63 and ending with 1955–84. Yet he concluded that 'the case for the effectiveness of capital punishment as a deterrent hinges in *including* the post-1963 data in the sample'.[83]

Fourth: Have the appropriate statistical methods and mathematical functional form been employed to estimate the deterrent effects?

There has been much controversy over which mathematical functional form should be used to estimate the relationship between executions and homicides. This is a highly technical issue, but different findings have sometimes, although not always, resulted from using the raw data rather than logarithmic values of the variables as Ehrlich and Layson have done. They have been particularly criticized because this necessitates giving a value to the number of executions in all years, even if there were none.[84]

[82] P. Passell and J. B. Taylor, 'The Deterrence Controversy: A Reconsideration of the Time-Series Evidence', in H. Bedau and C. M. Pierce (eds), *Capital Punishment in the United States* (1976), pp. 359–371; and Bowers and Pierce, n. 64 above; see also, Zeisel, n. 53 above, p. 330.

[83] Layson, n. 60 above, p. 596; and n. 59 above, pp. 82–83. Fox and Radelet, n. 75 above, quote Layson as having told a Congressional Committee that 'If I exclude all the data [after] 1960, I do find that evidence for the deterrent effect of capital punishment is very "weak" or even "nonexistent" ', p. 41. See also Brian Forst, 'Capital Punishment and Deterrence: Conflicting Evidence', *Journal of Criminal Law and Criminology* 74 (1983), pp. 927–942 at 930–931, and Justine A. Freeman, *Murder and Economics: A Literature Review* (1993).

[84] Layson gives the value of one execution for those years in which none occurred on the rather doubt-

Fifth: Are all the relevant variables taken into account when attempting to control for those other factors that might affect both the homicide rate and the execution rate?

The answer to this, of course, depends to a great extent on the theory which it is believed best explains homicide rates. However, even within the econometric framework it has been contended that the analyses so far conducted have been seriously biased because they have omitted important variables which might explain the homicide rate or execution rate or both. This is a particular problem with the cross-sectional analysis of states that are likely to differ in very many ways. An example is gun ownership, which one study found to have a statistically significant effect upon the homicide rate, although it found no effect was produced by executions.[85] Other factors that are extremely difficult to measure are facets of the more general social climate, such as migration, the effectiveness of informal social controls, the extent of alcohol abuse, the degree of communal integration, and the extent to which there is a 'sub-culture of violence' or alternative modes of relieving frustrations other than violence. Of course, it is not possible to state a priori what effect their inclusion would have on the relationship between homicide and execution rates, whether negative or positive.

8. Implications for Policy

However, the absence of sufficient controls, when taken in conjunction with the other problems mentioned above, should lead any dispassionate analyst to conclude from the findings of these studies that it is not prudent to accept the hypothesis that capital punishment deters murder to a marginally greater extent than does the threat and application of the supposedly lesser punishment of life imprisonment. Indeed, it is quite incorrect to conclude, when statistically significant negative coefficients have been found, that they constitute proof of *deterrence* as such. They may be *consistent* with a deterrent hypothesis, but there are often alternative explanations. The same applies to interpreting positive coefficients as proof of a brutalizing effect. Layson's original claim that his study provides 'solid support for the deterrent hypothesis' has to be contrasted with Ehrlich's far more cautious statement that 'the results obtained from my own studies do not constitute a proof of the theory as they are subject to all the limitations of positive analysis, statistical inference and design, and the data used'.[86] And indeed, when pressed during his testimony before a Congressional Committee, Layson also conceded that he did not 'regard [his] evidence . . . as conclusive'.[87]

---

ful assumption that people did not actually believe the probability was zero in the period when there was a moratorium on executions. Both Ehrlich and Layson have claimed that the logarithmic form best fits the data, having undertaken the standard test.

[85] Gary Kleck, 'Capital Punishment, Gun Ownership, and Homicide', *American Journal of Sociology* 84 (1979), pp. 882–908.

[86] Ehrlich, 'On Positive Methodology', n. 77 above, p. 125.

[87] Statement of Professor Layson, *Capital Punishment: Hearings on H.R. 2837 and H.R. 343 before the*

It still seems right to echo the conclusions of the Panel set up by the American National Academy of Sciences published twenty-three years ago: 'Any policy use of scientific evidence on capital punishment will require extremely severe standards of proof. The non-experimental research to which the study of the deterrent effects of capital punishment is necessarily limited will almost certainly be unable to meet those standards of proof.'[88] It has also been astutely pointed out that the data analysed so far 'are not sufficiently strong to lead researchers with different prior beliefs to reach a consensus regarding the deterrent effects of capital punishment'.[89] The implications of this conclusion for policy depend ultimately on moral and political views of what standards of proof are required. Most of those who favour abolition (assuming that they are not opposed to execution under any circumstances) would demand proof that executions have a substantial marginal deterrent effect. Thus, the leading American academic abolitionist Professor Hugo Adam Bedau has recently stated that, although it is hard to find a moral argument why the most atrocious of killers should not forfeit their lives, the evidence of research strongly supports the view that capital punishment 'exceed[s] what is necessary to achieve whatever legitimate goals a system of punishment has'—in other words, as much deterrence as can be achieved can be achieved without resorting to capital punishment. His argument is very persuasive:

Anyone who studies the century and more of experience without the death penalty in American abolitionist jurisdictions must conclude that these jurisdictions have controlled criminal homicide and managed their criminal justice system, including their maximum security prisons with life-term violent offenders, at least as effectively as have neighbouring death penalty jurisdictions. The public has not responded to abolition with riot and lynching; the police have not become habituated to excessive use of lethal force; prison guards, staff and visitors are not at greater risk; surviving victims of murdered friends and loved ones have not found it more difficult to adjust to their grievous loss.[90]

Those retentionist countries that rely on the deterrent justification should face the fact that if capital punishment were to be used to try to obtain its maximum possible deterrent effect, it would have to be enforced mandatorily, or at least with a high degree of probability, and therefore on a substantial scale across most categories of homicide. This is not an option for democratic states bound by the rule of law, concern for humanity, and respect for human rights. One wonders, therefore, whether those states that do retain the death penalty for some limited class of murders

---

Subcommittee on Criminal Justice of the House Committee on the Judiciary, 99th Congress (1987), pp. 311 and 316; quoted in Ronald J. Tabak, 'How Empirical Studies can Affect Positively the Politics of the Death Penalty', *Cornell Law Review* 83 (1998), pp. 1431–1447 at 1432.

[88] Blumstein *et al.*, n. 80 above, pp. 62–63.

[89] W. S. McManus, 'Estimates of the Deterrent Effect of Capital Punishment: The Importance of the Researcher's Prior Beliefs', *Journal of Political Economy* 93 (1985), pp. 417–425 at 425.

[90] Hugo Adam Bedau, 'Abolishing the Death Penalty even for the Worst Murderers', in Austin Sarat (ed), *The Killing State: Capital Punishment in Law, Politics, and Culture* (1999), pp. 40–59 at 47–49.

and murderers, imposed in a somewhat haphazard and arbitrary way on only some of them, can really claim that such a policy is justified by its general deterrent effects. As Chapter 8 shows, at least as far as the United States is concerned, fewer and fewer citizens support capital punishment on the grounds of its supposed general deterrent value. Looked at this way, the balance of evidence favours the abolitionist position.

8

A Question of Opinion or a Question of Principle?

1. THE ROLE OF PUBLIC OPINION

(a) Public Opinion and the Politics of Abolition

Public opinion is quite frequently cited as a major factor in the decision whether to abolish, retain, or reinstate the death penalty. For example, government officials in Japan,[1] several countries of the former USSR,[2] China,[3] Thailand,[4] and elsewhere have stated that the strength of public opinion in favour of capital punishment militates against its abolition. Sometimes the argument is that abolition without public support would undermine confidence in the law and perhaps lead to private vengeance.[5] Sometimes, more generally, that the state must express 'the will of the people',[6] or that it is anti-democratic for legislatures to ignore strong public sentiment.[7]

The extent to which governments base penal policy on the attitudes expressed by the general population depends, of course, upon their political ideology and the

---

[1] See Marc J. Bossuyt, *The Administration of Justice and the Human Rights of Detainees*, Report to the United Nations (1987), E/CN.4/Sub.2/1987/20, p. 25.

[2] See, for example, A. S. Mikhlin, *The Death Penalty in Russia* (1999), pp. 170–173, and Serhiy Holovatiy, 'Abolishing the Death Penalty in Ukraine: Difficulties Real or Imagined?', in Council of Europe, *The Death Penalty: Abolition in Europe* (1999), pp. 139–151 at 143–147.

[3] See Hu Yunteng, 'On the Death Penalty at the Turning of the Century', in M. Nowak and Xin Chunying (eds), *EU–China Human Rights Dialogue: Proceedings of the Second EU–China Legal Experts' Seminar Held in Beijing on 19 and 20 October 1998* (2000), pp. 88–94 at 93. It should be noted, however, that one Chinese contributor to the EU–China Human Rights Dialogue in Beijing in May 2001 stated that the death penalty had been abolished for ordinary theft in 1997, despite public opinion being strongly against this reform (personal knowledge).

[4] In a public opinion poll of 1,357 Bangkok residents interviewed in April 2001, 88.6% said that Thailand still needed to carry out executions, *The Nation*, 26 Apr. 2001.

[5] For example, in the debate leading up to abolition in France (see Ch. 2 p. 25), this argument was used by the then Minister of Justice, M. Peyrefitte; see G. Picca, 'La peine de mort: Un problème politique et social', *Revue Internationale de Droit Pénal* 68 (1987), pp. 435–450 at 448. It was also employed by the government of Tanzania in 1994 to head off a challenge to capital punishment; it was said that if 'progressive' criminal policy 'jumped too far ahead of the population', the people would resort to 'mob justice'. *Republic* v. *Mbushuu et al.* [1994] 2 LRC 335 (High Court of Tanzania), p. 349.

[6] A view expressed by Botswana, for example. See Bossuyt, n. 1 above, p. 24.

[7] The United States has, for example, declared in a report to the United Nations Human Rights Committee that 'the majority of citizens through their freely elected officials have chosen to retain the death penalty for the most serious crimes, a policy which appears to represent the majority sentiment of the country'. UN doc. CCPR/C/81/Add.4. (1994), para. 139.

sources from which they believe the authority of law should emanate. Nearly all the countries of the Middle East and North Africa, for example, are adamant that the retention of the death penalty is the clear commandment of Islam. On the other hand, in Western liberal parliamentary democracies where laws are based on the mandate given to elected representatives it is not incumbent on legislators to follow popular opinion. In France, Germany, the United Kingdom, and Canada abolition of the death penalty took place even though a majority of popular opinion was opposed to it.[8] These countries have since held steadfastly to the view—despite strong differences of opinion—that popular sentiment alone should not determine penal policy, that task being the responsibility of elected representatives exercising their own judgement. The Parliaments of Canada and the United Kingdom have both rejected several attempts to reinstate capital punishment, despite the fact that in both countries the polls showed substantial majorities in favour of a return to capital punishment, although the level of support has recently declined.[9] Similarly, in Austria all the political parties are united in opposition to the death penalty even though 'a considerable segment of the population somewhat favours' it.[10]

In several 'new' states, as mentioned in Chapter 2, it has been the President or the Minister of Justice who has, through an act of political leadership, promulgated the abolition of the death penalty on the grounds that it was a violation of human rights. It will be recalled that abolition has sometimes been linked specifically with the over-throw of totalitarian and repressive regimes, such as in Italy and Germany after the Second World War, in Romania after the fall of Ceauşescu, and in Cambodia after

[8] On the situation in France, see Picca, n. 5 above, p. 449, and Robert Badinter, *L'Abolition* (2000), who notes on p. 301 that on the morning of the debate on abolition *Le Figaro* (17 Sept. 1981) published an opinion poll which showed that 62% of respondents favoured the death penalty, with 33% against. When asked whether they were in favour of capital punishment for particularly atrocious crimes, 73% replied 'yes'. On Germany, see M. Mohrenschlager, 'The Abolition of Capital Punishment in the Federal Republic of Germany: The German Experience', *Revue Internationale de Droit Pénal* 58 (1987), pp. 509–519 at 513, and Richard J. Evans, *Rituals of Retribution: Capital Punishment in Germany 1600–1987* (1996), pp. 801–804, and Statistical Appendix at 935; on Canada, Ezzat A. Fattah, 'Canada's Successful Experience with the Abolition of the Death Penalty', *Canadian Journal of Criminology* 25 (1987), pp. 421–431.

[9] According to the British Social Attitudes Survey, the proportion of respondents in favour of the death penalty for murder in the course of a terrorist act was 77% in 1985 and 70% in 1994; for murder of a policeman, 71% in 1985 and 67% in 1994; and for other murders, 66% in 1985 and 59% in 1994. In the 1999 survey, 57% agreed (28% strongly) with the statement 'For some crimes, the death penalty is the most appropriate sentence' (*British Social Attitudes: Who Shares New Labour Values? The 16th Report* (1999)). This suggests that the conclusion reached in the mid-1990s that 'A solid three in five people remain in favour of reintroducing capital punishment for all murders' is showing some signs of change. See also Lindsay Brook and Ed Cape, 'Libertarianism in Retreat', in Roger Jowell *et al.* (eds), *British Social Attitudes: The 12th Report* (1995), p. 194. In the debates in the Canadian Parliament in June 1987 several speakers quoted figures from surveys, ranging from 60% to 83% in favour. *Report of Canadian Commons Debates*, 5 June, col. 6803, 18 June, col. 7309, 25 June, 1987, col. 7594. In 1995 a national opinion poll found 44% to be strongly in favour, and 25% moderately in favour of reinstating the death penalty: 18% were strongly opposed. See AI, *Death Penalty News*, Sept. 1995, AI Index: ACT 43/03/95. Yet by 2001 polls found that only about half (48–52%) of Canadians supported the death penalty and 46–7% were opposed. See Death Penalty Information Center, *Summaries of Public Opinion Poll Findings*, www.death-penaltyinfo.org/Polls.html.

[10] See Roland Miklau, 'The Death Penalty: A Decisive Question', *United Nations Crime Prevention and Criminal Justice Newsletter* 12 and 13 (Nov. 1986), pp. 39–42 at 39.

the demise of Pol Pot's infamous reign. Similarly, several of the countries with new constitutions which emphasize that all citizens have the right to life have declared capital punishment to be an unacceptable violation of that principle, whatever the majority of the public might claim to want. Hence, capital punishment has been abolished on these grounds by a number of supreme courts, such as in Hungary, Ukraine, Namibia, and South Africa. Thus, when the Constitutional Court of South Africa abolished capital punishment, on the grounds that it was incompatible with a human rights culture enshrined in that country's new constitution, it recognized that 'the majority of South Africans agree that the death penalty should be imposed in extreme cases of murder'.[11]

Quite a different view of representative government has been taken in the United States. In some states the question of capital punishment has been put to the popular vote in referendums. For example, the electorate of Oregon abolished the death penalty in 1964 but voted to reinstate it in 1978 and (after that law had been found unconstitutional) again in 1984. Similarly, California reinstated capital punishment after a plebiscite.[12] In approving the legislation of states under the revised capital statutes in *Gregg* v. *Georgia* and other cases in 1976, the majority of the United States Supreme Court clearly held the view that the fact that state legislators had revised their laws in order to ensure that capital punishment could be enforced against the most egregious type of murderer was an expression of public sentiment that could not be overridden by an abstract judgement that capital punishment was 'cruel and unusual punishment' per se. This is because the Court considers public opinion as one of the barometers for deciding whether the death penalty violates 'evolving standards of decency'—a criterion used to determine whether punishments should be regarded as 'cruel and unusual'.[13] Furthermore, as was noted in Chapter 2 (page 68), leading politicians in the United States in recent years, from candidates for the Presidency and state governorships downwards, have felt inhibited from taking a stand against capital punishment for fear of its impact on their chances of election. In addition, the fact that candidates for the posts of public prosecutor as well as judge in many states must stand for election favours those who respond positively to public sentiments on the death penalty. There is no doubt, therefore, that in the United States the status of capital punishment is very dependent on the state of public opinion. To what extent may it be liable to change?

(b) The Nature of Public Opinion

The concept of public opinion is undoubtedly open to a number of interpretations. It is commonly used to denote opinions gathered through polls or other surveys. These record immediate opinions and responses, which are, of course, affected by the nature and specificity of the questions posed, their order in the sequence of questioning, the

[11] *State* v. *Makwanyane* [1995] (3) S.A. 391, quoted in William A. Schabas, 'Public Opinion and the Death Penalty', Paper presented to the EU–China Seminar on Human Rights, Beijing, 10–12 May 2001.
[12] See Hugo Adam Bedau, *Death is Different* (1987), pp. 153–163.
[13] See Sarah T. Dike, *Capital Punishment in the United States* (1982), p. 60.

socio-political context within which the survey takes place, and the socio-economic, race, and gender composition of the sample. There is, for example, evidence from Germany and Spain that the proportion of people favouring the death penalty has fluctuated considerably when questions have been asked in the aftermath of outbreaks of terrorist violence.[14] Strength of feelings or commitment may also vary. In Great Britain, for example, in 1992, 74 per cent of all respondents to a survey agreed with the statement that death was 'the most appropriate penalty for some crimes', but only 43 per cent 'agreed strongly'.[15] Seven years later support had dropped to 57 per cent, with 28 per cent agreeing 'strongly'.[16] It is also the case that support for the death penalty in abstract gives no indication of what level of executions is expected or will be tolerated. Over a quarter of a century ago Marc Ancel called for a 'more complete sociological study' of the reactions of the public to executions, but it has yet to be carried out.[17]

It has, however, been noted that while opinion in the United States suggests that there is strong support for the death penalty, there is no clamour for executions as such. Indeed, very often some of those awaiting death may evoke a good deal of sympathy.[18] Research also shows that very few persons would support the death penalty as a mandatory punishment to be applied to every case of murder and that questions therefore need to be carefully targeted towards specific categories.[19] Indeed, according to some leading researchers:

Increased support for the death penalty may be more of a reflection of the desire for the execution of a Ted Bundy [a notorious serial killer] and other celebrity criminals than for the execution of more typical and more obscure condemned inmates . . . We suspect, therefore, that recent trends in survey data on death penalty opinions are largely a function of changes in the way respondents conceptualise a particular crime.[20]

---

[14] Mohrenschlager, n. 8 above, p. 513; Evans, n. 8 above, p. 802; and A. Beristain, 'La sanction capitale en Espagne: Referénce spéciale à la dimension religieuse Chrétienne', *Revue Internationale de Droit Pénal* 58 (1987), pp. 613–636, at 620–622.

[15] *British Social Attitudes Cumulative Sourcebook* (1992), table B-2.

[16] *British Social Attitudes: Who Shares New Labour Values? The 16th Report* (1999).

[17] United Nations, *Capital Punishment* (1962).

[18] Bedau, n. 12 above, p. 146.

[19] For example, in the United States a telephone poll carried out by Media General/Associated Press in 1986 showed that, of 1,251 adults, 29% of respondents endorsed the statement 'In general, do you feel the death penalty should be allowed for all murder cases?' This is of course not the same as 'Do you think that all murderers, whatever the circumstances, should be sentenced to death?' See US Department of Justice, *Report to the Deputy Attorney General on Capital Punishment and the Sentencing Commission* (13 Feb. 1987), Appendix B, 'Public Opinion and the Death Penalty'. See also Frances Cullen, Bonnie S. Fisher, and Brandon Applegate, 'Public Opinion about Punishment and Corrections', in M. Tonry (ed), *Crime and Justice: A Review of Research*, vol. 27 (2000), Chicago: University of Chicago Press, pp. 1–79 at 17–18, quoting a study in Florida which showed that, depending on the facts (in a vignette) given to respondents, support for the offender's execution 'ranged from a low of 29.4% for one vignette to a high of 93.2% for another . . . only 13.1% of the [366] respondents favored capital punishment in all cases'. For further details, see Alexis M. Durham, H. Preston Elrod, and Patrick T. Kinkade, 'Public Support for the Death Penalty: Beyond Gallup', *Justice Quarterly* 13 (1996), pp. 705–736.

[20] James Alan Fox, Michael J. Radelet, and Julie L. Bonsteel, 'Death Penalty Opinion in the Post-*Furman* Years', *New York University Review of Law and Social Change* 18 (1990–1), pp. 499–528 at 510–511.

This was certainly the case in relation to the 'Oklahoma bomber', Timothy McVeigh (see page 243 below). Researchers have insisted, therefore, that 'pollsters should clearly delineate the elements of the crime when soliciting a respondent's attitude to the death penalty, rather than leaving it to the respondent to "fill in" the gory details'.[21] And even though polls may give the impression that a large majority of persons support capital punishment under aggravated circumstances of the kind which are to be found in the statutes of most American states, the behaviour of prosecutors and jurors suggests that it is only in the most egregious cases that there is any high degree of consensus about who should be sentenced to death.[22] Similarly, polls in Russia have shown that only a very small proportion of those questioned (6.6 per cent) favoured the complete abolition of capital punishment. Yet, of all those who replied, most (69.1 per cent) 'believed that the death penalty should be applied only in the most extreme instances and as infrequently as possible'.[23]

Lastly, it is evident that support for the death penalty is much higher among the more powerful in society than the less powerful. In the United States, for example, capital punishment is favoured more often by whites, the more wealthy, and by males, Republicans, and conservatives than by blacks, poorer people, women, Democrats, and liberals. It has been suggested that the degree of support will depend, at least in part, on the relative confidence of citizens from different social strata or ethnic groups that they will be treated fairly by the criminal justice system.[24]

It has also been shown that when respondents are presented with an alternative to the death penalty (admittedly a severe one) their support for capital punishment declines. A series of studies in the United States, begun by Professor Bowers, has asked members of the public whether they would support the death penalty if the alternative were life imprisonment without possibility of parole and with restitution to the relatives of the victim. These surveys have shown, in seven states, that no more

[21] *Ibid.*, p. 515.

[22] In one study people were given descriptions of three cases in which the defendants had been sentenced to death. Despite the fact that the majority stated that they were in favour of capital punishment in general, no more than 15% recommended that any one of the defendants in these cases should be sentenced to death. This study by Phoebe Ellsworth is quoted in Phoebe C. Ellsworth and Lee Ross, 'Public Opinion and Capital Punishment: A Close Examination of the Views of Abolitionists and Retentionists', *Crime and Delinquency* 29 (1983), pp. 116–169 at 139.

[23] See Mikhlin, n. 2 above, pp. 170–173.

[24] See Robert M. Bohm, 'American Death Penalty Opinion, 1936–1986: A Critical Examination of the Gallup Polls', in R. M. Bohm (ed), *The Death Penalty in America: Current Research* (1991), pp. 113–143 at 135; Steven E. Barkan and Steven F. Cohn, 'Racial Prejudice and Support for the Death Penalty by Whites', *Journal of Research in Crime and Delinquency* 31 (1994), pp. 202–209; Robert L. Young, 'Race, Conceptions of Crime and Justice, and Support for the Death Penalty', *Social Psychology Quarterly* 54 (1991), pp. 67–75; and Fox, Radelet, and Bonsteel, n. 20 above, pp. 506–508. According to the Gallup Organization Poll Analysis of 2 Mar. 2001, 'Two-Thirds of Americans Support the Death Penalty': 'Roughly 70% of whites support the death penalty in recent polls, while less than a majority of non-whites do . . . Men more than women tend to support the death penalty, typically by about 10 percentage points . . . The latest polls shows support among older Americans around 70%, while support among those under 30 is in the low 60s . . . 79% of Republicans say they favor the death penalty compared with 52% of democrats'. See www.gallup.com/poll/releases/pr010302.asp. See also Samuel R. Gross, 'Update: American Public Opinion on the Death Penalty—It's Getting Personal', *Cornell Law Review* 83 (1998), pp. 1448–1475 at 1451.

than 43 per cent, and often no more than a quarter of respondents, would favour the death penalty if this alternative were available.[25] When asked specifically whether the penalty for murder should be death or life imprisonment without the possibility of parole, a poll taken in February 2001 showed that only 52 per cent were in favour of capital punishment (a proportion which has been quite consistent since as long ago as 1985).[26]

Professor Bowers has concluded from the fact that support for the death penalty declined, when 'life-means-life' was given as the alternative, that many members of the public did not support the death penalty per se, but rather were concerned that they should be sufficiently protected. In other words, their opinion was based more on utilitarian than on retributive considerations. This view was supported by evidence from the Capital Jury Project, that when given the choice between death and life without parole plus restitution, jurors preferred the latter by a majority of 59 per cent to 29 per cent, with 12 per cent undecided.[27] And Austin Sarat's discussion of his interviews with jurors in a case where the defendant was sentenced to death revealed that 'None of them believed that executions served as a deterrent to others and none embraced a purely retributivist rationale for capital punishment . . . they were overwhelmingly concerned with incapacitation as a goal of punishment.' Indeed, they did not expect the person concerned to be executed. As one of the jurors aptly and tellingly put it: 'We all pretty well knew when you vote for death you don't necessarily or usually get death. Ninety-nine per cent of the time, they don't put you to death. You sit on death row and get old.'[28]

The same may be true of many legislators. According to a study in Tennessee, 95 per cent of a sample of 40 state legislators had said that they favoured the death penalty, but only 53 per cent said that they would not prefer the alternative of life without parole plus work and payments of restitution.[29]

---

[25] William Bowers, 'Capital Punishment and Contemporary Values: People's Misgivings and the Court's Misperceptions', *Law and Society Review* 27 (1993), pp. 157–175. Also, Richard C. Dieter, *Sentencing for Life: Americans Embrace Alternatives to the Death Penalty*, A Report of the Death Penalty Information Center (1993), www.deathpenaltyifo.org.dpic.r07.html. Also R. M. Bohm, 'American Death Penalty Opinion: Past, Present, and Future', in J. A. Acker, R. M. Bohm, and C. S. Lanier (eds), *America's Experiment with Capital Punishment* (1998), pp. 25–46 at 42. However, it has been suggested that, because of the way the question was posed, these findings may have exaggerated the falling off of support for the death penalty. Thus, a survey which asked the 79% who had said they favoured capital punishment whether they would continue to do so if they knew that murderers would be given 'a true life sentence without the possibility of parole' found that 66% of them continued to say 'yes' and 20% said 'no'. This reduced the support for capital punishment among the whole sample from 79% to 60%. Reported in Gross, n. 24 above, at 1456–1457

[26] See www.gallup.com/poll/indicators/inddeath_pen.asp. Also, Death Penalty Information Center, *Summaries of Recent Poll Findings*, www.deathpenaltyinfo.org/Polls.html.

[27] William J. Bowers and Benjamin D. Steiner, 'Death by Default: An Empirical Demonstration of False and Forced Choices in Capital Sentencing', *Texas Law Review* 77 (1999), pp. 605–717 at 706.

[28] Austin Sarat, *When the State Kills: Capital Punishment and the American Condition* (2001), pp. 147 and 149. See also, Benjamin D. Steiner, William Bowers, and Austin Sarat, 'Folk Knowledge and Legal Action: Death Penalty Judgements and the Tenet of Early Release in a Culture of Mistrust and Punitiveness', *Law and Society Review* 33 (1999), pp. 461–503.

[29] See John T. Whitehead, ' "Good Ol' Boys" and the Chair: Death Penalty Attitudes of Policy Makers in Tennessee', *Crime and Delinquency* 44 (1998), pp. 245–256. It should be noted that 33% defi-

As the Death Penalty Information Center pointed out, many Americans who support the death penalty appear to be unaware that most states do have life sentences with no possibility of parole for twenty-five years.[30] The optimistic view, therefore, is that more information on this issue could have the effect of changing attitudes towards a pro-abolitionist position.[31] But, of course, such an alternative would make the price of abolition very high. It is one thing to favour the *availability* of life imprisonment without the possibility of parole in any sentencing system that would replace capital punishment. It is quite another to make the alternative to a death sentence a *mandatory* sentence of such severity. If the latter were to be the policy, it is likely that far more persons would be convicted of capital murder and thus a much greater number of persons would be incarcerated for a lifetime than ever would be executed.

(c) Changing Public Opinion

As all other research on people's attitudes shows, there is a large gap between the sort of 'off the top of the head opinion' which is tapped by opinion polls conducted on the telephone or in the street, and the complex weighing up of considerations of the kind that juries have to undertake. Most members of the public have been found to possess very limited knowledge about the circumstances in which murder takes place, the characteristics of murderers, and all aspects of capital punishment.[32] Without such knowledge their immediate opinions are a dubious basis upon which to form policy, as they are in other areas of criminal justice. Empirical investigations to assess the so-called 'Marshall hypothesis' have arisen from Justice Marshall's opinion in *Furman* v. *Georgia* that 'it is imperative for constitutional purposes to attempt to discern the probable opinion of an informed electorate', for, as Robert Bohm has pointed out, 'Marshall believed that, given information about the death penalty, "the great mass of citizens would conclude . . . that the death penalty is immoral and therefore unconstitutional".'[33] Thus, if they were made more aware of the true facts, public opinion would shift towards the abolitionist position.

The major issue which has therefore emerged in studies of public opinion is whether the provision of knowledge about the death penalty would be an effective means of changing popular views. The object has been to get behind the raw data of the polls in order to try to tap the socio-psychological determinants of attitudes.[34] A series of studies of students in a mid-western university by Robert Bohm and his

nitely preferred the alternative and 16% said they didn't know. Also that support for the death penalty fell far less among a sample of prosecutors, 67% of whom did not prefer the alternative sentence; p. 251.

[30] Dieter, n. 25 above.

[31] See Kenneth C. Haas and J. A. Inciardi, 'Lingering Doubts about Capital Punishment', in K. C. Haas and J. A. Inciardi (eds), *Challenging Capital Punishment* (1988), pp. 11–28.

[32] Ellsworth and Ross, n. 22 above, pp. 139–145.

[33] Bohm, n. 25 above, p. 31.

[34] See U. Zvekic and T. Kubo, 'Main Trends in Research on Capital Punishment (1979–1986)', in *The Death Penalty: A Bibliographical Research* (1988), pp. 533–554 at 542; also in *Revue Internationale de Droit Pénal* 58 (1987).

colleagues revealed that, despite taking a special class on the death penalty, increased knowledge had little effect on the opinions of students who supported capital punishment on the grounds of retribution, because the knowledge was often assimilated in a biased way 'in support of previously held emotionally based opinions'. While not being entirely pessimistic, the researchers concluded that opinions on the death penalty are far more difficult to change through instruction than is often assumed.[35] Students questioned some two to three years later about whether they were in favour of or against the death penalty had 'rebounded to near their initial pre-test opinion'. Bohm hypothesized that 'perhaps it was because death penalty opinions are based primarily on emotion rather than on cognition and that, in the long run, cognitive influences on death penalty opinions give way to emotional factors'.[36] Other studies, however, have pointed to the fact that, if supporters of the death penalty were provided with information about the lack of proof of its unique deterrent effect, a relatively small, but a still significant, proportion have said that they would change their opinion. The Gallup Poll data in the United States suggest that if supporters were convinced that abolition of the death penalty would not increase the homicide rate, the proportion in favour would drop from 70 to 55 per cent.[37]

The suggestion that attitudes to the death penalty are so deeply embedded that they are impervious to the impact of information about its administration and effects has to be placed alongside the fact that, in many countries, opinions have changed, and quite markedly, over relatively short periods of time. A prime example is the United States. The polls differ by several percentage points here and there, but the trends are clear, whichever poll one considers. In 1953 opinion polls showed 66 per cent in favour of the death penalty. By 1965 this had fallen to around only 40 per cent. Yet, according to the National Opinion Research Center, by 1977 it had risen to 67 per cent and by 1994 to 74 per cent.[38] Then came a downturn in support. According to the Gallup Poll, it fell from a high of 80 per cent in 1994 back to 71 per cent in 1999 and dropped further to 65 per cent in mid-2001.

Opinion polls have differed, according to the questions asked, as to whether deterrence really is the primary reason why people favour capital punishment or only one among a number of other reasons, most notably retribution.[39] Several studies in the 1980s suggested that deterrence was given as the justification because it appeared

[35] R. M. Bohm, L. J. Clark, and A. F. Aveni, 'Knowledge and Death Penalty Opinions: A Test of the Marshall Hypotheses', *Journal of Research in Crime and Delinquency* 28 (1991), pp. 360–387; R. M. Bohm, R. E. Vogel, and A. A. Maisto, 'Knowledge and Death Penalty Opinion: A Panel Study', *Journal of Criminal Justice* 21 (1993), pp. 29–45; R. M. Bohm and R. E. Vogel, 'A Comparison of Factors Associated with Uninformed and Informed Death Penalty Opinions', *ibid.* 22 (1994), pp. 125–143.

[36] Bohm, n. 25 above, pp. 40–41.

[37] See H. Zeisel and A. M. Gallup, 'Death Penalty Sentiment in the United States', *Journal of Quantitative Criminology* 5 (1989), pp. 285–296.

[38] Support for the death penalty had increased for all social groups, although black people, the poor, and women continued to be considerably less in favour of the death penalty than white people, the wealthy, and males. See Anne L. Pastore and Kathleen Maguire (eds), *Sourcebook of Criminal Justice Statistics—1999* (2000), table 2.61.

[39] The Gallup Poll found that among those in favour of capital punishment only 22% gave deterrence as their reason. See Zeisel and Gallup, n. 37 above. The survey results were reproduced in US Department

to provide a 'scientific and socially acceptable reason for supporting the death penalty', when what really underlay support for capital punishment was 'strongly held moral and political ideals', value and belief systems 'deeply anchored in a person's personality'. These have an 'emotional, symbolic function' rather than stemming from 'a set of reasoned beliefs',[40] and during the early 1990s researchers noted that 'as support for the death penalty has increased so has willingness to endorse retribution as a motive'.[41]

Polls taken by the Gallup organization in February 2001 found that 48 per cent of those who supported the death penalty for murder did so because it was 'an eye for an eye/They took a life/Fits the crime', a further 6 per cent because 'they deserve it', and another 3 per cent for other 'justice' reasons. Thus, well over half the respondents chose retributive reasons. Another 20 per cent said they supported it because it 'saves taxpayers money/cost associated with prison', which may also indicate retributive sentiments (they are not worth paying for), while only 10 per cent endorsed it as a 'deterrent for potential crimes/sets an example'.

Similarly, a telephone survey of 386 police chiefs and county sheriffs, randomly chosen, from across the United States in 1995 found that two-thirds of them did not believe that capital punishment significantly reduces the number of homicides, largely it seems because 82 per cent of them did not think that murderers thought about possible punishments. Thus only one-third of these police chiefs supported it because they thought it was effective, while 58 per cent supported it 'in principle' even though they did not believe it was effective in practice. A mere 4 per cent were not in favour of capital punishment.[42]

This might help to explain the great swings in public opinion on capital punishment that have occurred over the past forty years in the United States. The high level of support for capital punishment, which peaked in the early to mid-1990s, was not fuelled by a larger proportion of population coming to believe that the death penalty had a general deterrent effect.[43] It was the result of a 'backlash' against a surge in the homicide rate—a 'retributive surge'.[44]

---

of Justice, *Sourcebook of Criminal Justice Statistics—1986* (1987), pp. 99–105. The Media General/Associated Press Poll, however, reported that 33% endorsed 'deter others' and a further 43% 'protect society'.

[40] For example, T. R. Tyler and R. Weber, 'Support for the Death Penalty: Instrumental Response to Crime, or Symbolic Attitude?', *Law and Society Review* 17 (1982), pp. 21–46; E. A. Fattah, 'Perceptions of Violence, Concern about Crime, Fear of Victimization and Attitudes to the Death Penalty', *Canadian Journal of Criminology* 21 (1979), pp. 22–38; Ellsworth and Ross, n. 22 above, pp. 145–157.

[41] Phoebe C. Ellsworth and Samuel R. Gross, 'Hardening of the Attitudes: Americans' Views on the Death Penalty', *Journal of Social Issues* 50(2) (Summer 1994), pp. 19–25.

[42] See Richard C. Dieter, 'The Death Penalty is not an Effective Law Enforcement Tool', repr. in David L. Bender *et al.* (eds), *Does Capital Punishment Deter Crime?* (1998), pp. 22–38 at 28–34.

[43] A point noted by Ellsworth and Gross in 1994. See n. 41 above, p. 27.

[44] Robert Bohm declared that 'a detailed analysis of the 90 per cent increase in death penalty support since 1966 has yet to be written'. But he notes that between four months prior to the *Furman* decision and four months afterwards, support for the death penalty increased by 7 percentage points and opposition to it dropped by 10 percentage points. He concluded: 'Although other factors have had an effect, it appears that significant public discontent with the *Furman* decision was decisive. With few exceptions, death penalty support has been increasing steadily ever since'. See Bohm, n. 25 above, pp. 25–46 at 29.

Now that the homicide rate has fallen dramatically, it may be that public opinion will be affected by other issues, most importantly by the question of fairness and justice in the administration of capital punishment. Professors Ellsworth and Gross noted in 1994 that although 'a large proportion of the American public . . . believe the death penalty is unfair, [they] support it nonetheless'.[45] This may be changing. The 2001 Gallup Poll revealed that only about half of those surveyed believed that the death penalty is 'applied fairly in this country today' and at least 80 per cent believed that at least one innocent person has been executed in the last five years, and only 6 per cent said that a person 'who was, in fact, innocent of the crime he or she was charged with' had never been executed within the last twenty years.[46] There is evidence to suggest that even supporters of the death penalty believe that the execution of innocent people is unacceptable, whatever other benefits they think capital punishment provides.[47] Furthermore, regardless of views for or against the death penalty, Americans, according to the polls, believe that the best argument against the death penalty (73 per cent in a 1997 survey) is that innocent people may be wrongly convicted and executed. A Gallup survey in 1995 found that the proportion of respondents in favour of capital punishment fell from 77 to 57 per cent when told that 'some experts estimate that one out of a hundred people who have been sentenced to death were actually innocent'.[48] It may be that increased knowledge that wrongful convictions have occurred on a substantial scale (as demonstrated conclusively by the Columbia University study, see pages 135–136 above); the acceptance by political leaders such as Governor Ryan of Illinois that innocent persons have come close to death but for fortuitous discovery of the truth; and proof through scientific methods such as DNA that some innocent persons have indeed been executed, will have a powerful effect on American public opinion.

Indeed, there would appear to be a substantial body of non-ideologically committed opinion in the United States that can be affected in one direction or another by information about crime and the impact of punishment. Attitudes towards the death penalty are more complex than has been often supposed: 'opinion can best be viewed as a set of ordered priorities, the order of which changes with time and circumstances'.[49] Certainly, both Professor Hans Zeisel and the Gallup organization expressed the view that such changes are more emotional than rational, linked to 'the widely observed increase in personal fears, dissatisfaction with society in general, and feelings of helplessness'.[50] For example, people may generally oppose the death penalty yet be in favour of it when shocked by a particularly horrifying crime. So, when the Gallup organization asked a national sample of United States citizens

---

[45] See n. 41 above.

[46] See Gallup Organization, *Poll Topics: Death Penalty*, at www.gallup.com/poll/indicators/inddeath_pen.asp.

[47] See David Weinstock and Gary E. Schwartz, 'Executing the Innocent: Preventing the Ultimate Injustice', *Criminal Law Bulletin* 34 (1998), pp. 328–347 at 335–341.

[48] Reported in Gross, n. 24 above, p. 1464.

[49] See M. Warr and M. Stafford, 'Public Goals of Punishment and Support for the Death Penalty', *Journal of Research in Crime and Delinquency* 21 (1984), pp. 95–111 at 106.

[50] See n. 37 above, pp. 294–295.

whether they believed that Timothy McVeigh should be executed for the murders he committed in the Oklahoma bombing, 79 per cent said 'yes' including 22 per cent who, although generally opposed to capital punishment, thought that McVeigh nevertheless should be executed.[51]

Despite what appears to be a relatively high level of 'abstract' support for the death penalty in America, this does not so readily translate into practice when citizens find themselves confronted with having to make the awful decision as a member of a jury. In other words, as Samuel Gross has put it, 'views may be less predictable in concrete cases than they seem in the abstract'.[52] Hugo Adam Bedau has poignantly pointed out that although jurors are screened to make sure that they do not oppose capital punishment in principle, they still only hand down death sentences in about one in 10 capital cases. He concluded with the telling remark: 'There is no clearer evidence than this of the essentially *symbolic* role of the death penalty at present.'[53]

(d) Abolition and its Effect on Public Opinion

There appears to be no necessary connection between the degree of public support for the death penalty and the incidence of homicide. The majority of the public in favour of capital punishment is much higher in the United Kingdom and Japan, which both have comparatively low homicide rates, than it is in the Scandinavian countries, where the homicide rate is about 3.5 times higher. Yet among those countries with relatively low homicide rates, some are abolitionist, like Spain, Austria, and the United Kingdom, while others retain the death penalty, such as Japan and the People's Republic of China. Yet even in Japan, where a high proportion favour the death penalty on retributive and deterrent grounds, as many as 40 per cent of those who favoured retention said that the death penalty could be abolished in future if the situation were to change.[54]

The evidence from north European countries suggested that once the abolitionist policy becomes embedded in the national consciousness, sentiments in favour of the death penalty gradually diminish in the general population irrespective of changes in the homicide rate.[55] For example, while a substantial majority of German

[51] See www.gallup.com/poll/indicators/inddeath_pen.asp. McVeigh represents an 'extreme case' which no doubt tests the consciences of many who are opposed to the death penalty. It was, for example, reported that Professor Hugo Adam Bedau admitted that he personally was willing to see McVeigh and those like him executed so long as all others not like McVeigh were spared the death penalty. See Robert J. Lifton and Greg Mitchell, *Who Owns Death? Capital Punishment, the American Conscience, and the End of Executions* (2000), 'The McVeigh Exception', pp. 220–221.

[52] Gross, n. 24 above, p. 1448.

[53] H. A. Bedau (ed), *The Death Penalty in America: Current Controversies* (1997), p. 86.

[54] Official Public Opinion Poll of the Government of Japan, Prime Minister's Office, Minister's Secretary (Management and Co-ordination Agency) (1994), with an English summary. According to the article 'Japan in Dock for "Inhuman" Treatment on Death Row', *The Guardian* (26 Feb. 2001), the Japanese Minister of Justice claimed that 80% of the Japanese people 'say the death penalty is imperative'.

[55] Franklin E. Zimring and Gordon Hawkins, *Capital Punishment and the American Agenda* (1986), pp. 10–15 and 21–22.

citizens supported capital punishment just prior to and after abolition, support had fallen to only 24 per cent by 1992.[56] In Ireland also the majority of the population has turned resolutely against capital punishment. A referendum held in June 2001 voted by a majority of 62 to 37 per cent in favour of an amendment to the Constitution prohibiting the Irish Parliament from enacting 'any law providing for the imposition of the death penalty'.[57]

A number of countries that have abolished the death penalty have done so partly as a result of the concerted organization of an influential and particularly well-informed body of opinion. This has often been mediated through the authoritative pronouncements of official Commissions of Inquiry, in so far as they have dispassionately reviewed the evidence. Effective campaigns have drawn the attention of the public and policy-makers to those defects of capital punishment that create the greatest unease, namely the inevitability of mistakes,[58] and an unacceptable degree of arbitrariness in its infliction. It is therefore usually of great importance to abolitionist movements to gain the support of elite opinion formers, especially among those who influence and administer the criminal justice system.

A survey carried out in the United States of 600 lawyers in the mid-1980s found two-thirds to be in favour of executing those persons currently on death row.[59] Times may in this respect be changing. For, although the powerful American Bar Association (ABA) has never taken a stand against the death penalty on principle (it 'takes no position'), it has recently condemned the way in which it has been put into effect in law and practice. In 1997 the ABA passed a resolution calling for a moratorium on executions 'until the jurisdiction implements policies and procedures . . . intended to (1) ensure that death penalty cases are administered fairly and impartially, in accordance with due process, and (2) minimize the risk that innocent people may be executed'.[60] If the Commissions set up to examine this issue in several states all conclude, as did the Illinois Governor's Commission in April 2002, that 'no system given human nature and frailties, could ever be devised that would work perfectly and guarantee absolutely that no innocent person is ever again sentenced to death',[61] then American lawyers as a professional group may well come to embrace the principled human rights position against capital punishment.

---

[56] Hans-Jörg Albrecht, 'The Death Penalty in China from a European Perspective' in Manfred Nowak and Xin Chunying (eds), *EU–China Human Rights Dialogue: Proceedings of the Second EU–China Legal Experts' Seminar Held in Beijing on 19 and 20 October 1998* (2000), pp. 95–118 at 115. Also, Evans, n. 8 above, pp. 797, 802–804, and 935–937.

[57] AI, *Death Penalty News*, June 2001, AI Index: ACT 53/003/2001, p. 2.

[58] For a survey of probable mistaken convictions in capital cases in the United States, see Hugo Adam Bedau and Michael L. Radelet, 'Miscarriages of Justice in Potentially Capital Cases', *Stanford Law Review* 40 (1987), pp. 21–179.

[59] *ABA Journal* 71 (1985), at 44. At much the same time a small-scale survey in India discovered strong support among university and college teachers, doctors, and, to a lesser extent, lawyers. See N. L. Mitra, 'Capital Punishment in the Indian Sub-continent', *Revue Internationale de Droit Pénal* 58 (1987), pp. 451–474.

[60] Quoted from Sarat, n. 28 above, p. 254.

[61] Illinois, *Report of the Governor's Commission on Capital Punishment: George H. Ryan Governor* (Apr. 2002), p. 207.

2. A QUESTION OF PRINCIPLE

At the end of the day, public opinion as such—meaning essentially an expression of *sentiment*—towards a policy or practice cannot, as the international human rights lawyer William Schabas has insisted, determine an issue which many believe must be dealt with on the basis of principle. In a recent paper read at the UN–China Human Rights Seminar in Beijing in May 2001, he quoted with approval the judgments of the President of the South African Constitutional Court, Arthur Chaskalson:

> Public opinion may have some relevance to the enquiry, but in itself is no substitute for the duty vested in the Courts to interpret the Constitution and to uphold its provisions without fear or favour. If public opinion were to be decisive, there would be no need for constitutional adjudication. The protection of rights could then be left to parliament, which has a mandate from the public, and is answerable to the public for the way its mandate is exercised . . . The very reason . . . for vesting the power of judicial review in the courts, was to protect the rights of minorities and others who cannot protect their rights adequately through the democratic process. Those who are entitled to claim this protection include the social outcasts and marginalised people in our society. It is only if there is a willingness to protect the worst and weakest amongst us that all of us can be secure that our own rights will be protected.[62]

Furthermore, Professor Schabas noted that

> the Judicial Committee of the Privy Council set an interesting example when it affirmed that its members were simply shocked at the notion of prolonged detention prior to execution [in the case of *Pratt et al.* v. *Attorney General for Jamaica*, see page 112 above]. They cited no polls, no legislative trends'. What is of greater significance is that 'Their judgment has made public opinion, even if it did not follow it'.[63]

This, of course, is a good example of how the nature of the administration of capital punishment (rather than the death penalty itself) was interpreted as a human rights violation. As noted in Chapter 1, not every country has subscribed to the view that there should be an international human rights norm banning capital punishment for serious crimes in all circumstances, and this is undoubtedly a serious bone of contention in international deliberations on the subject. However, the abundant and growing evidence about how the death penalty is enforced—which has revealed degrees of cruelty, violating human rights, and many breaches of the legal principles that demand the equitable, proportionate, impartial, and unbiased administration of criminal justice—may one day convince even those governments that would (in their ideal world) favour capital punishment that it cannot safely and properly be administered in human societies founded on the principles of human rights, equality, and justice.

---

[62] *State* v. *Makwanyane* (1995) (3) SA 391, at para. 88.
[63] Schabas, n. 11 above.

Appendix 1
List of Abolitionist and Retentionist Countries

Afghanistan	Indonesia	Rwanda
Algeria	Iran (Islamic Republic)	Saint Kitts and Nevis
Bahamas	Iraq	Saint Lucia
Bahrain	Japan	Saint Vincent and the
Bangladesh	Jordan	Grenadines
Belarus	Kazakhstan	Saudi Arabia
Botswana	Kenya	Sierra Leone
Burundi	Kuwait	Singapore
Cameroon	Kyrgyzstan	Somalia
Chad	Lebanon	Sudan
China	Lesotho	Syrian Arab Republic
Comoros	Liberia	Taiwan Province of China
Cuba	Libyan Arab Jamahiriya	Tajikistan
Democratic People's	Malawi	Thailand
Republic of Korea	Malaysia	Trinidad and Tobago
Democratic Republic of	Mongolia	Uganda
the Congo	Morocco	United Arab Emirates
Egypt	Nigeria	United Republic of
Equatorial Guinea	Oman	Tanzania
Ethiopia	Pakistan	United States of America
Ghana	Palestine	(38 states and federal
Guatemala	Philippines	and military law)
Guinea	Qatar	Uzbekistan
Guyana	Republic of Korea	Vietnam
India	Russian Federation	Yemen
		Zambia
		Zimbabwe

Note: The above-mentioned countries and territories retain the death penalty for ordinary crimes. Most of them are known to have carried out executions during the ten years before 2001. In some cases, however, it is difficult to ascertain whether or not executions have in fact been carried out.

TABLE A1.2

Status of capital punishment in December 2001: countries and territories that are retentionist but can be considered abolitionist de facto (total 34)

Country or territory	Date of last execution	Country or territory	Date of last execution
Antigua and Barbuda	1989	Madagascar	1958
Armenia	1991	Maldives	1952
Barbados	1984	Mali	1980
Belize	1986	Mauritania	1989
Benin	1989	Myanmar	1989
Bhutan	1964	Nauru	1968[c]
Brunei Darussalam	1957	Niger	1976
Burkina Faso	1989	Papua New Guinea	1950
Central African Republic	n.a.	Samoa	1962
Congo	1982	Senegal	1967
Dominica	1986	Sri Lanka	1976
Eritrea[a]	1989	Suriname	1982
Gabon	1981	Swaziland	1989
Gambia[b]	1981	Togo	1979
Grenada	1978	Tonga	1982
Jamaica	1988	Tunisia	1991
Lao People's Democratic Republic	1989	Turkey	1984

Notes: n.a. = information not available.

   [a] Eritrea became independent in 1993.

   [b] Gambia abolished the death penalty in Apr. 1993, it was reinstated by the military regime in Aug. 1995.

   [c] Year in which independence was achieved. No executions have taken place since that time. The date of the last execution prior to independence is not available.

TABLE A1.3

Status of capital punishment in December 2001: countries and territories that are completely abolitionist (total 75)

Country or territory	Date of abolition for all crimes	Date of abolition for ordinary crimes	Date of last execution
Andorra	1990		1943
Angola	1992		n.a.
Australia	1985	1984	1967
Austria	1968	1950	1950
Azerbaijan	1998		1993
Belgium	1996		1950
Bolivia	1995/1997[a]		1974
Bulgaria	1998		1989
Cambodia	1989		n.a.
Canada	1998	1976	1962
Cape Verde	1981		1835
Colombia	1910		1909
Costa Rica	1877		n.a.
Côte d'Ivoire	2000		1960
Croatia	1990		1987
Czech Republic	1990		n.a.
Denmark	1978	1933	1950
Djibouti	1995		1977[b]
Dominican Republic	1966		n.a.
East Timor	1999		1999[b]
Ecuador	1906		n.a.
Estonia	1998		1991
Finland	1972	1949	1944
France	1981		1977
Georgia	1997		1994
Germany	1949/1987[c]		1949/1981[c]
Guinea Bissau	1993		1986
Haiti	1987		1972
Honduras	1956		1940
Hungary	1990		1988
Iceland	1928		1830
Ireland	1990		1954
Italy	1994	1947	1947
Kiribati	1979		1979[b]
Liechtenstein	1987		1785
Lithuania	1998		1995

TABLE A1.3 (*continued*):

Country or territory	Date of abolition for all crimes	Date of abolition for ordinary crimes	Date of last execution
Luxembourg	1979		1949
Macedonia (former Yugoslav Republic of)	1991		n.a.
Malta	2000	1971	1943
Marshall Islands	1986		1986[b]
Mauritius	1995		1987
Micronesia (Federated States of)	1986		1986[b]
Monaco	1962		1847
Mozambique	1990		1986
Namibia	1990		1988
Nepal	1997	1990	1979
Netherlands	1982	1870	1952
New Zealand	1989	1961	1957
Nicaragua	1979		1930
Norway	1979	1905	1948
Palau	1994		1994[b]
Panama	1922		1903
Paraguay	1992		1928
Poland	1997		1988
Portugal	1976	1867	1849
Republic of Moldova	1995		1989
Romania	1989		1989
San Marino	1865	1848	1468
São Tomé and Principe	1990		1975[b]
Seychelles	1993	1979	1976[b]
Slovakia	1990		n.a.
Slovenia	1989		1957
Solomon Islands	1978	1966	1966[d]
South Africa	1997	1995	1991
Spain	1995	1978	1975
Sweden	1972	1921	1910
Switzerland	1992	1942	1944
Turkmenistan	1999		1997
Tuvalu	1978		1978[b]
Ukraine	1999		1997

TABLE A1.3 (*continued*):

Country or territory	Date of abolition for all crimes	Date of abolition for ordinary crimes	Date of last execution
United Kingdom of Great Britain and Northern Ireland	1998	1965	1964
Northern Ireland	1998	1973	1961
Uruguay	1907		n.a.
Vanuatu	1980		1980 [b]
Vatican City State	1969		n.a.
Venezuela	1863		n.a.

Notes: n.a. = information not available.

[a] According to the Constitution of Bolivia of 1967, amended in 1995, Article 17 prohibits the use of the death penalty. Despite this prohibition, the Penal Code of 1973 provided for capital punishment. To bring the law into line with the amended Constitution of 1995, the Bolivian Congress formally abolished the death penalty in 1997.

[b] Year in which independence was achieved. The date of the last execution prior to independence is not available.

[c] The death penalty was abolished in the Federal Republic of Germany (FRG) in 1949 and in the German Democratic Republic (GDR) in 1987. The last execution in the FRG was in 1949; the last execution in the GDR was 1981.

[d] Before that year.

Appendix 1

Table A1.4

Status of capital punishment in December 2001: countries that are abolitionist for ordinary crimes only (total 14)

Country	Date of abolition for ordinary crimes	Date of last execution
Albania	2000	1995
Argentina	1984 (1921)[a]	1916
Bosnia-Hercegovina	1997	n.a.
Brazil	1979 (1882)[b]	1855
Chile	2001	1985
Cyprus	1983	1962
El Salvador	1983	1973
Fiji	1979	1964
Greece	1994	1972
Israel	1954	1962
Latvia	1999	1996
Mexico	n.a.	1930
Peru	1979	1979
Yugoslavia	2001	1989

Notes: n.a. = information not available.

[a] The death penalty was abolished in Argentina in 1921 but re-introduced in 1976 for a number of offences but no judicial death sentences were imposed.

[b] The death penalty was abolished in Brazil in 1882 but re-introduced in 1969 for political crimes only until 1979, when the death penalty was again abolished.

TABLE A1.5

Countries and territories that have abolished capital punishment since 1985 (total 49)

Year	Country or territory	Offences for which capital punishment was abolished	
		All offences	Ordinary offences
1985	Australia	x	
1987	German Democratic Republic	x	
1987	Haiti	x	
1987	Liechtenstein	x	
1989	Cambodia	x	
1989	New Zealand	x	
1989	Romania	x	
1989	Slovenia	x	
1990	Andorra	x	
1990	Croatia	x	
1990	Czech Republic	x	
1990	Hungary	x	
1990	Ireland	x	
1990	Mozambique	x	
1990	Namibia	x	
1990	São Tomé and Principe	x	
1990	Slovakia	x	
1991	Macedonia (former Yugoslav Republic of)	x	
1992	Angola	x	
1992	Paraguay	x	
1992	Switzerland	x	
1993	Guinea Bissau	x	
1993	Seychelles	x	
1994	Greece	x	
1994	Italy	x	
1994	Palau	x	
1995	Djibouti	x	
1995	Mauritius	x	
1995	Republic of Moldova	x	
1996	Belgium	x	
1995/1997[a]	Bolivia	x	
1997	Bosnia-Hercegovina		x
1997	Georgia	x	
1997	Nepal	x	

TABLE A1.5 (*continued*):

Year	Country or territory	Offences for which capital punishment was abolished	
		All offences	Ordinary offences
1997	Poland	x	
1997	South Africa	x	
1998	Azerbaijan	x	
1998	Bulgaria	x	
1998	Canada	x	
1998	Estonia	x	
1998	Lithuania	x	
1998	United Kingdom of Great Britain and Northern Ireland	x	
1999	East Timor	x	
1999	Latvia		x
1999	Turkmenistan	x	
1999	Ukraine	x	
2000	Côte d'Ivoire	x	
2000	Malta	x	
2001	Chile		x

[a] See Table A1.3 note a.

TABLE A1.6

Death penalty status at the end of December 2001 (developments between 1994 and 2001) (total 194)

Complete abolitionist	75
Have remained totally abolitionist	52[a]
Have become totally abolitionist:	
From abolitionist for ordinary crimes	6[b]
From retentionist but abolitionist de facto	4[c]
From retentionist	13[d]
TOTAL	23
Abolitionist for ordinary crimes	14
Have remained abolitionist for ordinary crimes	9[e]
Have become abolitionist for ordinary crimes:	
From abolitionist	0
From retentionist but abolitionist de facto	2[f]
From retentionist	3[g]
TOTAL	5
Retentionist but abolitionist de facto	34
Have remained abolitionist de facto	17[h]
With no death sentences reported	14[i]
With death sentences reported	3[j]
Have become abolitionist de facto:	
From abolitionist	1[k]
From abolitionist for ordinary crimes	0
From retentionist	16[l]
With no death sentences reported	5[m]
With death sentences reported	11[n]
TOTAL	17
Retentionist	71
Have remained retentionist with executions	55[o]
No executions recorded since 1994	6[p]
Have reverted from abolitionist de facto status to retentionist by resuming executions	10[r]

[a] Andorra, Angola, Australia, Austria, Cambodia, Cape Verde, Colombia, Costa Rica, Croatia, Czech Republic, Denmark, the Dominican Republic, Ecuador, Finland, France, Germany, Guinea Bissau, Haiti, the Holy See, Honduras, Hungary, Iceland, Ireland, Kiribati, Liechtenstein, Luxembourg, the Marshall Islands, Micronesia (Federated States of), Monaco, Mozambique, Namibia, the Netherlands, New Zealand, Nicaragua, Norway, Panama, Paraguay, Portugal, Romania, San Marino, São Tomé and Principe, Seychelles, Slovakia, Slovenia, Solomon Islands, Sweden, Switzerland, the former Yugoslav Republic of Macedonia, Tuvalu, Uruguay, Vanuatu, Venezuela.

[b] Canada, Italy, Malta, Nepal, Spain, and the United Kingdom of Great Britain and Northern Ireland.

[c] Belgium, Bolivia, Côte d'Ivoire, Djibouti.

d Azerbaijan, Bulgaria, East Timor, Estonia, Georgia, Lithuania, Mauritius, Poland, the Republic of Moldova, Palau, South Africa, Turkmenistan, Ukraine.

e Argentina, Brazil, Cyprus, El Salvador, Fiji, Greece, Israel, Mexico, Peru.

f Bosnia-Hercegovina, Chile.

g Albania, Latvia, Yugoslavia.

h Bhutan, Brunei Darussalam, Central African Republic, the Congo, Grenada, Madagascar, Maldives, Mali, Nauru, Niger, Papua New Guinea, Samoa, Senegal, Sri Lanka, Suriname, Togo, Tonga.

i Bhutan, Brunei Darussalam, the Central African Republic, the Congo, Grenada, Madagascar, Maldives, Nauru, Niger, Samoa, Senegal, Suriname, Togo, Tonga.

j Mali, Papua New Guinea, Sri Lanka.

k The Gambia.

l Antigua and Barbuda, Armenia, Barbados, Belize, Benin, Burkina Faso, Dominica, Eritrea, Gabon, Jamaica, Lao People's Democratic Republic, Mauritania, Myanmar, Swaziland, Tunisia, Turkey.

m Eritrea, Gabon, Lao People's Democratic Republic, Tunisia, Swaziland.

n Antigua and Barbuda, Armenia, Barbados, Belize, Benin, Burkina Faso, Dominica, Jamaica, Mauritania, Myanmar, Turkey.

o Afghanistan, Algeria, Bangladesh, Belarus, Botswana, Cameroon, China, Cuba, Democratic People's Republic of Korea (no executions reported), Democratic Republic of the Congo, Egypt, Equatorial Guinea, Ethiopia, Guyana, India, Indonesia, Iran (Islamic Republic of), Iraq, Japan, Jordan, Kazakhstan, Kuwait, Kyrgyzstan, Lebanon, Lesotho, Liberia, the Libyan Arab Jamahiriya, Malaysia, Mongolia, Nigeria, Oman, Pakistan, Palestine, Republic of Korea, Rwanda, Saint Lucia, Saint Vincent and the Grenadines, Saudi Arabia, Sierra Leone, Singapore, Somalia, Sudan, Syrian Arab Republic, Taiwan Province of China, Tajikistan, Thailand, Uganda, United Arab Emirates, United Republic of Tanzania, United States of America, Uzbekistan, Vietnam, Yemen, Zambia, Zimbabwe.

p Chad, Ghana, Kenya, Malawi, Morocco. Also included here is the Russian Federation, which formally ceased executions in 1996 in expectation of abolishing the death penalty.

q Bahamas, Bahrain, Burundi, the Comoros, Guatemala, Guinea, Philippines, Qatar, Saint Kitts and Nevis, Trinidad and Tobago.

Appendix 2
Ratification of International Treaties

Countries that have signed or ratified Protocol No. 6 to the European Convention for the Protection of Human Rights and Fundamental Freedoms (ECHR), the Second Optional Protocol to the International Covenant on Civil and Political Rights (ICCPR), and/or the Protocol to the American Convention on Human Rights (ACHR), and countries that have already abolished the death penalty completely or for ordinary crimes and ratified the American Convention on Human Rights (Art.4.3 bars the reimposition of the death penalty once it has been abolished)

TABLE A2.1

Country (by region)	Protocol No. 6 ECHR	Second Optional Protocol to the ICCPR	Protocol to the ACHR	ACHR
Australia		R (1990)		
Nepal		R (1998)		
New Zealand		R (1990)		
Latin America and the Caribbean				
Argentina				R (1984)
Bolivia				R (1979)
Brazil			R (1996)	R (1992)
Chile		S (2001)	S (2001)	R (1990)
Colombia		R (1997)		R (1973)
Costa Rica		R (1998)	R (1998)	R (1970)
Dominican Republic				R (1993)
Ecuador		R (1993)	R (1998)	R (1977)
El Salvador				R (1978)
Haiti				R (1977)
Honduras		S (1990)		R (1977)
Mexico				R (1981)
Nicaragua		S (1990)	R (1999)	R (1979)
Panama		R (1993)	R (1991)	R (1978)
Paraguay			R (2000)	R (1989)
Peru				R (1978)
Uruguay		R (1993)	R (1994)	R (1985)
Venezuela		R (1993)	R (1993)	R (1977)
Eastern Europe				
Albania	R (2000)			
Armenia	S (2001)			
Azerbaijan	S (2001)	R (1999)		

Table A2.1 *(continued)*:

Country (by region)	Protocol No. 6 ECHR	Second Optional Protocol to the ICCPR	Protocol to the ACHR	ACHR
Bosnia-Hercegovina		R (2001)		
Bulgaria	R (1999)	R (1999)		
Croatia	R (1997)	R (1995)		
Czech Republic	R (1992)			
Estonia	R (1998)			
Georgia	R (2000)	R (1999)		
Hungary	R (1992)	R (1994)		
Latvia	R (1999)			
Lithuania	R (1999)	S (2000)		
Poland	R (2000)	S (2000)		
Republic of Moldova	R (1997)			
Romania	S (1994)	R (1991)		
Russian Federation	S (1997)			
Slovakia	R (1992)	R (1999)		
Slovenia	R (1994)	R (1994)		
Turkmenistan		R (2000)		
The former Yugoslav Republic of Macedonia	R (1997)	R (1995)		
Urkaine	R (2000)			
Yugoslavia		R (2001)		
Africa				
Cape Verde		R (2000)		
Guinea-Bissau		S (2000)		
Mozambique		R (1993)		
Namibia		R (1994)		
Saõ Tomé and Principe		S (2000)		
Seychelles		R (1994)		
Western Europe				
Andorra	R (1996)			
Austria	R (1984)	R (1993)		
Belgium	R (1998)	R (1998)		
Cyprus	R (2000)	R (1999)		
Denmark	R (1983)	R (1994)		
Finland	R (1990)	R (1991)		
France	R (1986)			
Germany	R (1989)	R (1992)		
Greece	R (1998)	R (1997)		
Iceland	R (1987)	R (1991)		
Ireland	R (1994)	R (1993)		
Italy	R (1988)	R (1995)		

Country (by region)	Protocol No. 6 ECHR	Second Optional Protocol to the ICCPR	Protocol to the ACHR	ACHR
Liechtenstein	R (1990)	R (1998)		
Luxembourg	R (1985)	R (1992)		
Malta	R (1991)	R (1994)		
Monaco		R (2000)		
Netherlands	R (1986)	R (1991)		
Norway	R (1988)	R (1991)		
Portugal	R (1986)	R (1990)		
San Marino	R (1989)			
Spain	R (1985)	R (1991)*		
Sweden	R (1984)	R (1990)		
Switzerland	R (1987)	R (1994)		
United Kingdom of Great Britain and Northern Ireland	R (1999)	R (1999)		

R = ratified
S = signed
* Withdrew reservations in 1997.

Appendix 3
International Instruments

SAFEGUARDS GUARANTEEING PROTECTION OF THE RIGHTS OF
THOSE FACING THE DEATH PENALTY[1]

1. In countries which have not abolished the death penalty, capital punishment may be imposed only for the most serious crimes, it being understood that their scope should not go beyond intentional crimes with lethal or other extremely grave consequences.

2. Capital punishment may be imposed only for a crime for which the death penalty is prescribed by law at the time of its commission, it being understood that if, subsequent to the commission of the crime, provision is made by law for the imposition of a lighter penalty, the offender shall benefit thereby.

3. Persons below 18 years of age at the time of the commission of the crime shall not be sentenced to death, nor shall the death sentence be carried out on pregnant women, or on new mothers, or on persons who have become insane.

4. Capital punishment may be imposed only when the guilt of the person charged is based upon clear and convincing evidence leaving no room for an alternative explanation of the facts.

5. Capital punishment may only be carried out pursuant to a final judgment rendered by a competent court after legal process which gives all possible safeguards to ensure a fair trial, at least equal to those contained in article 14 of the International Covenant on Civil and Political Rights, including the right of anyone suspected of or charged with a crime for which capital punishment may be imposed to adequate legal assistance at all stages of the proceedings.

6. Anyone sentenced to death shall have the right to appeal to a court of higher jurisdiction, and steps should be taken to ensure that such appeals shall become mandatory.

7. Anyone sentenced to death shall have the right to seek pardon, or commutation of sentence; pardon or commutation of sentence may be granted in all cases of capital punishment.

8. Capital punishment shall not be carried out pending any appeal or other recourse procedure or other proceeding relating to pardon or commutation of the sentence.

9. Where capital punishment occurs, it shall be carried out so as to inflict the minimum possible suffering.

[1] Economic and Social Council resolution 1984/50

Additions to Safeguards as Agreed by the Economic and Social Council Resolution 1989/64

1. Affording special protection to persons facing charges for which the death penalty is provided by allowing time and facilities for the preparation of their defence, including the

adequate assistance of counsel at every stage of the proceedings, above and beyond the protection afforded in non-capital cases.

2. Providing for mandatory appeals or review with provisions for clemency or pardon in all cases of capital offence.

3. Establishing a maximum age beyond which a person may not be sentenced to death or executed.

4. Eliminating the death penalty for persons suffering from mental retardation or extremely limited mental competence, whether at the stage of sentence or execution.

Strengthening of the Safeguards as Agreed by the Economic and Social Council Resolution 1996/15.

The Council:

1. Encouraged Member States in which the death penalty had not been abolished to ensure that each defendant facing a possible death sentence was given all guarantees to ensure a fair trial, as contained in article 14 of the International Covenant on Civil and Political Rights, and bearing in mind the Basic Principles on the Independence of the Judiciary the Basic Principles on the Role of Lawyers, the Guidelines on the Role of Prosecutors, the Body of Principles for the Protection of All Persons under Any Form of Detention or Imprisonment, and the Standard Minimum Rules for the Treatment of Prisoners.

2. Also encouraged Member states in which the death penalty had not been abolished to ensure that defendants who did not sufficiently understand the language used in court were fully informed, by way of interpretation or translation, of all the charges against them and the content of the relevant evidence deliberated in court.

3. Called upon Member States in which the death penalty might be carried out to allow adequate time for the preparation of appeals to a court of higher jurisdiction and for the completion of appeal proceedings, as well as petitions for clemency, in order to effectively apply rules 5 and 8 of the safeguards guaranteeing protection of the rights of those facing the death penalty.

4. Also called upon Member States in which the death penalty might be carried out to ensure that officials involved in decisions to carry out an execution were fully informed of the status of appeals and petitions for clemency of the prisoner in question.

5. Urged Member States in which the death penalty might be carried out to effectively apply the Standard Minimum Rules for the Treatment of Prisoners, in order to keep to a minimum the suffering of prisoners under sentence of death and to avoid any exacerbation of such suffering.

INTERNATIONAL COVENANT ON CIVIL AND POLITICAL RIGHTS, G.A. RES. 2200A (XXI), 21 U.N. GAOR SUPP. (NO. 16) AT 52, U.N. DOC. A/6316 (1966), 999 U.N.T.S. 171, *ENTERED INTO FORCE* MAR. 23, 1976 (ARTICLES 6, 14, AND 15).

Article 6

1. Every human being has the inherent right to life. This right shall be protected by law. No one shall be arbitrarily deprived of his life.

2. In countries which have not abolished the death penalty, sentence of death may be imposed only for the most serious crimes in accordance with the law in force at the time of the commission of the crime and not contrary to the provisions of the present Covenant and to the Convention on the Prevention and Punishment of the Crime of Genocide. This penalty can only be carried out pursuant to a final judgement rendered by a competent court.

3. When deprivation of life constitutes the crime of genocide, it is understood that nothing in this article shall authorize any State Party to the present Covenant to derogate in any way from any obligation assumed under the provisions of the Convention on the Prevention and Punishment of the Crime of Genocide.

4. Anyone sentenced to death shall have the right to seek pardon or commutation of the sentence. Amnesty, pardon or commutation of the sentence of death may be granted in all cases.

5. Sentence of death shall not be imposed for crimes committed by persons below eighteen years of age and shall not be carried out on pregnant women.

6. Nothing in this article shall be invoked to delay or to prevent the abolition of capital punishment by any State Party to the present Covenant.

Article 14

1. All persons shall be equal before the courts and tribunals. In the determination of any criminal charge against him, or of his rights and obligations in a suit at law, everyone shall be entitled to a fair and public hearing by a competent, independent and impartial tribunal established by law. The press and the public may be excluded from all or part of a trial for reasons of morals, public order (ordre public) or national security in a democratic society, or when the interest of the private lives of the parties so requires, or to the extent strictly necessary in the opinion of the court in special circumstances where publicity would prejudice the interests of justice; but any judgement rendered in a criminal case or in a suit at law shall be made public except where the interest of juvenile persons otherwise requires or the proceedings concern matrimonial disputes or the guardianship of children.

2. Everyone charged with a criminal offence shall have the right to be presumed innocent until proved guilty according to law.

3. In the determination of any criminal charge against him, everyone shall be entitled to the following minimum guarantees, in full equality:

(a) To be informed promptly and in detail in a language which he understands of the nature and cause of the charge against him;

(b) To have adequate time and facilities for the preparation of his defence and to communicate with counsel of his own choosing;

(c) To be tried without undue delay;

(d) To be tried in his presence, and to defend himself in person or through legal assistance of his own choosing; to be informed, if he does not have legal assistance, of this right; and to have legal assistance assigned to him, in any case where the interests of justice so require, and without payment by him in any such case if he does not have sufficient means to pay for it;

(e) To examine, or have examined, the witnesses against him and to obtain the attendance and examination of witnesses on his behalf under the same conditions as witnesses against him;

(f) To have the free assistance of an interpreter if he cannot understand or speak the language used in court;

(g) Not to be compelled to testify against himself or to confess guilt.

4. In the case of juvenile persons, the procedure shall be such as will take account of their age and the desirability of promoting their rehabilitation.

5. Everyone convicted of a crime shall have the right to his conviction and sentence being reviewed by a higher tribunal according to law.

6. When a person has by a final decision been convicted of a criminal offence and when subsequently his conviction has been reversed or he has been pardoned on the ground that a new or newly discovered fact shows conclusively that there has been a miscarriage of justice, the person who has suffered punishment as a result of such conviction shall be compensated according to law, unless it is proved that the non-disclosure of the unknown fact in time is wholly or partly attributable to him.

7. No one shall be liable to be tried or punished again for an offence for which he has already been finally convicted or acquitted in accordance with the law and penal procedure of each country.

Article 15

1. No one shall be held guilty of any criminal offence on account of any act or omission which did not constitute a criminal offence, under national or international law, at the time when it was committed. Nor shall a heavier penalty be imposed than the one that was applicable at the time when the criminal offence was committed. If, subsequent to the commission of the offence, provision is made by law for the imposition of the lighter penalty, the offender shall benefit thereby.

2. Nothing in this article shall prejudice the trial and punishment of any person for any act or omission which, at the time when it was committed, was criminal according to the general principles of law recognized by the community of nations.

Bibliography

References to UN documents, such as resolutions and reports of committees and of the Special Rapporteur, as well as those of the Council of Europe and the European Community, were too numerous to include and can be found in the footnotes, as can the citations to reports from Amnesty International, Human Rights Watch, and other organizations. They can be easily traced by country or subject matters by using the Index. Only major reports from organizations are included in the Bibliography.

ACKER, J. R., 'Mandatory Capital Punishment for the Life Term Inmate who Commits Murder: Judgments of Fact and Value in Law and Social Sciences', *Criminal and Civil Confinement* 11–12 (1985), pp. 267–327.

—— 'Research on the Death Penalty: A Different Agenda: The Supreme Court, Empirical Research Evidence, and Capital Punishment Decisions, 1986–1989', *Law and Society Review* 27 (1993), pp. 65–87.

—— BOHM, R. M., and LANIER, C. S. (eds), *America's Experiment with Capital Punishment: Reflections on the Past, Present, and Future of the Ultimate Penal Sanction* (1998), Durham, NC: Carolina Academic Press.

—— and LANIER, C. S., 'The Dimensions of Capital Murder', *Criminal Law Bulletin* 29 (1993), pp. 379–417.

—— —— ' "Parsing this Lexicon of Death", Aggravating Factors in Capital Sentencing Statutes', *Criminal Law Bulletin* 30 (1994), pp. 107–152.

—— —— 'In Fairness and Mercy: Statutory Mitigating Factors in Capital Punishment Laws', *Criminal Law Bulletin* 30 (1994), pp. 299–345.

—— —— 'Matters of Life and Death: The Sentencing Provisions of the Capital Punishment Statutes', *Criminal Law Bulletin* 31 (1995), pp. 19–60.

—— —— 'Unfit to Live, Unfit to Die: Incompetence for Execution under Modern Death Penalty Legislation', *Criminal Law Bulletin* 33 (1997), pp. 107–150.

—— —— 'Beyond Human Ability?', in J. R Acker, R. M. Bohm, and C. S. Lanier (eds), *America's Experiment with Capital Punishment* (1998), pp. 77–115.

—— —— 'Introduction: America's Experiment with Capital Punishment', in J. R. Acker, R. M. Bohm, and C. S. Lanier (eds), *America's Experiment with Capital Punishment* (1998), pp. 5–21.

—— —— 'May God—or the Governor—Have Mercy: Executive Clemency and Executions in Modern Death-Penalty Systems', *Criminal Law Bulletin* 36 (2000), pp. 200–237.

—— and WALSH, E. R., 'Challenging the Death Penalty under State Constitutions', *Vanderbilt Law Review* 42 (1989), pp. 1299–1363.

ADAMS, J. C., 'Racial Disparity and the Death Penalty', *Law and Contemporary Problems* 61 (1998), pp. 153–170.

ADEYEMI, A. A., 'Death Penalty: Criminological Perspectives. The Nigerian Situation', *Revue Internationale de Droit Pénal* 58 (1987), pp. 485–502.

ADOLF, P. S., Note, 'Killing Me Softly: Is the Gas Chamber, or Any Other Method of Execution, "Cruel and Unusual Punishment"?', *Hastings Constitutional Law Quarterly* 22 (1995), pp. 815–866.

AGARWAL, R. S., and KUMAR, S. (eds), *Crime and Punishment in New Perspective* (1986), Delhi: Mittal Publications.

AI. See Amnesty International.

ALBRECHT, H.-J., 'The Death Penalty in China from a European Perspective', in M. Nowak and Xin Chunying (eds), *EU–China Human Rights Dialogue* (2000), Vienna: Verlag Österreich, pp. 95–118.

AL-HEWESH, SHEIK MOHAMMED IBN IBRAHIM, 'Shari'a Penalties and Ways of their Implementation in the Kingdom of Saudi Arabia', in *The Effects of Islamic Legislation on Crime Prevention in Saudi Arabia* (1980), Kingdom of Saudi Arabia in collaboration with UNSDRI, Rome, pp. 349–400.

AMERICAN BAR ASSOCIATION, *A Gathering Momentum: Continuing Impacts of the American Bar Association Call for a Moratorium on Executions* (Jan. 2000), Washington.

—— *Death Knell for the Death Penalty* (June 2000), Washington.

—— COLLEGE OF PHYSICIANS, HUMAN RIGHTS WATCH, NATIONAL COUNCIL TO ABOLISH THE DEATH PENALTY, AND PHYSICIANS FOR HUMAN RIGHTS, *Breach of Trust, Physician Participation in the United States* (1994), Philadelphia.

—— MEDICAL ASSOCIATION, 'Council on Ethical and Judicial Affairs. American Medical Association: Physician Participation in Capital Punishment', *Journal of the American Medical Association* 270 (1993), pp. 365–368.

—— SECTION OF INDIVIDUAL RIGHTS AND RESPONSIBILITIES, *Towards Greater Awareness: The American Bar Association Call for a Moratorium on Executions Gains Ground. A Summary of Moratorium Resolution Impact from January 2000 through July 2001* (Aug. 2001), Washington.

—— TASK FORCE ON REVIEW OF STATE CAPITAL CASES, *Toward a More Just and Effective System of Review in State Death Penalty Cases*, (1989), Washington.

American University Law Review, Note, 'The Death Penalty in Georgia: An Aggravating Circumstance' 30 (1981), pp. 835–861.

AMNESTY INTERNATIONAL (AI), *The Death Penalty: Amnesty International Report* (1979), AI Index: ACT 05/03/79.

—— *When the State Kills. The Death Penalty v. Human Rights* (1989), AI Index: ACT 51/07/89.

—— *The Machinery of Death: A Shocking Indictment of Capital Punishment in the United States* (1995), New York: Amnesty International USA.

AMSTERDAM, A, 'Selling a Quick Fix for Boot Hill', in Austin Sarat (ed), *The Killing State: Capital Punishment in Law, Politics, and Culture* (1999), pp. 148–183.

ANAGNOSTOPOULOS, I. G., and MAGLIVERAS, K. D., *Criminal Law in Greece* (2000), London: Kluwer Law International.

ANCEL, M., *The Death Penalty in European Countries* (1962), Strasbourg: Council of Europe.

ANDENAES, J., *Punishment and Deterrence* (1974), Ann Arbor: University of Michigan Press.

ANTOINE, R. B. M., 'International Law and the Right to Legal Representation in Capital Offence Cases—a Comparative Approach', *Oxford Journal of Legal Studies* 12 (1992), pp. 284–294.

—— 'The Judicial Committee of the Privy Council—An Inadequate Remedy for Death Row Prisoners', *International and Comparative Law Quarterly* 41 (1992), pp. 179–190.

APPELBAUM, P. S., 'Hypotheticals, Psychiatric Testimony, and the Death Sentence', *Bulletin of the American Academy of Psychiatry and Law* 12 (1984), pp. 169–177.

ARCHER, D., and GARTNER, R., *Violence and Crime in Cross-National Perspective* (2nd edn 1994), New Haven: Yale University Press.

ARKIN, S. D., 'Discrimination and Arbitrariness in Capital Punishment: An Analysis of Post-*Furman* Murder Cases in Dade County, Florida, 1973–76', *Stanford Law Review* 33 (1980), pp. 75–101.

ARRIENS, J. (ed), *Welcome to Hell: Letters and Other Writings by Prisoners on Death Row in the United States* (1991), Cambridge: Ian Faulkner Publishing.

AUSTRALIAN LAW REFORM COMMISSION, *Sentencing Penalties* Paper no. 30 (1987), Sydney.

BADINTER, R., *L'Abolition* (2000), Paris: Librairie Artheme Fayard.

BAILEY, W. C., 'An Analysis of the Deterrent Effect of the Death Penalty in North Carolina', *North Carolina Central Law Journal* 10 (1978), pp. 29–51.

—— 'Deterrence and the Death Penalty for Murder in Utah', *Journal of Contemporary Law* 5 (1978), pp. 1–20.

—— 'Deterrence and the Death Penalty for Murder in Oregon', *Williamette Law Review* 16 (1979), pp. 67–85.

—— 'The Deterrent Effect of the Death Penalty for Murder in California', *Southern California Law Review* 52 (1979), pp. 743–764.

—— 'The Deterrent Effect of the Death Penalty for Murder in Ohio', *Cleveland State Law Review* 28 (1979), pp. 51–81.

—— 'A Multivariate Cross-Sectional Analysis of the Deterrent Effect of the Death Penalty', *Sociology and Social Research* 64 (1980), pp. 183–207.

—— 'Capital Punishments and Lethal Assaults against Police', *Criminology* 19 (1982), pp. 608–625.

—— 'Murder and Capital Punishment in the Nation's Capital', *Justice Quarterly* 1–2 (1984), pp. 211–223.

—— 'The General Preventive Effect of Capital Punishment on Non-Capital Felonies', in R. M. Bohm (ed), *The Death Penalty in America: Current Research* (1991), pp. 21–38.

—— and PETERSON, R. D., 'Police Killings and Capital Punishment: The Post-*Furman* Period', *Criminology* 25 (1987), pp. 1–25.

—— —— 'Murder and Capital Punishment: A Monthly Time-Series Analysis of Execution Publicity', *American Sociological Review* 54 (1989), pp. 722–743.

—— 'Murder, Capital Punishment and Deterrence: A Review of the Evidence and an Examination of Police Killings', *Journal of Social Issues* 50(2) (Summer 1994), pp. 53–74.

BALDUS, D. C., 'The Death Penalty Dialogue between Law and Social Science', *Indiana Law Journal* 70 (1995), pp. 1033–1041.

—— PULASKI, C. A., Jr., WOODWORTH, G., and KYLE, F. D., 'Identifying Comparatively Excessive Sentences of Death: A Quantitative Approach', *Stanford Law Review* 33 (1980), pp. 1–74.

—— and WOODWORTH, G. 'Race Discrimination and the Death Penalty: An Empirical and Legal Overview', in J. R. Acker, R. M. Bohm, and C. S. Lanier (eds) *America's Experiment with Capital Punishment* (1998), pp. 385–415.

—— —— and PULASKI, C. A., Jr, 'Arbitrariness and Discrimination in the Administration of the Death Penalty: A Challenge to State Supreme Courts', *Stetson Law Review* 15 (1986), pp. 133–261.

—— —— —— *Equal Justice and the Death Penalty: A Legal and Empirical Analysis* (1990), Boston: Northeastern University Press.

—— —— —— 'Reflections in the "Inevitability" of Racial Discrimination in Capital Sentencing and the "Impossibility" of its Prevention, Detection and Correction', *Washington and Lee Law Review* 51 (1994), pp. 359–430.

—— —— YOUNG, G. L. and CHRIST, A. M., *The Disposition of Nebraska Capital and Non-Capital Homicide Cases (1973–1999): A Legal and Empirical Analysis,* Final report (amended) (10 Oct. 2001), mimeo.

BALDUS, D. C., WOODWORTH, G., ZUCKERMANN, D., WEINER, N. A., and BROFFITT, B., 'Racial Discrimination and the Death Penalty in the Post-*Furman* Era: An Empirical and Legal Overview, with Recent Findings from Philadelphia', *Cornell Law Review* 83 (1998), pp. 1638–1770.

—— —— —— —— —— 'The Use of Peremptory Challenges in Capital Murder Trials: A Legal and Empirical Analysis', Symposium: Race, Crime, and the Constitution, *University of Pennsylvania Journal of Constitutional Law* 3 (2001), pp. 3–170.

BANTEKAS, I., and HODGKINSON, P., 'Capital Punishment at the United Nations: Recent Developments', *Criminal Law Forum* 11(1) (2000), pp. 23–34.

BARBER, P. G., Note: '*People* v. *Smith:* Mandatory Death Laid to Rest', *Albany Law Review* 49 (1985), pp. 926–966.

BARKAN, S. E. and COHN, S. F., 'Racial Prejudice and Support for the Death Penalty by Whites', *Journal of Research in Crime and Delinquency* 31 (1994), pp. 202–209.

BARNETT, A., 'Some Distribution Patterns for the Georgia Death Sentence', *University of California, Davis, Law Review* 18 (1985), pp. 1327–1363.

BARRY, D. and WILLIAMS, E., 'Russia's Death Penalty Dilemmas', *Criminal Law Forum* 8 (1997), pp. 231–258.

BAYER, R. 'Lethal Injections and Capital Punishment: Medicine in the Service of the State', *Journal of Prison and Jail Health* 4(1) (1984), pp. 7–15.

BECCARIA, C., *On Crimes and Punishments* (1764), trans. H. Paolucci (1963), Indianapolis: Bobbs-Merrill.

BEDAU, H. A., 'Felony Murder Rape and the Mandatory Death Penalty: A Study in Discretionary Justice', *Suffolk University Law Review* 10 (1976), pp. 493–520.

—— *Death is Different* (1987), Boston: Northeastern University Press.

—— 'The Decline of Executive Clemency in Capital Cases', *New York University Review of Law and Social Change* 18 (1990–1), pp. 255–272.

—— 'The United States', in P. Hodgkinson and A. Rutherford (eds), *Capital Punishment: Global Issues and Prospects* (1996), pp. 45–76.

—— (ed), *The Death Penalty in America: Current Controversies* (1997), New York: Oxford University Press.

—— 'Abolishing the Death Penalty Even for the Worst Murderers', in Austin Sarat (ed), *The Killing State: Capital Punishment in Law, Politics, and Culture* (1999), pp. 40–59.

—— and PIERCE, C. M. (eds), *Capital Punishment in the United States* (1976), New York: AMS Press.

—— and RADELET, M. L., 'Miscarriages of Justice in Potentially Capital Cases', *Stanford Law Review* 40 (1987), pp. 21–179.

—— —— 'The Myth of Infallibility: A Reply to Markman and Cassell', *Stanford Law Review* 41 (1988), pp. 161–170.

BENDER, D. L., LEONE, B., *et al, Does Capital Punishment Deter Crime?* An Opposing Viewpoints Series (1998), San Diego: Greenhaven Press.

BENDREMER, F. J., BRAMNICK, G., JONES, J. C., and LIPPMAN, S. C., '*McCleskey* v. *Kemp:* Constitutional Tolerance for Racially Disparate Capital Sentencing', *University of Miami Law Review* 41 (1986), pp. 295–355.

BERGER, V., 'The Chiropractor as Brain Surgeon: Defense Lawyering in Capital Cases', *New York University Review of Law and Social Change* 18 (1990–1), pp. 245–254.

—— '*Herrera* v. *Collins:* The Gateway of Innocence for Death-Sentenced Prisoners Leads Nowhere', *William and Mary Law Review* 35 (1994), pp. 943–1023.

BERISTAIN, A., 'La sanction capitale en Espagne: Reférénce spéciale à la dimension religieuse Chrétienne', *Revue Internationale de Droit Pénal* 58 (1987), pp. 613–636.

BERK, R. A., BOGER, J. and WEISS, R. 'Research on the Death Penalty: Chance and the Death Penalty' and 'Rejoinder', *Law and Society Review* 27 (1993), pp. 89–110, 125–127.

BEYLEVELD, D., 'Identifying, Explaining and Predicting Deterrence', *British Journal of Criminology* 19 (1979), pp. 205–224.

BHAGWAT, A., 'The McCleskey Puzzle: Remedying Prosecutorial Discrimination against Black Victims in Capital Sentencing', in D. J. Hutchinson, D. A. Strauss, and G. R. Stone (eds), *The Supreme Court Review* (1999), Chicago: University of Chicago Press, pp. 145–192.

BIENEN, L. B., 'A Good Murder', *Fordham Urban Law Journal* 20 (1993), pp. 585–607.

—— 'The Quality of Justice in Capital Cases: Illinois as a Case Study', *Law and Contemporary Problems* 61 (1998), pp. 193–217.

—— WEINER, N. A., ALLISON, P. D., and MILLS, D. L., 'The Reimposition of Capital Punishment in New Jersey: Felony Murder Cases', *Albany Law Review* 54 (1990), pp. 709–817.

—— —— DENNO, D. W., ALLISON, P. D., and MILLS, D. L., 'The Re-imposition of Capital Punishment in New Jersey: The Role of Prosecutorial Discretion', *Rutgers Law Review* 41 (1988), pp. 27–372.

BIRNBAUM, M., *Nigeria: Fundamental Rights Denied: Report of the Trial of Ken Saro-Wiwa and Others* (June 1995), London: Bar Human Rights Committee of England and Wales, Law Society of England and Wales, and Article 19, the International Centre against Censorship.

BLACK, T., and ORSAGH, T., 'New Evidence on the Efficacy of Sanctions as a Deterrent to Homicide', *Social Science Quarterly* 58 (1978), pp. 616–630.

BLACKSHIELD, A. R., 'Capital Punishment in India', *Journal of the Indian Law Institute* 21 (1979), pp. 137–226.

BLUME, J. H., EISENBERG, T., and JOHNSON, S. L., 'Post-*McCleskey* Racial Discrimination Claims in Capital Cases', *Cornell Law Review* 83 (1998), pp. 1771–1810.

—— GARVEY, S., and JOHNSON, S. L., 'Future Dangerousness in Capital Cases: Always "at Issue" ', *Cornell Law Review* 86 (2001), pp. 397–410.

BLUMSTEIN, A., COHEN, J., and NAGIN, D. (eds), *Deterrence and Incapacitation* (1978), Washington: National Academy of Sciences.

BOAZ, J. E., 'Summary Processes and the Rule of Law: Expediting Death Penalty Cases in Federal Courts', *Yale Law Journal* 95 (1985), pp. 349–370.

BOHM, R. M. (ed), *The Death Penalty in America: Current Research* (1991), Academy of Criminal Justice Sciences, Northern Kentucky University Cincinnati: Anderson Pub. Co.

—— 'American Death Penalty Opinion, 1936–1986: A Critical Examination of the Gallup Polls', in R. M. Bohm (ed), *The Death Penalty in America: Current Research* (1991), pp. 113–143.

—— 'The Economic Costs of Capital Punishment: Past, Present and Future', in J. R. Acker, R. M. Bohm, and C. S. Lanier (eds), *America's Experiment with Capital Punishment* (1998), pp. 437–458.

—— 'American Death Penalty Opinion: Past, Present, and Future', in J. R. Acker, R. M. Bohm, and C. S. Lanier (eds), *America's Experiment with Capital Punishment* (1998), pp. 25–46.

—— CLARK, L. J., and AVENI, A. F., 'Knowledge and Death Penalty Opinions: A Test of the Marshall Hypotheses', *Journal of Research in Crime and Delinquency* 28 (1991), pp. 360–387.

—— and VOGEL, R. E., 'A Comparison of Factors Associated with Uninformed and Informed Death Penalty Opinions', *Journal of Criminal Justice* 22 (1994), pp. 125–143.

BOHM, R. M., VOGEL, R. E., and MAISTO, A. A., 'Knowledge and Death Penalty Opinion: A Panel Study', *Journal of Criminal Justice* 21 (1993), pp. 29–45.

BONNER, R. A., 'Death Penalty', *Annual Survey of American Law* (1984), pp. 493–513.

BONNIE, R. J., 'Dilemmas in Administering the Death Penalty: Conscientious Abstention, Professional Ethics, and the Needs of the Legal System', *Law and Human Behavior* 14 (1990), pp. 67–90.

—— 'Grounds for Professional Abstention in Capital Cases: A Reply to Brodsky', *Law and Human Behavior* 14 (1990), pp. 99–102.

—— 'Preserving Justice in Capital Cases while Streamlining the Process of Collateral Review', *University of Toledo Law Review* 23 (1991), pp. 99–116.

BOSSUYT, M. J., *The Administration of Justice and the Human Rights of Detainees*, Report to the United Nations (1987), E/CN.4/ Sub.2/1987/20.

BOWERS, W. J., 'The Pervasiveness of Arbitrariness and Discrimination under Post-*Furman* Capital Statutes', *Journal of Criminal Law and Criminology* 74 (1983), pp. 1067–1110.

—— 'The Effect of Executions is Brutalization, not Deterrence', in K. C. Haas and J. A. Inciardi (eds), *Challenging Capital Punishment* (1988), pp. 49–89.

—— 'Capital Punishment and Contemporary Values: People's Misgivings and the Court's Misperceptions', *Law and Society Review* 27 (1993), pp. 157–175.

—— 'The Capital Jury Project: Rational, Design, and Review of Early Findings', *Indiana Law Review* 70 (1995), pp. 1043–1102.

—— and PIERCE, G. L., 'The Illusion of Deterrence in Isaac Ehrlich's Research on Capital Punishment', *Yale Law Journal* 85 (1975), pp. 187–208.

—— with PIERCE, G. L., and McDEVITT J. F., *Legal Homicide: Death as Punishment in America, 1864–1982* (2nd edn 1984), Boston: Northeastern University Press.

—— SANDYS, M. and STEINER, B. D., 'Foreclosed Impartiality in Capital Sentencing: Juror's Predispositions, Guilt-Trial Experience, and Premature Decision-Making', *Cornell Law Review* 83 (1998), 1476–1556.

—— and STEINER, B. D, 'Choosing Life or Death: Sentencing Dynamics in Capital Cases', in J. R. Acker, R. M. Bohm, and C. S. Lanier (eds), *America's Experiment with Capital Punishment* (1998), pp. 309–349.

—— —— 'Death by Default: An Empirical Demonstration of False and Forced Choices in Capital Sentencing', *Texas Law Review* 77 (1999), pp. 605–717.

—— —— and SANDYS, M., 'Death Sentencing in Black and White: An Empirical Analysis of the Role of Jurors' Race and Jury Racial Composition', *University of Pennsylvania Journal of Constitutional Law* 3 (2001), pp. 171–272.

BOXER, J. T., 'China's Death Penalty: Undermining Legal Reform and Threatening National Economic Interest', *Suffolk Transnational Law Review* 22 (1999), pp. 593–618.

BRENNAN, W. J., Jr. 'Neither Victims nor Executioners', *Notre Dame Journal of Law, Ethics and Public Policy: Symposium on Capital Punishment* 8 (1994), pp. 1–9.

BRIGHT, S. B., 'Death by Lottery—Procedural Bar of Constitutional Claims due to Inadequate Representation of Indigent Defendants', *West Virginia Law Review* 92 (1990), pp. 679–695.

—— 'Counsel for the Poor: The Death Sentence not for the Worst Crime, but the Worst Lawyer', *National Legal Aid and Defender Cornerstone* 13(3) (1991), pp. 8–10.

—— 'Counsel for the Poor: The Death Sentence not for the Worst Crime, but the Worst Lawyer', *Yale Law Journal* 103 (1994), pp. 1835–1883.

—— 'The Politics of Crime and the Death Penalty: Not "Soft on Crime", but Hard on the Bill of Rights', *Saint Louis University Law Journal* 39 (1995), pp. 479–503.

—— 'Casualties of the War on Crime: Fairness, Reliability and the Credibility of the Criminal Justice System', *University of Miami Law Review* 51 (1997), pp. 413–424.

—— 'The Politics of Capital Punishment: The Sacrifice of Fairness for Executions', in J. R. Acker, R. M. Bohm, and C. S. Lanier (eds) *America's Experiment with Capital Punishment* (1998), pp. 117–135.

—— 'Symposium. Restructuring Federal Courts: Habeas: Elected Judges and the Death Penalty in Texas. Why Full Habeas Corpus Review by Independent Federal Judges is Indispensable to Protecting Constitutional Rights', *Texas Law Review* 78 (2000), pp. 1805–1837.

BRITISH MEDICAL ASSOCIATION, *Medicine Betrayed: The Participation of Doctors in Human Rights Abuses*, Report of a Working Party (1992), London: Zed Books.

BRODSKY, S. L., 'Professional Ethics and Professional Morality in the Assessment of Competence for Execution: A Response to Bonnie', *Law and Human Behavior* 14 (1990), pp. 91–97.

BROOK, L. and CAPE, E., 'Libertarianism in Retreat', in R. Jowell, J. Curtis, A. Park, L. Brook, and D. Ahrendt (eds), *British Social Attitudes: The 12th Report* Social and Community Planning Research (1995), Aldershot: Dartmouth Publishing, pp. 191–209.

BURNS, G. B., 'The Right to Effective Assistance of a Psychiatrist under *Ake* v. *Oklahoma*', *Criminal Law Bulletin* 30 (1994), pp. 429–457.

BUTLER, R., 'Dying for Counsel', *New Law Journal* 144 (1994), pp. 1743–1745.

BYERS, K. A., 'Incompetency, Execution, and the Use of Antipsychotic Drugs', *Arkansas Law Review* 47 (1994), pp. 361–391.

CALABRESI, S. G., and LAWSON, G., 'Equity and Hierarchy: Reflections on the Harris Execution', *Yale Law Journal* 102 (1992), pp. 255–279.

CALLANS, P. J., 'Sixth Amendment: Assembling a Jury Willing to Impose the Death Penalty: A New Disregard for a Capital Defendant's Rights', *Journal of Criminal Law and Criminology* 76 (1985), pp. 1027–1050.

CALVERT, E. R., *Capital Punishment in the Twentieth Century* (5th edn. 1972), London: Putnam.

CAMINKER, E., and CHEMERINSKY, E., 'The Lawless Execution of Robert Alton Harris', *Yale Law Journal* 102 (1992), pp. 225–254.

CANADA, *A Graphical Overview of Crime and the Administration of Criminal Justice in Canada 1998* (2000), Ottawa: Ministry of Industry.

CANTOR, D., and COHEN, L. E., 'Comparing Measures of Homicide Trends: Methodological and Substantive Differences in the Vital Statistics and Uniform Crime Report Time-Series (1933–1975)', *Social Science Research* 9 (1980), pp. 121–145.

CARROLL, J. E., Note, 'Images of Women and Capital Sentencing among Female Offenders: Exploring the Outer Limits of the Eighth Amendment and Articulated Theories of Justice', *Texas Law Review* 75 (1997), pp. 1413–1451.

CASCELLS, W., CURRAN, W. J., and HYG, S. M., 'Doctors, the Death Penalty and Lethal Injections', *New England Journal of Medicine* 307 (1982), pp. 1532–1533.

CERNA, C. M., 'The Death Penalty and the Jurisprudence of the Inter-American System for the Protection of Human Rights', Paper presented to the Conference on the Death Penalty, University of Galway, Sept. 2001.

CHEN GUANGZHONG, 'On the System of Death Sentences with Two Year Suspension of Execution in China's Legal System of Criminal Justice', *Study of Law* 4 (1986), pp. 59–64.

CHEN XINLIANG, 'The Implementation of the Death Penalty', in Chen Guangzhong (ed), *The*

Death Penalty in the United Nations Standards and China's Legal System of Criminal Justice (1998), Beijing: Legal Publishing House, ch. 18.

CHIROUF, L., 'Defying World Trends: Saudi Arabia's Extensive Use of Capital Punishment', Paper presented to the 1st World Congress against the Death Penalty, Strasbourg, 21–3 June 2001.

CHRISTOPH, J. B., *Capital Punishment and British Politics* (1962), London: Allen & Unwin.

COCHRAN, J. K., CHAMLIN, M. B., and SETH, M., 'Deterrence or Brutalization? An Impact Assessment of Oklahoma's Return to Capital Punishment', *Criminology* 32 (1994), pp. 107–134.

COHEN, J., *The Criminal Process in the People's Republic of China 1949–1963*, Cambridge, Mass.: Harvard University Press.

Columbia Law Review, Note, 'Distinguishing among Murders when Assessing the Proportionality of the Death Penalty' 85 (1985), pp. 1786–1807.

CONSTANZO, M., and CONSTANZO, S., 'Jury Decision Making in the Capital Penalty Phase: Legal Assumptions, Empirical Findings, and a Research Agenda', *Law and Human Behavior* 16 (1992), pp. 185–201.

COOK, P. J., and SLAWSON, D. B., *The Cost of Processing Murder Cases in North Carolina* (May 1993), Durham, NC: Terry Stanford Institute of Public Policy, Duke University.

COPELAND, R., Comment, 'Getting it Right from the Beginning: A Critical Examination of Current Criminal Defense in Texas and Proposal for a Statewide Public Defender System', *St. Mary's Law Journal* 32 (2001), pp. 493–540.

COUNCIL OF EUROPE, *The Abolition of the Death Penalty: Answers to Questionnaires*, Report of the Committee on Legal Affairs and Human Rights of the Parliamentary Assembly of the Council of Europe (1994), Strasbourg.

—— *The Death Penalty: Abolition in Europe* (1999), Strasbourg: Council of Europe Publishing.

CULLEN, F., FISHER, B. S., and APPLEGATE, B., 'Public Opinion about Punishment and Corrections', in M. Tonry (ed), *Crime and Justice: A Review of Research*, vol. 27 (2000), Chicago: Chicago University Press, 1–79.

CURRAN, W. J., and CASCELLS, W., 'The Ethics of Medical Participation in Capital Punishment by Intravenous Drug Injection', *New England Journal of Medicine* 302 (1980), pp. 226–230.

—— and HYG, S. M., 'Psychiatric Evaluations and Mitigating Circumstances in Capital Punishment Sentencing', *New England Journal of Medicine* 307 (1982), pp. 1431–1432.

DANDO, S., *Shikei Haishi-ron (On Abolishing the Death Penalty)* (4th edn 1995), Tokyo: Yūhikeku.

DAVIS, M., *Justice in the Shadow of Death: Rethinking Capital and Lesser Punishments* (1996), Lanham, Md.: Rowman & Littlefield.

DEATH PENALTY INFORMATION CENTER, *Innocence and the Death Penalty: Assessing the Dangers of Mistaken Executions* (1993), Washington.

—— *Sentencing for Life: Americans Embrace Alternatives to the Death Penalty* (1993), Washington, D.C.

—— *Millions Misspent: What Politicians Don't Say About the High Cost of the Death Penalty* (rev. May 1994), Washington.

—— *The Future of the Death Penalty in the U.S.: A Texas-Sized Crisis* (1994), Washington.

—— *Mental Retardation and the Death Penalty*, www.deathpenaltyinfo.org/topics.htm

DECKER, S. H., and KOHFELD, C. W., 'A Deterrence Study of the Death Penalty in Illinois, 1933–1980', *Journal of Criminal Justice* 12 (1984), pp. 367–377.

DEITCHMAN, M. A., KENNEDY, W. A., and BECKHAM, J. C., 'Self-Selection Factors in the Participation of Mental Health Professionals in Competency for Execution Evaluations', *Law and Human Behavior* 15 (1990), pp. 287–303.

DENNO, D. W., 'Is Electrocution an Unconstitutional Method of Execution? The Engineering of Death over a Century', *William and Mary Law Review* 35 (1994), pp. 551–692.

—— 'Testing *Penry* and its Progeny', *American Journal of Criminal Law* 22 (1994), pp. 1–75.

—— 'Getting to Death: Are Executions Constitutional?', *Iowa Law Review* 82 (1997), pp. 319–417.

—— 'Execution and the Forgotten Eighth Amendment', in J. R. Acker, R. M. Bohm, and C. S. Lanier (eds), *America's Experiment with Capital Punishment* (1998), pp. 547–577.

—— 'Adieu to Electrocution', *Ohio Northern University Law Review* 26 (2000), pp. 655–688.

—— 'When Legislatures Delegate Death: The Troubling Paradox behind State Uses of Electrocution and Lethal Injection and what it Says about Us', *Ohio State Law Journal* 63 (2002), pp. 63–260.

DIETER, R., 'The Death Penalty is not an Effective Law Enforcement Tool', repr. in D. L. Bender and B. Leone *et al.* (eds), *Does Capital Punishment Deter Crime?* (1998), pp. 22–38.

DIKE, S. T., *Capital Punishment in the United States: A Consideration of the Evidence*, (1982) Hackensack, NJ: National Counsel on Crime and Delinquency.

DIX, G. E., 'Appellate Review of the Decision to Impose Death', *Georgetown Law Journal* 68 (1979), pp. 97–161.

—— 'Expert Prediction Testimony in Capital Sentencing: Evidentiary and Constitutional Questions', *American Criminal Law Review* 19 (1981), pp. 1–48.

—— 'Psychological Abnormality and Capital Sentencing: The New "Diminished Responsibility".' *International Journal of Law and Psychiatry* 7 (1984), pp. 249–267.

DREWRY, G., 'The Politics of Capital Punishment', in G. Drewry and C. Blake (eds), *Law and the Spirit of Inquiry* (1999), The Hague: Kluwer Law International, pp. 137–159.

DUMBUTSHENA, E., 'The Death Penalty in Zimbabwe', *Revue Internationale de Droit Pénal* 58 (1987), pp. 521–532.

DURHAM, A. M., ELROD, H. P., and KINKADE, P. T., 'Public Support for the Death Penalty: Beyond Gallup', *Justice Quarterly* 13 (1996), pp. 705–736.

EDWARDS, W. J., 'Capital Punishment and Mental Disability: *Amici Curiae* Brief in *Penry v. Johnson*', *Criminal Law Forum* 12 (2001), pp. 267–276.

EHRLICH, I. 'The Deterrent Effect of Capital Punishment: A Question of Life and Death', *American Economic Review* 65 (1975), pp. 397–417.

——'Deterrence: Evidence and Inference', *Yale Law Journal* 85 (1975), pp. 2089–27.

—— 'Capital Punishment and Deterrence: Some Further Thoughts and Additional Evidence', *Journal of Political Economy* 85 (1977), pp. 741–788.

—— 'On Positive Methodology, Ethics, and Polemics in Deterrence Research', *British Journal of Criminology* 22 (1982), pp. 124–139.

ELLIOTT, R., 'Social Science Data and the APA (American Psychology Association): The *Lockhart* Brief as a Case in Point', *Law and Human Behavior* 15 (1991), pp. 59–76.

ELLSWORTH, P. C., 'To Tell what we Know or Wait for Godot?', *Law and Human Behavior* 15 (1991), pp. 77–90.

—— and GROSS, S. R., 'Hardening of Attitudes: Americans' Views on the Death Penalty', in

H. A. Bedau (ed), *The Death Penalty in America: Current Controversies* (1997), pp. 90–115. Also in *Journal of Social Issues* 50 (Summer 1994), pp. 19–25.

—— Ross, L., 'Public Opinion and Capital Punishment: A Close Examination of the Views of Abolitionists and Retentionist', *Crime and Delinquency* 29 (1983), pp. 116–169.

ELMAN, L., Jr., Note, 'Peremptory Challenges under *Batson* v. *Kentucky:* Equal Protection under the Law or an Unequal Application of the Law', *Criminal and Civil Confinement* 20 (1994), pp. 481–538.

EVANS, G. L., '*Perry* v. *Louisiana* (1990): Can a State Treat an Incompetent Prisoner to Ready him for Execution?', *Bulletin of the American Academy of Psychiatry and Law* 19 (1991), pp. 249–270.

EVANS, R. J., *Rituals of Retribution: Capital Punishment in Germany 1600–1987* (1996), Oxford: Oxford University Press.

EWING, C. E,. ' "Dr Death" and the Case for an Ethical Ban on Psychiatric and Psychological Predictions of Dangerousness in Capital Sentencing Proceedings', *American Journal of Law and Medicine* 8 (1983), pp. 407–428.

EWING, C. P., 'Preventive Detention and Execution: The Constitutionality of Punishing Future Crimes', *Law and Human Behavior* 15 (1991), pp. 139–163.

—— ' "Above all Do No Harm": The Role of Health and Mental Health Professionals in the Capital Punishment Process', in J. R. Acker, R. M. Bohm, and C. S. Lanier (eds), *America's Experiment with Capital Punishment* (1998), pp. 431–476.

FARBER, N. J., ABOFF, B. M., WEINER, J., DAVIS, E. B., BOYER, E. G., and UBEL, P. A, 'Physicians' Willingness to Participate in the Process of Lethal Injection for Capital Punishment', *Annals of International Medicine*, 135(10) (2001), pp. 884–888.

FATTAH, E. A., *A Study of the Deterrent Effects of Capital Punishment with Special Reference to the Canadian Situation* (1972), Canada: Department of the Solicitor General.

—— 'Perceptions of Violence, Concern about Crime, Fear of Victimization and Attitudes to the Death Penalty', *Canadian Journal of Criminology* 21 (1979), pp. 22–38.

—— 'Canada's Successful Experience with the Abolition of the Death Penalty', *Canadian Journal of Criminology* 25 (1987), pp. 421–431.

—— 'The Use of the Death Penalty for Drug Offences and for Economic Crime', *Revue Internationale de Droit Pénal* 58 (1987), pp. 723–736.

FAUST, R., RUBINSTEIN, T. J., and YACKLE, L. W., 'The Great Writ in Action: Empirical Light on the Federal Habeas Corpus Debate', *New York University Review of Law and Social Change* 18 (1990–1), pp. 637–710.

FELDMAN, M., MALLOUH, K. and LEWIS, D. O., 'Filicidal Abuse in the Histories of 15 Condemned Murderers', *Bulletin of the American Academy of Psychiatry and Law* 14 (1986), pp. 345–352.

FELTOE, G., 'Extenuating Circumstances: A Life and Death Issue', *Zimbabwe Law Review* 4 (1987), pp. 60–87.

FINCH, M., and FERRARO, M., 'The Empirical Challenge to Death Qualified Jurors: On Further Examination', *Nebraska Law Review* 65 (1986), pp. 21–74.

FINKS, T. O., 'Lethal Injection: An Uneasy Alliance of Law and Medicine', *Journal of Legal Medicine* 4 (1983), pp. 383–403.

FITZGERALD, E., 'The Commonwealth Caribbean', in P. Hodgkinson and A. Rutherford (eds), *Capital Punishment: Global Issues and Prospects* (1996), pp. 143–153.

—— 'Savings Clauses and the Colonial Death Penalty Regime', in Prison Reform International *et al.*, *Commonwealth Caribbean Human Rights Seminar*, 12–14 Sept. 2000 (2001), Paris: Penal Reform International, pp. 113–126.

FITZPATRICK, J., and MILLER, A., 'International Standards on the Death Penalty: Shifting Discourse', *Brooklyn Journal of International Law* 19 (1993), pp. 273–366.

FITZSIMMONS, C. A., '*Whitmore* v. *Arkansas*: Execution of an Individual, without a Prior Mandatory Appellate Review, Denied Scrutiny', *Criminal and Civil Confinement* 18 (1992), pp. 203–229.

FOLEY, L. A., and POWELL, R. S., 'The Discretion of Prosecutors, Judges, and Juries in Capital Cases', *Criminal Justice Review* 7 (1982), pp. 10–22.

FOLEY, T. J., 'The New Arbitrariness: Procedural Default in Federal Habeas Claims in Capital Cases', *Loyola of Los Angeles Law Review* 23 (1989), pp. 193–212.

FORST, B. E., 'The Deterrent Effect of Capital Punishment: Cross-Sectional Analysis of the 1960s', *Minnesota Law Review* 61 (1977), pp. 743–767.

—— 'Capital Punishment and Deterrence: Conflicting Evidence', *Journal of Criminal Law and Criminology* 74 (1983), pp. 927–942.

FOX, J. A., and RADELET, M. L., 'Persistent Flaws in Econometric Studies of the Deterrent Effect of the Death Penalty', *Loyola of Los Angeles Law Review* 23 (1989), pp. 29–44.

—— —— and BONSTEEL, J. L., 'Death Penalty Opinion in the Post-*Furman* Years', *New York University Review of Law and Social Change* 18 (1990–1), pp. 499–528.

FREE LEGAL ASSISTANCE GROUP (FLAG), 'Position Paper on the Death Penalty Bills', *Flag Newsletter*, Dec. 2001, Quezon City, Philippines.

FREEMAN, J. A., *Murder and Economics: A Literature Review* (1993), Department of Economics, University of Leicester.

GAO MING XUAN, *The Main Idea in General Provisions of the Criminal Law*, (in Chinese) (1986), Tianjin.

—— 'A Brief Dissertation on the Death Penalty in the Criminal Law of the People's Republic of China', *Revue Internationale de Droit Pénal* 58 (1987), pp. 399–405.

GARLAND, D., 'The Cultural Conditions of Capital Punishment', *Punishment and Society* 4 (2002).

GARVEY, S. P., JOHNSON, S. L., and MARCUS, P., 'Correcting Deadly Confusion: Responding to Jury Inquiries in Capital Cases', *Cornell Law Review* 85 (2000), pp. 627–651.

GAYLORD, M., and GALLIHER, J. F., 'Death Penalty Politics and Symbolic Law in Hong Kong', *Howard Journal of Criminal Justice* 33 (1994), pp. 19–37.

GEWIRTH, K. E., and DORNE, C. K., 'Imposing the Death Penalty on Juvenile Murderers: A Constitutional Assessment', *Judicature* 75(1) (1991), pp. 6–15.

GILLERS, S., 'The Quality of Mercy: Constitutional Accuracy at the Selection Stage of Capital Sentencing', *University of California, Davis, Law Review* 18 (1985), pp. 1037–1111.

GODFREY, M. J., and SHIRALDI, V., 'The Death Penalty may Increase Homicide Rates', repr. in D. L. Bender *et al.* (eds), *Does Capital Punishment Deter Crime?* (1999), pp. 47–52.

GOLDSTEIN, S. M., 'Chipping away at the Great Writ: Will Death Sentenced Federal Habeas Corpus Petitioners be Able to Seek and Utilise Changes in the Law?' *New York University Review of Law and Social Change* 18 (1990–1), pp. 357–414.

GOODMAN, D. S., 'Demographic Evidence in Capital Sentencing', *Stanford Law Review* 39 (1987), pp. 499–543.

GREEN, K. A., 'Statistics and the Death Penalty: A Break with Tradition', *Creighton Law Review* 21 (1987), pp. 265–301.

GREENBERG, D. F., and WEST, V., 'Siting the Death Penalty Internationally', Paper presented to the Annual Meeting of the Law and Society Association, Budapest, July 2001.

GREENBERG, J., 'Capital Punishment as a System', *Yale Law Journal* 91 (1982), pp. 908–936.

GROSS, S. R., 'Determining the Neutrality of Death Qualified Juries', *Law and Human Behavior* 8 (1984), pp. 7–29.

—— 'Race and Death: The Judicial Evaluation of Evidence of Discrimination in Capital Sentencing', *University of California, Davis, Law Review* 18 (1985), pp. 1275–1325.

—— 'Lost Lives: Miscarriages of Justice in Capital Cases', *Law and Contemporary Problems* 61 (1998), pp. 125–152.

—— 'Update: American Public Opinion on the Death Penalty—It's Getting Personal', *Cornell Law Review* 83 (1998), pp. 1448–1475.

—— and MAURO, R., 'Patterns of Death: An Analysis of Racial Disparities in Capital Sentencing and Homicide Victimization', *Stanford Law Review* 37 (1984), pp. 27–153.

—— —— *Death and Discrimination: Racial Disparities in Capital Sentencing* (1989), Boston: Northeastern University Press.

GRZESKOWIAK, A., 'Capital Punishment in Polish Penal Law', *United Nations Crime Prevention and Criminal Justice Newsletter* 12 and 13 (1986), pp. 43–46.

GUPTA, S.C., *Capital Punishment in India* (1986), New Delhi: Deep & Deep Publications.

HAAS, K. C., and INCIARDI, J. A. (eds), *Challenging Capital Punishment* (1988), Newbury Park: Sage.

—— —— 'Lingering Doubts about Capital Punishment', in K. C. Haas and J. A. Inciardi (eds), *Challenging Capital Punishment* (1988), pp. 11–28.

HAINES, H. H., *Against Capital Punishment. The Anti-Death Penalty Movement in America, 1972–1994* (1996), New York: Oxford University Press.

HALE, R. L., *A Review of Juvenile Executions in America*, Criminology Studies 3 (1997), Lewiston, NY: Edwin Mellen Press.

HANDS OFF CAIN, *Towards Abolition: The Law and Politics of the Death Penalty* (1998), Rome: Associazione Mariateresa Di Lascia.

HARDING, R. M., ' "Endgame": Competency and the Execution of Condemned Inmates—A Proposal to Satisfy the Eighth Amendment's Prohibition against the Infliction of Cruel and Unusual Punishment', *Saint Louis University Public Law Review* 14 (1994), pp. 105–152.

HATCHARD, J., and COLDHAM, S., 'Commonwealth Africa', in P. Hodgkinson and A. Rutherford (eds), *Capital Punishment: Global Issues and Prospects* (1996), pp. 155–191.

HAUCK, B., HENDRICKSON, C., and YOSLOV, Z., 'Symposium. The Death Penalty Debate: Capital Punishment Legislation in Massachusetts', *Harvard Journal on Legislation* 36 (1999), pp. 479–503.

HEILBRUN, A. B., Jr., FOSTER, A., and GOLDEN, J., 'The Death Sentence in Georgia 1947–1987: Criminal Justice or Racial Injustice', *Criminal Justice and Behavior* 16 (1989), pp. 139–153.

HERMAN, S. N., 'Why the Court Loves *Batson*: Representation-Reinforcement, Colorblindness and the Jury', *Criminal and Civil Confinement* 20 (1994), pp. 1807–1853.

HILLMAN, H., 'The Possible Pain Experienced during Execution by Different Methods', *Perception* 22 (1993), pp. 745–753.

HINSON, K,. 'Post-Conviction Determination of Innocence for Death Row Inmates', *SMU Law Review* 48 (1994), pp. 231–261.

HODGKINSON, P., and RUTHERFORD, A. (eds), *Capital Punishment: Global Issues and Prospects* (1996), Winchester: Waterside Press.

HOFFMAN, L. J., Note, 'The Madness of the Method: The Use of Electrocution and the Death Penalty', *Texas Law Review* 70 (1992), pp. 1039–1062.

—— 'Justice Dando and the "Conservative" Argument for Abolition', *Indiana Law Review* 72 (1996), pp. 21–24.

HOLLAND, N., 'Death Row Conditions: Progression toward Constitutional Protections', *Akron Law Review* 2 (1985), pp. 293–310.

HOLOVATIY, S., 'Abolishing the Death Penalty in Ukraine: Difficulties Real or Imagined?' Council of Europe, in *The Death Penalty: Abolition in Europe* (1999), Strasbourg: Council of Europe Publishing, pp. 139–151.

HOOD, R., 'Capital Punishment', in M. Tonry (ed), *The Handbook of Criminology* (1998), New York: Oxford University Press, pp. 739–776.

—— 'The Value of Statistical Returns and Empirical Research in Discussions on the Death Penalty', Paper presented to the EU–China Human Rights Seminar, Beijing, 11–12 May 2001.

HORVATH, T., 'L'Abolition de la peine de mort en Hongrie', *Revue Internationale de Criminologie et de Police Technique* 2 (1992), pp. 167–179.

HOSNI, N., 'La Peine de mort en droit égyptien et en droit islamique', *Revue Internationale de Droit Pénal* 58 (1987), pp. 407–420.

Howard Law Journal, Note, 'Safeguarding Eighth Amendment Rights with a Comparative Proportionality Review in the Imposition of the Death Penalty, *Pulley* v. *Harris*' 28 (1985), pp. 331–333.

HU YUNTENG, 'On the Death Penalty at the Turning of the Century', in M. Nowak and Xin. Chunying (eds), *EU–China Human Rights Dialogue* (2000), pp. 88–94.

ILLINOIS, *Report of the Governor's Commission on Capital Punishment: George H. Ryan Governor* (Apr. 2002).

INTERNATIONAL COMMISSION OF JURISTS, *Administration of the Death Penalty in the United States* (1996), Geneva.

JACKSON, B., and CHRISTIAN, D., *Death Row* (1980), Boston: Beacon Press.

JACOBY, J. E., and PATERNOSTER, R,. 'Sentencing Disparity and Jury Packing: Further Challenges to the Death Penalty', *Journal of Criminal Law and Criminology* 73 (1982), pp. 379–387.

JAPAN, *National Statement on Crime Prevention for Freedom, Justice, Peace and Development* (1985).

JEFFRIES, J. C., Jr., *Justice Lewis F. Powell, Jr.: A Biography* (1994), University of Virginia Press; New York: C. Scribners & Sons.

JOHNSON, R., 'Under Sentence of Death: The Psychology of Death Row Confinement', *Law and Psychology Review* 5 (1979), pp. 141–158.

—— *Condemned to Die: Life under Sentence of Death* (1981), Prospect Heights, Ill.: Waveland Press.

—— 'Institutions and the Promotion of Violence', in A. Campbell and J. J. Gibbs (eds), *Violent Transactions* (1986), Oxford: Blackwell, pp. 181–205.

—— *Death Work: A Study of the Modern Execution Process* (2nd edn 1998), Belmont, Calif.: Wadsworth Publishing.

—— 'Life under Sentence of Death: Historical and Contemporary Perspectives', in J. R. Acker, R. M. Bohm, and C. S. Lanier (eds), *America's Experiment with Capital Punishment* (1998), pp. 507–529.

—— and CARROLL, J. L., 'Litigating Death-Row Conditions, the Case for Reform', in I. P. Robbins (ed), *Prisoners and the Law* (1985), pp. 8–15.

JOWELL, R., CURTICE, J., PARK, A., and THOMSON, K., *British Social Attitudes: Who Shares New Labour Values? The 16th Report* (1999), Aldershot: Ashgate Publishing.

JÜRGENSEN, C., 'Egypt: Death Penalty after Unfair Trials' (2001), Paper presented to the 1st World Congress against the Death Penalty, Strasbourg, 21–3 June 2001.

KAHNEMAN, D., SLOVIC, P., and TVERSKY, A. (eds), *Judgment under Uncertainty: Heuristics and Biases* (1982), Cambridge: Cambridge University Press.

KAINE, T., 'Capital Punishment and the Waiver of Sentence Review', *Harvard Civil Rights— Civil Liberties Law Review* 18 (1983), pp. 483–524.

KAISER, G., 'Capital Punishment in a Criminological Perspective', *United Nations Crime Prevention Criminal Justice Newsletter* 12 and 13 (1986), pp. 10–18.

KAPLAN, J., 'Administering Capital Punishment', *University of Florida Law Review* 36 (1984), pp. 177–192.

KATO, WARREN M., Note and Comment, 'The Juvenile Death Penalty', *Journal of Juvenile Law* 18 (1997), pp. 112–149.

KEATING, J., 'Out of Sight, Out of Mind', *Amicus Journal* 3 (2001), pp. 15–19.

KEIL, T. J., and VITO, G. F., 'Kentucky Prosecutor's Decision to Seek the Death, Penalty: A LISREL Approach', in R. M. Bohm (ed), *The Death Penalty in America: Current Research* (1991), pp. 53–68.

KEYES, D., EDWARDS, W. and PERSKE, R. 'People with Mental Retardation are Dying, Legally at least 44 have been Executed,' *Journal of Mental Retardation* 40(3) (2002), pp. 243–244..

KILLINGLEY, J., 'Note on *Shafer* v. *South Carolina*', *Amicus Journal* 3 (2001), pp. 20–21.

KING, A., 'Legal Aid and Access to Justice', in Penal Reform International *et al.*, *Commonwealth Caribbean Human Rights Seminar*, 12–14 Sept. 2000 (2001), London, pp. 49–59.

KIRCHMEIER, J. L., 'Another Place beyond Here: The Death Penalty Moratorium Movement in the United States', *University of Colorado Law Review* 73 (2002), pp. 2–116.

KIRKPATRICK, J., 'The Relevance of Customary International Norms to the Death Penalty in the United States', *Georgia Journal of International and Comparative Law* 25 (1995), pp. 1–16.

KLECK, G. 'Capital Punishment, Gun Ownership, and Homicide', *American Journal of Sociology* 84 (1979), pp. 882–908.

—— 'Racial Discrimination in Criminal Sentencing', *American Sociological Review* 46 (1981), pp. 783–805.

KLEIN, L. R., FORST, B., and FILATOV, V., 'The Deterrent Effect of Capital Punishment: An Assessment of the Evidence', in A. Blumstein, J. Cohen, and D. Nagin (eds), *Deterrence and Incapacitation* (1978), pp. 336–360.

KNISKERN, E. M., 'Does *Ford* v. *Wainwright*'s Denial of Executions of the Insane Prohibit the State from Carrying out its Criminal Justice System?', *Southern University Law Review* 26 (1999), pp. 171–195.

KOBIL, D. T., 'The Evolving Role of Clemency in Capital Cases', in J. A. Acker, R. M. Bohm, and C. S. Lanier (eds), *America's Experiment with Capital Punishment* (1998), pp. 531–546.

KOH, H. H., 'Paying "Decent Respect" to World Opinion on the Death Penalty', *UC Davis Law Review* 35 (2002), pp. 1085–1131.

KRIEGER, J., *The Oxford Companion to Politics of the World* (2001), New York: Oxford University Press.

KRÜGER, H. C., 'Protocol No. 6 to the European Convention on Human Rights', in Council of Europe, *The Death Penalty: Abolition in Europe* (1999), Strasbourg: Council of Europe Publishing.

LAYSON, S. A., 'Homicide and Deterrence: A Re-examination of the United States Time-Series Evidence', *Southern Economic Journal* 52 (1985), pp. 68–69.
—— 'United States Time-Series Homicide Regressions with Adaptive Expectations', *Bulletin of the New York Academy of Medicine* 62 (1986), pp. 589–600.
—— *Statement of Professor Layson to Capital Punishment: Hearings on H.R. 2837 and H.R. 343 before the Subcommittee on Criminal Justice of the House Committee on the Judiciary, 99th Congress* (1987).
LEDEWITZ, B. L, 'The New Role of Statutory Aggravating Circumstances in American Death Penalty Law', *Duquesne Law Review* 22 (1984), pp. 317–396.
—— 'Sources of Injustice in Death Penalty Practice: The Pennsylvania Experience', *Dickinson Law Review* 95 (1991), pp. 651–690.
LEHRFREUND, S., 'The Death Penalty and the Continuing Role of the Privy Council', *New Law Journal* 149 (1999), pp. 1299–1301.
—— 'The Commonwealth Caribbean and Evolving International Attitudes towards the Death Penalty', in Penal Reform International *et al.*, *Commonwealth Caribbean Human Rights Seminar*, Fort George Hotel, Belize City, 12–14 Sept. 2000 (2001), Paris: Penal Reform International, pp. 75–90.
—— 'International Legal Trends and the "Mandatory" Death Penalty in the Commonwealth Caribbean', *Oxford University Commonwealth Law Journal* 1 (2001), pp. 171–194.
LEMPERT, R., 'Desert and Deterrence: An Assessment of the Moral Bases of the Case for Capital Punishment', *Michigan Law Review* 79 (1981), pp. 1177–1231.
—— 'The Effect of Executions on Homicides: A New Look in an Old Light', *Crime and Delinquency* 29 (1983), pp. 88–115.
LEONE, U., 'International Bibliography on Capital Punishment', *Revue Internationale de Droit Pénal* 58 (1987), pp. 823–914.
LESSER, W., *Pictures at an Execution* (1993), London: Harvard University Press.
LEVINE, M.,'The Adversarial Process and Social Science in the Courts: *Barefoot* v. *Estelle*', *Journal of Psychiatry and Law* 12 (1984), pp. 147–181.
LEWIS, D. O., *Guilty by Reason of Insanity: A Psychiatrist Explores the Minds of Killers* (1999), London: Arrow.
—— and BARD, J. S., 'Multiple Personality and Forensic Issues', *Psychiatric Clinics of North America* 41(3) (1991), pp. 741–756.
—— PINCUS J. H., BARD, B., RICHARDSON, E., PRICHEP, L. S., FELDMAN, M., and YEAGER, C., 'Neuropsychiatric, Psychoeducational, and Family Characteristics of 14 Juveniles Condemned to Death in the United States', *American Journal of Psychiatry* 145 (1988), pp. 584–589.
—— —— FELDMAN, M., JACKSON, L., and BARD, B., 'Psychiatric, Neurological, and Psycho-educational Characteristics of 15 Death Row Inmates in the United States', *American Journal of Psychiatry* 143 (1986), pp. 838–845.
LIEBMAN, J. S., 'More than "Slightly Retro": The Rehnquist Court's Rout of Habeas Corpus Jurisdiction in *Teague* v. *Lane*', *New York University Review of Law and Social Change* 18 (1990–1), pp. 537–635.
—— FAGAN, J., WEST, V., and LLOYD, J., 'Capital Attrition: Error Rates in Capital Cases, 1973–1995', *Texas Law Review* 78 (2000), pp. 1771–1803.
—— —— GELMAN, A., WEST, V., DAVIES, G., and KISS, A,. *A Broken System, Pt. II: Why is*

There So Much Error in Capital Cases, and What Can be Done About It? (Feb. 2002), Columbia Law School Publications.

LIFTON, R. J., and MITCHELL, G., *Who Owns Death? Capital Punishment, the American Conscience, and the End of Executions* (2000),. New York: HarperCollins.

LIPPMAN, M., McCONVILLE, S., and YERUSHALMI, M., *Islamic Criminal Law and Procedure* (1988), London: Praeger.

LIU HAINAN, 'The Effect on the Capital Punishment by the Chinese Traditional Theory of the Criminal Law', in M. Nowak and Xin Chunying (eds), *EU–China Human Rights Dialogue* (2000), Vienna: Verlag Österreich, pp. 99–120.

LOMBARDI, G., SLUDER, R. L.,and WALLACE, D., 'Mainstreaming Death-Sentenced Inmates: The Missouri Experience and its Legal Significance', *Federal Probation* 61(2) (1997), 3–11.

LUGINBUHL, J., 'Comprehension of Judge's Instructions in the Penalty Phase of a Capital Trial: Focus on Mitigating Circumstances', *Law and Human Behavior* 16 (1992), pp. 203–218.

—— and HOWE, J., 'Discretion in Capital Sentencing Instructions: Guided or Misguided?', *Indiana Law Journal* 70 (1995), pp. 1161–1181.

MACKAY, R. D., 'Post-Hinckley Insanity in the USA', *Criminal Law Review* (1988), pp. 88–96.

MACKEY, S., *The Saudis: Inside the Desert Kingdom* (1987), London: Harrap.

McFARLAND, S. G., 'Is Capital Punishment a Short-Term Deterrent to Homicide? A Study of the Effects of Four Recent American Executions', *Journal of Criminal Law and Criminology* 74 (1983), pp. 1014–1032.

McMANUS, W. S.,'Estimates of the Deterrent Effect of Capital Punishment: The Importance of the Researcher's Prior Beliefs', *Journal of Political Economy* 93 (1985), pp. 417–425.

MAGEE, D., *Slow Coming Dark: Interviews on Death Row* (1982), London: Quartet.

MAILER, N., *The Executioner's Song* (1979), London: Hutchinson.

MANN, C. R., *Unequal Justice: A Question of Color* (1993), Bloomington: Indiana University Press.

MANSON, A., '*Kindler* and the Courage to Deal with American Convictions', *Criminal Reports* 8 C.R. (4th) (1991), pp. 68–81.

MARKMAN, S. J., and CASSELL, P. G., 'Protecting the Innocent: A Response to the Bedau–Radelet Study', *Stanford Law Review* 41 (1988), pp. 121–160.

MARQUART, J. W., EKLAND-OLSON, S., and SORENSEN, J. R., 'Gazing into the Crystal Ball: Can Jurors Accurately Predict Dangerousness in Capital Cases?', *Law and Society Review* 23 (1989), pp. 449–468.

—— —— —— *The Rope, the Chair, and the Needle: Capital Punishment in Texas, 1923–1990* (1994), Austin: University of Texas Press.

—— and SORENSEN, J. R., 'Institutional and Postrelease Behavior of *Furman*-Commuted Inmates in Texas', *Criminology* 26 (1988), pp. 677–693.

MARSHALL, L. C., 'In Spite of Meese', *Journal of Criminal Law and Criminology* 85 (1994), pp. 261–280.

MARSHALL, T. R., 'Public Opinion and the Rehnquist Court', *Judicature* 74 (6) (1991), pp. 322–329.

MELLO, M., and PERKINS, P. J., 'Closing the Circle: The Illusion of Lawyers for People Litigating for their Lives at the Fin de Siècle', in J. R. Acker, R. M. Bohm, and C. S. Lanier (eds), *America's Experiment with Capital Punishment* (1998), pp. 245–284.

MELTSNER, M., *Cruel and Unusual: The Supreme Court and Capital Punishment* (1973), New York: Random House.

MIHALIK, J., 'The Death Penalty in Bophuthatswana: A New Deal for Condemned Prisoners?', *South African Law Journal* 107 (1990), pp. 465–489.

MIKLAU, R., 'The Death Penalty: A Decisive Question', *United Nations Crime Prevention and Criminal Justice Newsletter* 12 and 13 (1986), pp. 39–42.

MIKHLIN, A. S., *The Death Penalty in Russia* (1999), London: Simmonds & Hill and Kluwer Law International.

MILLER, K. S., and RADELET, M. L., *Executing the Mentally Ill: The Criminal Justice System and the Case of Alvin Ford* (1993), London: Sage.

MILLER, R. D., 'Evaluation of and Treatment to Competency to be Executed: A National Survey and an Analysis', *Journal of Psychiatry and Law* (Spring 1988), pp. 67–90.

MISHAN, E. J., 'The Lingering Debate on Capital Punishment', *Encounter* (Feb. 1988), pp. 61–75.

MITRA, N. L., 'Capital Punishment in the Indian Sub-continent', *Revue Internationale de Droit Pénal* 58 (1987), pp. 451–474.

MOCAN, H. N., and GITTINGS, R. K, 'Pardons, Executions and Homicide', unpub. paper, University of Colorado at Denver, Department of Economics.

MOHRENSCHLAGER, M., 'The Abolition of Capital Punishment in the Federal Republic of Germany: The German Experience', *Revue Internationale de Droit Pénal* 58 (1987), pp. 509–519.

MOLDRICH, D., *Hangman—Spare that Noose* (1983), Colombo: D. Moldrich.

MONTHY, J.T., Comment, 'Internal Perspectives on Chinese Human Rights Reform: The Death Penalty in the PRC', *Texas International Law Journal* 33 (1998), pp. 189–212.

MOSSMAN, D., 'Assessing and Restoring Competency to be Executed: Should Psychiatrists Participate?', *Behavioral Sciences and the Law* 5 (1987), pp. 397–405.

—— 'The Psychiatrist and Execution Competency: Fording Murky Ethical Waters', *Case Western Law Review* 43 (1992), pp. 1–95.

MOURAD, FAROUK ABDUL RAHMAN, 'Effect of the Implementation of the Islamic Legislation on Crime Prevention in the Kingdom of Saudi Arabia: A Field Research', in *The Effects of Islamic Legislation in Crime Prevention in Saudi Arabia* (1980), Rome: UNSDRI pp. 494–567.

MURPHY, E. L., 'Application of the Death Penalty in Cook County', *Illinois Bar Journal* (Oct. 1984), pp. 90–95.

NAKELL, B., and HARDY, K. A., *The Arbitrariness of the Death Penalty* (1987), Philadelphia: Temple University Press.

NATHANSON, S., 'Does it Matter if the Death Penalty is Arbitrarily Administered?', *Philosophy and Public Affairs* 14 (1985), pp. 149–164.

NATIONAL COALITION TO ABOLISH THE DEATH PENALTY, *Survey of State Legislation*, (annual), Washington.

NAUDE, B., *Criminal Justice and the Death Penalty in South Africa: A Criminological Study* (1992), Pretoria Institute of Criminology, mimeo.

NESBIT, C. A., 'Managing Death Row', *Corrections Today* (July 1986), pp. 90–106.

—— HOWARD, P. L., and WALLACE, S. M., *Managing Death-Sentenced Inmates: A Survey of Practices* (1989), Washington: American Correctional Association.

NIRMAL, C. J. (ed), *Human Rights in India,: Historical, Social and Political Perspectives* (1999), Oxford: Oxford University Press.

NOWAK, M., 'Is the Death Penalty an Inhuman Punishment?', in T. S. Orlin, A. Rossas, and M. Scheinin (eds), *The Jurisprudence of Human Rights Law: A Comparative Interpretive Approach* (2000), Abo Akademi University Institute of Human Rights, pp. 27–45.

—— and XIN CHUNYING (eds), *EU–China Human Rights Dialogue: Proceedings of the Second EU–China Legal Experts Seminar Held in Beijing on 19 and 20 October 1998* (2000), Studienreihe des Ludwig Boltzmann Instituts für Menschenrechte, vol. iv., Vienna: Verlag Österreich.

NSEREKO D. D. N., and GLICKMAN, M. J. A., 'Capital Punishment in Botswana', *United Nations Crime Prevention and Criminal Justice Newsletter* 12 and 13 (1986), pp. 51–53.

OFFICER, J. (ed), *If I should die . . . A Death Row Correspondence* (1999), Cheltenham: New Clarion Press.

OLMESDAHL, M. C. J., 'Predicting the Death Sentence', *South African Journal of Criminal Law and Criminology* 6 (1982), pp. 201–218.

ORGANIZATION FOR SECURITY AND COOPERATION IN EUROPE (OSCE), *The Death Penalty in the OSCE Area: A Survey, January 1998–June 1999*, Review Conference, Sept. 1999, Office of Democratic Institutions and Human Rights, OD/HR Background Paper 1999/1 (1999), Warsaw: OSCE/ODIHR.

O'SHEA, K. A., *Women and the Death Penalty in the United States, 1990–1998* (1999), London: Praeger.

PALMER, M., 'The People's Republic of China', in P. Hodgkinson and A. Rutherford (eds), *Capital Punishment: Global Issues and Prospects* (1996), pp. 105–141.

PANNICK, D., *Judicial Review of the Death Penalty* (1982), White Plains, NY: Sheridan.

PASSELL, P., 'The Deterrent Effect of the Death Penalty: A Statistical Test', *Stanford Law Review* 28 (1975), pp. 61–80.

—— and TAYLOR, J. B., 'The Deterrence Controversy: A Reconsideration of the Time-Series Evidence', in H. Bedau and C. M. Pierce (eds), *Capital Punishment in the United States* (1976), pp. 359–371.

PASTORE, A. L., and MAGUIRE, K., (eds), *Sourcebook of Criminal Justice Statistics—1999* (2000), Washington: US Department of Justice.

PATAKI, G. E. (Governor of New York State), 'The Death Penalty as a Deterrent', repr. in David L. Bender *et al.* (eds), *Does Capital Punishment Deter Crime?* (1998), pp. 10–13.

PATERNOSTER, R., 'Race of Victim and Location of Crime: The Decision to Seek the Death Penalty in South Carolina', *Journal of Criminal Law and Criminology* 74 (1983), pp. 754–785.

—— 'Prosecutorial Discretion in Requesting the Death Penalty: A Case of Victim-Based Racial Discrimination', *Law and Society Review* 18 (1984), pp. 437–478.

—— 'Prosecutorial Discretion and Capital Sentencing in North and South Carolina', in R. M. Bohm (ed), *The Death Penalty in America: Current Research* (1991), pp. 39–52.

—— 'Assessing Capriciousness in Capital Cases', *Law and Society Review* 27 (1993), pp. 111–123.

PETERSON, R. D., and BAILEY, W. C., 'Is Capital Punishment an Effective Deterrent for Murder? An Examination of Social Science Research', in J. R Acker, R. M. Bohm, and C. S. Lanier (eds), *America's Experiment with Capital Punishment* (1998), pp. 157–182.

PHILLIPS, D. P., 'The Deterrent Effect of Capital Punishment: New Evidence on an Old Controversy', *American Journal of Sociology* 86 (1980), pp. 139–148.

—— 'Strong and Weak Research Designs for Detecting the Impact of Capital Punishment on Homicide', *Rutgers Law Review* 33 (1981), pp. 790–798.

—— and HENSLEY, J. E., 'When Violence is Rewarded or Punished: The Impact of Mass Media Stories on Homicide', *Journal of Communications* (Summer 1984), pp. 101–116.

PHILLIPS, R. T. M., 'Professionalism, Mental Disability, and the Death Penalty: The Psychiatrist as Evaluator: Conflicts and Conscience', *New York Law School Review* 41 (1996), pp. 189–199.

PICCA, G., 'La Peine de mort: Un problème politique et social', *Revue Internationale de Droit Pénal* 68 (1987), pp. 435–450.

PIERCE, G. R., and RADELET, M. L., 'Race, Region, and Death Sentencing in Illinois, 1988–1997', Appendix to Illinois, *Report of the Governor's Commission on Capital Punishment: George H. Ryan Governor* (2002).

POJMAN, L. P., and REIMAN, J., *The Death Penalty, For and Against* (1998), Lanham, Md.: Rowman & Littlefield.

POTAS, I., and WALKER, J., *Capital Punishment,* Trends & Issues in Crime and Criminal Justice No. 3 (1987), Canberra: Australia Institute of Criminology.

PREJEAN, H., *Dead Man Walking* (1993), London: Fount.

PROKOSCH, E., 'The Death Penalty versus Human Rights', in Council of Europe, *The Death Penalty: Abolition in Europe* (1999), Strasbourg: Council of Europe Publishing, pp. 17–27.

RADELET, M. L. 'Racial Characteristics and the Imposition of the Death Penalty', *American Sociological Review* 46 (1981), pp. 918–927.

—— (ed), *Facing the Death Penalty* (1989), Philadelphia: Temple University Press.

—— 'Physician Participation', in P. Hodgkinson and A. Rutherford (eds.), *Capital Punishment: Global Issues and Prospects* (1996), pp. 243–260.

—— 'The Role of Organized Religions in Changing Death Penalty Debates', in *William and Mary Bill of Rights Journal* 9 (2000), pp. 201–214.

—— 'More Trends toward Moratoria on Executions', *Connecticut Law Review* 33 (2001), pp. 845–860.

—— and AKERS, R. L., 'Deterrence and the Death Penalty: The Views of Experts', *Journal of Criminal Law and Criminology* 87(1) (1996), pp. 1–11.

—— and BEDAU, H. A., 'The Execution of the Innocent', *Law and Contemporary Problems* 61 (1998), pp. 105–124.

—— —— PUTNAM, C. E., *In Spite of Innocence: Erroneous Convictions in Capital Cases* (1992), Boston: Northeastern University Press.

—— and BORG, M. J., 'The Changing Nature of Death Penalty Debates', *Annual Review of Sociology* 26 (2000), pp. 43–61.

—— and PIERCE, G. L., 'Race and Prosecutorial Discretion in Homicide Cases', *Law and Society Review* 19 (1985), pp. 587–621.

—— and VANDIVER, M., 'Race and Capital Punishment: An Overview of the Issue', *Crime and Social Justice* 25 (1986), pp. 94–113.

—— —— and BERARDO, F. M., 'Families, Prisons, and Men with Death Sentences', *Journal of Family Issues* 4 (1983), pp. 593–612.

—— and ZSEMBIK, B. A., 'Executive Clemency in Post-*Furman* Capital Cases', *University of Richmond Law Review* 27 (1993), pp. 289–314.

RADIN, M. J., 'Cruel Punishment and Respect for Persons: Super Due Process for Death', *Southern California Law Review* 53 (1980), pp. 1143–1185.

RADZINOWICZ, L., *A History of English Criminal Law and its Administration*, vol. iv, *Grappling for Control* (1968), London: Stevens & Sons.

—— *See* United States Senate (1970).

—— *Adventures in Criminology* (1999), London: Routledge.

—— and HOOD, R., *A History of English Criminal Law*, vol. v, *The Emergence of Penal Policy* (1986), London: Stevens & Son.

RAOUL WALLENBERG INSTITUTE OF HUMAN RIGHTS AND HUMANITARIAN LAW, *The Abolition of the Death Penalty in South Africa*, Report No. 23 (1997), Lund.

REDO, S. M., *United Nations Position on Drugs Crimes*, UNAFEI Resource Material no 27 (1985).

REINHARDT, S., 'The Supreme Court, the Death Penalty, and the *Harris* Case', *Yale Law Journal* 102 (1992), pp. 205–223.

ROBERTS, M. M. (ed), *Out of Night: Writings from Death Row* (1994), Cheltenham: New Clarion Press.

ROBERTS, N., 'Death Penalty Developments around the World', *Amicus Journal* 3 (2001), 5–6.

ROBINSON, D. A., and STEPHENS, O. H, 'Patterns of Mitigating Factors in Juvenile Death Penalty Cases', *Criminal Law Bulletin* 28 (1992), pp. 246–275.

ROSCOE POUND—SHORTER AMERICAN TRIAL LAWYERS FOUNDATION, *The Penalty of Death*, Final Report, Annual Chief Justice Earl Warren Conference on Advocacy in the United States, Washington (1980).

ROTHMAN, S., and POWERS, S., 'Execution by Quota?', *Public Interest* (1994), pp. 3–17.

RUBIN, P. H., 'The Death Penalty and Deterrence', *Phi Kappa Phi Forum* 82(1) (2002), pp. 10–12.

RUTHERFORD, A., 'Abolition: A Tale of Two Struggles', in P. Hodgkinson and A. Rutherford (eds), *Capital Punishment: Global Issues and Prospects* (1996), pp. 261–277.

SANDYS, M., 'Stacking the Deck for Guilt and Death: The Failure of Death Qualification to Ensure Impartiality', in J. R. Acker, R. M. Bohm, and C. S. Lanier (eds), *America's Experiment with Capital Punishment* (1998), Durham, NC: Carolina Academic Press, pp. 285–307.

SARAT, A., 'Violence, Representation, and Responsibility in Capital Trials: The View from the Jury', *Indiana Law Journal* 70 (1995), pp. 1103–1135.

—— (ed), *The Killing State: Capital Punishment in Law, Politics, and Culture* (1999), New York: Oxford University Press.

—— *When the State Kills: Capital Punishment and the American Condition* (2001), Princeton University Press.

SCHABAS, W. A., 'Note on *Kindler* v. *Canada* (Minister of Justice)', *American Journal of International Law* 87 (1993), pp. 128–133.

—— 'Execution Delayed, Execution Denied', *Criminal Law Forum* 5 (1994), pp. 180–193.

—— 'International Norms on Execution of the Insane and the Mentally Retarded', *Criminal Law Forum* 4 (1994), pp. 95–117.

—— 'Les Réserves des États-Unis d'Amérique au pacte international relatif aux droits civils et politiques en ce qui a trait à la peine de mort', *Revue Universelle des Droits de l'Homme* 6 (1994), pp. 137–150.

—— '*Soering*'s Legacy: The Human Rights Committee and the Judicial Committee of the Privy Council Take a Walk down Death Row', *International and Comparative Law Quarterly* 43 (1994), pp. 913–923.

—— 'The Death Penalty for Crimes Committed by Persons under Eighteen Years of Age', Paper presented at the European Conference: Monitoring Children's Rights, 1994, Ghent.

—— 'Invalid Reservations to the International Covenant on Civil and Political Rights: Is the United States Still a Party?', *Brooklyn Journal of International Law* 21 (1995), pp. 277–325.

—— *The Abolition of the Death Penalty in International Law* (2nd edn 1997), Cambridge: Cambridge University Press.

—— 'Symposium. Religion's Role in the Administration of the Death Penalty: Islam and the Death Penalty', *William and Mary Bill of Rights Journal* 9 (2000), pp. 223–236.

—— 'Public Opinion and the Death Penalty', Paper presented to the EU–China Seminar on Human Rights, Beijing, 10–12 May 2001.

—— 'From *Kindler* to *Burns*: International Law is Nourishing the Constitutional Living Tree', Paper presented at a Conference on Capital Punishment and International Human Rights Law, Galway, 20 Sept. 2001.

SCHECK, B., NEUFELD, P., and DWYER, J., *Actual Innocence: Five Days to Execution and Other Dispatches from the Wrongfully Convicted* (2000), New York: Doubleday.

SCHEININ, M., 'Capital Punishment and the International Covenant on Civil and Political Rights: Some Issues of Interpretation in the Practice of the Human Rights Committee', Paper presented to the EU–China Human Rights Seminar, Beijing, 10–12 May 2001.

SCHWARTZ, B., 'Death TV? Is there a Press Right of Access to News that Allows Television of Executions?', *Tulsa Law Journal* 30 (1994), pp. 305–353.

SEAY, P. A., 'Law, Crime, and Punishment in the People's Republic of China: A Comparative Introduction to the Criminal Justice and Legal System of the People's Republic of China', *Indiana International and Comparative Law Review* 9 (1998), pp. 143–153.

SELLIN, T., (ed), *The Death Penalty* (1959), Philadelphia: American Law Institute.

—— *The Death Penalty: Retribution or Deterrence?*, UNAFEI Resource Material Series no. 13 (1977), Tokyo, pp. 41–52.

—— *The Penalty of Death* (1980), Beverly Hills, Calif.: Sage.

SHELEFF, L. S., *Ultimate Penalties: Capital Punishment, Life Imprisonment, Physical Torture* (1987), Columbus: Ohio State University Press.

SHOWALTER, C. R., and BONNIE, R. J., 'Psychiatrists and Capital Sentencing: Risks and Responsibilities in a Unique Legal Setting', *Bulletin of the American Academy of Psychiatry and Law* 12 (1984), pp. 153–167.

SIMON, J., and SPAULDING, C., 'Tokens of our Esteem: Aggravating Factors in the Era of Deregulated Death Penalties', in Austin Sarat (ed), *The Killing State: Capital Punishment in Law, Politics and Culture* (1999) pp. 81–136.

SINGH, M. P., 'Capital Punishment: Perspective and the Indian Context', in R. S. Agarwal and S. Kumar (ed.), *Crime and Punishment in New Perspective* (1986), pp. 28–39.

SKOLNICK, A. A., Note 'Physicians in Missouri (but not Illinois) Win Battle to Block Physician Participation in Executions', *Journal of the American Medical Association* 274(7) (1995), p. 524.

SKOVORON, S. E., SCOTT, J. E., and CULLEN, F. E., 'The Death Penalty for Juveniles: An Assessment of Public Support', *Crime and Delinquency* 35 (1989), pp. 546–561.

SMALL, M. A., and OTTO, R. K., 'Evaluations of Competency to be Executed: Legal Contours and Implications for Assessment', *Criminal Justice and Behavior* 18 (1991), pp. 146–158.

SNELL, T L., *Capital Punishment 2000* (2001), Washington: US. Department of Justice, Bureau of Justice Statistics.

SORENSEN, J. R.,and MARQUART, J. W., 'Prosecutorial and Jury Decision-Making in Post-

Furman Texas Capital Cases', *New York University Review of Law and Social Change* 18 (1990–1), pp. 743–776.

—— and PILGRIM, R. L., 'An Actuarial Risk Assessment of Violence Posed by Capital Murder Defendants', *Journal of Criminal Law and Criminology* 90 (2000), pp. 1251–1270.

—— WALLACE, D. H., and PILGRIM, R. L., 'Empirical Studies on Race and Death Penalty Sentencing: A Decade after the GAO Report', *Criminal Law Bulletin* 36 (2001), pp. 395–408.

SPANGENBERG GROUP, *A Study of Representation of Capital Cases in Texas,* Report (1993), Boston, Mass.

SPREGER, M., Note, 'A Critical Evaluation of State Supreme Court Proportionality Review in Death Sentencing Cases', *Iowa Law Review* 73 (1988), pp. 719–741.

STACK, S., 'Publicized Executions and Homicide', *American Sociological Review* 52 (1987), pp. 532–540.

STEIKER, C. S., and STEIKER, J. M., 'ABA's Proposed Moratorium. Defending Categorical Exemptions to the Death Penalty: Reflections on the ABA's Resolutions Concerning the Execution of Juveniles and Persons with Mental Retardation', *Law and Contemporary Problems* 61 (1998), pp. 89–104.

—— —— 'Judicial Developments in Capital Punishment Law', in J. R. Acker, R. M. Bohm, and C. S. Lanier (eds), *America's Experiment with Capital Punishment* (1998), pp. 47–75.

STEIN, G. M., 'Distinguishing among Murders when Assessing the Proportionality of the Death Sentence', *Columbia Law Review* 85 (1985), pp. 1786–1807.

STEINER, B. D., BOWERS, W., and SARAT A., 'Folk Knowledge and Legal Action: Death Penalty Judgements and the Tenet of Early Release in a Culture of Mistrust and Punitiveness', *Law and Society Review* 33 (1999), pp. 461–503.

STEPHEN, J. F., 'Capital Punishments', *Fraser's Magazine* 69 (1864), pp. 753–772.

STEVENSON, B. A., 'Capital Punishment in the United States', in Penal Reform International *et al., Commonwealth Caribbean Human Rights Seminar* (2001), Paris: Penal Reform International, pp. 61–73.

—— and FRIEDMAN, R. E., 'Deliberate Indifference: Judicial Tolerance of Racial Bias in Criminal Justice', *Washington and Lee Law Review* 51 (1994), pp. 509–527.

STREIB, V. L., 'Juvenile Death Penalties: The Beginning of the End of a Scandalous American Practice', Paper presented at the 1986 Annual Meeting of the American Society of Criminology, Atlanta, Ga.

—— *Death Penalty for Juveniles* (1987), Bloomington: Indiana University Press.

—— 'Imposing the Death Penalty on Children', in K. C. Haas and J. A. Inciardi (eds), *Challenging Capital Punishment* (1988), pp. 245–267.

—— 'Perspectives on the Juvenile Death Penalty in the 1990s', in S. Randall Humm *et al.* (eds), *Child, Parent, and State: Law and Policy Reader* (1994), pp. 646–656.

—— *Capital Punishment of Female Offenders: Present Death Row Inmates and Death Sentences and Executions of Female Offenders, January 1, 1973 to September 15, 1995* (1995), Cleveland, Ohio: Cleveland Marshall College of Law.

—— *The Juvenile Death Penalty Today: Present Death Row Inmates under Juvenile Death Sentences and Death Sentences and Executions for Juvenile Crimes, January 1 1973 to September 15, 1995* (1995), Cleveland, Ohio: Cleveland Marshall College of Law.

—— 'Executing Women, Children, and the Retarded: Second Class Citizens in Capital Punishment', in J. R. Acker, R. M. Bohm, and C. S. Lanier (eds), *America's Experiment with Capital Punishment* (1998), pp. 201–221.

—— 'Moratorium on the Death Penalty for Juveniles', *Law and Contemporary Problems* 61(1998), pp. 55–74.

—— *The Juvenile Death Penalty Today: Death Sentences and Executions for Juvenile Crimes, January 1 1973 to December 31 2000.* Available solely on the Internet, http://www.law.onu.edu/faculty/streib/juvdeath.pdf.

Supreme Court Yearbook (annual), Washington: *Congressional Quarterly*.

SVENSSON, M., 'State Coercion, Deterrence and the Death Penalty in the PRC', Paper presented to the Annual Meeting of the Association for Asian Studies, Chicago, 22–5 Mar. 2001.

TABAK, R. J., 'The Death of Fairness: The Arbitrary and Capricious Imposition of the Death Penalty in the 1980's', *New York University Review of Law and Social Change* 14 (1986), pp. 797–848.

—— 'Is Racism Irrelevant? Or should the Fairness in Death Sentencing Act be Enacted to Substantially Diminish Racial Discrimination in Capital Sentencing?', *New York University Review of Law and Social Change* 18 (1990–1), pp. 777–806.

—— 'How Empirical Studies can Affect Positively the Politics of the Death Penalty', *Cornell Law Review* 83 (1998), pp. 1431–1447.

—— Commentary, 'Finality without Fairness: Why we are Moving towards Moratoria on Executions, and the Potential Abolition of Capital Punishment', *Connecticut Law Review* 33 (2001), pp. 733–763.

TAY, S. S. C., 'Human Rights, Culture, and the Singapore Example', *McGill Law Journal* 41 (1996), pp. 743–780.

TIFFT, L. L., 'Capital Punishment Research, Policy and Ethics: Defining Murder and Placing Murderers', *Crime and Social Justice* 21 (1982), pp. 61–68.

—— 'Reflections on Capital Punishment and the "Campaign against Crime" in the People's Republic of China', *Justice Quarterly* 2 (1985), pp. 127–137.

—— 'The Death Penalty and the "Fairy Ring"' in Council of Europe, *The Death Penalty: Abolition in Europe* (1999), Strasbourg: Council of Europe Publishing, pp. 29–34.

TRINIDAD, *The Death Penalty in Trinidad and Tobago*, Report of the Commission of Enquiry into the Death Penalty (Chairman Elton A. Prescott) (1990).

TROMBLEY, S., *The Execution Protocol* (1993), London: Century.

TRUOG, R. D., and BRENNAN, T. A., 'Participation of Physicians in Capital Punishment', *New England Journal of Medicine* 329 (1993), pp. 1346–1349, and correspondence 330 (1994), pp. 935–937.

TURACK, D. C., 'The New Chinese Criminal Justice System', *Cardozo Journal of International and Comparative Law* 7 (1999), pp. 49–70.

TUTTLE, E. O., *The Crusade against Capital Punishment in Great Britain* (1961), London: Quadrangle Books.

TYLER, T. R., and WEBER, R., 'Support for the Death Penalty: Instrumental Response to Crime, or Symbolic Attitude?', *Law and Society Review* 17 (1982), pp. 21–46.

ULATE, R., 'The Death Penalty: Some Observations on Latin America', *United Nations Crime Prevention and Criminal Justice Newsletter* 12 and 13 (Nov. 1986), pp. 27–31.

UNITED KINGDOM, *Royal Commission on Capital Punishment 1949–1953, Report*, Cmd 8932, 1953, London: Her Majesty's Stationery Office.

UNITED NATIONS, *Capital Punishment*, Report prepared by M. Ancel (1962), New York.

—— *Capital Punishment, Developments 1961–1965*, Report prepared by N. Morris, New York.

UNITED NATIONS, 'United Nations Action in the Field of Capital Punishment', *United Nations Crime Prevention and Criminal Justice Newsletter* 12 and 13 (1986), pp. 2–4.

UNITED STATES OF AMERICA, COMMITTEE ON THE JUDICIARY, *Innocence and the Death Penalty: Assessing the Danger of Mistaken Executions*, Staff Report by the Subcommittee on Civil and Constitutional Rights, One Hundred and Third Congress, First Session (1993), Washington.

UNITED STATES OF AMERICA, DEPARTMENT OF JUSTICE, *Capital Punishment*, Bureau of Justice Statistics (annual), Washington.

—— *Sourcebook of Criminal Justice Statistics*, Bureau of Justice Statistics (annual), Washington.

—— *Report to the Deputy Attorney General on Capital Punishment and the Sentencing Commission* (1987), Appendix B, Public Opinion and the Death Penalty, Washington.

—— *The Federal Death Penalty System: A Statistical Survey (1988–2000)* (12 Sept. 2000), Washington.

—— *The Federal Death Penalty System: Supplementary Data, Analysis and Revised Protocols for Capital Case Review* (6 June 2001).

UNITED STATES OF AMERICA, GENERAL ACCOUNTING OFFICE, *Death Penalty Sentencing: Research Indicates Pattern of Racial Disparities*, GAO/GDD-90-57 (1990), Washington.

UNITED STATES SENATE, *Hearings to Abolish the Death Penalty* (1970), Statement by Sir Leon Radzinowicz before the Sub-Committee on Criminal Laws and Procedures of the Committee on the Judiciary, 19th Congress, 2nd Session on S. 1760 (20, 21 Mar., and 2 July 1968), Washington.

UROFSKY, M. L., 'A Right to Die: Termination of Appeal for Condemned Prisoners', *Journal of Criminal Law and Criminology* 75 (1984), pp. 553–582.

VAN DEN BERG, G. P., 'The Soviet Union and the Death Penalty', *Soviet Studies* 35 (1983), pp. 154–174.

—— 'Judicial Statistics in a Period of Glasnost', *Review of Socialist Law* 13 (1987), pp. 299–311.

—— 'Russia and Other CIS States', in P. Hodgkinson and A. Rutherford (eds), *Capital Punishment: Global Issues and Prospects* (1996), pp. 77–103.

VAN DEN HAAG, E., ' Justice, Deterrence and the Death Penalty', in J. R. Acker, R. M. Bohm, and C. S. Lanier (eds), *America's Experiment with Capital Punishment* (1998), pp. 139–156.

—— and CONRAD, J., *The Death Penalty: A Debate* (1983), New York: Plenum.

VANDIVER, M., 'Capital Juror Interviews', in Amnesty International, *The Machinery of Death: A Shocking Indictment of Capital Punishment in the United States* (1995), New York: Amnesty International USA, pp. 75–78.

—— 'The Impact of the Death Penalty on the Families of Homicide Victims and of Condemned Prisoners', in J. R. Acker, R. M. Bohm, and C. S. Lanier (eds), *America's Experiment with Capital Punishment* (1998), pp. 477–505.

VAN DUIZEND, R., 'Comparative Proportionality Review in Death Sentence Cases', *State Court Journal* 8(3) (1984), pp. 9–13 and 21–23.

Virginia Law Review, Note, 'The Executioner's Song: Is there a Right to Listen?' 69 (1983), pp. 373–401.

VITIELLO, M., '*Payne* v. *Tennessee*: A "Stunning *Ipse Dixit*" ', *Notre Dame Journal of Law, Ethics and Public Policy* 8 (1994), pp. 165–280.

VITO, G. F., KOESTER, P., and WILSON, D. G., 'Return of the Dead: An Update on the Status of *Furman*-Commuted Death Row Inmates', in R. M. Bohm (ed), *The Death Penalty in America: Current Research* (1991), pp. 89–99.

—— WILSON, D. G., and LATESSA, E. J., 'Comparison of the Dead: Attributes and Outcomes of *Furman*-Commuted Death Row Inmates in Kentucky and Ohio', in R. M. Bohm (ed), *The Death Penalty in America: Current Research* (1991), pp. 101–111.

VOGELMAN, L., 'The Living Dead: Living on Death Row', *South African Journal on Human Rights* 5(2) (1989), pp. 183–195.

WALKER, N., 'The Efficacy and Morality of Deterrence', *Criminal Law Review* (1979), pp. 125–144.

WALLACE, D. H., 'The Need to Commute the Death Sentence: Competency for Execution and Ethical Dilemmas for Mental Health Professionals', *International Journal of Law and Psychiatry* 15 (1992), pp. 317–337.

—— and SORENSEN, J. R., 'Missouri Proportionality Review: An Assessment of a State Supreme Court's Procedures in Capital Cases', *Notre Dame Journal of Law, Ethics and Public Policy: Symposium on Capital Punishment* 8 (1994), pp. 281–315.

WARR, M., and STAFFORD, M., 'Public Goals of Punishment and Support for the Death Penalty', *Journal of Research in Crime and Delinquency* 21 (1984), pp. 95–111.

WARREN, MARK, *The Death Penalty in Canada: Facts, Figures and Milestones* (2001), London: Amnesty International.

WAZIR, A., 'Quelques aspects de la peine de mort en droit pénal islamique', *Revue Internationale de Droit Pénal* 58 (1987), pp. 421–429.

WECHSLER, H., 'The Model Penal Code and the Codification of American Criminal Law', in R. Hood (ed), *Crime, Criminology, and Public Policy: Essays in Honour of Sir Leon Radzinowicz* (1974), pp. 419–468, London: Heinemann.

WEINSTOCK, D., and SCHWARTZ, G. E., 'Executing the Innocent: Preventing the Ultimate Injustice', *Criminal Law Bulletin* 34 (1998), pp. 328–347 at 335–341.

WEISBERG, R., 'Deregulating Death', *Supreme Court Review* (1983), pp. 305–395.

WELD, W. F., and CASSELL, P., *Report to the Deputy Attorney-General on Capital Punishments and the Sentencing Commission* (1987), Washington: US Department of Justice.

WELSH, JAMES, *Mental Retardation and the Death Penalty*, Amnesty International, AI Index: ACT 75/002/2001.

WHITE, W. S., 'Defendants who Elect Execution', *University of Pittsburgh Law Review* 48 (1987), pp. 855–877.

—— *The Death Penalty in the Nineties: An Examination of the Modern System of Capital Punishment* (2nd edn 1994), Ann Arbor: University of Michigan Press.

WHITEHEAD, J. T., ' "Good Ol' Boys" and the Chair: Death Penalty Attitudes of Policy Makers in Tennessee', *Crime and Delinquency* 4 (2) (1998), pp. 245–256.

WILLIAMS, C. W., 'The Federal Death Penalty for Drug-Related Killings', *Criminal Law Bulletin* 27 (1991), pp. 387–415.

WILLIAMS, F. P., III, and MCSHANE, M. D., 'Inclinations of Prospective Jurors in Capital Cases', *Sociology and Social Research* 74(2) (1990), pp. 85–94.

WILLS, G., 'The Dramaturgy of Death', *New York Review of Books,* 21 June 2001.

WINDLESHAM, LORD, *Responses to Crime*, vol. 3 (1996), Oxford: Oxford University Press.

WOHLWEND, R., 'The Efforts of the Parliamentary Assembly of the Council of Europe', in Council of Europe, *The Death Penalty: Abolition in Europe* (1999), Strasbourg: Council of Europe Publishing.

WOLPIN, K. A., 'Capital Punishment and Homicide in England: A Summary of Results', *American Economic Review* 68 (1978), pp. 422–427.

YACKLE, L. W., 'The American Bar Association and Federal Habeas Corpus', *Law and Contemporary Problems* 61 (1998), pp. 171–192.

YAO ZAOHUI, *New Crimes Emerging in the Process of China's Development and the Strategic Policies and Measures to be Taken,* UNAFEI Resource Material Series no. 30 (1986).

YOUNG, R. L., 'Race, Conceptions of Crime and Justice, and Support for the Death Penalty', *Social Psychology Quarterly* 54 (1991), pp. 67–75.

YU SHUTONG, 'Le Système de la peine capitale dans le droit pénal chinois', *Revue Internationale de Droit Pénal* 58 (1987), pp. 689–695.

ZAFFARONI, E. R., 'Executions Without Due Process', *Revue Internationale de Droit Pénal* 58 (1987), pp. 785–795.

ZEISEL, H., 'The Deterrent Effects of the Death Penalty: Facts v. Faith', *Supreme Court Review* (1976), pp. 317–343.

—— Comment, *American Journal of Sociology* 86 (1980), pp. 168–169.

—— 'Race Bias in the Administration of the Death Penalty: The Florida Experience', *Harvard Law Review* 95 (1981), pp. 456–468.

—— and GALLUP, A. M., 'Death Penalty Sentiment in the United States', *Journal of Quantitative Criminology* 5 (1989), pp. 285–296.

ZIMRING, F. E., 'Research on the Death Penalty: The Liberating Virtues of Irrelevance', *Law and Society Review* 17 (1993), pp. 9–17.

—— 'The Executioner's Dissonant Song: On Capital Punishment and American Legal Values', in Austin Sarat (ed), *The Killing State: Capital Punishment in Law, Politics and Culture* (1999), pp. 137–147.

—— and HAWKINS, G., *Capital Punishment and the American Agenda* (1986), Cambridge: Cambridge University Press.

ZVEKIC, U., and KUBO, T., 'Main Trends in Research on Capital Punishment (1979–1986)', in *The Death Penalty: A Bibliographical Research* (1988), Rome: UNSDRI, pp. 533–554.

Cases Cited

Atkins v. Virginia	122 S.Ct. 2242 (2002)
Bachan Singh v. State of Punjab	2 SCJ 474 (1980), 1 SCR 145 (1983)
Baptiste v. Grenada	CR 38/00 (2000)
Barefoot v. Estelle	463 U.S. 880 (1983)
Batson v. Kentucky	476 U.S. 79 (1986)
Berthill Fox v. The Queen	UKPC 13 (2002)
Blystone v. Pennsylvania	494 U.S. 299 (1990)
Breard v. Greene	140 L.Ed.2d 529 (US Supreme Court 1998)
Bryan v. Moore	528 U.S. 960 (US Supreme Court 1999) 528 U.S. 1133; 145 L.Ed.2d 927 (2000).
Burdine v. Johnson	231 F.3d 950 (Fifth Circuit Texas 2000)
Burdine v. Johnson	No. 99-21034 (United States Court of Appeal for the Fifth Circuit 2001)
Callins v. Collins	114 S.Ct. 1127 (1994)
Campbell v. Trinidad and Tobago	21 July 1999, unreported
Campbell v. Wood	18 F.3d 662 (1994)
Cantu-Tzin v. Johnson	162 F.3d 295 (United States Court of Appeals for the Fifth Circuit 1998)
Catholic Commission for Justice and Peace in Zimbabwe v. Attorney General	14 Human Rights Law J., 323 (1993)
Chambers v. Bowersox	175 F.3d 560 (8th Circuit 1998)
Chandler v. United States of America	218 F.3d 1305 (2000)
Coker v. Georgia	433 U.S. 584 (1977) (plurality opinion)
Coleman v. Thompson	111 S.Ct. 2546 (1991)
Commonwealth v. Fahy	516 A.2d 689 (1986)
Commonwealth v. Logan	1549 A.2d 531 (1988)
Commonwealth v. Moser	549 A.2d 76 (Pa. 1988)
Commonwealth v. Smith	540 A.2d 246 (1988)
Connecticut Board of Pardons v. Dumschat	452 U.S. 458 (1981)
Dawson v. the State	274 Ga. 327 (2001) Supreme Court of Georgia
Eddings v. Oklahoma	455 U.S. 104 (1982)
Elledge v. Florida	525 U.S. 944 (1998)
Fierro v. Gomez	865 F. Supp. 1387 (N.D.Cal. 1994)
Fierro v. Gomez	77. F.3d 301 (9th Circuit 1996)
Ford v. Wainwright	477 U.S. 399 (1986)
Fowler v. North Carolina	420 U.S. 969 (1975)
Furman v. Georgia	408 U.S. 238 (1972) (per curiam)
Germany v. United States of America, LaGrand case	International Court of Justice, Judgment 27/07/2001, Press release 2001/16
Godfrey v. Georgia	446 U.S. 420 (1980)

R v. Mattan   *The Times*, 5 March 1998

Ramjattan v.
    Trinidad and Tobago   *The Times*, 1 April 1999

Reid v. Jamaica   Report of the Human Rights Committee, UN Doc.
A/45/40, vol. 2 (1990)

Republic v. Mbushuu alias
    Dominic Mnyaroje   Criminal Sessions Case No. 44 of 1991, [1994] Tanzanian
    and Kalai Sangula   Law Reports 146–173

Ring v. Arizona   122 S.Ct. 2428 (2002)

Roberts v. Louisiana   428 U.S. 325 (1976)

Robinson v. Jamaica   Report of the Human Rights Committee, UN Doc.
A/44/40 (1989)

Rose and others v. Jamaica   CR 66/99 (1999)

Ruiz v. Estelle   679 F.2d. 1115 (1982)

Saldano v. Texas   530 U.S. 1212 (2000)

Schlup v. Delo   115 S.Ct. 851 (1995)

Shafer v. South Carolina   121 S.Ct. 1263 (2001)

Shashi nayar v. UOI   [1992] 1SCC 96

Simmons v. South Carolina   114 S.Ct. 2187 (1994)

Soering v. UK   161 Eur.Ct. H.R. (ser. A) 34 (1989)

Spaziano v. Florida   468 U.S. 447 (1984)

Spence and Hughes v.   Criminal Appeal No. 20 of 1998, Eastern Caribbean Court
    The Queen   of Appeal (2001)

Stanford v. Kentucky   492 U.S. 361 (1989)

State v. T. Makwanyane and   Case No. CCT/3/94
    M. McHunu   Constitutional Court of South Africa

Strickland v. Washington   466 U.S. 668 (1984)

Sumner v. Shuman   483 U.S. 66 (1987)

Teague v. Lane   499 U.S. 288 (1989) No. 44 (1991)

Thompson v. Oklahoma   108 S.Ct. 2687 (1988)

Trop v. Dulles   356 U.S. 86, 101 (1958)

Turner v. Murray,
    Director, Virginia
    Department of Corrections   476 U.S. 28 (1986)

United States v. Burns   2001 SCC 7. File No.: 26129 (2001) Supreme Court of
Canada

Wainwright v. Sykes   433 U.S. 72 (1977)

Walton v. Arizona   497 U.S. 639 (1990)

Washington v. Harper   494 U.S. 210 (1990)

Weeks v. Angelone   528 U.S. 225 (2000)

Weems v. United States   217 U.S. 349, 378 (1910)

Whitmore v. Arkansas   495 U.S. 149 (1990)

Wilkins v. Missouri   492 U.S. 937 (1989) (companion case)

Wilson v. Smith   No. 86-1751 (E.D. LA Feb. 12, 1990)

Woodson v. North Carolina   428 U.S. 280 (1976)

Zant v. Stephens   462 U.S. 862 (1983)

Index

Index